Promoting Peace with Information

Promoting Peace with Information

TRANSPARENCY AS A TOOL OF SECURITY REGIMES

Dan Lindley

PRINCETON UNIVERSITY PRESS

PRINCETON AND OXFORD

Published by Princeton University Press, 41 William Street, Princeton, New Jersey 08540

In the United Kingdom: Princeton University Press, 3 Market Place, Woodstock, Oxfordshire OX20 1SY

Library of Congress Cataloging-in-Publication Data
    Lindley, Dan, 1961–
    ]Promoting peace with information : transparency as a tool of security regimes / Dan Lindley.
    p.   cm.
    Includes bibliographical references and index.
    ISBN-13: 978-0-691-12943-3 (hardback : alk. paper)
    ISBN-10: 0-691-12943-6 (hardback : alk. paper)
    1. Transparency in government.   2. Peace-building.   3. International agencies.
    I. Title.
    JC598.L56 2007
    352.8'8—dc22   2006035857

British Library Cataloging-in-Publication Data is available

This book has been composed in Sabon

Printed on acid-free paper. ∞

press.princeton.edu

Printed in the United States of America

10   9   8   7   6   5   4   3   2   1

*This book is dedicated to Hannah Alice Lindley
and Ethan Ledyard Lindley,
to all children,
and to those who want them to grow up in peace.*

Contents

List of Tables   *ix*

Preface and Acknowledgments   *xi*

CHAPTER ONE
Promoting Peace with Information   1

CHAPTER TWO
Theory, Methods, and Case Selection   17

CHAPTER THREE
The Concert of Europe: Forum Diplomacy
and Crisis Management   55

CHAPTER FOUR
The United Nations Force in Cyprus   86

CHAPTER FIVE
The United Nations Disengagement Observer Force
in the Golan Heights   118

CHAPTER SIX
The United Nations Transition Assistance Group
for Namibia   142

CHAPTER SEVEN
The United Nations Transitional Authority in Cambodia   155

CHAPTER EIGHT
Conclusion   180

Appendix A: Information Operations in Recent U.N.
Peacekeeping Missions   197

Appendix B: Insights on Transparency from the Open Skies,
Strategic Arms Control, and Non-Proliferation Regimes   215

Bibliography   237

Index   269

Tables

TABLE 2-1. Types of Transparency   21

TABLE 2-2. Effects of Opacity and Transparency on Mis/Calculation, Deterrence, and War   34

TABLE 2-3. Summary of Hypotheses   43

TABLE 3-1. Findings by Hypothesis   82

TABLE 4-1. Findings by Hypothesis   112

TABLE 5-1. Summary of the Areas of Separation and Limitation   128

TABLE 5-2. Findings by Hypothesis   138

TABLE 6-1. Findings by Hypothesis   152

TABLE 7-1. Findings by Hypothesis   176

TABLE 8-1. Summary of Findings by Case and Hypothesis   182

TABLE 8-2. Information Conditions and Likely Operational Effectiveness of Transparency in U.N. Peacekeeping Operations   184

Preface and Acknowledgments

THIS BOOK began when my initial dissertation topic underwent creative implosion. The original idea, "The Formation, Effectiveness, and Demise of Collective Security Systems," looked at the Concert of Europe, League of Nations, and United Nations and tried to explain the life-cycles of collective security systems. It was a huge topic, and it muddied the issue of most interest, that of effectiveness. There is a considerable amount of great power politics in the formation and demise of collective security systems, and looking at their ebb and flow is a good way to take the pulse of great power politics. What do these systems actually do, however, to promote peace while they are around?

With an abiding interest in applying institutional theories to issues of war and peace, the clarifying revelation that came to me was to see if transparency might be a contribution of security regimes. Informational arguments occupy a large place in the institutionalist repertoire, but how well do they apply in the realm of security?

This book attempts to answer that question. I have run hypotheses about transparency up the flagpole, testing them by seeing if, and how well, two of the most prominent security regimes used transparency to manage problems and promote peace. Here I report the results.

Whatever I have achieved, it would not have been possible without the help of a large number of people. I owe the greatest debt to Professors Stephen Van Evera and Barry Posen. Their many comments and marginalia over the years epitomized scholarly insight, and the time they spent trying to help me make sense well exceeded their professional responsibilities. They have more than earned their pay, my respect, and my gratitude. Professor Kenneth Oye, my third reader, was always helpful, constructive, and to the point. The contribution of these three to my education goes well beyond thesis and paper comments and continues to this day. I am still trying to figure out what mental algorithms they bring to bear when they construct and parse apart arguments. Their ability to get quickly to the core of arguments is formidable.

My graduate student colleagues never failed to help when asked. I was lucky to go to school with Taylor Seybolt and Jane Kellett as well as Eric Heginbotham, Clifford Bob, Jonathan Ladinsky, and Daryl Press. David Nickles of the Harvard History Department commented several times on my pre-Concert and Concert chapters. In addition, I frequently availed myself of Professor George Rathjens and the New Directions in Security Studies Working Group to sharpen my ideas.

Looking back, I must thank Professor Martin Sherwin at Tufts, who helped teach me about nuclear weapons. In Washington, everyone I ever worked for reaffirmed my faith that working on security issues was the right thing to do and that many good people worked on these issues both in and out of government. This includes Bill Ratchford, Steve Goose, John Pike, Paul Stares, Ken Flamm, and Josh Epstein, all of whom helped me take the next step.

I wish to thank George Rathjens, Harvey Sapolsky, MIT's Defense and Arms Control Studies Program (now Security Studies Program), the MacArthur Foundation, and MIT's Department of Political Science for numerous years of financial support. The International Security Program of the (now Belfer) Center for Science and International Affairs (CSIA) at Harvard University's John F. Kennedy of School of Government saw me through the home stretch of the dissertation with a two-year fellowship that greatly increased my productivity. The Carnegie Corporation of New York and their Commission on Preventing Deadly Conflict supported the project on internal conflicts that I worked on at the CSIA.

Several colleagues at the CSIA provided valuable comments and critiques of my work, especially Mike Brown, as well as Rachel Bronson, Miriam Fendius Elman, Matt Evangelista, Christopher Layne, Sean Lynn-Jones, John Matthews, Chantal de Jonge Oudraat, Jo Spear, and Bradley Thayer.

Many people at the U.N. helped me with my research. In New York, I owe particular thanks to Lena Yacoumopoulou, as well as Kevin Kennedy, Fred Eckhard, and Henry Breed. In later research, Simon Davies, Eleanor Beardsley, Susan Manuel, Frederick Schottler, and David Wimhurst were all helpful and forthcoming.

On Cyprus, almost everyone I met at the U.N. Peacekeeping Force in Cyprus (UNFICYP) was very helpful and generous—certainly beyond every reasonable expectation. I never figured out why UNFICYP was so forthcoming, giving me access to any operational documents or U.N. officials I wished, and so credit must go to those at the top who set the tone. I especially refer to General Ahti Vartiainen, who lent assistance in many ways and to Waldemar Rokoszewski, a true expert on Cyprus. I also am grateful to the staff of the operations branch, who never seemed to be bothered by my continued note-taking presence. I grew fond of the booming British voice of Lieutenant Colonel Nick Parker, the mellifluous Argentinean accent of Major Marcelo Rozas-Garay, and the laugh of the hard-working Major Edgar Wallig from Austria. The three formed a great team and exemplified the multinational ideal of the U.N. I also thank Gustave Feissel, Colonel Ian Talbot, Lieutenant Colonel Andrew Snowdon, Lieutenant Colonel Jorges Tereso, Major Andrew Barnard, Major Walsh, and Bombardiers Raymond Cowie and Elwyn Jones.

My visit to the U.N. Disengagement Observer Force (UNDOF) was assisted by General Johannes Kosters, Captain Ken-Ichi Kawazu, and the enthusiastically helpful Captain Richard Deschambault. Among others at the U.N. Truce Supervision Organization (UNTSO), Zenon Carnapas, Anthony French, and General R. M. Kupolati were generous with their time. Mikael Lindvall from the U.N. Interim Force in Lebanon (UNIFIL) came down to Israel during a troubled period to give me a lengthy briefing. I also thank General Kosters and Captain Deschambault for allowing me to take notes on some of UNDOF's documents.

I also thank Michael Doyle of International Peace Academy, and William Durch and Tory Holt of the Stimson Center. Francis X. Stenger, Deputy Division Chief for Open Skies Treaty at the DOD Defense Threat Reduction Agency (DTRA), was very supportive and informative.

At Notre Dame, Jim McAdams, Tony Messina, Andy Gould, Keir Lieber, Al Tillery, and David Singer have all given their time in providing comments. James Thompson and Matthew Flynn have helped with my research. The Joan B. Kroc Institute for International Peace Studies has been very generous with financial and moral support.

I received many helpful comments during presentations of various aspects of this work. I presented my analysis of the Concert of Europe at the Program on International Politics, Economics, and Security, University of Chicago, December 1999, and at the American Political Science Association conference in September 2002. I am grateful for the helpful comments of Charles Lipson, Alexander Wendt, Duncan Snidal, Daniel Drezner, and Charles Kupchan.

I presented various aspects of my U.N. peacekeeping chapters at the Peace Studies Program of Cornell University in March 1999; at the CSIA of Harvard University in April 1999; at the MIT Security Studies Program in May 1999; and at the Seminar on Protracted Conflict at the Project on Negotiation at the Harvard Law School in May 1998. I presented my research on Cyprus at the Eastern Mediterranean University, Famagusta, North Cyprus, in March 1998; at the U.S. Central Intelligence Agency, Washington, D.C., in December 1997; at the University of Minnesota in October 1997; and at the Intercollege in Nicosia, Cyprus, in April 1997. Various portions were presented at the American Political Science Association conferences in 1994, 1995, 2000, and 2002; at the New England Political Science Association conferences in 1993 and 1995; and at the International Studies Association Conference in 1999. Research and parts of the book contributed to the following publications, while comments on these articles helped the book: "Avoiding Tragedy in Power Politics: The Concert of Europe, Transparency, and Crisis Management," *Security Studies* 13, no. 2 (Winter 2003/4): 195–229; "Untapped Power? The Status of U.N. Information Operations," *International Peacekeeping* 11, no. 4 (Winter 2004): 608–24; "UNDOF: Operational Analysis and Lessons Learned," *Defense and Security Analysis* 20, no. 2 (June 2004): 153–64; and "Cooperative Airborne Monitoring: Opening the Skies to Promote Peace, Protect the Environment, and Cope with Natural Disasters," *Contemporary Security Policy* 27, no. 2 (August 2006): 325–43. I thank all the discussants, reviewers, and other contributors to the foregoing efforts.

I thank Teresa Lawson for her excellent and insightful editing of my manuscript.

I thank a number of people at Princeton University Press, including the supportive Chuck Myers, senior acquisitions editor, and Lucy Day Werts Hobor, associate production editor and a friend of books. Princeton brought Linda Truilo on board as my copy editor, and I engaged Jim Curtis to serve as indexer. This whole team has been a pleasure to work with. The external reviewers for the book were superb, and one went beyond the call of duty in constructively helping me improve my theory section.

Last and most important, I would like to thank Daniel A. Lindley, Jr. and Lucia Woods Lindley for their support for so many years, support which helped me make the choices I have so enjoyed. I thank Jennifer King Lindley for putting up with me and for reading and helping edit the manuscript—my now excised footnotes about the meaning of life are a still-running joke. I thank Amy Hoyt Lindley for teaching me about independence and self-sufficiency. I thank Helen Stokes Lindley for staying grounded and for being my buddy. And I thank Granny and Popso for always being there. Without them, I might have passed the fail-safe point long ago. My children, Ethan and Hannah, now appear to be entrusted with the recall code.

Dan Lindley, September 4, 2006

Promoting Peace with Information

CHAPTER ONE

Promoting Peace with Information

AFTER MORE THAN twenty years of civil war, foreign interference, and massacres by the Khmer Rouge, Cambodia finally seemed ready for peace. In 1991, a peace agreement was signed by the principle parties, and the United Nations sent peacekeepers to Cambodia to help maintain the cease-fire and rebuild the war-torn country. The U.N.'s prime objective was to hold an election to seal the peace with a new democratic government. Success depended on the U.N.'s ability to teach the country about elections, monitor the elections, and legitimize the results with a high turnout. A number of wild and false rumors and fears, however, threatened to jeopardize the elections. Some potential voters suspected that the ballot-marking pencils contained radio beacons that broadcast to satellites, revealing who had voted for whom. Others feared spying by secret electronic eyes in the polling places. With radio and other educational efforts, the U.N. defused these rumors about what the Khmer Rouge and others were imagined to be doing to sabotage the elections, assured voters that the ballots would be secret, and taught the Cambodians about democracy. The turnout was a resounding 90 percent.

What happened here? The U.N. used accurate information to calm false rumors. This is but one example of a security regime increasing transparency—what adversaries know about each other's intentions, capabilities, and actions—to promote peace. There are many ways institutions can increase transparency and promote peace, ranging from providing a forum to broadcasting, inspecting, verifying, and monitoring.

Almost 200 years earlier, transparency also helped one of the first security regimes promote peace—though not in the way many think. At the end of 1814 and into 1815, the great powers of Europe met together in Vienna in what would become the first international crisis management forum in history: the Concert of Europe. Russia's occupation of Poland and Prussian claims to Saxony caused a growing crisis. Supporting Prussia's designs on Saxony with blustery belligerence, Tsar Alexander of Russia said in October 1814, "I have two hundred thousand men in the duchy of Warsaw. Let them drive me out if they can! I have given Saxony to Prussia. . . . If the King of Saxony refuses to abdicate, he shall be led to Russia; where he will die."[1] In December, Prince Hardenburg of Prussia

---

[1] A letter from the Prince de Talleyrand to King Louis XVII, Vienna, October 25, 1814, in Duc de Broglie, ed., *Memoirs of the Prince de Talleyrand*, Raphael de Beaufort, trans., vol. 2 (New York, NY: Putnam's, 1891), 277.

said that Austrian, British, and French resistance to his plans was "tanta-mount to a declaration of war." British Viscount Castlereagh termed this "a most alarming and unheard-of menace."[2] Talk of war swept through Vienna.

On January 3, 1815, Austria, Britain, and France signed a secret treaty to counter Russia and Prussia. Castlereagh revealed the treaty to Alexan-der the next day. Faced with hardened opposition, Russia forced Prussia to back down, and this quickly resolved the crisis. The great powers used the new forum to communicate threats and reach bargains far more rap-idly than they could before. Information exchanged during forum diplo-macy clarified the stakes at issue and the balance of power. Increased transparency did not calm fears, the most commonly imagined effect of transparency. Instead, it enhanced coercive diplomacy and bargaining.

International institutions in which states cooperate to prevent war are called security regimes. One of the main tools at a security regime's dis-posal is increasing transparency. Scholars and policymakers often assume that increased transparency reduces unwarranted fears, misperceptions, and miscalculation, but few have examined how transparency is provided or how it operates in practice.

This book answers two main questions about transparency: How and when do security regimes increase transparency? How and when do these efforts to increase transparency promote peace?

I examine the role of transparency in crisis management by the Concert of Europe and in several different U.N. peacekeeping operations. While there are many different security regimes, these cases allow examination of the provision and effects of transparency in a variety of contexts. The Concert brought diplomats together in a forum to manage crises, something they had never done before. Today, in U.N. operations, peacekeepers more actively generate and exchange information. Findings based on these cases have global importance. Today, there are many forums from the Associa-tion of Southeast Asia Nations (ASEAN) to the African Union, and pro-posals for additional forums often cite the Concert as a model.[3] In 2005, some sixteen U.N. and ten non-U.N. peacekeeping missions around the world monitored cease-fires and elections, verified disarmament and arms control agreements, and patrolled buffer zones and other areas of conflict.[4]

The mechanisms for providing transparency vary greatly, as do trans-parency's effects. As this book demonstrates, sometimes transparency suc-ceeds in promoting peace, sometimes it fails, and sometimes it makes

[2] C. K. Webster, ed., *British Diplomacy 1813–1815: Select Documents Dealing with the Reconstruction of Europe* (London: G. Bell, 1921), 277–78.

[3] See note 5 in this chapter as well as note 87 in chap. 3.

[4] Alex J. Bellamy and Paul D. Williams, "Who's Keeping the Peace? Regionalization and Contemporary Peace Operations," *International Security* 29, no. 4 (Spring 2005): 166–67.

things worse. By helping figure out how and when security regimes can make transparency work, this book bolsters scholarship on security institutions, advances emerging debates about transparency, and helps policymakers more effectively use regimes to promote peace.

WHY STUDY TRANSPARENCY AND SECURITY REGIMES?

There are three practical and scholarly reasons for studying security regimes and transparency. The first is policy relevance. States have turned to security regimes to help prevent war for the past two hundred years. Recent years have seen renewed interest in the two types of security regimes examined here: peacekeeping and forums. Wherever one stands on debates about security regimes' ultimate influence in international relations, such discussion consumes considerable attention and resources from decision-makers. Second, security regimes in general are understudied by academics, and the large policy-oriented literature on peacekeeping remains a surprisingly theory-free zone. Few scholars have used the subject to develop and test international relations theories. Third, transparency is a reasonably manipulable product for security regimes, and transparency in the context of security regimes is understudied. Knowledge about transparency also helps us understand the role and practice of public diplomacy, because it too aims to influence the information environment. Thus, figuring out whether and how transparency contributes to security regimes' effectiveness will help policymakers use them better and will advance international relations scholarship on several fronts. I discuss these three points in turn, looking first at the topic of security regimes in policy and scholarly debates, then explaining the specific focus on transparency.

Security Regimes and Policy

Security regimes are of perennial concern to policymakers. Every time a major war ends, the participants set up a security regime to help prevent a "next" war. The Napoleonic Wars were followed by the Concert of Europe; World War I by the League of Nations; and World War II by the United Nations. Similarly, the end of the Cold War rekindled enthusiasm for the U.N. and sparked a number of new peacekeeping operations. Over time, the number of security regimes has grown, ranging from the Open Skies agreement in Europe to the African Union.

Security regimes are of immediate interest to today's leaders. The 1990s were marked by a surge of debate and new policies focused on the U.N. and other security regimes. To replace the North Atlantic Treaty Organization

(NATO) or supplement the U.N., a number of analysts proposed new security forums modeled after the Concert of Europe.[5] Others proposed strengthening the U.N. and moving it closer toward being an ideal all-against-any-aggressor collective security system.[6]

These proposals for new forums and the initial post–Cold War enthusiasm for the U.N., followed by the U.N.'s troubles in Bosnia and Somalia, provoked a backlash. Critics charged that peacekeeping is useless or counterproductive: that it makes peace only between those who want peace; that it works only between small countries; or that it prevents adversaries from negotiating an end to their dispute by removing the strongest incentive to compromise, the pain of continuing war.[7]

---

[5] Proponents of concerts include Andrew Bennett and Joseph Lepgold, "Reinventing Collective Security after the Cold War and Gulf Conflict," *Political Science Quarterly* 108, no. 2 (Summer 1993); Gregory Flynn and David J. Scheffer, "Limited Collective Security," *Foreign Policy,* no. 80 (Fall 1990); Douglas M. Gibler, "East or Further East?" *Journal of Peace Research* 36, no. 6 (November 1999); James Goodby, "Commonwealth and Concert: Organizing Principles of Post-Containment Order in Europe," *Washington Quarterly* 14, no. 3 (Summer 1991); James E. Goodby, "A New European Concert: Settling Disputes in CSCE," *Arms Control Today* 21, no. 1 (January/February 1991); Robert Jervis, "International Primacy: Is the Game Worth the Candle?" *International Security* 17, no. 4 (Spring 1993); Charles A. Kupchan and Clifford A. Kupchan, "Concerts, Collective Security, and the Future of Europe," *International Security* 16, no. 1 (Summer 1991); Charles Lipson, "Is the Future of Collective Security Like the Past?," pp. 109–10, 125 in George Downs, ed., *Collective Security beyond the Cold War* (Ann Arbor: University of Michigan Press, 1994); Lipson, "Are Security Regimes Possible? Historical Cases and Modern Issues," in Efraim Inbar, ed. *Regional Security Regimes: Israel and Its Neighbors* (Albany, NY: State University of New York Press, 1995) (Lipson's positive interpretation of the Concert is echoed by Robert J. Lieber's contribution to this volume as well); John Mueller, "A New Concert of Europe," *Foreign Policy,* no. 77 (Winter 1989–90); William Odom, "How to Create a True World Order: Establish a Concert of Great Powers," *Orbis* 39, no. 2 (Spring 1995); Richard Rosecrance, "A New Concert of Powers," *Foreign Affairs* 71, no. 2 (Spring 1992); W. R. Smyser, "Vienna, Versailles, and Now Paris: Third Time Lucky?" *Washington Quarterly* 14, no. 3 (Summer 1991); and Philip Zelikow, "The New Concert of Europe," *Survival* 34, no. 2 (Summer 1992).

[6] Proponents of stronger, more ideal, forms of collective security include Gene M. Lyons, "A New Collective Security: The United Nations in Theory and Practice," *The Washington Quarterly* 17, no. 2 (Spring 1994); Edward Luck,"Making Peace," *Foreign Policy,* no. 89 (Winter 1992–93); Brian Urquhart, "The United Nations: From Peace-Keeping to a Collective System?" in Adelphi Paper 265 (London: International Institute for Strategic Studies, Winter 1991/1992); and Robert Wright, "Bold Old Vision: The Case for Collective Security," *The New Republic,* January 25, 1993.

[7] Critiques include Richard Betts, "Systems for Peace or Causes of War? Collective Security, Arms Control, and the New Europe," *International Security* 17, no. 1 (Summer 1992); Charles L. Glaser, "Future Security Arrangements for Europe: Why NATO Is Still Best," in Downs, ed., *Collective Security;* Dennis C. Jett, *Why Peacekeeping Fails* (New York: Palgrave, 2001); Josef Joffe, "Collective Security and the Future of Europe: Failed Dreams and Dead Ends," *Survival* 34, no. 1 (Spring 1992); Michael Lind, "Twilight of the U.N.," *The New Republic,* October 30, 1995, p. 25–33; and Lind, "Peacefaking: The Case Against U.N.

As a result of these critiques and real-world failures, U.N. peacekeeping declined in the mid-1990s, but demand for these operations soon returned. The number of U.N. military personnel and civilian police jumped from 10,000 in 1987–91 to 78,000 in mid-1993, falling back to around 10,000 in 1999 and rising again to almost 66,000 in May 2005. Accordingly, costs for peacekeeping rose from the typical Cold War level of less than $300 million per year to $640 million in 1989 to $3.6 billion in 1993, dropping to about $1.0 billion in 1998, and rising to $4.47 billion for the year July 2004–June 2005.[8]

Despite this history and these policy debates, few scholars have stepped back to take a theoretically informed look at security regimes. With peacekeeping in particular, much analysis is directed at policymakers, but the subject is little used to test and develop international relations theories. Some scholarly debates about security institutions are heated, but do not contribute detailed analysis.[9]

Security Regimes and Scholarship

The study of security regimes is the study of how institutions affect security policies and the probability of war. This intersection of two core streams of international relations scholarship—liberal institutionalism and security studies—remains largely uncharted. Those who study institutions have contributed greatly to the political science subfield of international political economy, but relatively little to security studies. Few institutionalists have a background in security studies.

Regime theory originated in the subfield of international political economy (IPE), and theoretically driven work on international institutions

---

'Peacemaking,'" *The New Republic,* November 8, 1993, pp. 14–17; Hans J. Morgenthau, *Politics among Nations: The Struggle for Power and Peace,* 5 ed. rev. (New York: Knopf, 1973), pp. 417–23; and Kenneth W. Thompson, "Collective Security Reexamined," *American Political Science Review* 47, no. 3 (September, 1953). See also Richard Bernstein, "Sniping Is Gnawing at U.N.'s Weakness as a Peacekeeper: The Optimism Has Faded," *The New York Times,* June 21, 1993, p. A10.

[8] See United Nations Peacekeeping Operations, "Background Note: 1 March 2001" at www.un.org/peace/bnote010101.pdf; "Composition of Peacekeeping Staff," at www.un.org/Depts/dpko/dpko/pub/pdf/2.pdf; "United Nations Peacekeeping from 1991 to 2000: Statistical Data and Charts" at www.un.org/Depts/dpko/dpko/pub/pko.htm; "UN Peace Operations, Year in Review: 2002," at www.un.org/Depts/dpko/yir/english; and "United Nations Peacekeeping Operations Background Note," May 31, 2005 at www.un.org/Depts/dpko/dpko/bnote.htm.

[9] See John J. Mearsheimer, "The False Promise of International Institutions," *International Security* 19, no. 3 (Winter 1994/95), and Robert O. Keohane and Lisa L. Martin, "The Promise of Institutionalist Theory," (and other responses) in *International Security* 20, no. 1 (Summer 1995).

continues to be dominated by the IPE subfield. Work here started with the question, Do regimes matter? It moved on to the questions, How and under what conditions do regimes matter?[10] Stephan Haggard and Beth Simmons wrote that regimes could be shown to matter if case studies showed that decision-makers

> were actually concerned with reputation, reducing transactions costs, the need for transparency, and so forth, when facing decisions about regime creation and compliance. . . . An even stronger claim [could be made if such analysis showed that regimes] can alter actors' interests and preferences. . . . Surprisingly little work of this kind has been done.[11]

That statement is still true, particularly in security studies. That work is the aim of this book.

Robert Keohane, a leading international political economist and proponent of international institutions, laments the lack of attention that the field of international relations has paid to security regimes—a concern echoed more recently by David Lake.[12] The best work on security regimes is by Robert Jervis, Charles Lipson, and Charles Kupchan and Clifford Kupchan, who have used the Concert of Europe to discuss transparency and other peace-promoting effects of institutions such as the promotion of rules and norms.[13] I advance this research program by focusing on transparency and expanding the analysis to U.N. peacekeeping. Other scholars of security regimes examine how institutional momentum, persistence, or form affect states' policies. For example, John Duffield brings institutional analysis to bear on the contentious issue of weapons procurement within NATO.[14]

---

[10] Stephen D. Krasner, ed., *International Regimes* (Ithaca, NY: Cornell University Press, 1983).

[11] Stephan Haggard and Beth A. Simmons, "Theories of International Regimes," *International Organization* 41, no. 3 (Summer 1987): 514.

[12] See Robert Keohane, "Institutional Theory and the Realist Challenge after the Cold War," in David A. Baldwin, ed., *Neorealism and Neoliberalism: The Contemporary Debate* (New York: Columbia University Press, 1993); and David Lake "Beyond Anarchy: The Importance of Security Institutions," *International Security* 26, no. 1 (Summer 2001): 129–30.

[13] Robert Jervis, "Security Regimes," in Krasner, ed., *International Regimes;* Jervis, "From Balance to Concert: A Study of International Security Cooperation." In Kenneth Oye, ed., *Cooperation Under Anarchy* (Princeton, NJ: Princeton University Press 1986; Kupchan and Kupchan, "Concerts, Collective Security, and the Future of Europe;" Charles Lipson, "International Cooperation in Economic and Security Affairs," *World Politics* 37, no. 1 (October 1984); and Lipson, "Is the Future of Collective Security Like the Past?" See also Janice Gross Stein, "Detection and Defection: Security 'Regimes' and the Management of International Conflict," *International Journal* 40, no. 4 (Autumn 1985).

[14] John S. Duffield, "NATO Force Levels and Regime Analysis," *International Organization* 46, no. 4 (Autumn 1992); and Duffield, *Power Rules: The Evolution of NATO's*

Some of the most insightful work on institutions and information comes from literatures on cooperation and bargaining, and security issues are especially prominent in the bargaining literature. Cooperation theorists have identified a number of barriers to cooperation among states and have studied how actors can overcome these hurdles. Barriers to cooperation include deadlock, inability or unwillingness to forecast or take into account the long-term consequences of policies (theorists call this inability a short shadow of the future), large numbers of actors that cause collective action problems, uncertainty about the costs and benefits of cooperation, and insufficient capabilities to monitor compliance with agreements and punish defectors (which in turn increases the likelihood of cheating and defection). Regimes can promote cooperation by giving states forums for discussion and helping them bargain and horse trade across different issue areas (issue linkage). Regimes can increase the shadow of the future, reduce transaction costs, and increase the amount of information available to actors.[15]

Conventional Force Posture (Stanford, CA: Stanford University Press, 1995). See also Barbara Koremenos, Charles Lipson, and Duncan Snidal, eds., *The Rational Design of International Institutions, special issue of International Organization* 55, no. 4 (Autumn 2001); Helga Haftendorn, Robert O. Keohane, and Celeste A. Wallander, eds., *Imperfect Unions: Security Institutions over Time and Space* (Oxford: Oxford University Press, 1999); Lisa L. Martin, *Coercive Cooperation: Explaining Multilateral Economic Sanctions* (Princeton, NJ: Princeton University Press, 1992); Martin, "Institutions and Cooperation: Sanctions During the Falklands Islands Conflict," *International Security* 16, no. 4 (Spring 1992); Benjamin Miller, "Explaining Great Power Cooperation in Conflict Management," *World Politics* 45, no. 1 (October 1992); Miller, "Explaining the Emergence of Great Power Concerts," *Review of International Studies* 20, no. 4 (October 1994); and Roger K. Smith, "Explaining the Non-Proliferation Regime: Anomalies for Contemporary International Relations Theory," *International Organization* 41, no. 2 (Spring 1987).

[15] Exemplars, emphasizing those relevant to security issues, include Robert Axelrod, *The Evolution of Cooperation* (New York: Basic Books, 1984); Jonathon Bendor, "Uncertainty and the Evolution of Cooperation," *The Journal of Conflict Resolution* 37, no. 4 (December 1993): 709–34; George W. Downs and David M. Rocke, *Tacit Bargaining, Arms Races, and Arms Control* (Ann Arbor, MI: University of Michigan Press, 1990); Matthew Evangelista, "Cooperation Theory and Disarmament Negotiations in the 1950s," *World Politics* 42, no. 4 (July 1990); James D. Fearon, "Signaling versus the Balance of Power and Interests: An Empirical Test of a Crisis Bargaining Model," *Journal of Conflict Resolution,* 38, no. 2 (June 1994); Robert O. Keohane, "The Demand for International Regimes," in Krasner, *International Regimes,* 159–67; Helen V. Milner, *Interests, Institutions, and Information: Domestic Politics and International Relations* (Princeton, NJ: Princeton University Press,1997); James D. Morrow, "Modeling the Forms of International Cooperation: Distribution vs. Information, *International Organization* 48, no. 3 (Summer 1994); Elinor Ostrom, *Governing the Commons: The Evolution of Institutions for Collective Action* (Cambridge: Cambridge University Press, 1990); and Stein, "Detection and Defection," as well as many of the contributions in Kenneth Oye, ed., *Cooperation Under Anarchy* (Princeton, NJ.: Princeton University Press, 1986), especially the following: Oye, "Explaining Cooperation under Anarchy: Hypotheses and Strategies"; Robert Jervis, "From Balance to

Bargaining theorists have focused on why states fail to arrive at negotiated settlements to their conflicts, why this sometimes leads to war, and how war is itself a bargaining process. Even though the word "transparency" may not be frequently or explicitly used, the arguments in this burgeoning literature often hinge on the quality of information available to the actors. For example, war may result if two sides disagree about their relative power, or if both sides cannot credibly commit to peace due to an inability to monitor the agreement. In the first case, increased transparency may help states calculate their relative power, better predict the outcome of a possible war, and negotiate to avoid that war. In the second case, increased transparency can help verify an accord, making commitments to that accord more credible and enforceable.[16]

By serving as forums, by monitoring, or by otherwise increasing information, regimes can increase transparency. Transparency in turn can reduce uncertainties about others' actions, intentions, and capabilities, and can help states calculate the consequences of their policies. Transparency can increase the ability to identify defectors and help states identify the payoffs from cooperation (or defection).[17]

This literature review, and the citations in the methods chapter, make clear that many different literatures talk about the effects of false information and transparency in similar ways despite their different angles and

---

Concert"; Stephen Van Evera, "Why Cooperation Failed in 1914"; George W. Downs, David M. Rocke, and Randolph M. Siverson, "Arms Races and Cooperation"; and Robert Axelrod and Robert O. Keohane, "Achieving Cooperation under Anarchy: Strategies and Institutions."

[16] James D. Fearon, "Bargaining, Enforcement, and International Cooperation," *International Organization* 52, no. 2, (Spring 1998): 269–305; Fearon, "Rationalist Explanations for War," *International Organization* 49, no. 3 (Summer 1995): 379–414; Robert Powell, "Bargaining Theory and International Conflict," *Annual Review of Political Science* 5 (2002): 1–30; Dan Reiter, "Exploring the Bargaining Model of War," *Perspectives on Politics* 1, no. 1 (March 2003): 27–43; James D. Morrow, "Capabilities, Uncertainty, and Resolve: A Limited Information Model of Crisis Bargaining," *American Journal of Political Science* 33, no. 4 (November 1989): 941–72. In the first article of this note, Fearon says that interstate bargaining increasingly takes place in the context of regimes and argues that "regimes deserve greater attention as *forums for bargaining* rather than primarily as institutions that aid monitoring and enforcement" (emphasis in original, p. 298).

[17] These are core arguments in the institutionalist literature, cited earlier, and they are also discussed prominently in the field of development economics. See for example, Thomas Blanton, "The World's Right to Know," *Foreign Policy* (July/August 2002); Philip Bowring, "Through a Glass, Darkly," *Development Dialogue*, no. 1 (1998); Michel Camdessus, *From Crisis to a New Recovery: Excerpts from Selected Addresses* (Washington, DC: International Monetary Fund, 1999), Scott B. MacDonald, "Transparency in Thailand's 1997 Economic Crisis: The Significance of Disclosure," *Asian Survey* 38, no. 7 (July 1998): 688–702; Andreas Kluth, "In Praise of Rules: A Survey of Asian Business," *The Economist*, April 7, 2001; and the work of Transparency International at www.transparency.org.

methods. The apparent differences among the political psychologists, rationalists, institutionalists, and qualitative causes of war scholars obscure these similarities, and cross-citations are rarer than they should be.

The Focus on Transparency

The first reason I focus on transparency as a tool of regimes is because of its relevance to issues of war and peace. Due to the effects described earlier, many believe that the promise of transparency can help seal a peace agreement or cease-fire. Transparency may also reduce arms races and security spirals, reduce misperceptions and miscalculations that can lead to war, and help adversaries bargain their way to agreements.

The second reason to focus on transparency is that it should be something relatively easy for security regimes to provide. Realist critics of institutions are correct that the U.N. is incapable of sending divisions of troops to quell a crisis. Security regimes are not that powerful. One should not ignore, however, other benefits that regimes may offer.

Increasing transparency means exchanging or providing information. Compared to sending forces, increasing transparency is relatively easy for regimes to accomplish. This is true whether one is looking at cost, logistics, institutional or technical expertise, number of necessary personnel, or political sensitivity.[18] Transparency is a fairly manipulable variable in the realm of security. Whatever good that security regimes can do in a dangerous world should be studied and welcomed.

Finally, transparency is of growing interest to scholars and policymakers. As mentioned, Jervis, Lipson, and Kupchan and Kupchan have led the study of transparency as applied to security regimes, while John Lewis Gaddis is the leading historian grappling with the subject. They have developed arguments about different peace-promoting effects of transparency ranging from calming arms races to reducing miscalculation.[19] These arguments are the conventional wisdom for arms controllers and institutionalists.

---

[18] Similar efficiency and bang for the buck arguments are made about public diplomacy.

[19] Jervis, "From Balance to Concert," 73–76; Kupchan and Kupchan, "Concerts, Collective Security, and the Future of Europe," 136; and Lipson, "Is the Future of Collective Security Like the Past?" 109–10, 125. Gaddis's work on transparency includes "The Long Peace: Elements of Stability in the Postwar International System," in Sean M. Lynn-Jones, ed., *The Cold War and After: Prospects for Peace* (Cambridge, MA: MIT Press, 1991), 25 and *The Long Peace: Inquiries into the History of the Cold War* (Oxford: Oxford University Press, 1987), chap. 7, "Learning to Live with Transparency: The Emergence of a Reconnaissance Satellite Regime." See also Charles L. Glaser, "Political Consequences of Military Strategy: Expanding and Refining the Spiral and Deterrence Models," *World Politics* 44, no. 4 (July 1992) and Robert Jervis, "Arms Control, Stability, and Causes of War," *Political Science Quarterly* 108, no. 2 (Summer 1993).

A new wave of scholarship by Ann Florini, James Marquardt, Ronald Mitchell, Bernard Finel, and Kirsten Lord has begun to explore arguments about the potentially negative effects of transparency. These findings suggest that transparency may exacerbate tensions, make bargaining more difficult, and even lead to conflict.[20] Bargaining theorists are also developing arguments about the negative effects of transparency and about the conditions under which transparency helps or hurts cooperation. Some argue that noisy information and uncertainty can hurt cooperation even when the parties want cooperation, but help cooperation when the parties are hostile. Others argue that transparency can remove peace-promoting ambiguity and encourage deadlock or even preventive war.[21] Within and across various literatures, the debate is engaged between transparency optimists and pessimists. This is one of the first attempts to lay out and test these conflicting contentions about transparency.

CASES AND METHODS

To learn about the provision of transparency and its effects in a range of contexts, I study the Concert of Europe and several U.N. peacekeeping operations. The Concert was the first multilateral crisis management forum. I study the role of transparency as the forum handled its first five crises from 1814 into the middle 1830s. While the Concert is 200 years

---

[20] Bernard I. Finel and Kristin M. Lord, eds., *Power and Conflict in the Age of Transparency* (New York, NY: Palgrave, 2000); Ann Florini, "The End of Secrecy," *Foreign Policy* 111 (Summer 1998): 60–61; James Marquardt, "Why Transparency in International Relations Is Not What It Appears To Be," Ph.D. diss., University of Chicago, 1998; Ronald Mitchell, "Sources of Transparency: Information Systems in International Regimes," *International Studies Quarterly* 42, no. 1 (March 1998): 109–30. See also John C. Baker, Kevin M. O'Donnell, and Ray A. Williamson, eds., *Commercial Observation Satellites: At the Leading Edge of Global Transparency* (Santa Monica, CA: RAND, 2001). There are increasingly vast literatures on the general subject of information and politics. See the website of the Institute of Communications Studies at the University of Leeds in Great Britain: www.leeds.ac.uk/ics/index.htm. This site includes subsections on a number of areas, including terrorism and propaganda, at www.leeds.ac.uk/ics/terrorism.htm as well as very up-to-date syllabi of courses on communications, the media, propaganda, and information warfare from Dr. Phillip Taylor, a leading scholar on these issues, at www.leeds.ac.uk/ics/pt1.htm.

[21] Bendor, "Uncertainty and the Evolution of Cooperation"; Xavier Jarque, Clara Ponsati, and Jozsef Sakovics, "Mediation: Incomplete Information Bargaining with Filtered Information," *Journal of Mathematical Economics* 39, no. 7, (September 2003): 805; and Curtis S. Signorino, "Simulating International Cooperation under Uncertainty: The Effects of Symmetric and Asymmetric Noise," *Journal of Conflict Resolution* 40, no. 1 (March 1996): 152–205.

old, its lessons help us predict what will happen when forums convene to confront crises or when adversaries with few means of communication, such as North and South Korea, meet.

The four peacekeeping cases consist of two exemplars each of the two main types of U.N. operations: traditional and multifunctional.[22] Traditional operations monitor buffer zones and verify areas of limited armaments, as in the cases of the United Nations Peacekeeping Force in Cyprus (UNFICYP) and the United Nations Disengagement Observer Force (UNDOF) on the Golan Heights. Multifunctional (or complex) operations organize and monitor elections, and take on other tasks to administer a conflict area. I assess these in the cases of the United Nations Transition Assistance Group (UNTAG) in Namibia and the United Nations Transitional Authority in Cambodia (UNTAC).

I study these cases for two reasons. First, they are historically significant and policy relevant. Second, the crises, incidents, and activities within the cases provide multiple observations of, and variations in, the variables that I study: regime activity, transparency, and levels of tension between adversaries. To examine these variables, I first develop a number of hypotheses on the provision and various possible effects of transparency. I then test these hypotheses by process tracing events within each case to see whether the regimes increased transparency and to assess the effects of any transparency provided. I explain methods and case selection in detail in the next chapter.

Why should these cases have anything to do with transparency? Prior to the Concert, multilateral meetings between states happened at peace conferences, but crisis diplomacy was limited to bilateral exchanges. In contrast, multilateral meetings should increase transparency because they allow more states to exchange information more easily. To assess whether this is true, and to determine the effect of any transparency provided on crisis management, I not only examine five crises confronted by the Concert, but I also compare Concert diplomacy with diplomacy prior to its formation. The ability to compare diplomacy before and after the Concert distills the effects of forum diplomacy and makes the Concert a valuable case for understanding how multilateral forums work.

U.N. peacekeepers may increase transparency by patrolling buffer zones, verifying arms control agreements, and monitoring elections. A central

---

[22] For typologies of peacekeeping operations, see William J. Durch, "Keeping the Peace: Politics and Lessons of the 1990s," in William J. Durch, ed., *UN Peacekeeping, American Politics and the Uncivil Wars of the 1990s* (New York: St. Martin's): 3–10, and Paul F. Diehl, Daniel Druckman, and James Wall, "International Peacekeeping and Conflict Resolution: A Taxonomic Analysis with Implications," *The Journal of Conflict Resolution,* 32, no. 1 (February 1998): 33–55.

purpose of these activities is to generate, provide, or exchange information about adversaries' capabilities, intentions, and actions. From the very beginning, peacekeeping has been about transparency:

> UN OBSERVERS. Their beat—no man's land. Their job—to get the facts straight. A frontier incident, an outbreak of fighting. . . . Which nation is responsible, whose story is true? The UN must know. So its peace patrols keep vigil to prevent flareups, supervise truces, investigate and report.
> —UN Department of Public Information poster, c. 1960[23]

Does this actually promote peace?

FINDINGS

Testing hypotheses about transparency across these cases generates a range of findings that indicate when transparency can most easily be increased, and what transparency's effects will be. These findings advance academic debates on the Concert, peacekeeping, international institutions, cooperation, and bargaining. They also provide the basis for a number of policy recommendations.

I find that the Concert often modestly increased transparency. This made coercive bargaining easier, while sometimes highlighting deadlock. Transparency helped bring peaceful endings to two crises, and it led to peaceful standoffs in two other cases. For example, during the Poland-Saxony crisis, three states made a secret alliance, revealed it the next day, and successfully coerced two other states into backing down. I argue that such a quick exchange of information would have been impossible prior to the forum.

With transparency, the Concert made power politics work more quickly and peacefully. This argument occupies the middle ground between Concert optimists who find that the Concert transformed European politics and call it the "best example of a security regime"[24] and those of recent Concert pessimists who find nothing to support institutional arguments.[25]

---

[23] Quoted in Walter Dorn, "Blue Sensors: Technology and Cooperative Monitoring in UN Peacekeeping," SAND 2004-1380 (Albuquerque, NM: Sandia National Laboratories, April 2004): 9.

[24] Paul W. Schroeder, *The Transformation of European Politics: 1763–1848* (Oxford: Oxford University Press, 1994); and Jervis, "Security Regimes," 178, respectively.

[25] Korina Kagan, "The Myth of the European Concert: The Realist-Institutionalist Debate and Great Power Behavior in the Eastern Question, 1821–41," *Security Studies* 7, no. 2 (Winter 1997–1998).

Because transparency helped coercion or clarified the existence of schisms, the cases reveal darker sides of transparency that contrast with the conventional wisdom of the arms control and liberal advocacy communities that transparency is a prescription for peace. Transparency did not overcome realpolitik, it just made it work better. At several points, transparency aggravated the crises and heightened the odds of war. While at first this might seem to support transparency pessimists, communication of positions and threats were also necessary to resolve the crisis.

Turning to the peacekeeping operations, I argue that traditional U.N. operations that monitor buffer zones face many previously unidentified barriers to their attempts to increase transparency. Scholars such as Michael Doyle may be too quick to assume that transparency works well in traditional operations.[26] For example, a close examination at UNDOF's inspection system reveals a number of deficiencies. The personnel, procedures, and equipment look good on paper but are not sufficient to monitor adequately the elaborate arms control agreement on the Golan Heights. These flaws suggest that the verification procedures in arms control agreements have to be carefully thought out, down to a fine-grained level of detail. This case also shows that it is hard for a regime to increase transparency when the adversaries already know a good deal about each other. When this is true, the regime cannot add much value to the flow of information.

The UNFICYP case reveals that efforts to increase transparency may not be able to overcome strong biases and enemy-imaging of adversaries.[27] For example, there is sometimes uncertainty about the nature of military construction along the buffer zone: is a fortification being repaired (allowed) or upgraded (not allowed)? Each side often fears the worst about the other. In theory, transparency could reduce these fears when they are unwarranted and exacerbated by uncertainty. In reality, several incidents reveal that each side is so suspicious that UNFICYP may not assuage fears no matter what it says in its reports. On the other hand, UNFICYP often uses information to coerce aggressors and troublemakers into backing down, thus preventing incidents from escalating.

In contrast, multifunctional operations show more promise. In Namibia and Cambodia, where there were scanty media outlets and poorly

---

[26] Michael W. Doyle, *UN Peacekeeping in Cambodia: UNTAC's Civil Mandate*, International Peace Academy Occasional Paper Series (Boulder, CO: Lynne Rienner, 1995): 76, 98.

[27] For more on enemy-imaging, see Patrick G. Coy and Lynne M. Woehrle, eds., *Social Conflicts and Collective Identities* (Lanham, MD: Rowman and Littlefield, 2000); and Richard K. Herrmann, "Image Theory and Strategic Interaction in International Relations," in David O. Sears, Leonie Huddy, and Robert Jervis, eds., *Oxford Handbook of Political Psychology* (Oxford: Oxford University Press, 2003), chap. 9.

informed and often illiterate citizens, information campaigns by UNTAG and UNTAC helped these operations succeed. In both cases, harmful rumors abounded, and the U.N. stopped these rumors with superior information firepower. As shown earlier, during the Cambodian elections of 1991, U.N. radio broadcasts reassured Cambodians that their votes would be kept secret. Other transparency-increasing mechanisms, including puppet shows, singers, and town meetings, taught voters about the U.N.'s mission and refuted rumors of violence that might have thwarted the elections. Transparency helped generate turnouts of 96 and 90 percent in these two operations' elections.

These peacekeeping missions suggest that efforts to increase transparency work best under the following conditions:

- there are poor information environments where the regime can more easily add value to existing information;
- adversaries are not so plagued by biases that new information cannot shift perceptions;
- adversaries are sufficiently weak relative to the U.N. so that they cannot thwart the U.N.'s efforts;
- the U.N. has sufficient resources and adequate procedures in place to accomplish its mandate.

These conditions for success are also likely to apply to information operations and public diplomacy, including efforts by the U.S. Department of Defense and State Department.[28]

POLICY IMPLICATIONS

The study of forum diplomacy helps predict what will happen when states that do not regularly consult are brought together. Despite the Internet and globalization, there are still areas like the Korean Peninsula and parts of Africa where adversaries scarcely communicate. Many analysts extol the virtues of concert-like forums, and my findings help make clear what we should expect from their recommendations.[29] Forums beat

[28] U.S. Army, Field Manual, FM 34–37, *Strategic, Departmental, and Operational IEW Operations* Preliminary Draft (1997), chap. 3, Land Information Warfare Activity (LIWA), available at www.fas.org/irp/doddir/army/fm34-37_97/3-chap.htm; U.S. Army, Center for Army Lessons Learned, "Task Force Eagle Information Operations(IO)," CALL Newsletter 03-18 (2003), available at www.globalsecurity.org/military/library/report/call/call_03-18_toc.htm; and U.S. Department of State, Under Secretary for Public Diplomacy and Public Affairs, available at www.state.gov/r.

[29] See fn. 5 in this chapter.

the alternative of no forums, but only because forum diplomacy enhances tough bargaining.

The peacekeeping cases offer a number of lessons for both traditional buffer zone–monitoring and multifunctional democracy-promoting operations. While promoting democracy is a task now almost taken for granted at the U.N., the mandates of several recent U.N. and NATO missions include establishing and supervising buffer zones. These include operations in Kosovo-Serbia, Eritrea-Ethiopia, and inter-Congo.

The first lesson is that policymakers and U.N. officials should recognize the value of increasing transparency to the success of some of their peacekeeping operations. There is institutional resistance to wielding information in ways that may affect conflicts. These fears remain, even though many in the U.N. recognize the successes of UNTAC and UNTAG. These missions showed that active information operations and transparency can reduce tensions, defuse crises, and help peacekeepers fulfill their mandates.

U.N. information efforts remain deficient. For example, in the U.N. Mission in Eritrea and Ethiopia (UNMEE), the U.N. broadcasts about its mission for one hour a week on Eritrean radio, but it is denied access to Ethiopian radio, and has no independent radio facilities. This study suggests that conditions in UNMEE's area of operations might be ripe for increased information efforts and transparency: the local information environment is poor, and uncertainties remain about the mission, the border, and the activities of the adversaries.

Second, peacekeepers can expand their transparency-increasing roles to new roles and missions. For example, peacekeepers could go beyond often-passive border patrols and post-hoc incident reports and try to increase transparency proactively. By monitoring each sides' policies and statements, peacekeepers and truth squads could combat dangerous falsehoods, rumors, and myths with relevant facts. This would combat false fears and fear-mongering as well as help get the adversaries operating with more common and accurate information.

Third, the U.N. should experiment with limited peacekeeping operations that seek only to increase transparency in cases where a full scale peacekeeping operation is not possible or desirable. A U.N. news radio station located near a troubled area might do some good if it helped reduce fears, correct misperceptions, and deflate myths held by each side.

In all cases, new doctrines, procedures, and equipment would have to be provided to bolster the small in-house information and media departments that are organic to most peacekeeping operations. Operations need enhanced expertise and information-gathering capabilities to separate myth from fact adequately and to provide tension-reducing information. Unfortunately, there is resistance within the U.N. to the development of these capabilities. Perhaps this book will bolster the forces of change.

STRUCTURE OF THE BOOK

Chapters 1 and 2 introduce the subject, the hypotheses, and the methodology. Chapter 3 begins by reviewing diplomacy and crisis management before the Concert of Europe. This provides a baseline, which I then use to assess how well the Concert used the new tool of forum diplomacy to manage its first five crises. Chapters 4 and 5 examine traditional buffer zone–monitoring operations in two cases: UNFICYP and UNDOF. Chapters 6 and 7 shift the peacekeeping focus to multifunctional operations that sponsor and monitor elections. I examine UNTAG and UNTAC, respectively. Chapter 8 concludes the book, summarizing my findings and presenting their implications for scholars and policymakers.

To help extend my findings and explore their limits, one appendix assesses the state of U.N. information operations in several recent missions while a second appendix looks at the role of transparency in mini-cases ranging from the Open Skies regime and strategic arms control, to the non-proliferation regime.

CHAPTER TWO

Theory, Methods, and Case Selection

METHODS HELP US ANSWER "What causes what?" questions about politics in a way that is systematic and that promises replicability. Methods establish standards for testing hypotheses, measuring variables, and making valid arguments about how the world works. Replicability and validity are tough to come by, but achieving them is a noble aim because they help scholars cumulate knowledge and they provide policymakers with more reliable insights.

Some variables like gross national product and geographic proximity are fairly easy to measure, while others such as ideas and norms are harder to visualize and evaluate. Transparency lies on the opaque side of this continuum. It is difficult to see transparency in action, because it is about who said what to whom, and how information affects the outcomes of crises and incidents. The trick in studying transparency, then, is to define terms precisely, to lay out clearly hypotheses about the causes and effects of transparency, and to explain their observable implications. These are the main goals of this chapter.

DEFINITION OF TRANSPARENCY

Transparency describes the availability of information about potential adversaries' actions, capabilities, and intentions. If information about potential adversaries is easy to obtain, and the amount and accuracy of information is high, then the world is said to be transparent. As transparency increases, completeness of information increases. If information about threats is difficult to acquire, the world is less transparent or more opaque. As transparency decreases, opacity increases, and incomplete information and uncertainty also increase.

The hypotheses spell out the different ways in which transparency can affect the probability of cooperation or deadlock, war or peace. Perhaps the effect of transparency that first comes to many people's minds is that it can calm arms races and reduce enemy-imaging between adversaries. A prevalent view in the liberal and arms control communities is that arms races are caused or exacerbated by incorrect worst-case analyses and that hostile relations are aggravated by exaggerated fears of the enemy.[1] When analyses and fears are indeed based on misperceptions, then transparency may reduce tensions and promote peace.[2] To those who think conflict is frequently based on misperception, transparency is viewed as an elixir of peace. Stephen Van Evera argues that "anything that makes the world more transparent will reduce the risk of war."[3] As we shall see, transparency has more complex effects.

There are four types of transparency, each corresponding to one of the four general ways by which states obtain information about their potential adversaries: cooperative, ambient, coerced, and unilateral.[4] I focus on *cooperative transparency,* which is the domain covered by most security regimes. Cooperative transparency is caused by states' institutionalized and

[1] For overviews of arms control arguments, see Arms Control Association, *Arms Control and National Security: An Introduction* (Washington, DC: Arms Control Association, 1989), 5–15; Coit D. Blacker and Gloria Duffy, eds., *International Arms Control: Issues and Agreements* (Stanford, CA: Stanford University Press, 1984, for the Stanford Arms Control Group), 335–38; Randall Forsberg, "The Freeze and Beyond," in Desmond Ball and Andrew Mack, eds., *The Future of Arms Control* (Sydney, Australia: Australian National University Press, 1987); George Rathjens, "The Dynamic of the Arms Race," *Readings from Scientific American: Progress in Arms Control?* (San Francisco, CA: W. H. Freeman, 1979); Thomas C. Schelling and Morton H. Halperin, *Strategy and Arms Control* (Washington, DC: Pergammon-Brassey's, 1985; originally published in 1975), chaps. 3 and 5, with a good discussion of verification in chap. 9; Geoffrey Blainey, *The Causes of War,* 3rd ed. (New York: Free Press, 1988), 135–41; Bernard Brodie, "On the Objectives of Arms Control," in Robert J. Art and Kenneth N. Waltz, eds., *The Use of Force,* 3rd ed. (Lanham, MD: University Press of America, 1988), 618–36; and Thomas C. Schelling, *Arms and Influence* (New Haven, CT: Yale University Press, 1966), chap. 7.

[2] Works exploring misperception and conflict include Nehemia Geva and Alex Mintz, eds., *Decisionmaking on War and Peace: The Cognitive-Rational Debate* (Boulder, CO: Lynne Rienner, 1997); Robert Jervis, "Hypotheses on Misperception," in G. John Ikenberry, ed., *American Foreign Policy: Theoretical Essays* (Glenview, IL: Scott, Foresman, 1989; reprint from *World Politics* 20, no. 3, April 1968); Robert Jervis, *Perception and Misperception in International Politics* (Princeton, NJ: Princeton University Press, 1976); Robert Jervis, Richard New Lebow, Janice Gross Stein, et al., *Psychology and Deterrence* (Baltimore, MD: Johns Hopkins University Press, 1985); Yuen Foong Khong, *Analogies at War: Korea, Munich, Dien Bien Phu, and the Vietnam Decisions of 1965* (Princeton, NJ: Princeton University Press, 1992); Jack S. Levy, "Misperception and the Causes of War, Theoretical Linkages and Analytical Problems" *World Politics* 36, no. 1 (October 1983); Jack S. Levy, "Loss Aversion, Framing Effects, and International Conflict: Perspectives from Prospect Theory," in Manus I. Midlarsky, ed., *Handbook of War Studies II* (Ann Arbor, MI: University of Michigan Press, 2000); and William Curti Wohlforth, *The Elusive Balance: Power and Perceptions during the Cold War* (Ithaca, NY: Cornell University Press, 1993).

[3] Stephen VanEvera, *Causes of War: Power and the Roots of Conflict* (Ithaca, NY: Cornell University Press, 1999), 34.

[4] While I categorize transparency here by its sources, it can also be categorized by its effects or functions as well as by the subject of the information being revealed. For example, Ann Florini lists deterrent, reassurance, and revelatory effects in "A New Role for Transparency," *Contemporary Security Policy* 18, no. 2 (August 1997): 59, while Antonia Handler Chayes and Abram Chayes list coordination, reassurance, and deterrence as functions in

cooperative efforts to increase transparency. Various cooperative mechanisms can be used to increase transparency, including sharing of information, meetings, discussion forums, buffer zones, verification provisions in treaties, and shared intelligence. These institutional mechanisms vary according to their formality—the extent of the regime's rules, bureaucracy, procedures, and functions. As a result, cooperative transparency has two main variants, *informal cooperative transparency* and *formal cooperative transparency*. For example, discussion forums like the Concert of Europe are less formal than U.N.-monitored buffer zones or onsite inspections.

The other three types include *ambient transparency*, which is caused by factors including the extent of global media coverage, relative ease of travel, and amount of trade and telecommunications, as well as information generated by nongovernmental organizations, think tanks, and universities. Although these factors are hard for policymakers to manipulate, an increase in any of them generally increases transparency. *Coerced transparency* occurs when states are forced to open up, as Iraq was forced to do after the Gulf War.

Unilateral transparency has three forms. The first is intelligence transparency, which is a state's independent and directed efforts to collect information. These efforts include satellites, spies, and other such methods to gather and assess information. The second is confrontational transparency, which is caused when states communicate in order to coerce or deter. When states coerce or deter, they may clarify their stakes in a given situation, clarify what actions they are willing to take to preserve their interest in those stakes, and clarify what capabilities (and allies) can be brought to bear to support those actions (and they may also be bluffing).[5] The third is proffered transparency, which is when states unilaterally reveal information in an effort to de-spiral conflicts and reassure others.[6]

There is sometimes overlap among the categories. For example, some security regimes such as the U.N. Special Commission on Iraq (UNSCOM)

"Regime Architecture: Elements and Principles," in Janne E. Nolan, ed., *Global Engagement: Cooperation and Engagement in the 21st Century* (Washington, DC: Brookings Institution Press, 1994), 65–130, esp. 81–84. By turning these effects, and others, into my hypotheses, I test how and under what conditions security regimes can achieve these results. The OTA classified transparency as macro or micro, depending on whether the information was about force structures and operational practices or about details like individual weapons designs; see U.S. Congress, Office of Technology Assessment, *Verification Technologies: Cooperative Aerial Surveillance in International Agreements,* OTA-ISC-480 (Washington, DC: U.S. Government Printing Office, July 1991), 22. See also Mitchell, "Sources of Transparency."

[5] On manipulation of risk, see Schelling, *Arms and Influence*.

[6] Kenneth W. Abbott, "'Trust but Verify': The Production of Information in Arms Control Treaties and Other International Agreements," *Cornell Journal of International Law* 26, no. 1 (Winter 1993): 4.

generate coerced transparency.[7] Bargaining during Concert crises was often confrontational. Even though states cooperatively joined in the forum's meetings, they often used the meetings to issue threats. It is also very important to note that just because the press or intelligence can be sources of transparency, they may also be prone to spreading misinformation, fostering and spreading biases, and so forth.

Moreover, the relationships among these types of transparency offer insight into how and when regime-provided transparency works best. A major finding of this book is that regimes can more easily provide transparency between adversaries when unilateral/intelligence and ambient transparency are low. This increases the ability of the regime to provide new and more accurate information.

Table 2-1 summarizes these types of transparency, underscoring that there are many sources of transparency and that this book focuses on cooperative transparency as provided by security regimes.

The Hypotheses

The questions this book answers are, Do security regimes increase transparency and does transparency promotes peace? If so how and when? This means that the causal chain I am investigating is as follows:

$$\text{Security Regimes} \rightarrow \text{Transparency} \rightarrow \text{Peace}$$

The first independent variable is security regimes. Transparency is a dependent and then an independent variable. The ultimate dependent variable is peace.[8]

To examine this causal chain systematically and explore the possible effects of transparency on conflict, I lay out and test hypotheses that explain the principal ways in which transparency may reduce or increase tensions and affect the probability of war. Transparency may affect bargaining about regime formation, decisions for war, crisis bargaining, threat assessments, likelihood of cheating on agreements, behavior of rogues and spoilers, and the functioning and operations of the regime itself.

These hypotheses are largely derived from the literatures on arms control, the security dilemma, international regimes, cooperation, and bargaining. For example, much thinking about transparency in security studies

---

[7] See Michael A. Levi and Michael E. O'Hanlon, *The Future of Arms Control* (Washington, DC: Brookings Institution, 2005) for a set of innovative policy recommendations urging leaders to move beyond traditional views of arms control and instead consider arms control as an asset to coercive diplomacy and the use of force.

[8] An independent variable causes things to happen and a dependent variable is the thing that is caused.

Table 2-1
Types of Transparency

Type	Definition	Examples
Cooperative	Agreed-upon sharing of information.	Security regimes of various types
Cooperative, informal	Exchanges of information where the nature of information offered or exchanged is not specified formally or in advance	Forums such as the Concert of Europe, military-military cooperation, G-8 meetings
Cooperative, formal	Treaties and agreements specify the nature of information gathered and exchanged	Onsite inspections, election monitoring, border and buffer zone patrols by peacekeepers, Open Skies agreements
Ambient	System and global level information sources	Mass media, trade, travel, NGOs
Coerced	Information that is coerced	UNSCOM in Iraq
Unilateral	Information gathered or offered by states	
Intelligence	State-level intelligence gathering	Satellites, spies
Confrontational	Information revealed to coerce or deter during a confrontation, standoff, or competition	Reciprocal missile and nuclear tests between India and Pakistan
Proffered	Information offered to de-spiral or reassure	Publicized arms reductions, such as Gorbachev's withdrawal of offensive bridging equipment[a]

[a]Timothy A. Mueller, Lt. Col, USAF, "Developing National Security Policy in the "'Gorbachev Era,'" National War College, March 31, 1989, p. 3, available at www.ndu.edu/library/n3/SSP-89-016.pdf

is found in the scholarship on arms control.[9] Advocates of arms control believe that regimes can increase transparency, and that the effects of transparency are to promote cooperation, reduce unwarranted fears and worst-case assumptions, and reduce miscalculation. While these assumptions

[9] Examples include Ashton B. Carter, William Perry, and John D. Steinbruner, *A New Concept of Cooperative Security* (Washington, DC: Brookings Institution, 1992), 38–41;

sum up the conventional and optimistic views of transparency, it is possible that their opposites are true. Perhaps regimes find it hard to increase transparency or end up spreading misinformation. Perhaps transparency confirms or increases fears instead of reducing them. As mentioned earlier, arguments about the negative and counterintuitive effects of transparency are emerging in the arms control, bargaining, and other literatures.

Where these negative effects seem plausible, I match hypotheses about the positive conflict-reducing effects of transparency with primed or counterhypotheses about the negative effects of transparency. This should not be construed, however, as setting up a horse-race between positive and negative effects of transparency. As we shall see, whether transparency has positive or negative effects cannot be determined on a blanket basis, because transparency's effects are often highly dependent on prior conditions. Further, the Concert demonstrates that even when transparency seems to aggravate crises, the ability to make clear threats can also help resolve crises.

To test my hypotheses, I infer predictions (observable implications) about what behavior one should expect in the cases if the hypothesis were true. I then examine the cases to see if they contain evidence of the predicted behavior(s). Predictions tell us what to look for when examining the evidence and they answer the question, How do we know transparency and its effects when we see them? Within a case study, determining how well the predictions fare is the best way to measure variables. My methods for testing the hypotheses are explained in more detail after I present the hypotheses.

Regimes Provide Transparency (H1)

The first hypothesis is that security regimes provide transparency. Transparency is about information, specifically how much is known about a

---

Richard A. Falkenrath, *Shaping Europe's Military Order: The Origins and Consequences of the CFE Treaty,* CSIA Studies in International Security No. 6 (Cambridge, MA: MIT Press 1995), 247–48; Ann Florini "The Evolution of International Norms," *International Studies Quarterly* 40, no. 3 (September 1996); Florini, "A New Role for Transparency"; Marquardt, "Why Transparency In International Relations Is Not What It Appears to Be;" United Nations, Office for Disarmament Affairs, *Report of the Secretary-General: Study on Ways and Means of Promoting Transparency in International Transfers of Conventional Arms* (New York: United Nations, 1992), esp. 23–24; Edward L. Warner III and David A. Ochmanek, *Next Moves: An Arms Control Agenda for the 1990s* (New York: Council on Foreign Relations Press, 1989), 124–26; Timothy E. Wirth, "Confidence and Security-Building Measures," in Robert D. Blackwill and F. Stephen Larrabee, eds., *Conventional Arms Control and East-West Security* (Durham, N.C.: Duke University Press, for the Institute for East-West Security Studies, 1989).

potential adversary's political and military capabilities and intentions. Transparency does not just happen; an agent or mechanism is always required to generate information, provide information, or facilitate the flow of information between the states or parties involved. Examples of mechanisms include peacekeepers, forums, and buffer zones. Without this hypothesis, I would be assuming, not examining, the first half of the causal chain that security regimes do in fact increase transparency:

$$\text{Security Regimes} \rightarrow \text{Transparency} \rightarrow \text{Peace.}$$

Observable Implications. Because security regimes must use mechanisms to generate, provide, or facilitate the exchange of information, I will look for their use in the cases. The use of information mechanisms is the main observable implication of H1. If no mechanism is used, the security regime cannot be increasing transparency. Security regimes could use a variety of mechanisms, alone or in combination, to provide transparency. They include the following:

- conferences
- summits
- liaisoning
- observation and monitoring missions
- inspection and verification missions
- demarcation lines
- buffer zones
- demilitarized zones
- restricted activity zones
- incident reports
- information and anti-propaganda campaigns
- radio, television, print, and other media
- organized sharing of intelligence
- organized sharing of information

Observable implications extend beyond identification of the mechanism. If the security regime provides new information or facilitates the exchange of information, then the actors to or among whom the information is distributed should also be identifiable. Further, the content of the information provided or exchanged should be identifiable and describable. For example, the information might be about the numbers and disposition of forces in buffer zones and limited force areas; it might determine the exact location of a border, help chains of command within countries to identify rogue actors, outline the various different interpretations of an incident and show which versions are supported by the facts gathered during the post-incident investigation, and so forth. Finally, the information provided will show up in the statements and assessments of the actors involved.

If the content of the information is hard to identify, then post hoc assessments by the actors involved and by historians and analysts assume greater importance. These assessments can be used to fill in the blanks and answer questions that would help indicate whether or not the regime provided information. When a transparency mechanism is used, I want to answer: What did the actors learn and how did it affect their behavior? Actors should recount history using the information that the regime provided, and this history should describe the role of the information provided (for H1 and some combination of the other hypotheses to be confirmed).

This hypothesis would be discredited if the security regime tried to use a mechanism to increase transparency and it provided little or no information. Finding that transparency had little or no effect would also serve to discredit the other hypotheses. This is not, however, a horse race to determine winning and losing hypotheses. It is an endeavor to tell the truth about transparency in order to advance scholarship and help policymakers.[10]

REGIMES SPREAD MISINFORMATION (H1')

One should not assume that regimes generate or transmit accurate information only. Regimes may be used to spread misinformation, or they may themselves spread misinformation. If this happens in the cases, we should identify specific instances of misinformation in the transparency mechanisms. Support would be bolstered if the actor who spread the misinformation and his or her intent could be identified.[11]

Anticipated Transparency Promotes Cooperation (H2)

The second hypothesis is that the promise or anticipation of transparency promotes cooperation. States create regimes to take advantage of their benefits, and one benefit is increased transparency.[12] The anticipation of increased transparency provided by a security regime promotes coopera-

---

[10] For more on my views about those who know the answers ahead of time and do not tell the truth, see Dan Lindley, "The Arrogance of the Dogmatic Left and Right" at www .nd.edu/~dlindley/handouts/arroganceofleftandright.html.

[11] Jervis, *The Logic of Images in International Relations*.

[12] The informational benefits of regimes have been a core theme in the literature on regime formation and design for a number of years. See Kenneth W. Abbott and Duncan Snidal, "Why States Act through Formal International Organizations," *The Journal of Conflict Resolution* 42, no. 1 (February 1998): 3–32; Robert O. Keohane, *After Hegemony: Cooperation and Discord in the World Political Economy* (Princeton, NJ: Princeton University Press, 1984); Keohane, "The Demand for International Regimes," in Krasner, *International Regimes;* Koremenos, Lipson, and Snidal, *The Rational Design of International Institutions;* Mitchell, "Sources of Transparency"; and James D. Morrow, "The Forms of International Cooperation," *International Organization* 48, no. 3 (Summer 1994): 400.

tion by increasing states' incentives to enter into agreements and to form a regime or accept a role for a security regime.

To illustrate how this works, fears of cheating diminish the willingness of states to enter into or stick with peace treaties, confidence-building measures, arms control, and other agreements. Transparency reduces fears of cheating and increases the incentives to cooperate by increasing the ability to detect cheating.[13] While this is perhaps the primary way anticipated transparency would help the formation of a regime, a number of other possible benefits of transparency may spur regime formation, including reduced miscalculation, reduced fears and worst-casing, and better ability to detect and deter rogues and spoilers on either side. These regime-provided effects are covered by separate hypotheses later, and I defer discussion of their logics until then.

Although I focus on transparency, transparency and incomplete information are not, of course, the sole causes of war or impediments to bargaining. States may be bent on war, and some problems are indivisible. Commitment problems and some conflictual aspects of power transitions may have little to do with information, though often both are related to uncertainty and incomplete information about the future. Likewise, there are a number of nontransparency-related ways of solving commitment problems, promoting peace, and facilitating bargaining. These include security guarantees, economic or political incentives, and coercion, any of which may supplement or supercede transparency in sealing bargains or deterring war.[14]

Observable Implications.   To assess hypothesis H2, I will look for evidence in the cases where states' willingness to sign an agreement increased after the promise of increased transparency by a security regime was extended. The reasons for this willingness will be found in the potential benefits that the regime and increased transparency will bring. For example, states may be seeking cooperation but must not trust each other enough to come to an agreement—much like a prisoners' dilemma. When this is so, states will fear cheating and will insist on adequate verification or monitoring before signing a peace treaty or a cease-fire or agreeing to an election or other tension-reducing agreement. This insistence will be evinced in speeches, negotiations, policy statements, debates, and so forth. States

[13] Abbott, "'Trust but Verify,'" 4, 28–29. See also the discussion of H5: "Transparency Reduces Cheating, Rogue, and Spoiler Problems."

[14] Dale C. Copeland, *The Origins of Major War* (Ithaca, NY: Cornell University Press, 2000); Fearon, "Rationalist Explanations for War"; Robert Powell, "The Inefficient Use of Power: Costly Conflict with Complete Information," *American Political Science Review* 98, no. 2 (May 2004): 231–41; Barbara F. Walter, *Committing to Peace: The Successful Settlement of Civil Wars* (Princeton, NJ: Princeton University Press, 2002).

may also seek increased transparency to control rogues or reduce security spirals.

The anticipation of increased transparency may hinder cooperation and lessen the likelihood of regime formation. For example, militaries and politicians may fear that intrusive verification or monitoring by peacekeepers will hinder their operational flexibility or their ability to keep classified information private. The conventional wisdom of arms controllers is that insufficient monitoring makes bargaining harder because it increases fears of cheating. Similarly, many cooperation and bargaining theorists write that private or incomplete information makes it harder to locate bargains.[15] These views suggest that transparency will generally promote cooperation, but this hypothesis explores counterarguments.

Transparency is about who knows how much about whom, and thus transparency has potentially severe distributional consequences.[16] This can hinder cooperation in a number of circumstances. Increases in transparency will be more likely to hurt cooperation if the parties are in the domain of relative gains,[17] while they will be more likely to spur cooperation in the domain of absolute gains. Revisionist states and actors may have little to gain and much to lose from transparency, especially if their plans depend on secrecy and surprise.

Defenders also have large incentives to bluff and act determined to impose high costs in case of an attack. These bluffs may help deterrence, but they may also increase the odds of conflict because they raise tensions and because their associated audience costs make it hard to back down.[18] Weak states may depend more on bluffing than strong states, and so strong states will tend to value transparency, while weak states are more threatened by

---

[15] Fearon, "Bargaining, Enforcement, and International Cooperation," esp. 285, 290; Walter, *Committing to Peace;* and see also fn. 1 in this chapter.

[16] Morrow, "The Forms of International Cooperation," 388.

[17] Relative gains concerns are discussed in Joseph M. Grieco, "Anarchy and the Limits of Cooperation: A Realist Critique of the Newest Liberal Institutionalism," *International Organization* 42, no. 3 (Summer 1988): 487–90; Charles Lipson, "International Cooperation in Economic and Security Affairs," *World Politics* 37, no. 1 (October 1984); Mearsheimer, "False Promise of International Institutions," 9–14, esp 12–13; Oye, *Cooperation Under Anarchy;* and Kenneth Waltz, *Theory of International Politics* (New York: Random House, 1979), chap. 6, esp. pp. 105–6, 118.

[18] Paul K. Huth, "Deterrence and International Conflict: Empirical Findings and Theoretical Debates," *Annual Review of Political Science* 2 (1999), 30–31. Engaging wider audiences and risking greater audience costs may, however, reveal information, signal resolve, and lower the probability of war. See Kenneth A. Schultz, "Domestic Opposition and Signaling in International Crises," *American Political Science Review,* 92, no. 4 (December 1998): 829–44.

transparency.[19] Military issues are acutely permeated by a sense of relative gains, boosting states' incentives to guard private information, misrepresent themselves to others, and fear transparency.[20] These points are not necessarily consistent—there may be strong states that are revisionists and that want to bluff—but they do highlight a number of conditions under which states may fear transparency.

Two pieces of evidence must be found in the cases to support this contention. First, parties must hesitate or refuse to form a regime or use its services. Second, the basis for this refusal or hesitation will be because they fear that the effect of the regime-to-be will deepen information asymmetries, or that resulting transparency will disproportionately benefit others or hurt their ability to keep information private.

Transparency Promotes Cooperation and Prevents Conflict (H3)

The third hypothesis is that increased transparency promotes peaceful outcomes from ongoing strategic interactions, including bargaining, coercion, and decisions for war. The qualitative causes of war and rationalist bargaining literatures contain a number of arguments in which uncertainty and miscalculations about threats, capabilities, actions, and resolve hinder negotiations and increase the likelihood of conflict and war. When incomplete information and miscalculation worsen strategic interaction, transparency can facilitate bargaining and promote peace.

As for qualitative causes of war, scholars such as Van Evera and Blainey note that anything that makes estimates of coercive and deterrent power less accurate increases the probability of deterrence failure through offensive or defensive optimistic miscalculation.[21] For rationalists such as Fearon and Powell, incomplete information and uncertainty hinders bargaining that would prevent costly war.[22] I discuss these two schools and their arguments in turn.

Optimistic miscalculation, the belief that one is stronger than one actually is, takes two forms. First, revisionist powers may believe their target for conquest is less powerful than it really is. This is *offensive* optimistic miscalculation, and it may cause deterrence to fail because the revisionist

[19] Branislav L. Slantchev, "The Principle of Convergence in Wartime Negotiations," *American Political Science Review* 97, no. 4 (November 2003): 621–32, esp. 627, 630.

[20] Fearon, "Rationalist Explanations for War." In contrast to these arguments about why states have incentives to bluff, Anne E. Sartori argues in *Deterrence by Diplomacy* (Princeton, NJ: Princeton University Press, 2005) that states usually have powerful incentives not to bluff. A reputation for honesty builds credibility, which helps diplomacy and deterrence.

[21] Blainey, *Causes of War;* and Van Evera, *Causes of War.*

[22] Fearon, "Rationalist Explanations for War"; and Powell, "Bargaining Theory and International Conflict."

does not know enough about its victim's capabilities or willpower to be deterred. For example, Germany's hope that Britain would not enter the coming war made it more belligerent than it otherwise would have been in the crisis leading up to World War I. Had Britain been clearer about its commitments, or had Germany possessed better information, the crisis might not have led to wide-scale war. Second, a status quo power may believe it enjoys greater safety than it really does, and this is *defensive* optimistic miscalculation. Here, deterrence fails because the status quo power is defensively overconfident, underestimates its adversary, and does not take enough action to deter or prepare successfully for attack. An example is India's optimistic assessment of Chinese intentions and capabilities prior to the unexpected and devastating Chinese attack of October 1962.[23]

Blainey sums up his miscalculation argument with this: "[M]ost wars were likely to end in the defeat of at least one nation which had expected victory." He later adds, "Any factor which increases the likelihood that nations will agree on their relative power is a potential cause of peace."[24] Transparency is one of those factors.

Rationalist bargaining scholars highlight a number of mechanisms by which incomplete information can increase conflict and lead to war. The main argument they make is that war is such a costly enterprise that if states had perfect information about each other's capabilities, resolve, and intentions, then they could reach a deal before incurring the costs of war. The ex post costs of war create an ex ante bargaining space. The only reason a bargain is not realized is that there is incomplete information and inability to calculate the costs of war, ex ante.[25] Sources of this incomplete information include deliberate misrepresentation either to hide or exaggerate capabilities for political or military effect, secrecy, misperceptions, and opacity.[26] For these scholars, war is itself an extended bargaining session that reveals information. Over time, wars end when

[23] Yaacov Vertzberger, "India's Strategic Posture and the Border War Defeat of 1962: A Case Study in Miscalculation," *The Journal of Strategic Studies* 5, no. 3 (September 1982).

[24] Blainey, *Causes of War*, 144–45, 294.

[25] Fearon, "Rationalist Explanations for War," 383–84; as well as Reiter, "Exploring the Bargaining Model of War"; James D. Fearon and David D. Laitin, "Explaining Interethnic Cooperation," *American Political Science Review* 90, no. 4 (December 1996): 715–35; Morrow, "Capabilities, Uncertainty, and Resolve"; William Reed, "Information, Power, and War," *American Political Science Review* 97, no. 4 (November 2003): 633–41; and Alastair Smith and Allan C. Stam, "Bargaining and the Nature of War," *Journal of Conflict Resolution* 48, no. 6 (December 2004): 783–813. Countering arguments that incomplete information is necessary for war is Branislav L Slantchev, "The Power to Hurt: Costly Conflict with Completely Informed States," *American Political Science Review* 97, no. 1 (February 2003): 123–33.

[26] Fearon, "Rationalist Explanations for War," 390–401, 383–84; as well as Reiter, "Exploring the Bargaining Model of War"; Morrow, "Capabilities, Uncertainty, and Resolve," 943–45 and 954; and Smith and Stam, "Bargaining and the Nature of War," 784–87.

enough information is exchanged for one side to realize that it must capitulate.[27] Despite different language, rationalist arguments about incomplete information leading to war have much in common with Blainey's conclusion that miscalculation results in at least one side ending up with an unexpected outcome that it could have avoided with better information.[28]

Rationalists also argue that incomplete information can make bargaining slower, inefficient, and less likely to be successful. Incomplete information and uncertainty hurt the ability of adversaries to signal their positions, actions, capabilities, intentions, and resolve during negotiations. When this is so, increased transparency should be able to improve signaling and facilitate bargaining.[29] Similarly, incomplete information can lead states to demand too much in a negotiation, increasing the odds of deadlock and conflict.[30]

Ken Oye argues that deadlock may result more often from the absence of mutual interest than from unwarranted fears, security dilemmas, accidents, or miscalculations.[31] Even when cooperation seems impossible, however, this does not mean that war is inevitable or that transparency is

[27] Darren Filson and Suzanne Werner, "A Bargaining Model of War and Peace: Anticipating the Onset, Duration, and Outcome of War," *American Journal of Political Science* 46, no. 4, (October 2002): 819–838; Mark Irving Lichbach, "Information, Trust, and Power: The Impact of Conflict Histories, Policy Regimes, and Political Institutions on Terrorism," draft paper, University of Maryland, College Park, MD, October 15, 2004; R. Harrison Wagner, "War and the State: Rethinking the Theory of International Politics," draft paper, University of Texas, Austin, TX, October 2005; and Reiter, "Exploring the Bargaining Model of War."

[28] For more discussion comparing and contrasting rationalist and miscalculation arguments about the causes of war, see Dan Lindley and Ryan Schildkraut, "Is War Rational? The Extent of Miscalculation and Misperception as Causes of War," draft paper, University of Notre Dame, available at www.nd.edu/~dlindley/.

[29] Fearon, "Bargaining, Enforcement, and International Cooperation"; Ariel Rubinstein, "Perfect Equilibrium in a Bargaining Model," *Econometrica* 50, no. 1 (January 1982): 97–109; Ariel Rubinstein, "A Bargaining Model with Incomplete Information about Time Preferences," *Econometrica* 53, no. 5 (September 1985): 1151–72; Signorino, "Simulating International Cooperation under Uncertainty."

Although it is beyond the capacity of this study to examine these claims, some scholars argue that regime type affects transparency and the abilities to signal effectively and make credible commitments. See Peter F. Cowhey, "Domestic Institutions and the Credibility of International Commitments: Japan and the United States, *International Organization* 47, no. 2 (Spring 1993): 299–326; James D. Fearon, "Domestic Political Audiences and the Escalation of International Disputes," *American Political Science Review* 88, no. 3 (September 1994): 577–92; Charles Lipson, *Reliable Partners: How Democracies Have Made a Separate Peace* (Princeton, NJ: Princeton University Press, 2003); and Kenneth A. Schultz, "Do Democratic Institutions Constrain or Inform? Contrasting Two Institutional Perspectives on Democracy and War," *International Organization* 53, no. 2 (Spring 1999): 233–66.

[30] Powell, "Bargaining Theory and International Conflict," 10–11.

[31] Oye, *Cooperation under Anarchy,* 7.

irrelevant. By helping sides understand that they have deadlocked and how they got to that point, transparency can help in two ways. First, transparency can improve each side's assessment of the other's relative commitment and strength. This might help each side live with deadlock if they were to realize that escalation would be too costly, and both sides were deterred. Second, such an understanding can break the deadlock by helping one side successfully coerce short of the use of force. Coercion is a bargain of sorts.

Observable Implications. Cases will confirm H3 if negotiations succeed or if wars are prevented because of new information provided by the regime. This new information will reduce incomplete information and miscalculation and will increase the range of acceptable bargaining outcomes ("win-sets") of the parties.[32] This should speed up bargaining and increase the likelihood of success. Although it is hard to ascertain specific odds of success in negotiations, cases studies and process tracing can provide examples of regime-provided information causing turning points in negotiations.

Those who have offensively optimistically miscalculated will come to recognize more fully the costs of war, and these higher costs will be a factor in spurring negotiations and locating a bargain. Those who are on the verge of aggression due to optimistic miscalculation will change their plans and desist once they learn through the regime that those plans were based on faulty assumptions and information. The readiness of forces may be relaxed, forces pulled back, and alerts canceled.

States who have defensively and optimistically miscalculated and who are more vulnerable than they thought will change their bargaining positions and plans accordingly once they learn from the regime that those plans were based on faulty assumptions and information. Such states may make concessions, appease, or bandwagon, or they may balance. Concessions, appeasement, and bandwagoning are marked by conceding to the demands of the revisionist or joining it in carrying out its plans. Signs of balancing include building up forces, redeploying forces better to counter the newly recognized threat, and making new alliances. War may be prevented and conflict reduced through enhanced deterrence or finding a bargain.

In all cases, H3 will hold true only if policy changes occur due to information provided by the regime. This information will be about the capabilities, resolve, and bargaining positions of adversaries, and it may

---

[32] Robert D. Putnam, "Diplomacy and Domestic Politics: The Logic of Two-Level Games," reprinted in Evans, Peter B., Harold K. Jacobson, and Robert D. Putnam, eds., *Double-Edged Diplomacy: International Bargaining and Domestic Politics* (Berkeley, CA: University of California Press, 1993).

have been deliberately obscured prior to the use or actions of the regime. Support will be strengthened if actors explain these changes with reference to this new information.

H3′: TRANSPARENCY HINDERS COOPERATION AND CAUSES CONFLICT

Transparency may cause war or hinder cooperation by removing ambiguities that bolstered deterrence and sustained deadlock, smoothed negotiations, or helped parties maintain blissful (or at least calming) ignorance. Transparency may also help a revisionist to plan its attack. I discuss these points in turn.

Rationalists and others are increasingly exploring the extent to which noise, incomplete information, and uncertainty actually help cooperation and prevent conflict. For example, uncertainty can lead a state to overestimate its adversary, and this would help deterrence.[33] In such cases, transparency would hurt deterrence as it reduced positive overestimation and revealed a more easily conquered prize for a revisionist state. States may also underestimate their adversaries, and new information that revealed a more powerful adversary could increase incentives for preventive war.[34] Likewise, incomplete information may help maintain a deadlock or standoff. Non-optimal, but still short of war.

Morrow notes that incomplete information is a necessary precondition to have something to bargain about; it is a key cause of inefficiency and conflict.[35] Incomplete information and shaded truth, however, can also help adversaries reach a compromise. In part, this is because parties are tempted, especially in the opening phases of negotiations, to start with overly ambitious opening gambits. This can lead to deadlock or spikes in tension. The essence of mediation can be to filter information as both sides learn more about each other and themselves.[36] As shown in the UNDOF case, U.S. Secretary of State Henry Kissinger prevented deadlock by limiting information exchange as he mediated between the Syrians and Israelis after the 1973 War. Because each side initially took positions that the other would find unacceptable, he feared that too much information would lead each side to walk away.

Negotiations are often marked by phases in which things seem to get worse before they get better. This is due to the multiple effects of

[33] Jack S. Levy, "Political Psychology and Foreign Policy," in Sears, Huddy, and Jervis, *Oxford Handbook of Political Psychology*, 261.

[34] Bendor, "Uncertainty and the Evolution of Cooperation"; Morrow, "Capabilities, Uncertainty, and Resolve," 955; Signorino, "Simulating International Cooperation under Uncertainty"; and Slantchev, "The Principle of Convergence in Wartime Negotiations."

[35] Morrow, "Capabilities, Uncertainty, and Resolve," 944.

[36] Jarque, Ponsati, and Sakovics, "Mediation: Incomplete Information, Bargaining with Filtered Information," 805.

transparency. It can first clarify how bad things are with respect to relative power, grievances, or resolve and/or it may reveal how unrealistic initial goals may have been. Once these costs and clarifications are on the table, however, they may then increase the incentives to compromise—if the negotiations survive.[37]

Transparency may remove a related form of peace-promoting ambiguity. Some "secrets," such as Israel's undeclared nuclear capability, are less irritating because of their ambiguous status. When norms and standards are not shared, familiarity can breed contempt, and transparency can make things worse.[38] It is also possible that transparency and too much information can create deadlock in negotiations, or overload leaders, making it hard to read their adversary's signals and making crisis management harder.[39]

Looked at more generally, noise and uncertainty cause a regression toward the mean among actors caught in repeated prisoner's dilemmas. Among populations of players with nasty strategies who would otherwise defect, incomplete information can lead to "accidental" cooperation. On the other hand, among populations of players with otherwise nice strategies, uncertainty can lead to accidental defections. In both cases, noise dilutes strategies and average outcomes veer toward a mean of mixed strategies. Incomplete information can hurt cooperation even when the parties want cooperation, but potentially help cooperation when the parties are hostile.[40]

In other words, transparency helps nice players stay nice, but at the cost of keeping mean players mean. While this may not be an irrelevant contribution in a world fraught with noise (and assuming mean players are mean to the bone), this reflects the critiques of those who think peacekeeping and institutions more generally are symptoms rather than causes in international relations.[41]

At its most brutal, Barry Posen argues that transparency may help a revisionist to plan an attack by identifying enemy weaknesses or plans. He

[37] Roger Fisher and William Ury, with Bruce Patton, *Getting to Yes: Negotiating an Agreement without Giving In,* 2nd ed. (New York: Penguin, 1991), 6.

[38] Florini, "End of Secrecy," *Foreign Policy* III (Summer 1998): 60; and Gaddis, *Long Peace,* p. 225.

[39] See Bernard I. Finel and Kristin M. Lord, "The Surprising Logic of Transparency," in Finel and Lord, eds., *Power and Conflict in the Age of Transparency* New York: Palgrove 2000; reprinted from *International Studies Quarterly* 43, no. 2 (June 1999): 315–39. On overload, see also Ole R. Holsti, *Crisis Escalation War* Montreal, Canada: McGill-Queens University Press, 1972, chap. 3.

[40] Bendor, "Uncertainty and the Evolution of Cooperation," 731.

[41] Betts, "Systems for Peace or Causes of War?; Richard Betts, "The Delusion of Impartial Intervention," *Foreign Affairs* 73, no. 6 (November/December 1994); and Mearsheimer, "False Promise of International Institutions."

suggests that intrusive inspections could help attack planning by revealing the lay of the land, secret defensive positions, and so forth.[42]

Observable Implications. To confirm H3', the cases should show that when the regime increases transparency, it weakens deterrence, pushes deadlock into conflict, and/or deadlocks negotiations. Evidence would be strengthened if it were also shown that incomplete information and uncertainty bolster deterrence, sustain deadlock, or facilitate negotiations. If transparency does help plan aggression, then information provided by the regime should be shown to contribute to the offensive military planning of a state or adversary, leading it to an attack that it previously thought unwise.

According to many deductively sound arguments, transparency (or incomplete information) can correlate with any outcome: peace, war, or something in between. So if incomplete information can produce war, deadlock, or help negotiations, and if transparency can reverse these effects, how do we know what is causing what and whether H3 or H3' is being confirmed? This conundrum is more apparent than real because there is a continuum of conflict severity between successful bargaining, deadlock, and war. I am analyzing processes along this continuum whereby things are either getting better or worse because of transparency (or incomplete information and uncertainty). If process tracing shows that increases in transparency push toward successful bargaining and away from war, then H3 is confirmed. If transparency increases conflict, then H3' is confirmed.

NOTE ON THE OPPOSING AND CONDITIONAL EFFECTS OF TRANSPARENCY

It is clear by now that transparency and its inverses of opacity, incomplete information, and uncertainty can have a variety of different effects depending on whether opacity causes over- or underestimation, and whether the actors are status quo (nice) or non–status quo (revisionist or mean). This is the logic behind the laying out of both positive and negative hypotheses about transparency. Table 2-2 shows some of the major ways in which miscalculation and accurate calculation can affect the probability of war between status quo and non–status quo actors. I could make a similar table for most of the effects of transparency, but this one makes the point that transparency can help or hurt, depending on the circumstances.[43] Casting debates about transparency as being engaged between

---

[42] Barry R. Posen, "Crisis Stability and Conventional Arms Control," *Daedalus* 120, no. 1 (Winter 1991): 228. Relatedly, one-sided information dominance is a cornerstone in U.S. plans to exploit the Revolution in Military Affairs (RMA).

[43] A complementary table is found in Signorino, "Simulating International Cooperation under Uncertainty," 193; see also Andrew Kydd, "Game Theory and the Spiral Model," *World Politics,* 49, no. 3 (April 1977): 371–400, esp. 389–93.

TABLE 2-2
Effects of Opacity and Transparency on Mis/Calculation, Deterrence, and War

	Overestimates SQ adversary's power and/or intentions (Opacity)	Underestimates SQ adversary's power and/or intentions (Opacity)	Accurately estimates SQ adversary's power and/or intentions (Transparency)	Overestimates NSQ adversary's power and/or intentions (Opacity)	Underestimates NSQ adversary's power and/or intentions (Opacity)	Accurately estimates NSQ adversary's power and/or intentions (Transparency)
SQ Power	1. Minor effects on chance of war; may spur unnecessary balancing, tension	2. Minor effects on chance of war; deterrence is weak	3. Minor effects on chance of war	4. Reduces chance of war, spurs balancing, and helps deterrence or spurs bandwagoning	5. Increases chance of war, reduces balancing, weakens deterrence	6. Reduces chance of war, spurs balancing, and helps deterrence or spurs bandwagoning
NSQ Power	7. Reduces chance of war, deterrence strengthened, likely to spur arms build-up	8. Increases chance of war, opens optimistic window of opportunity	9. Indeterminate, depending on balance of power (and risk tolerance). Increases chance of war if NSQ power confirms that it is stronger, reduces chance of war if NSQ power discovers it is weaker.	10. Reduces chance of war, deterrence strengthened, likely to spur arms build-up	11. Increases chance of war, opens optimistic window of opportunity	12. Indeterminate, depending on balance of power (and risk tolerance). Increases chance of war if NSQ power confirms that it is stronger, Reduces chance of war if NSQ power discovers it is weaker.

Note: SQ = status quo; NSQ = non-status quo (revisionist)

If one assumes that transparency helps an aggressor plan, then one might also assume that it should help the status quo power to identify the revisionist. In other words, if both powers are awake, entry no. 6 occurs at the same time as entry 9. Unfortunately, the literature on surprise attacks suggests that vulnerability to surprise is a nearly perpetual condition due in part to opacity, but especially due to cognitive, organizational, and bureaucratic blinders. Many surprise attacks are preceded by enough signals to prevent surprise, but these signals are ignored or misread. See fn. 44 for further reading.

transparency optimists and pessimists is useful because it reflects the literature. This table, however, serves as a reminder that such casting can oversimplify and that the effects of transparency can be highly dependent on prior conditions.[44]

Transparency Reduces Unwarranted Fears and Worst-case Assumptions (H4)

The fourth hypothesis is that increased transparency lessens unwarranted fears and reduces worst-case assumptions. Incomplete information and uncertainty allow for threat assessments that overestimate an adversary's hostility, and these are, according to Jack Levy, "one of the most common and important forms of misperception."[45] This misperception in turn worsens the security dilemma, escalates spirals and arms races, and increases tension and conflict. With increased transparency, states may replace worst-case assumptions with facts. Transparency can thereby reduce unwarranted fears, tensions, and security spirals, reducing the likelihood of war and increasing the likelihood of cooperation.

At the heart of this hypothesis is the spiral model. The spiral model depicts an action-reaction, tit-for-tat arms race (or other hostile escalation) in which each side escalates responding to real and anticipated actions on the other side. Arms races and escalations are both symptoms and causes of tension and conflict. The fundamental cause of spirals is anarchy, because states must provide for their own security and cannot escape the security dilemma. Transparency becomes relevant, however, when spirals are aggravated by uncertainty and incomplete information about present and future actions, capabilities, and intentions. In an uncertain and anarchic world, states seek insurance by making worst-case assumptions.[46] Spirals are also affected by psychological and perceptual dynamics, and by the indistinguishability of weapons that can be used for both offense

---

[44] See Richard K. Betts, *Surprise Attack: Lessons for Defense Planning* (Washington, DC: Brookings Institution, 1982), 120–27; Jervis, *Perception and Misperception in International Politics*, 270–79, 291–96; Ephraim Kam, *Surprise Attack: The Victim's Perspective* (Cambridge, MA: Harvard University Press, 1988), 128–29; Ernest R. May, "Conclusions: Capabilities and Proclivities," in Ernest R. May, ed., *Knowing One's Enemies: Intelligence Assessment Before the Two World Wars* (Princeton, NJ: Princeton University Press, 1986), 529, 537–42; Patrick Morgan, "The Opportunity for Strategic Surprise," in Klaus Knorr and Patrick Morgan, eds., *Strategic Military Surprise: Incentives and Opportunities* (New Brunswick, NJ: Transaction Books, 1983); Roberta Wohlstetter, *Pearl Harbor: Warning and Decision* (Stanford, CA: Stanford University Press, 1962), 386–96.

[45] Jack S. Levy, "The Causes of War: A Review of Theories," in Philip E. Tetlock, Jo L. Husbands, Robert Jervis, Paul C. Stern, and Charles Tilly, eds., *Behavior, Society, and Nuclear War*, vol. 1 (New York: Oxford University Press, 1989), 280.

[46] Jervis, *Perception and Misperception*, chap. 3.

and defense. In some cases, transparency can mitigate cognitive misperceptions and misperceptions of the offense-defense balance and the nature of some weaponry.[47]

George Rathjens writes, "Action-reaction phenomenon, stimulated in most cases by uncertainty about an adversary's intentions and capabilities, characterizes the dynamics of the arms race."[48] Similarly, George Downs, David Rocke, and Randolph Siverson argue,

> Imperfect intelligence can inspire an arms race that would not take place in the presence of perfect information, and can permit one to continue when it is "unjustified. . . ." Imperfect intelligence expands the range of games that can lead to arms races by raising the possibility that one side will think the other side has defected even though this may not have occurred.[49]

Unwarranted fears and worst-case assumptions are not simply caused by rational responses to uncertainty and anarchy, but can also be affected by motivational orientations toward trust or fear or toward revisionism or peace, perceptual biases, and other psychological dynamics.[50] Because transparency is about the quality of incoming information available to actors and not cognitive distortions of information after it has been received, transparency can better reduce fears when the source of those fears is external factors like opacity or bluffing rather than such factors as an actor's internal makeup. Nonetheless, the psychological literature does suggest that biases can sometimes be changed by new incoming information, especially when that information is vivid and forceful.[51]

Prime examples of spirals made worse by incomplete information and uncertainty are the Cold War bomber and missile gaps, which occurred when the United States vastly overestimated Soviet bomber and missile

---

[47] On the ability of transparency to affect cognitive misperceptions, see fn. 51 in this chapter.

[48] Rathjens, "Dynamic of the Arms Race," p. 42; see also fn. 1 in this chapter.

[49] Downs, Rocke, and Siverson, "Arms Races and Cooperation," in Oye, *Cooperation under Anarchy*, 134–35.

[50] Jonathon Bendor, Roderick M. Kramer, and Suzanne Stout, "When in Doubt . . . Cooperation in a Noisy Prisoner's Dilemma," *The Journal of Conflict Resolution* 35, no. 4 (December 1991): 691–719; Jervis, *Perception and Misperception*; Robert Jervis, "War and Misperception," *The Journal of Interdisciplinary History* 18, no. 4 (Spring 1988): 675–700; Kydd, "Game Theory and the Spiral Model," 389–93; Jack S. Levy, "Misperception and the Causes of War, Theoretical Linkages and Analytical Problems," *World Politics* 36, no. 1 (October 1983): 76–99; Signorino, "Simulating International Cooperation under Uncertainty," 155, 185.

[51] Jervis, "Hypotheses on Misperception"; and Levy, "Political Psychology and Foreign Policy."

capabilities, increasing tensions and worsening the nuclear arms race. The Cold War also provides an exemplar of transparency calming fears. Gaddis contends that the reconnaissance revolution "may rival in importance the 'nuclear revolution' that preceded it" in explaining the long peace of the Cold War. For example, satellites helped prevent recurrence of the bomber gap and missile gap panics.[52] While the Cold War arms race may be the first thing that comes to mind when thinking about spirals, a number of scholars also apply the spiral model to ethnic conflict.[53]

Observable Implications.   The primary prediction of this hypothesis is that threat assessments become more benign after a regime increases transparency. With increased transparency, revised assessments should be based on new facts and information provided or facilitated by the security regime with the mechanisms listed earlier. Threat assessments characterized by worst-case assumptions and unwarranted fears should suggest grave danger from an adversary, the inevitable threat of war, an implacably hostile enemy, and so forth. Hard facts and conservative estimates will be scanty or lacking. Instead, insider revelations or post hoc analyses should indicate that the threat assessment was indeed based on assumptions, assertions, guesses, extrapolations, and so forth.

H4′: TRANSPARENCY CONFIRMS FEARS

In some cases, worst-case fears may be confirmed by new information. Not all dire threat assessments are wrong. If H4′ is true, then the regime's transparency mechanisms will confirm the gravity of the threat and the accuracy of the suspicions. This does not mean that transparency caused the underlying conflict, or will necessarily make it worse. Furthermore, it may well be the task of the regime to uncover violations or report information related to threat assessments, and its credibility may well depend on reporting the truth even if that risks exacerbating the situation. While it seems likely that reducing unwarranted fears will reduce tension, table 2-2 makes clear that the effects of increased transparency and more accurate threat assessments may also be to increase the odds of conflict,

---

[52] Quote in Gaddis, "Long Peace," 232; see also chap. 7, "Learning to Live with Transparency: The Emergence of a Reconnaissance Satellite Regime"; and Jane Kellett Cramer, *National Security Panics: Overestimating Threats to National Security,* Ph.D. diss. MIT, Cambridge, MA, 2002.

[53] Fearon and Laitin, "Explaining Interethnic Cooperation"; Stuart J. Kaufmann, "Spiraling to Ethnic War: Elites, Masses, and Moscow in Moldova's Civil War," *International Security,* 21, no. 2 (Autumn 1996): 108–38; and Barry R. Posen, "The Security Dilemma and Ethnic Conflict," in Michael E. Brown, ed., *Ethnic Conflict and International Security* (Princeton, NJ: Princeton University Press, 1993).

depending on whether the parties are revisionist(s) and what their prior assessments were.

Transparency Reduces Cheating, Rogue, and Spoiler Problems (H5)

The fifth hypothesis is that transparency reduces cheating, rogue, and spoiler problems. This hypothesis is about the ability of transparency to help control provocative and hostile action, while the prior two hypotheses focus on the ability of transparency to push outcomes from strategic interaction toward peace and to calm threat assessments, respectively.

Incomplete information encourages defection and provocation in several ways. First, it hinders the ability to detect defection and retaliate, increasing the incentives to defect in the first place. Second, it makes it harder for regimes to control rogues on their own side, and more difficult for the other side to decide if a provocative act is due to rogue behavior or deliberate policy. Third, uncertainty surrounding the nature and motives of potential spoilers makes them harder for peacekeepers to control. Fourth, incomplete information within conflict zones makes it easier for hate-mongers to perpetrate hostile myths. Transparency can reduce all these problems. Finally, international regimes also have a special informational tool that supplements transparency. They can use information to shed a public spotlight on hostile behavior, and this tool can shame and coerce actors into changing their behavior. I discuss these points in turn.

A key argument in the institutionalist, cooperation, and bargaining literatures is that institutions promote cooperation and deter cheating because they can monitor agreements and increase transparency. Transparency increases the odds that defection will be detected, and this then affords the opportunity for retaliation.[54] A key factor is that there is something to defect from in the first place. Without an agreement (in my cases, to attend a multilateral forum during crises or abide by the agreement that installed a peacekeeping operation), then defection is harder to define and identify. In this way, agreements help send signals and increase transparency, even when they are broken.

Jervis summarizes how transparency can identify and prevent defection:

> Cooperation is made more likely not only by changes in payoffs but also by increases in the states' ability to recognize what others are doing—called "transparency" in the literature on regimes. Coupled with the ability to act on this information, transparency can produce a situation in which, in effect, the choices of CD and DC [one cooperates, the other

[54] For citations on this, see chapter 1, fns. 15, 16, and 17.

defects] are effectively ruled out. Short periods of defection may occur; but if they can be detected and countered, the only real alternatives are CC and DD [both cooperate or both defect].[55]

Michael Doyle echoes this with his argument that traditional peacekeeping operations use transparency to promote cooperation and compliance by solving coordination games and by sufficiently altering the payoffs in prisoners' dilemma games to turn them into coordination games.[56] My research shows this is likely to be more true in multifunctional operations.

Fears of cheating are particularly high in the security arena. Compared to economic cooperation, there is a "special peril" of defection in security affairs.[57] In contrast to cheating in economic agreements, cheating on security agreements can lead to conquest by an aggressor and to "game over" for the victim. This was the fear of those in the 1980s who thought the Soviets might rapidly break out of the ABM Treaty by upgrading their air defenses into ballistic missile defenses. Although the bar for reassurance is raised in security affairs, once states are assured that compliance can be adequately monitored, they are more likely to make agreements (as noted in H2).

Rogues engage in provocative behavior unsanctioned by their leaders or government. Informational issues related to rogues are fourfold. First, governments may have a hard time identifying and thus controlling rogue behavior within their own ranks due to lack of internal transparency and accountability. This is seen in the Cyprus case. A second issue is that it may be hard for adversaries to differentiate rogue behavior from deliberate policy. As Fearon and Laitin point out, intergroup information is harder to come by than intragroup information. If someone from ethnic group A engages in provocative behavior, and all that group B knows is that the provocateur is from group A, group B is more likely to want to punish group A as a whole. In contrast to limiting retaliation to the provocateur, group punishment increases the likelihood of violence spiraling upward.[58] This dynamic helped start the Seven Years War in America, as I show in chapter 3. A third factor exacerbates this problem. Even if the side with the provocateur promises to punish that individual, the other side will not necessarily know if punishment has indeed been meted out, or

[55] Jervis, "From Balance to Concert,'" in Oye, *Cooperation under Anarchy,* 73; his excellent discussion of transparency spans pp. 73–76. Lipson concurs that poor information hinders cooperation in "Are Security Regimes Possible?" 5. See also the discussion of transparency and arms control on p. 9.

[56] Doyle, *UN Peacekeeping in Cambodia,* 98, fn. 139.

[57] Lipson, "International Cooperation in Economic and Security Affairs," 14; and Stein, "Coordination and Collaboration: Regimes in an Anarchic World," 128.

[58] Fearon and Laitin, "Explaining Interethnic Cooperation," 719.

how genuinely the provocateur's side is trying to suppress violence more generally.[59] Finally, negative noise, such as a false belief that an adversary broke an agreement or intentionally committed a hostile action, can spark conflict.[60] A regime involving monitoring, verification, and inspections can ameliorate all these issues.

Spoilers are related to rogues, but their main goal is to undermine a peace agreement or peace process. Confronting spoilers is made more difficult because of uncertainties surrounding their goals, resolve, leadership, and unity. In the absence of this knowledge, it is harder for peacemakers to craft appropriate strategies.[61] Thus, a major task for peacemakers is to generate more information about who is threatening the peace and why.

The final problem is that ethno-nationalist leaders and hate-mongers bent on conflict can exploit uncertainty about the nature of threats to stir up their domestic constituencies and incite conflict. Media monopolies exacerbate this danger. Slobodan Milosevic's mobilization against his neighbors and the Hutu's use of radio Milles Collines are frequently cited examples.[62] When these problems arise, one remedy is to try to break media monopolies and provide more accurate information to the targeted area.[63]

International regimes can sometimes bring the international spotlight to bear on provocative behavior. This can promote peace by creating a shaming effect and by increasing the likelihood of international censure and sanction. Examples of beneficent coercion through information disclosure and dissemination are found in the work of NGOs who promote good governance by publicizing pollution, corruption, human rights abuses, and other evils.[64]

---

[59] Andrew Kydd and Barbara F. Walter, "Sabotaging the Peace: The Politics of Extremist Violence," *International Organization* 56, no. 2 (Spring 2002): 266.

[60] Bendor, "Uncertainty and the Evolution of Cooperation"; and Signorino, "Simulating International Cooperation under Uncertainty," 155, 193. Signorino calls actions by rogues and factions "negative noise," which is false information that makes things seem worse than they are.

[61] Stephen John Stedman, "Spoiler Problems in Peace Processes," *International Security* 22, no. 2 (Fall 1997): 5–53, esp. 7, 17, and 44–53.

[62] Rui J. P. de Figueiredo, Jr., and Barry R. Weingast, "The Rationality of Fear: Political Opportunism and Ethnic Conflict," in Barbara F. Walter and Jack Snyder, eds., *Civil Wars, Insecurity, and Intervention* (New York: Columbia University Press, 1999), 261–302, esp. 277–80; V. P. Gagnon, Jr., "Ethnic Nationalism and International Conflict: The Case of Serbia," *International Security* 19, no. 3 (Winter 1994/95): 130–66; and Kaufmann, "Spiraling to Ethnic War."

[63] Dan Lindley, "Collective Security Organizations and Internal Conflicts," in Michael Brown, ed., *The International Dimensions of Internal Conflict* (Cambridge, MA: MIT Press, 1996), 537–68; and Jack Snyder and Karen Ballentine, "Nationalism and the Marketplace of Ideas," *International Security*, 21, no. 2 (Fall 1996): 5–40.

[64] See Ann M. Florini, ed., *The Third Force: The Rise of Transnational Civil Society* (Washington, DC: Carnegie Endowment for International Peace, 2000); Florini, "A New

Observable Implications. If H5 is supported, then there will be evidence in the cases that the regime identified and gathered information on cheaters, rogues, and spoilers, and that this regime-provided information was used to coerce, suppress, punish, or retaliate against these actors. The foregoing discussion makes clear many of the specifics, for example, that information can affect inter- and intragovernmental and inter- and intragroup relations. Showing that potential defectors were in fact deterred can be problematic, however. Not only is it hard to prove a negative, which is always difficult in the study of deterrence, but also few potential defectors are likely to cry uncle, fess up to malignant intentions, or admit their inability to carry through.

There is no H5' as I cannot readily see how transparency could help cheaters, rogues, and spoilers. If these actors did use the regime to spread myths and false information, that would not be about transparency helping them; instead H1': Regimes spread misinformation would kick in.

Transparency about the Regime Increases its Effectiveness (H6)

The sixth hypothesis is that regimes can increase transparency about their own functions to reduce fears about its operations, clarify its purposes, and increase its effectiveness. States or parties involved with a peacekeeping operation may harbor fears about the operation, be uncertain about why it is there, or suspect the operation of working for or having bias toward the other side. These uncertainties may make the operation vulnerable to rumors and disinformation campaigns that will hamper its effectiveness. Parties may need to be educated about aspects of the operation's mission such as what democracies are, how to vote, and so forth. The operation may remedy these problems with an information campaign to increase transparency about itself and to teach people about its mission(s). I dub information operations about a peacekeeping operation's purposes "self-transparency."[65]

Role for Transparency;" Margaret E. Keck and Kathryn Sikkink, *Activists Beyond Borders: Advocacy Networks in International Politics* (Ithaca, NY: Cornell University Press, 1998); and Wolfgang H. Reinicke, *Global Public Policy: Governing without Government?* (Washington, DC: Brookings Institution, 1998); as well as the project "National Security and Open Government: Striking the Right Balance" at the Campbell Public Affairs Institute of the Maxwell School at Syracuse University, at www.maxwell.syr.edu/campbell/opengov/; the National Security Archive-based freedominfo.org at the George Washington University (funded by George Soros's Open Society Initiative), with many studies and reports as well as links to similar organizations worldwide at www.freedominfo.org/; and especially the anti-corruption work of Transparency International at www.transparency.org/.

[65] There is little theoretical work on "self-transparency," but for an excellent book devoted to information operations in U.N. peacekeeping operations, see Ingrid A. Lehmann, *Peacekeeping and Public Information: Caught in the Crossfire* (London: Frank Cass, 1999).

This hypothesis is more applicable to formal regimes like peacekeeping, which has agents on the ground trying to accomplish complex tasks. Informal regimes such as forums are less likely to kindle fears or require explanation. Formal regimes are also more likely to be able to wage an information campaign.

Observable Implications. To see if H6 is supported in the cases, I will look for evidence that the regime (e.g., peacekeepers) is aware that the operation is the subject of malicious rumors and misinformation or that its functions need explanation. The regime will embark on an information campaign using transparency mechanisms to correct this misinformation. The evidence will confirm that the information reached its target population and affected their behavior in ways favoring the mission.

Summary of Hypotheses

Table 2-3 summarizes my hypotheses. Some may want to merge hypotheses where they see overlap, while others may want to break hypotheses into component parts where they see them capturing several discrete effects. For example, threat assessments affected by incomplete information hurt bargaining, and so one might be tempted to fold H4 into H3. One might want to break out cheating from rogues and spoilers, and thus change H5 from one hypothesis to two. I recognize these concerns, and I have tried many permutations ranging from four hypotheses (with no counter-hypotheses) to eight (with many counter-hypotheses). The end result reflects my goal of providing a comprehensive set of hypotheses on the provision and effects of transparency, with each hypothesis reflecting a major set of arguments in the relevant literatures. I have tried to steer between oversimplifying and overcomplexifying.

To illustrate, much is made of uncertainty leading to worst-casing in the arms control and bargaining literatures. The ability of transparency to reduce this effect deserved being a separate hypothesis. Although worst-casing affects bargaining, folding worst-casing into the bargaining hypothesis would have obscured much more than it clarified and left many wondering what happened to this core theory about the way transparency is supposed to work. In contrast, I put cheating, rogues, and spoilers into one hypothesis because the underlying logic in the hypothesis is the same for all three: information can coerce better behavior. By creating a drizzle of hypotheses, separating these out would have obscured more than it clarified.

TABLE 2-3
Summary of Hypotheses

Hypothesis	Applies to	Main question used to examine hypothesis in the case studies:
Regimes provide transparency (H1) Regimes spread misinformation (H1′)	Ability of regime to generate, provide, or transmit *new and accurate information*	Does the regime use a transparency mechanism to help exchange or generate information, and is the information accurate?
Anticipated transparency promotes cooperation (H2) Anticipated transparency hinders cooperation (H2′)	Effects of anticipated transparency on *negotiations to establish the regime*	Does the promise of regime-provided transparency promote cooperation?
Transparency promotes cooperation and prevents conflict (H3) Transparency hinders cooperation and causes conflict (H3′)	Effects of new information from the regime on *bargaining,* coercion, and decisions for war	Does transparency promote peaceful outcomes within strategic interactions?
Transparency reduces unwarranted fears and worst-case assumptions (H4) Transparency confirms fears (H4′)	Effects of new information from the regime on *threat assessments,* including arms levels, arms races, spirals, likelihood of future hostile actions, and overall level of tensions and suspicions	Does transparency reduce or confirm fears about the adversary's actions, capabilities, and intentions?
Transparency reduces cheating, rogue, and spoiler problems (H5)	Effects of new or anticipated information from the regime to detect, deter, reverse, or retaliate for *defections,* including *cheating,* or actions by *rogues and spoilers*	Is the regime detecting defection and does this lead to more lawful behavior or reciprocity? Is the threat of detection deterring defection?
Transparency about the regime (or self-transparency) increases its effectiveness (H6)	Effects of information activities by the *regime to explain its purposes* and operations	Is the regime or its purposes misunderstood or feared, and is it using information to correct this and help its mission?

Methodology for Testing the Hypotheses

I test the hypotheses using the comparative case study method and process-tracing. By asking the same questions of each case, I generate comparative case studies.[66] The comparative case study method strengthens findings by assessing evidence in the same way across cases.

The main questions I ask of each case are indicated in Table 2-3. For example, to evaluate H1 consistently across cases, I ask, Does the regime use a transparency mechanism to help exchange or generate information, and is the information accurate? The specific evidence I look for is found under each hypothesis's observable implications. For a regime to provide transparency, as specified by H1, I must identify the mechanisms that the regime uses to provide or generate information.

To increase replicability and clarity, I report my findings in tables at the end of each chapter.[67] These tables refer to the pages on which the evidence for each finding is found, guiding the reader to each piece of evidence that informs my conclusions. A summary table in the conclusion (chap. 8) aggregates the findings for each case and hypothesis, and highlights the variations in findings across the cases. These variations help tell us about when the provision and effects of transparency will best promote peace.

My goal is to track new information provided or exchanged by the regime, and to correlate that new information with changes in behavior by the actors involved. To do this, I process-trace crises and incidents to

---

[66] See Henry E. Brady and David Collier, eds., *Rethinking Social Inquiry, Diverse Tools, Shared Standards* (Lanham, MD: Rowman and Littlefield, 2004); David Collier and James Mahoney, "Insights and Pitfalls: Selection Bias in Qualitative Research," Research Note, *World Politics* 49, no. 1 (October 1996): 56–91; Harry Eckstein, "Case Study and Theory in Political Science," in F. I. Greenstein and N. W. Polsby, eds., *Handbook of Political Science,* vol. 7 (Reading, MA: Addison-Wesley, 1975); Alexander L. George and Timothy McKeown, "Case Studies and Theories of Organizational Decision Making," *Advances in Information Processing in Organizations,* vol. 2 (Greenwich, CT: JAI Press, 1985), 35; Alexander L. George, "Case Studies and Theory Development," in Paul Gordon Lauren, ed., *Diplomacy: New Approaches in History, Theory, and Policy* (New York: Free Press, 1979), 43–68; Alexander L. George and Andrew Bennett, *Case Studies and Theory Development in the Social Sciences* (Cambridge, MA: MIT Press, 2005); John Gerring, *Social Science Methodology: A Critical Framework,* (Cambridge, England: Cambridge University Press, 2001); Gary King, Robert O. Keohane, and Sidney Verba, *Designing Social Inquiry: Scientific Inference in Qualitative Research* (Princeton, NJ: Princeton University Press, 1994); Arend Lijphart, "The Comparable-Cases Strategy in Comparative Research," *Comparative Political Studies* 8, no. 2 (July 1975); James Mahoney and Gary Goertz, "The Possibility Principle: Choosing Negative Cases in Comparative Research," *American Political Science Review* 98, no. 4 (November 2004): 653–69; and Stephen Van Evera, *Guide to Methods for Students of Political Science* (Ithaca, NY: Cornell University Press, 1997).

[67] King, Keohane, and Verba, *Designing Social Inquiry,* 26–27.

evaluate the predictions and determine the influence of regimes and transparency. "Process-tracing" means looking carefully at what caused the crisis and what made the crisis unfold as it did. In particular, I examine turning points in crises and see if the security regime and transparency played a role. Although I do not use extensive games or similar diagrams to tell my stories, turning points are the same as the inflection points represented in extensive games.[68]

Crises are where we see regimes in action and where we see relations between adversaries shift from peace to tension and then back toward peace or on to war. Crises put the study variables into play, and this helps us understand whether the causal chain of security regimes →transparency→peace holds true.[69] Glenn H. Snyder and Paul Diesing point out that "a crisis distills many of the elements that make up the essence of politics in the international system. It is a 'moment of truth' when the latent product of all these central elements [power configurations, interests, images, and alignments] become manifest in decision and action."[70]

To address the question of how much of the world can the theory help us explain,[71] I make a point with my hypotheses to examine the positive and negative effects of transparency. I am explicit and detailed with the observable implications for each hypothesis, increasing the likelihood that I will correctly identify the provision and effects of transparency and that others can replicate these findings. In the case studies, I try to be honest about competing and complementary explanations. Whatever role transparency plays, I explain the major factors at work in a crisis or incident from power to norms. To help ensure that the regime really did increase transparency and that transparency really did have x or y effect, I often ask counterfactuals in my cases.[72] Symptoms that I have avoided "curve-fitting" are the reports of "no evidence" in my cases, as are the

[68] Robert Bates et al., *Analytic Narratives* (Princeton, NJ: Princeton University Press, 1998). See also Khong, *Analogies at War,* for the use of extensive game-type diagrams to make arguments about how analogies proved crucial in turning points.

[69] For more on process-tracing, see the sources in fn. 66 of this chapter.

[70] Glenn H. Snyder and Paul Diesing, *Conflict among Nations: Bargaining, Decision Making, and System Structure in International Crises* (Princeton, NJ: Princeton University Press, 1977), 4.

[71] King, Keohane, and Verba, *Designing Social Inquiry,* 101.

[72] This method is similar to that suggested by Goldstein and Keohane for assessing the impact of ideas in foreign policy in Judith Goldstein and Robert O. Keohane, "Ideas and Foreign Policy: An Analytical Framework," in Goldstein and Keohane, eds., *Ideas and Foreign Policy: Beliefs, Institutions, and Political Change* (Ithaca, NY: Cornell University Press, 1993), esp. 29. See also King, Keohane, and Verba, *Designing Social Inquiry,* 88; and Philip E. Tetlock and Aaron Belkin, eds., *Counterfactual Thought Experiments in World Politics: Logical, Methodological and Psychological Perspectives* (Princeton, NJ: Princeton University Press, 1996).

variations in evidence within and between the cases where the successes, failures, and irrelevancies of transparency come to life.[73]

CASE SELECTION

To examine the provision of transparency by a forum, I study the first five crises confronted by the Concert of Europe: the dispute between Poland and Saxony in 1814–15, the rebellions in Naples and Spain in the early 1820s, the revolt in Greece in the early 1820s, and the Belgian crisis in the early 1830s. To examine transparency in U.N. peacekeeping, I study two traditional peacekeeping operations in which lightly armed U.N. forces patrol a buffer zone: the United Nations Peacekeeping Force in Cyprus (UNFICYP) and the United Nations Disengagement Observer Force (UNDOF) in the Golan Heights. I also study two multifunctional operations in which U.N. forces and personnel rebuild war-torn countries by promoting democracy, monitoring elections, disarming factions, and other efforts. These cases are the United Nations Transitional Authority in Cambodia (UNTAC) and the United Nations Transition Assistance Group in Namibia (UNTAG).

I selected these cases because they let me assess the provision and effects of transparency in a range of settings, they offer variation on all the variables and substantial within-case variance, they are data-rich, and they are important for scholars and policymakers. I explain these selection criteria in turn, and conclude by talking about other security regimes that I either exclude or survey more briefly.

Variance

This is the first extensive investigation of transparency provided by security regimes. For this reason, and to generate the most theoretical leverage and policy insight, it is important to look at an array of cases to see how various mechanisms for providing transparency function under different conditions. The Concert of Europe and my U.N. cases evince variance at all the steps in my causal chain of security regimes: → transparency → peace. The cases have variance in the presence or activities of the regime, and the level of transparency provided by the regime's activities is variable and discernable, as is the influence of transparency on the level of tension between adversaries.

The Concert is a relatively informal regime, while the U.N. and its instrument of peacekeeping are more formal. Scholars of international in-

---

[73] Bates et al., *Analytic Narratives*, 231–32.

stitutions note that a primary way that regimes vary is according to how formally they are designed.[74] More formal regimes have more elaborate rules and procedures. In this analysis of transparency, the more formal the regime, the more actively the regime itself generates or exchanges information.

As indicated earlier in table 2-1, *informal* regimes such as forums like the Concert of Europe have no buildings, no secretariat or other employees, and few formal rules governing behavior. They are decentralized, highly flexible, and confront a range of problems on an ad hoc basis. Forums are informal because states simply meet to discuss the problems they face. Compared to pre-forum diplomacy, where diplomats met separately, forums facilitate communication, and transparency may be increased as the actors exchange information while bargaining.

The Concert offers a wonderful opportunity for measuring the presence of the security regime and its influence on diplomacy. The Concert was the first peacetime multilateral crisis management forum in history. This allows for an easy comparison of pre-Concert, non-forum diplomacy with forum diplomacy. Per Mill's "method of difference," in which cases for comparison are chosen to be similar in all ways but the study variable, I examine the first partition of Poland in 1772 because it is the closest crisis to the Concert (1814) in terms of date, stakes, and actors.[75] A chief difference is the existence of the forum. This comparison offers analytical leverage and variance that few other Concert scholars have exploited. I also examine whether the promise of transparency motivated diplomats to form the Concert.

In looking at five crises within the Concert, I use process-tracing to assess the extent to which communications were facilitated by the forum, and I ask the counterfactual: what would have happened in the absence of the forum? Analysis of the first partition of Poland helps answer this counterfactual question. Between and within the five crises, there is variance in the level of activity of the regime in that some crises were resolved almost exclusively within the forum (Poland-Saxony), while the outcomes for other crises also depended on diplomatic dispatches (Greek) and meetings outside of the forum (Belgium).

Finally, the five crises I assess offer variance in the levels of tension— the ultimate dependent variable in my causal chain. The crises include revolutions in neighboring states and territorial disputes. Their gravity ranges from major war scares to fits of pique—often at different times

---

[74] See Abbott and Snidal, "Why States Act through Formal International Organizations"; and Koremenos, Lipson, and Snidal, eds., *Rational Design of International Institutions*.

[75] John Stuart Mill, *The Logic of the Moral Sciences* (London: Duckworth, 1987), 68– 69; Van Evera, *Guide to Methods*, 68–69.

within the same crisis. The analytical task is determining whether the regime helped defuse these incidents and whether transparency had anything to do with it.

More *formal* regimes such as the U.N. and its peacekeeping operations have buildings, bureaucracies, budgets, hierarchies, standard operating procedures, and formal rules. Here the mechanisms to generate or exchange information include the activities of traditional peacekeeping missions such as patrols, monitoring of buffer zones, and verification of arms control agreements and of disarmament. Multifunctional operations also may conduct patrols and verify disarmament, but their functions extend to the monitoring of elections and the proactive shaping of the information environment with educational and media campaigns. Thus, the U.N. cases differ from the Concert in terms of formality and from each other in terms of functions and the mechanisms that they use to provide transparency.

For the U.N. cases, the first step in assessing variation in the presence or activities of the regime is to examine whether the promise of transparency provided by the regime was a factor in signing the peace or counterfactual deal that led to the mission. I then review the U.N. mandates for each mission and examine the extent to which each of the activities in the mandate relies on transparency for its success. As mentioned, activities range from patrolling buffer zones, arms control inspections, disarmament, and election monitoring. Crises and incidents range from intergroup violence and threats of violence to malicious rumors and harassment along buffer zones. Again, the analytical task is to see if transparency plays a role in the regime's activities at each juncture, and whether transparency affected the outcomes.

Each of my cases, five crises during the Concert of Europe and four U.N. peacekeeping operations, contain many subcases in the form of incidents, crises, and subcrises. For example, in the crisis surrounding Belgian independence starting in 1830, France had to be convinced to leave Belgium, then persuaded not to intervene again. Finally, France and Britain coordinated a joint intervention into Belgium. U.N. peacekeeping missions have a number of mandated tasks, and each operation usually confronts many incidents related to each of those tasks. In short, there is substantial within-case variance. This increases the number of observations and the robustness of my conclusions.[76]

The proof about variance is in the pudding. The cases provide evidence of transparency playing strong, moderate, weak, and nonexistent roles in ways that increased, decreased, and did not affect tensions in a wide

[76] Gerring, *Social Science Methodology,* 190–91; King, Keohane, and Verba, *Designing Social Inquiry,* 217–30; and Van Evera, *Guide to Methods,* 47, 61–63.

range of circumstances. There are positive cases and negative cases in this analysis.[77]

I have not picked hard cases, easy cases, extreme cases, or crucial cases. I picked cases that were important on scholarly and policy dimensions, which I thought would contain variation in all my variables, and about which there was enough information to process-trace about transparency. Perhaps these are easy cases for transparency because there was no great power war during the Concert period, only moderate conflict on Cyprus—and almost none since 1974: no war in the Golan Heights, and the elections in Cambodia and Namibia were successful. On the other hand, these may all be hard cases because they are all instances of regimes operating in the realm of security. Institutions have a much more difficult time being effective in this realm than in economics and other issue areas.[78] Another reason that it is hard to judge whether these are hard or easy cases is that it is difficult to tell a priori whether it is easy or hard for a regime to increase transparency, to know how much of a role transparency played in the cases compared to other influences on crisis and incident outcomes, or even to predict the effects of transparency. As the hypotheses suggest, increases in transparency can reduce or increase tension depending on the information revealed, the aims of the actors, and other circumstances. In the end, I think there are instances in the cases that lend themselves to the provision and peaceful effects of transparency, and other times when the regimes and transparency are less successful or fail outright. This variation helps us learn about the provision and effects of transparency.

Data Richness

Another criteria for case selection was data richness. As the observable implications for the hypotheses suggest, evaluating hypotheses on transparency requires figuring out how the regime influenced the information that was exchanged or generated, and what effect that information had. Learning who said what to whom and with what effect involves a fine-grained level of process-tracing.

As for the Concert, because I have failed to raise Castlereagh, Metternich, and Alexander at seances, the chapter is based on primary materials such as letters and memoirs as well as the large historical and political science literature on the subject. There is a wealth of data and debate on the Concert.

On the U.N., my data is best for UNFICYP and UNDOF, where I conducted extensive field research on both sides of both buffer zones, which

---

[77] Mahoney and Goertz, "The Possibility Principle," 653–69.
[78] Lipson, "International Cooperation in Economic and Security Affairs."

included interviews, access to peacekeeping sites, and access to diplomatic and operational documents. A solid literature has developed for UNTAC, and it includes several books devoted solely to its information operations. The literature is less developed for UNTAG. The UNTAG and UNTAC chapters are bolstered with primary sources including operational records and interviews with a number of U.N. officials involved with both missions at the U.N. headquarters in New York.

Unfortunately, scholarship is more scanty on newer missions and it is often not detailed enough to offer transparency-related insights. It is often hard to find operational details about newer missions, much less details (or even summary assessments) regarding information operations. For example, to write two pages on UNMEE, I collected hundreds of news items and U.N. reports in about eight inches of folders, and I conducted a number of phone interviews. In the absence of field research, operational details are hard to come by on the newer missions.

Scholarly and Policy Importance of the Cases

Cases were also chosen for their scholarly and policy relevance as students, scholars, and policymakers are the main audiences for this book. Although it began almost 200 years ago, the Concert lives on as it continues to inspire the development and understanding of international organizations. The Concert of Europe was formed in 1814–15 to help preserve Europe's hard-won peace. It was the first peacetime multilateral crisis management forum as well as the institutional precursor of the League of Nations and the United Nations.[79] As mentioned earlier, the end of the Cold War sparked over a dozen calls for Concert-based or Concert-like structures to replace or supplement NATO and the U.N.[80] The Concert has influenced the thinking of scholars and policymakers on other regimes as diverse as the Group of Seven/Eight (G7/G8), the Association of Southeast Asian Nations (ASEAN), the Organization of African Unity (OAU), the African Union (AU), and the Economic Community of West African States (ECOWAS).[81] While recommendations for forums are plentiful, scholarly

[79]G. John Ikenberry, *After Victory: Institutions, Strategic Restraint, and the Rebuilding of Order after Major Wars* (Princeton, NJ: Princeton University Press, 2001).

[80]See chap. 1, n. 5.

[81]In addition to many of the citations in fn. 5 of chap. 1, see also: Amitav Acharya, "A Concert of Asia?" *Survival* 41, no. 3 (Autumn 1999); Armstrong Matiu Adejo, "From OAU to AU: New Wine in Old Bottle?" paper prepared for CODESRIA's 10th General Assembly on "Africa in the New Millennium," Kampala, Uganda, December 8–12, 2002; Aspen Institute, *Managing Conflict in the Post–Cold War World: The Role of Intervention*, Report of the Aspen Institute Conference, August 2–6, 1995 (Washington, DC: Aspen Institute, 1996); Nicholas Khoo and Michael L.R. Smith, "A 'Concert of Asia?'" *Policy Review* 108 (August/September 2001); Winrich Kühne, with Jochen Prantl, "The Security Council and

analyses of the effects of forums on diplomacy are not. Fearon notes that interstate bargaining increasingly takes place in the context of regimes and argues that "regimes deserve greater attention as *forums for bargaining* rather than primarily as institutions that aid monitoring and enforcement."[82] This book addresses this gap.

Finally, international relations theorists often rely on the Concert to develop theories about security institutions. Robert Jervis called the Concert the "best example of a security regime."[83] John Gerring calls certain cases "paradigm" cases that have high "analytic utility."[84] Nazi Germany is a paradigm case for studies of fascism, for example, and a study lacking that case would be suspect. The Concert is a paradigm case in the literature on security regimes.

The U.N. is the most prominent present-day security regime and its most visible function is peacekeeping. Again, this is a paradigm case with high policy relevance. To learn the most from my U.N. cases, I picked operations that seemed most typical for their genre: UNFICYP and UNDOF for traditional missions, and UNTAG and UNTAC for multifunctional missions. Although there are wide variations among U.N. and other peacekeeping operations, these missions are likely to share many characteristics with what would be deployed in either the traditional or multifunctional context.[85] Moreover, the lessons from these two types of operations

the G8 in the New Millennium: Who is in Charge of International Peace and Security?" Stiftung Wissenschaft Und Politik (SWP), Research Institute for International Affairs, 5th International Workshop (June 30–July 1, 2000), Berlin, Germany; Gani Joses Yoroms and Emmanuel Kwesi Aning, "West African Regional Security in the Post Liberian Conflict Area: Issues and Perspectives," CDR Working Paper 97.7 (November 1997), Institute for International Studies Department for Development Research (former Centre for Development Research), Copenhagen, Denmark; Mark W. Zacher, "The Conundrums of Power Sharing: The Politics of Security Council Reform," prepared for the conference on the United Nations and Global Security, Centre of International Relations, Liu Institute for Global Issues, University of British Columbia (January 18–19 2003), Vancouver, BC, Canada.

[82] Fearon, "Bargaining, Enforcement, and International Cooperation," 298, emphasis in original.

[83] Jervis, "Security Regimes," 178.

[84] Gerring, *Social Science Methodology,* 192–93; 219. He also calls paradigm cases "crucial cases," but this does not correspond with the way in which other scholars use the term "crucial case" to mean most and least-likely cases. Gerring discusses this meaning of "crucial case" on p. 220.

[85] For example, Ingrid Lehmann argues that UNTAG was a model for many of the multifunctional missions that followed, *Peacekeeping and Public Information,* 28, as does Michael Doyle, Senior Fellow, International Peace Academy in an interview, April 19, 1996. Mark Thompson and Monroe Price write that UNTAC's information practices set a precedent for a number of operations in their "Introduction" to Monroe E. Price and Mark Thompson, eds., *Forging Peace: Intervention, Human Rights and the Management of Media Space* (Bloomington, IN: Indiana University Press, 2002), 1. For typologies of peacekeeping operations, see fn. 22 of chap. 1.

should offer much to various peacekeeping, border monitoring, and democracy promotion operations of the Organization for Security and Co-operation in Europe (OSCE), the AU, the European Union (EU), ECOWAS, and other regional security organizations and coalitions.

Mini-Cases and Excluded Cases

I cover some regimes and newer peacekeeping operations with mini–case studies in the appendices. Their purpose is to explore the wider applicability and limits of my findings, and to probe what other cases might contribute to the study of transparency. In the appendices, I first review three recently launched peacekeeping operations: the United Nations Mission in Ethiopia and Eritrea (UNMEE), the United Nations Organization Mission in the Democratic Republic of Congo (MONUC), and the United Nations Interim Administration Mission in Kosovo (UNMIK). I then examine the Open Skies Treaty, the Strategic Arms Limitation Talks (SALT I and SALT II), the Anti-Ballistic Missile Treaty (ABMT), the Nuclear Non-Proliferation Treaty (NPT), and the associated International Atomic Energy Agency (IAEA). My main cases let me make arguments about forums, peacekeeping, and public diplomacy/information operations, and the mini-cases of other regimes help assess the tradeoffs in my case selection.

Time and space meant that some regimes were left aside. These include the peacekeeping, democracy promotion, and other security-related activities of various regional organizations and coalitions, including the EU, the AU, ECOWAS, ASEAN, the Organization of American States (OAS), and historical cases such as the League of Nations and Organization of African Unity (OAU). Absent field research, the study of regional organizations is hard because they lack the wealth of primary and secondary data sources that are available for the Concert and U.N. Their activities are generally not as salient as those of the U.N. The number of non-U.N. peace operations is growing, however, and the lessons from this study should assist these activities.[86]

A host of additional arms control and confidence-building agreements such as the Conventional Forces in Europe Treaty (CFE) and the Missile Technology Control Regime (MCTR) are not covered.[87] The Federation of American Scientists' website lists some sixty-seven arms control treaties and agreements, underscoring the Nathan Hale aspect of

---

[86] Bellamy and Williams, "Who's Keeping the Peace?" 157–95.

[87] See lists of arms control agreements at the Federation of American Scientists' and Arms Control Association websites: www.fas.org/nuke/control/ and www.armscontrol.org/treaties/, respectively.

this book: "I regret that I have but one life to give for this phase of my research program."[88]

While most of the excluded regimes and all the mini-cases are worthy of more study, many of these do not meet my case-selection criteria as well as those of the Concert and U.N. For example, the League of Nations is not as historically significant or as policy relevant as the U.N., and scholars of security regimes pay much more attention to the Concert than the League.

Arms control agreements have a number of benefits, and many of these benefits are tied to verification and transparency,[89] but most arms control regimes do not deal with crises and incidents, and it is harder to detect how they affect levels of tension between adversaries. Hence, variance on my independent and dependent variables is more difficult to obtain or observe. Nonetheless, I examine the Open Skies regime, SALT I/ II and the ABMT, and the NPT/IAEA to see what roles transparency played in their formation, and in how well they accomplished their objectives. Of these, transparency is most salient in the NPT/IAEA cases of Iran, Iraq, and North Korea. This is because transparency has been impossible to provide at a sufficiently high level to calm suspicions, and suspicions are high mostly due to the fact that those countries deserve/d to be suspected as proliferators in the first place.

LIMITS AND OPPORTUNITIES

My goal is not to provide a comprehensive history of the Concert, nor a general theory of peacekeeping, and I do not claim that a focus on transparency will yield either of these. As with all theories, transparency is a lens that brings some elements of a story into sharper view, at the risk of obscuring other elements. Because I am aware of the tradeoffs of this focus, I have tried to be fair in my cases by acknowledging the multiple purposes of the Concert and of the various peacekeeping techniques and activities in each of my peacekeeping cases.

It turns out that focusing on transparency and telling "who told what to whom" stories inevitably reveal much about the Concert's politics and purposes, and about the range of techniques involved in peacekeeping. What follows are stories about the ideologies and alliances of Concert

---

[88] Nathan Hale really said, "I regret that I have but one life to lose for my country" before he was hanged by the British as a spy during the Revolutionary War.

[89] For lists of arms control agreements, see the Arms Control Association website at www.armscontrol.org/treaties/ and the Federation of American Scientists website at www.fas.org/nuke/control/.

states, and about peacekeepers interposing themselves between combatants, confronting shootings in buffer zones, and using puppets to educate people about elections. Focusing on transparency helps us understand these stories. Being honest about the successes, failures, and irrelevancies of transparency in the context of each regime's activities helps us see how well institutionalist arguments apply to the realm of security, and contributes to theory-building, cumulation of knowledge, and wise policy-making.

CHAPTER THREE

The Concert of Europe: Forum Diplomacy and Crisis Management

THE CONCERT OF EUROPE was the first peacetime multilateral crisis management forum. States before the Concert were limited to bilateral diplomacy, and never met together to manage crises. Compared to prior pre-forum diplomatic practice, the chief benefit of meeting together should be the quicker exchange of information. A greater flow of information should mean increased transparency—what states know about each other's intentions and capabilities.

The reason is that in situations involving three or more states, bilateral diplomacy slows communications and poses coordination problems. For example, if five states are limited to bilateral diplomacy, there have to be ten separate meetings for each to meet each other only once. Imagine trying to exchange views as one might in a Parent-Teachers Association or a faculty meeting, without actually convening. In contrast, multilateral forum diplomacy speeds communications and lowers the transactions costs for exchanging information, and thus increases transparency. Meeting in the same place should also facilitate backroom deals between subsets of the participants. As Austrian foreign minister Count Wenzel Lothar Metternich said in anticipation of an 1821 meeting with British secretary of state Viscount Robert Stewart Castlereagh, "I shall achieve more in a few days . . . than in six months of writing."[1]

The questions that this chapter raises are: Did the Concert facilitate the exchange of information and increase transparency? If so, what effects did transparency have on crisis management?

To answer these questions, I first investigate diplomacy and crisis management in the eighteenth century. Examining how well crises were managed under pre-Concert conditions helps reveal what effect the Concert of Europe had on causing peace. I set this eighteenth-century performance benchmark in three parts.

The first examines the general conditions under which diplomacy was conducted during the eighteenth century. Transparency-increasing mechanisms we now take for granted were minimal in the eighteenth century:

[1] Roy Bridge, "Allied Diplomacy in Peacetime: The Failure of Congress 'System,' 1815–1823," in Alan Sked, ed., *Europe's Balance of Power: 1815–1848* (London: Macmillan, 1979), 47.

states employed small diplomatic corps and bureaucracies, travel was slow, and there were no peacetime forums for conducting diplomacy. The second is a short case study of the outbreak of the Seven Years War in America. This case illustrates how lack of transparency can help cause war. Rogue actors used faulty and unverifiable stories to foment war; they exploited opacity to peddle bad information. Uncertain borders led to disputes. Plausible counterfactuals suggest that greater transparency or a Concert-like forum might have prevented the war.

The third part is a brief case study of the crisis surrounding the first partition of Poland in 1772. Even more than the Seven Years' War, this case serves as a control case for analysis of the Concert's crises. This is because the first partition of Poland is as close as possible to a Concert episode in time, geography, actors, stakes, and severity. During the first partition of Poland, as in many Concert episodes, a crisis arose on the periphery of Europe, and the resulting tensions among the great powers threatened general war. Despite lacking a Concert-like forum, the great powers worked through some complicated diplomacy and prevented a general war. This success for bilateral, Concert-less diplomacy and its similarity to the Concert's crises casts doubt on whether the Concert transformed crisis management or European politics more generally.[2]

I spend the rest of the chapter examining how the Concert handled the first five crises it confronted: the dispute over who would control Poland and Saxony during the Congress of Vienna in 1814–15, the liberal rebellions in Naples and Spain in the early 1820s, the nationalist revolt in Greece against Turkey also in the early 1820s, and the establishment of Belgian independence and neutrality in the early 1830s.

In the Poland-Saxony and Belgian cases, the Concert added value to diplomacy by increasing transparency, as predicted by H1. The effect of the increased transparency was to clarify power balances and deadlocks. This prevented miscalculation and helped states make coercive threats that ended these crises, as contended by H3. Thus, the most visible contribution of forum diplomacy and transparency was to facilitate realpolitik. Realpolitik or power politics is self-interested diplomacy, frequently supported by the threat or use of force. It contrasts with behavior constrained or informed by norms or rules that promote enlightened self-interest (helping oneself by helping others) and that discourage threats or use of force.[3]

The Concert clarified the existence of deadlock in a minor way in the Naples and Spain cases, causing a schism between Britain and the other

[2] This transformation is the core argument of Schroeder in *Transformation of European Politics*.

[3] According to the Oxford English Dictionary, realpolitik is "practical politics; policy determined by practical, rather than moral or ideological considerations."

Concert powers. Here, transparency mildly increased conflict, as predicted by H3′, which contends that transparency can increase tensions during bargaining. Forum diplomacy was little used in the Greek case.

DIPLOMACY IN THE EIGHTEENTH CENTURY

Diplomacy is a basic way of increasing transparency. It is one of the first mechanisms that states turn to in order to learn more about their adversaries. The foundations for modern, bureaucratized diplomacy took years to develop, with much progress made in the eighteenth century. States in the 1600s began to handle "outside threats [with an] emphasis on acquiring information. Permanent embassies were established; secret agents and spies were hired; knowledgeable merchants and travelers were questioned."[4] Diplomats were not systematically recruited and paid to serve their state prior to the eighteenth century. Strange as it may now seem, the few diplomats who were posted abroad were often paid by the host government. France had five officials in its foreign ministry in 1661, but the ministry grew during the 1700s to include cartographic, financial, cryptographic, correspondence, legal, and archival departments.[5] In 1695, Russia had no permanent representatives abroad. By 1721, it had twenty-one missions abroad, although by 1800 this number had declined to fourteen. In 1702, there were four representatives from abroad in Russia, and eleven by 1719.[6]

In the mid-eighteenth century, dispatches traveled at a maximum of 100 kilometers per day. It took about three weeks for news to travel from London to Venice.[7] The European road network grew swiftly during the eighteenth century, and when the stagecoach system was developed, it hastened communications and enabled meaningful diplomatic discussion by dispatch. With permanent diplomats and sufficiently speedy communications, continuous diplomacy became possible. In the hands of a capable diplomatic corps, an organized and continuous flow of information about

---

[4] Joseph R. Strayer, *On the Medieval Origins of the Modern State* (Princeton, NJ: Princeton University Press, 1970), 96. He goes on to discuss the shortcomings of these early efforts, some of which are discussed below and many of which were not very well addressed until the eighteenth century.

[5] Keith Hamilton and Richard Langhorne, *The Practice of Diplomacy: Its Evolution, Theory, and Administration* (New York: Routledge, 1995), 73–74.

[6] M. S. Anderson, *Europe in the Eighteenth Century: 1713–1783*, 2nd ed. (London: Longman, 1976), 198–99.

[7] Fernand Braudel, *Civilization and Capitalism, 15th–18th Centuries: The Structures of Everyday Life, The Limits of the Possible*, vol. 1 (New York: Harper and Row, 1979), 424–27.

other states could be relayed back to the home state. The state could respond with instructions that were less likely to have been overtaken by events.

Precursors to Concert practices fell into place during the eighteenth century. There were peace conferences following several of the many wars of the time.[8] The practice of mediation also became widespread. Kalevi Holsti lists six instances of mediation from the Peace of Nystadt in 1721 to the end of the war of Bavarian Succession in 1779. He, however, argues that mediation was most often a device for states to save face after "issues had already been resolved on the battlefield" and that "there are no cases on record where formal mediation actually prevented a war."[9] Between 1713 and 1814 there were no crisis management conferences, but states were developing the institutional capacity and physical infrastructure to conduct concert diplomacy.[10]

Seven Years War in America

The lead-up to the Seven Years War between Britain and France in America during the 1750s highlights the dangers of opacity. Concert diplomacy and other means of increasing transparency would have lowered the probability of war.

In the mid-1700s, the expansion of the British colonies in Eastern North America made tension inevitable with its less-populated French neighbor

[8] For example, the Congresses of Soissons (1728–1729), Aix-la-Chapelle (1745), and Breda (1746). See Richard Langhorne, "The Development of International Conferences, 1648–1830," *Studies in History and Politics*, 2, no. 2 (1981/1982): 73–75.

[9] Kalevi J. Holsti, *Peace and War: Armed Conflict and International Order 1648–1989* (Cambridge, England: Cambridge University Press, 1991), 111–12.

[10] Other sources consulted for this section include M. S. Anderson, "Eighteenth-Century Theories of the Balance of Power," in Ragnild Hatton and M. S. Anderson, eds., *Studies in Diplomatic History* (London: Longman Group, 1970); Anderson, *Europe in the Eighteenth Century,* 174–215; Sir Herbert Butterfield, "Diplomacy," in Hatton and Anderson, *Studies in Diplomatic History;* Inis Claude, *Swords into Plowshares: The Problems and Progress of International Organization,* 4th ed. (New York: McGraw-Hill, 1984), 21–27; Gordon A. Craig and Alexander A. George, *Force and Statecraft: Diplomatic Problems of Our Time,* 2nd ed. (New York: Oxford University Press, 1990), 22–24; Leo Gershoy, *From Despotism to Revolution: 1763–1789* (New York: Harper, 1944), chap. 7; F. H. Hinsley, *Power and the Pursuit of Peace: Theory and Practice in the History of Relations Between States* (Cambridge, England: Cambridge University Press, 1967), 153–196; Holsti, *Peace and War,* chaps. 3–5; Richard Langhorne, "The Regulation of Diplomatic Practice: The Beginnings to the Vienna Convention on Diplomatic Practice, 1961," *Review of International Studies,* 18, no. 1 (January 1992): 4–5; Langhorne, "Development of International Conferences," 65–77; Paul Gordon Lauren, *Diplomats and Bureaucrats: The First Institutional Responses to Twentieth-Century Diplomacy in France and Germany* (Stanford, CA: Hoover Institution Press, 1976), chap. 1; and Schroeder, *Transformation of European Politics,* 3–11.

to the west. Britain and France sought to control the Ohio River Valley, a vital transit link for the French, and the next open territory to the west of the British colonies. Each side engaged in arms races to build forts faster than the other and thus control territory. Attacks followed to oust each other's forts and forces. On one level, this is a straight contest over resources—a contest taking place while both sides were on the verge of world war.

Opacity, however, exacerbated misperceptions, caused miscalculations, and made specific catalysts of the war, including territorial contests and rogue activity, harder to rectify. Britain and France frequently misinterpreted each other's actions as aggressive and their own as defensive. Both had different maps of the same areas, were hampered by slow communications, and the central governments could not monitor their own hawkish, expansionist underlings. These opacity-related problems contributed to the start of the war.

While tension was inevitable, perhaps war was not. Britain and France attempted to dampen their incipient conflicts throughout the Western Hemisphere, most notably by establishing a joint Delimitation Commission in 1750 to settle land claims where their colonies bumped up against one another. As looking at old maps reminds us, there was great uncertainty about the state of the world in this period—especially about relatively undeveloped land. The goal of the commission was to promote peace by establishing a base truth or common version about where rivers and boundaries actually were. Thus, the goal of the commission was to increase transparency, but it had limited powers and could not resolve what should have been objective differences between British and French maps.

The map problem became dangerous in 1753 when France began to fortify the Ohio territory, land that was claimed by both powers. The British responded in February 1754 with an eviction notice and began to build a counter-fortification at the fork of the Ohio River (now Pittsburgh). The French forcibly ousted the British in April 1754 while they were still building the fort. Tensions rose, but at this point, neither side wanted war.

Opacity helped cause the crisis escalate into a war. First, each side thought itself to be supporting the status quo, and so each side perceived its own actions to be aimed at deterrence while viewing the other's moves as compellent. Neither understood the other's intentions and ultimate goals. To the French, their successful attack on a new British fort, Fort Necessity, in July 1754 repelled intruders into their Ohio area. Many British saw it as an indication that Louis the XV was pursuing maximum objectives around the world, even at the risk of major war.

Second, rogue hawks influenced policy at several key junctures. Governor Shirley of Massachusetts contributed to Britain's overly pessimistic assessment of French motives by falsely reporting to London in 1754 that the French had begun to settle in Massachusetts.[11] Governor Dinwiddie of Virginia and Governor Duquesne of New France had commercial interests in Ohio. In communications to their home governments, both overemphasized Ohio's importance while exaggerating threats to the area. Their claims were hard to verify and their influence went unchecked by their central governments in part because few channels of communication existed and because communications were so slow (news from Fort Necessity took two months to reach London).

Greater inter- and intragovernmental transparency would have reduced the influence of the hawks in precipitating the war. A forum, in particular, would have sped up diplomacy and allowed Britain and France to clarify their misperceptions. Instead, after a series of skirmishes and a small naval engagement, Britain declared war on France in May 1756.[12] As many of the causes of the war lie in a series of misperceptions and miscalculation, a reasonable counterfactual suggests that greater transparency might have prevented war by helping to bargain, reduce fears, and control rogues. This case therefore offers some support to H3: Transparency promotes cooperation.

THE FIRST PARTITION OF POLAND

On October 6, 1768, war erupted between Russia and Turkey when Russian troops pursued Polish rebels across the Polish border and into the then Turkish-held town of Balta. At the time, Poland, though technically sovereign and neutral, was Russia's puppet, while the Ottoman Empire extended north through what is now Romania up to Poland.

In spring and summer 1769, Russia won a series of military victories. Russia occupied Bessarabia and the Danubian principalities of Moldavia and Wallachia on the Austrian frontier. By mid-1770, Russia had begun to conquer the Crimea, stirred up a revolt in southern Greece (Morea), and, after sailing from the Baltic, had sunk the Turkish fleet (with British help) at Chesme in the Mediterranean.

Austria feared being dragged into this war along its eastern borders, and Prussia in turn feared what might become a larger European war. Starting in August 1769, Austria and Prussia began discussions over a number

---

[11] Had the joint Delimitation Commission stuck around long enough to tell London that the French were not in fact colonizing Massachusetts, this information would have contradicted Shirley's falsehoods. This would have been an early example of a regime disclosing information to coerce rogues into backing down, the contention of H5, and might have helped delay or prevent the Seven Years War.

[12] This account is drawn from Richard Smoke, *Controlling Escalation* (Cambridge, MA: Harvard University Press, 1977), chap. 8.

of issues, including exchanging articles of neutrality, possible mediation of the Russo-Turkish war, and initial ideas for a partition of Poland. In the partition, Russia would be given some of Poland as compensation for backing off from Turkey and withdrawing from the Danubian principalities that it now occupied. Austria and Prussia would gain Polish territory as well.

Although Russia continued South and conquered Crimea on July 1, 1771, domestic politics, an epidemic, fear of peasant revolt, and continued unrest in Poland led Russia to become more conciliatory; it began to see partition as a viable choice to end the stresses of war.

A further prod to Russia came on July 6, when Turkey took up Austria's offer of alliance. Although Frederick believed that Austria actually would not be willing to fight for its new ally, he renewed his push for partition of Poland with Russia. Russia viewed the Austro-Turkish treaty with greater alarm.[13] Its fears were exacerbated when it learned that Turkey sent silver to Austria, as payments in accord with their not-so-secret treaty. Russia learned this from Frederick (who knew it would alarm Russia), who learned it from the French, whose government in Paris had been informed of the shipment by the British ambassador in Constantinople.[14] This was the final straw for Russia, which finally accepted a Prussian plan for partition in January of 1772. Austria resisted the plan for several months, but it eventually gave in as Russia and Prussia offered ever-larger shares of Poland.

The turning points in the three-year-long crisis were three shifts in power: on the ground (Russia's victories), domestically (Russia's turmoil), and in alliances (Turkey with Austria). None required a security regime to make its effects known. In the end, Poland lost one-third of its territory and one-half of its population. Prussia achieved its goal of partitioning Poland and avoiding being dragged into war. Austria received the largest share of Poland, and the Russians withdrew their threatening forces from the Danubian Principalities and returned the territory to Turkey (but gave itself the role of protector of those lands).[15]

[13] Gershoy, *From Despotism to Revolution,* 174–81; Hajo Holborn, *A History of Modern Germany: 1648–1840* (Princeton, NJ: Princeton University Press, 1964), 253; Schroeder, *Transformation,* 15–16; Albert Sorel, *The Eastern Question in the Eighteenth Century: The Partition of Poland and the Treaty of Kainardji* (New York: Howard Fertig, 1969), 161–62.

[14] Albert Sorel, *Eastern Question in the Eighteenth Century: The Partition of Poland and the Treaty of Kainardji* (New York: Howard Fertig, 1969), 173. I cannot tell how long it took this information to flow from the British ambassador in Turkey (who learned of the shipment on July 25) to Paris to Austria and on to Russia.

[15] Additional sources used for this section include Anderson, *Europe in the Eighteenth Century,* 186–92; Arthur Hassall, *The Balance of Power, 1715–1789. Period VI* (New York: MacMillan, 1898); R. B. Mowat, *Europe, 1715–1815* (New York: Longmans, Green, 1929), 113–15.

The deal to partition Poland was a complicated and multilateral outcome—even though it resulted from a series of bilateral negotiations and maneuvers. A multilateral forum was not necessary to conduct the complicated diplomatic dance that preceded the partition, or to achieve the tripartite partition itself. States did not need a forum, or any added transparency that it might provide, to machinate, to be aware of each others' machinations, or to make a multilateral peace agreement.

Could a multilateral forum, like the later Concert of Europe, have changed the outcome? A plausible counterfactual argument can be made that multilateral diplomacy would have reduced tensions between Russia and Austria and hastened—but not changed—the eventual outcome. Austria and Prussia (and Russia to a lesser extent) had shared and overlapping interests. Multilateral diplomacy could well have revealed those common interests sooner and reduced the need for what seems to have been an inefficient and time-consuming level of manipulation. That said, Russia's victories and then domestic weakness arguably explain most of the changes in Austrian, Prussian, and Turkish policies during this episode. Multilateral diplomacy would have had little effect on these factors. In the end, all one can conclusively say is that sequential diplomacy was *sufficient* to produce a multilateral outcome and that multilateral diplomacy was not *necessary* to do so.

To what extent do these results offer a baseline for measuring increases in transparency provided by the Concert, and thus help assess the hypothesis that regimes can increase transparency (H1)?[16] The first partition of Poland suggests that there was already some transparency and diplomatic nimbleness without forum diplomacy. On the other hand, the first partition of Poland took a long time to negotiate. In contrast, several disputes during the Concert were resolved with relative alacrity. They probably would not have been resolved so fast without the use of multilateral forum diplomacy.

THE CONCERT OF EUROPE: FIVE CRISES

This section investigates how much the early nineteenth century's new practice of multilateral crisis management—called the Concert of Europe—helped states manage crises. I examine the five most significant crises the

---

[16] Usage note: To match evidence directly to hypotheses in my case studies, and to help the reader understand and replicate the findings reported in the summary tables at the end of each case (which themselves flow into the master summary table at the conclusion of the book), I frequently make explicit reference to the relevant hypotheses. Sometimes, I make a full notation along the lines of "this supports hypothesis H4, which contends that transparency reduces unwarranted fears." Because such lengthy explanations would get tedious,

Concert confronted in its early years: the crisis over Poland and Saxony in 1814–15, the rebellions in Naples and Spain in the early 1820s, the revolt in Greece also in the early 1820s, and the establishment of Belgian independence and neutrality in the early 1830s. According to most scholars of the Concert, it was most effective and coherent during its earliest years: 1814–15 through the early 1820s.[17]

I begin by sketching the origins and legal framework of the Concert. This will help determine the extent to which the promise of transparency to be provided by the Concert helped motivate the Concert's founders. To the extent this is true, it supports H2, which contends that the promise of transparency promotes cooperation. Then I examine the five crises to see if the Concert actually provided transparency (H1) and what effect this transparency had on crisis management. Whether transparency is found to help bargaining or calm fears bears on H3 and H4. Because the Concert is an informal regime with relatively few rules and procedures, cheating and self-transparency (H5 and H6) are not likely to be as important.

THE FORMATION OF THE CONCERT

The Concert of Europe took form through a series of military, political, and ideological treaties. Tracing these treaties shows that the Concert had its roots in the wartime alliance against Napoleon. It owes much of its

---

and because the hypothesis and its effects are often clear from the context, at other times I refer more elliptically to the hypotheses and simply write, for example, "(H4)."

[17] Although the practice of multilateral peacetime diplomacy started by the Concert lived on, I side with scholars who argue that the Concert ended or was in decay by the early 1820s: they include Inis Claude, *Swords Into Plowshares*, 25, 31; Hinsley, *Power and the Pursuit of Peace*, 198–199; Jervis, "Security Regimes, 178; Langhorne, "The regulation of diplomatic practice," 318; Harold Nicholson, *The Congress of Vienna, A Study in Allied Unity: 1812–1822* (New York: Harcourt, Brace, and Company, 1946), 272–73; Richard N. Rosecrance, *Action and Reaction in World Politics: International Systems in Perspective* (Boston, MA: Little, Brown, 1963); H. G. Schenk, *The Aftermath of the Napoleonic Wars: The Concert of Europe–An Experiment* (New York: Howard Fertig, 1967), 213. Some argue that the Concert's effectiveness ended with the Crimean War, including Paul W. Schroeder, *Austria, Great Britain, and the Crimean War: The Destruction of the European Concert* (Ithaca, NY: Cornell University Press, 1972); and Richard B. Elrod, "The Concert of Europe: A Fresh Look at the International System," *World Politics* 27, no. 2 (January 1976): 159. Others contend that World War I marked the end of the Concert, including K. J. Holsti, "Governance with Government: Polyarchy in Nineteenth-Century European International Politics," in James N. Rosenau and Ernst-Otto Czempiel, eds., *Governance Without Government: Order and Change in World Politics* (Cambridge, England: Cambridge University Press, 1992), 50–51; and Paul Gorden Lauren, "Crisis Prevention in Nineteenth-Century Diplomacy," in Alexander George ed., *Managing U.S.-Soviet Rivalry: Problems of Crisis Prevention* (Boulder, CO: Westview, 1983), 36.

existence to the momentum of that alliance, to continued fear of a resurgent and possibly revolutionary France, and to the fear of liberal revolution more generally. These fears bound the Concert, and thus Walt's balance of threat theory explains most of the Concert's origins.[18]

Hopes for increased transparency, however, played a supporting role in spurring the Concert into existence. Because of this, H2, which contends that the anticipation of regime-provided transparency can promote cooperation, receives modest support. Britain's Foreign Minister Viscount Castlereagh, the prime architect of the Concert, expressed hope in his first trip to the continent in 1814 that the Concert-to-be would increase transparency:

> [M]any pretensions might be modified, asperities removed, and causes of irritation anticipated and met, by bringing the respective parties in unrestricted communications common to them all, and embracing in confidential and united discussion all the great points in which they were severally interested.[19]

This statement confirms H2, because Castlereagh expressed a general belief that a regime could promote peace with transparency. More specifically, Castlereagh's statement also indicates an understanding that transparency would enhance bargaining as predicted by H3, and reduce fears, as predicted by H4. Confirmation would be even stronger if I had found evidence that Castlereagh used these arguments to persuade others to sign on.

The first concrete step toward the Concert of Europe was the Treaty of Chaumont, signed by Austria, Britain, Prussia, and Russia just prior to Napoleon's first defeat and abdication in March 1814. The allies agreed to continue the war against France, each maintaining 150,000 troops in the field for service against France, and "most important, [it] united them for twenty years in jointly maintaining peace."[20]

In September 1814, the Congress of Vienna met to chart Europe's future, and this meeting is widely recognized as the birthplace of the Concert of Europe. The Congress's Final Act of June 1815—a lengthy, formal, and detailed document—covered over one hundred territorial, governance, legal, and other issues.

---

[18] Balance of threat theory posits that states ally with each other to secure themselves from threats. For more, see Stephen M. Walt, *The Origins of Alliances* (Ithaca, NY: Cornell University Press, 1987).

[19] Sir Charles Webster, *The Foreign Policy of Castlereagh, 1815–1822: Britain and the European Alliance* (London: G. Bell, 1947; first published in 1925), 56.

[20] Schroeder, *Transformation of European Politics,* 501. The Treaty was signed on March 9, 1814, and backdated to March 1. See also Frederick H. Hartmann, ed., *Basic Documents of International Relations* (Westport, CT: Greenwood Press, 1951), 1–4.

The defeat of Napoleon at Waterloo marked the next evolutionary step, when the allies signed the Second Treaty of Paris, on November 20, 1815. While singling out the dangers of Bonapartism, the allies also expressed more general fears about liberal revolution:

And as the same revolutionary principles which upheld the last criminal usurpation, might again, under other forms, convulse France, and thereby endanger the repose of other States; under these circumstances the High Contracting Parties . . . engage . . . to concert themselves . . . for the safety of their respective states, and for the general tranquillity of Europe.[21]

Further, the allies pledged to "renew their Meetings at fixed periods . . . for the purpose of consulting upon their common interests" to promote prosperity and maintain the "Peace of Europe."[22] The Concert of Europe thereby received formal recognition and its role as a discussion forum was codified.[23] The Quadruple Alliance was expanded to include France by the Treaty of Aix-la-Chapelle in October 1818.

Next, the Treaty of the Holy Alliance was signed by Austria, Prussia, and Russia on September 26, 1815. The most ideologically motivated of the various treaties of the period, it marked the beginning of the European Eastern-conservative vs. Western-more-liberal schism. The treaty stated that the "Three Contracting Monarchs" agreed to "take no other rule for their guidance" than the precepts of Christianity—"Justice, Charity, and Peace"—and to give each other aid and assistance "on all occasions and in all places."[24] Even though they did not take it seriously, all other European governments subsequently adhered to this treaty, except Turkey, the Papal States, and Great Britain.[25]

Two liberal revolutions in 1820 (Spain, January; Naples, July) prompted Russia's Tsar Alexander I to call a conference of the great powers in Troppau in October 1820. The resulting Troppau Protocol endorsed the use of force against revolutionary states and was signed only by Austria, Russia,

[21] Webster, *Foreign Policy of Castlereagh*, 54.

[22] Hartmann, *Basic Documents*, 5.

[23] René Albrecht-Carrié, *A Diplomatic History of Europe since the Congress of Vienna*, rev. ed. (New York: Harper and Row, 1973), 24; and Sir Charles Webster, *The Congress of Vienna: 1814–1815* (New York: Barnes and Noble, 1969; originally published by the British Foreign Office in 1919), 163.

[24] Hartmann, *Basic Documents*, 6–8.

[25] Albrecht-Carrié, *Diplomatic History of Europe*, 19; Henry A. Kissinger, *A World Restored: Metternich, Castlereagh, and the Problems of Peace 1812–1822*, (Boston, MA: Houghton Mifflin, 1973), 189–90; Nicholson, *The Congress of Vienna*, 250; and Webster, *Foreign Policy of Castlereagh*, 59.

and Prussia.[26] The rejection of the Protocol by the British Government[27] created "an open and public breach with the Alliance."[28]

By formalizing commitments and making states more explicitly express their views by voting on them, the Concert reduced ambiguity and heightened tensions with England. This incident, however, only mildly supports hypotheses about regimes increasing transparency (H1), and transparency increasing conflict during bargaining (H3'), because Britain would probably have distanced itself from any conservative intervention, regardless of procedures. Despite these initial schisms, Castlereagh said in 1816 that the practice of meeting together reduced what otherwise would have been a "cloud of prejudice and uncertainty." Although it is not clear what uncertainties (H3) or unwarranted fears (H4) were reduced, his assertion offers modest support for H4 due to the specificity of the word "prejudice" and the presumed effects of removing its cloud.[29]

First Crisis: Poland and Saxony, Late 1814–Early 1815

In this crisis, forum diplomacy helped Austria, France, and Great Britain quickly make an alliance and coerce Russia into ending the conflict. Clear diplomacy prevented Russia from miscalculating and led it to back down. This offers support for H3, which contends that transparency can reduce miscalculation and help bargaining achieve peaceful outcomes. Forum diplomacy increased transparency, and the effect of this increased flow of information was to facilitate power-political bargaining.

The most difficult and dangerous problem that arose during the Congress of Vienna involved the ultimate governance of the Duchy of Warsaw (Poland) and the Kingdom of Saxony. By the end of the Napoleonic Wars, Austria, Prussia, and Russia had already signed treaties (Teplitz, Kalisch, and Reichenbach) to partition Saxony, Poland, and other territories peacefully when the war was over. Russia, the dominant power in the region, wanted Poland and had 200,000 troops stationed there at war's end. Some of Poland, however, had been part of Prussia, and so to placate Prussia, Russia backed giving it long-coveted Saxony in exchange.

[26] This idea was first floated at the Congress of Aix-la-Chapelle by Tsar Alexander. Castlereagh vigorously objected to this notion of a conservative collective security system designed to interfere in the domestic politics of its members, and it never got off the ground at Aix. Webster, *Foreign Policy of Castlereagh*, 307–8.

[27] Harold Temperley, *The Foreign Policy of Canning, 1822–1827: England, The Neo-Holy Alliance, and the New World* (London: G. Bell, 1925), 73; and Webster, *Foreign Policy of Castlereagh*, 298–307, esp. 304.

[28] Webster, *Foreign Policy of Castlereagh*, 306.

[29] Ibid., 56–57.

Russia's plan amounted to a fait accompli and raised fears in England and Austria.[30] If Russia obtained Poland, Russian power would be projected deep into Central Europe. Central Europe would then no longer be strong enough to serve as a counterweight either to French or Russian expansion. Austria was concerned that Prussian expansion into Saxony would boost its influence throughout greater Germany and give Prussia a much longer border with Austria.

As resistance mounted from England, Austria, and France, Alexander became increasingly adamant. During an October 22, 1814, meeting between Alexander and France's representative, Prince Charles-Maurice de Talleyrand-Perigord, Alexander said, "I have two hundred thousand men in the duchy of Warsaw. Let them drive me out if they can! I have given Saxony to Prussia; and Austria consents." Talleyrand replied, "I do not know that. I should find it difficult to believe, it is so decidedly against her own interests. But can the consent of Austria give to Prussia what belongs to the King of Saxony?" Talleyrand had "reminded [Alexander] of the treaty by which the allies had agreed that the duchy of Warsaw should be shared by the three courts." Alexander retorted, "If the King of Saxony refuses to abdicate, he shall be led to Russia; where he will die. . . . You are always speaking to me of principles. Your public law is nothing to me: I don't understand all that. What do you think are all your parchments and treaties to me?"[31]

Thus Talleyrand and Alexander clarified their differences, made claims about relative power on the ground, and indicated how each viewed the stakes in the crisis. At this point, transparency was increasing tensions, as suggested by H3'.

Talk of impending war swept the Congress from October on into December. Despite quickly rising tensions, it became clear that Russia would not budge and would eventually receive the lion's share of Poland. The prospect of Russia's inevitable success in Poland frightened Prussia's Prince Carl Vincent von Hardenberg, as the agreed-upon support from Austria and Britain for his claims to Saxony were conditional on a less-lopsided outcome in Poland.

Having lost on Poland, Austria dug in its heels on Saxony, and tensions rose between Austria and Prussia. Castlereagh proposed to Prussia that it accept a limited part of Saxony and receive compensation elsewhere. This outcome was unacceptable to Prussia, and on December 30, Hardenberg stated that refusal of others to recognize its annexation of the whole of Saxony was "tantamount to a declaration of war." Castlereagh termed

---

[30] Schroeder, *Transformation of European Politics,* 524.

[31] Letter from the Prince de Talleyrand to King Louis XVII, Vienna, October 25, 1814, in de Broglie, *Memoirs of the Prince de Talleyrand,* 277.

this "a most alarming and unheard-of menace."[32] Here is another instance of clarification of positions increasing conflict, supporting the predictions of H3'.

Meanwhile, Talleyrand had offered an alliance with Austria and Britain on December 23. These rising tensions made Austria and Britain accept. On January 3, 1815, the three powers signed a secret treaty in which each promised to supply 150,000 troops in case of attack. The treaty strengthened the resolve of Metternich and Castlereagh in their continued discussions with Hardenberg, and Hardenberg began to yield.

Castlereagh met with Alexander on January 4, just one day after the treaty was signed. At this meeting, Alexander asked him if the rumors of the treaty were true, and Castlereagh answered in a way that "could have left him little doubt . . . and henceforward the Russian plenipotentiaries worked their hardest for a settlement." Alexander withdrew Russian support of Prussia's all-or-nothing position and urged a compromise partition of Saxony.[33] Prussia, the weakest of the great powers, lost its ally and was forced to accept a compromise in which it received two-fifths of Saxony and portions of the Rhineland. The quick formation and even quicker leak of the secret alliance was the turning point.

Coercion was successful. Plans were changed based on new information whose provision was facilitated by the regime, reducing miscalculation that might otherwise have caused Russia and Prussia to persist with their demands in the face of ever-more determined opposition.[34] Russia's bargaining position became more pliable, once the costs of its hard line were raised and made evident—all effects of transparency that support H3.

Assessment

To assess the role of transparency in this crisis, one must look at how the two problems that created the crisis were resolved: Russia's annexation of Poland and Prussia's claims to compensation. Russia succeeded while Prussia's claims were clipped back. In both cases, albeit with some risk, power relationships were made clear and then were no longer contested.

At first, the forum increased transparency, as hypothesized by H1, because it helped states clarify their positions. This increased tensions, as

[32] Webster, *British Diplomacy*, 277–78.

[33] Webster, *Congress of Vienna*, 135.

[34] General references for this section include Edward Vose Gulick, *Europe's Classic Balance of Power* (New York: Norton, 1955), 189–243; Kissinger, *A World Restored*, 152–74; Nicholson, *Congress of Vienna*, 148–81; Schroeder, *Transformation of European Politics*, 523–38; Albert Sorel, *L'Europe et la Révolution Française*, vol. 8 7th ed. (Paris: Plon, 1908), 393–401; Webster, *Congress of Vienna*, 117–41; Webster, *Foreign Policy of Castlereagh*, 122, 327–87.

predicted by H3', and led to balancing. The most crucial turning points were the events leading up to Prussia's diplomatic retreat. Concert diplomacy facilitated the making of the secret alliance and Concert diplomacy also let news of the alliance reach Alexander efficiently. As this would have been very difficult to achieve with such speed prior to forum diplomacy, this is clear evidence that the Concert increased transparency, supporting H1. Russia was successfully coerced, and when Prussia then backed down, its aggressive optimism was revealed to be something of a miscalculation; thus transparency reduced miscalculation and helped bargaining as predicted by H3. The complex dance between rising tensions, balancing, and successful coercion is simply realpolitik, aided by transparency.

Were norms or other institutional effects at work helping to resolve the crisis? Schroeder rejects the realpolitik argument altogether, arguing that "balance of power tactics were tried and failed." Yet he also says that Russia prevailed "hands down" with its fait accompli due to its "big battalions," and that power helped "force" concessions from Prussia.[35] If that is not realpolitik, what is? Schroeder writes that Russia forced concessions to save the alliance,[36] but that boils down to saving the alliance from Russia's own belligerent policy. Russia reduced the costs of its fait accompli by transferring those costs onto Prussia (by making Prussia accept less than it sought and less than it had been promised). Kissinger and Schroeder agree that no state truly wanted war, so some credit for the peaceful outcome of this episode is due to the shared moderation of the Concert states. Perhaps more remarkable is all the talk of war from states that had just endured and fought together during the Napoleonic Wars.

Second and Third Crises: The Rebellions in Naples and Spain

The liberal rebellions in Naples and Spain highlight the ideological jockeying over the purposes of the Concert. The crises made Britain's opposition to joint intervention against liberal revolution even more explicit. This created a schism in the Concert. As a result, these cases offer modest support for the predictions of H3', that transparency may increase conflict.

When a military-led revolution broke out in Spain in January of 1820, the only great power concerned at first was Russia. Having for years advanced the idea, particularly at the Congress of Aix-la-Chapelle in 1818, that the alliance should evolve into an antirevolutionary league, Russia soon called for a great power congress to confront the Spanish revolt. Russia's call languished until another revolt broke out in Naples in July.

[35] Schroeder, *Transformation of European Politics*, 537–38.
[36] Ibid., 558.

Naples adopted the same liberal constitution as that taken up by the Spanish revolutionaries. Austria wanted to intervene in Naples to restore conservative order in its Italian satellite. For France, this plan heightened the Franco-Austrian competition for influence in Italy, and so it began to seek a congress to restrain Austria. As at Aix, Britain opposed any allied steps toward a general policy of suppressing revolutions and it opposed a congress

Despite British opposition, a congress was held at Troppau in late 1820, with Russia, Austria, and Prussia represented by plenipotentiaries and France and Britain by observers. The three Eastern powers issued the Troppau Protocol on November 19, which stated in part,

> [a]ny state forming part of the European Alliance which may change its form of interior government through revolutionary means, and which might thus become a menace to other states, will automatically cease to form a part of the Alliance. . . . The Allied Powers . . . will employ every means to bring the offenders once more within the sphere of the Alliance. Friendly negotiations will be the first means resorted to, and if this fails, coercion will be employed.[37]

Lord Charles Stewart, the British representative, returned from a visit to Vienna to find himself presented with the Protocol already signed by Russia, Prussia, and Austria. He protested this fait accompli. Britain and France refused to sign. This shows how a document which was intended to express and consolidate norms instead ended up highlighting rifts in the Concert, as predicted by H3'.

Nonetheless, Austria's plans were blessed by the Troppau Protocol and Austria sent troops to crush the Naples revolt in early 1821. In theory, this joint blessing may have reduced miscalculation, promoted cooperation, and supported H3. In reality, there was little threat of war due to the intervention, blessing or not, hence little potential for miscalculation.

With regard to the revolt in Spain, Russia offered to lead an international army to quash the Spanish rebellion by sending its troops across Europe and into Spain. This was a threatening prospect for the other powers, especially Austria, and preventing Russian intervention was one reason that Metternich so quickly supported action by France. France at first wanted to keep the matter out of Alliance hands, but ended up supporting a Congress at Verona, which convened starting in October 1822.

Britain again objected to intervention. France, however, won the backing of the three Eastern powers, invaded Spain, and restored Ferdinand

---

[37] W. P. Cresson, *The Holy Alliance: The European Background of the Monroe Doctrine* (New York: Oxford University Press, 1922), 99. "European Alliance" refers to the Holy Alliance. Do the roots of the 1968 Brezhnev Doctrine go back almost 150 years?

VII in April 1823. Canning, Castlereagh's successor, obtained French assurances that the invasion would be temporary and that Portugal's independence would be respected.

The joint blessing to France made action in Spain more predictable, and helped keep Russia from marching across Europe. Thus, it is possible that forum diplomacy mildly reduced fears of Russian or French actions, and reduced any resulting miscalculation. This would support the predictions of H4 and H3. The clearest result of the diplomacy surrounding these revolutions, however, was to highlight schisms in the Concert caused by Britain's objections to the interventions, and this supports H3', which contends that transparency can increase tensions when it reduces uncertainty and clarifies positions.

The revolutions showed that "common action was no longer possible . . . because the insular and the Continental conceptions of danger had become incompatible."[38] When Britain rejected the Troppau Protocol, it started a "doctrinal controversy and propaganda war [that] would last for decades [and that produced] the first open break between Britain and the Holy Alliance."[39] Canning wrote of Verona, "The issue of Verona has split the one and indivisible alliance into three parts as distinct as the constitutions of England, France, and Muscovy . . . and so things are getting back to a wholesome state again. Every nation for itself and God for us all."[40] According to Temperley, Metternich thought the breach with England might end the Congress system.[41]

Assessment

Concert diplomacy helped clarify the great powers' intentions and it is possible, although unlikely, that the chance of war was diminished in the Spanish case. However improbable, Russia's scheme to march a Russian army through Europe to Spain raised tensions and the risks of accident and miscalculation. Concerted diplomacy helped dissuade Tsar Alexander

---

[38] Kissinger, *A World Restored*, 275.

[39] Schroeder, *Transformation of European Politics*, 611.

[40] Quoted in Norman Rich, *Great Power Diplomacy: 1814–1914* (New York: McGraw-Hill, 1992), 40.

[41] Temperley, *Foreign Policy of Canning*, 73. Other sources for this section include Bridge, "Allied Diplomacy"; Roger Bullen, "The Great Powers and the Iberian Peninsula, 1815–1848," in Alan Sked, ed., *Europe's Balance of Power*; Kissinger, *A World Restored*, 247–85; Irby C. Nichols, Jr., *The European Pentarchy and the Congress of Verona, 1822* (The Hague, Netherlands: Martinus Nijhoff, 1971); Walter Alison Philips, *The Confederation of Europe: A Study of the European Alliance, 1813–1823, as an Experiment in the International Organization of Peace*, 2nd ed. (New York: Longmans, Green, 1920), 164–66; Schroeder, *Transformation of European Politics*, 606–14, 621–628; Temperley, *Foreign Policy of Canning*, chaps. 1, 3, 4; and Webster, *Foreign Policy of Castlereagh*, 228–347.

from following through with his plan. By clarifying actions, the potential for miscalculation and unwarranted fears was possibly reduced, extending mild support to H3 and H4, respectively. With regard to the possible conflict between France and Austria over Italy, discussions, the Troppau declaration, and Russia's backing of Austria all made the small possibility of Franco-Austro conflict even more remote.

It is not clear, however, that Concert diplomacy added much to what regular diplomacy could have achieved. Other than when Britain was presented with a presigned declaration, I cannot identify moments where crisis resolution was greatly accelerated or where specific information really altered the course of events. In the end, the most threatened powers (Austria and France) intervened against the threats, and the least threatened power (Britain) stayed on the sidelines. No serious problems were averted or were even at stake. Britain's liberal position was known beforehand, and despite some grave language, Britain came back to the Concert in later episodes. Thus, it is not clear that the Concert did much to increase transparency (H1). If H1 is not really confirmed, this weakens support for the other hypotheses.

FOURTH CRISIS: THE REVOLT IN GREECE

The case of the early 1820s revolt of the Greeks against the Turks offers hints that the Concert facilitated a deception campaign. Britain and Austria used misinformation to persuade Russia not to intervene on behalf of the Greeks. Support for the contention that regimes can spread misinformation (H1′) is, however, diminished by the fact that the Britains and Austrians mostly used bilateral means and not the forum for transmitting false reports.

In early 1821, Christians in Greece and in the Danubian Principalities of Wallachia and Moldavia rebelled against their Muslim Turkish rulers. By March 1821, over one-third of the forty thousand Turks in Morea (Southern Greece) had been killed. This quickly led to Turkish counteratrocities, including the killing of the Orthodox Greek Patriarch of Constantinople at the door of his cathedral on Easter Sunday in April 1821.

Had this been another liberal revolution similar to those in Naples and Spain, the Concert powers might have been content to see the Sultan suppress the revolution. Russia, however, had traditionally viewed itself as the protector of the Orthodox faith and was motivated to intervene to protect its fellow faithful. Moreover, Russia and the Ottoman Empire had been competing for influence throughout the Balkans, the Caucasus, and around the Black Sea for years. Instead of wanting to crush the Greek rebellion, Russia wanted to intervene for solidarity and gain.

Austria feared Balkan turmoil on its doorstep, and wanted to keep Russia at arms-length. Britain preferred a weak Ottoman Empire to a strengthened Russia moving south into the Mediterranean. France favored restraining Russia as well.

In July 1821 Russia issued an ultimatum to the Turks insisting that they protect the rights of Christians, and breaking relations with the Turks. War seemed imminent. Austria's Metternich set out to convince the Tsar not to intervene. As British interests were now threatened, Castlereagh put the schisms over Naples and Spain aside and added his voice to Metternich's.

With Metternich in the lead, they appealed to the tsar's pro-Concert and antirevolutionary feelings. They reminded him of his pledges not to act unilaterally. They gave the tsar credit for creating the European Alliance and urged him not to wreck it. At the same time, they also tried to convince Alexander that the rebels were not Christian victims in need of being saved from the Muslim Turks. Instead, they painted the rebels as ordinary but dangerous liberal revolutionaries, whom Turkey was justified in crushing. Metternich arranged to send numerous slanted and exaggerated (if not false) diplomatic and police reports from around Europe to Alexander attesting to the spread of revolutionary sentiment and the dangers of revolution.[42] Patricia Kennedy Grimsted wrote that Metternich used "gross exaggeration and underhanded tactics" as part of his campaign. For example, he ordered the interception of diplomatic dispatches looking for evidence to undermine the tsar's most influential advisor, the pro-Greek Count Ioannis Capo d'Istria (or Capodistrias), by tying him to the Greek rebellion.[43] Metternich met Castlereagh in Hanover in October 1821, and they concocted to send similar messages to Russia.[44]

If this deception and propaganda plan were much aided by forum diplomacy, it might offer support for the hypothesis that regimes can spread misinformation (H1'). H1' is undercut, however, because Concert diplomacy itself should be downplayed. For example, Alexander had hoped that he could dominate the 1822 Congress of Verona with the subject of the revolt. He was foiled, and the Greek Revolt took a back seat to the situation in Spain, described earlier. While not completely off the table, "it was a matter of common courtesy not to mention Turkish difficulties at Verona." What was discussed regarding Greece was "anticlimactic," though the Conference did give Metternich the chance to continue spinning his tales of Greek-inspired revolutionaries in Europe to Alexander.[45] Instead of Concert diplomacy, it was non-forum communication such as

[42] Kissinger, *A World Restored*, 293 and 300.

[43] Patricia Kennedy Grimsted, *The Foreign Ministers of Alexander I: Political Attitudes and the Conduct of Russian Diplomacy, 1801–1825* (Berkeley, CA: University of California Press, 1969), 255.

[44] Temperley, *Foreign Policy of Canning*, 323.

[45] Nichols, *European Pentarchy*, 254 (the first quote is Nichols citing Friedrich von Gentz, the Austrian publicist).

Metternich's meeting with Castlereagh in Hanover and the exaggerated reports to Alexander that most influenced the course of events.

This incident, however, is one of the clearest examples of pro-Concert, non-unilateral norms actually affecting behavior and leading to an outcome that would not have happened in the absence of those norms. Ironically, the norms were part of the deception campaign.

By mid-1822, Alexander had been persuaded not to go to war, however morally satisfying or lucrative it might have been. He acted to save the alliance, his Holy Alliance. This is the turning point in the crisis, and it casts doubt on the value of Concert diplomacy in doing anything other than facilitating the deception that helped stop Alexander.

If forum diplomacy was not crucial, was Alexander a norm-driven idealist, or was he duped by others' misinformation? The answer bears on the issue of whether the Greek crisis is an information story at all, and whether there were such a thing as Concert norms as claimed by the optimists.

Schroeder calls Alexander's decision a "triumph of diplomacy over the use of force" and the "easiest and simplest" counter-realist example of a state that has "foregone concrete material advantages for the sake of moral principle."[46] On the other hand, Kissinger makes the tsar out to be a dupe and quotes Metternich as holding Alexander's pliability in contempt:

> After having robbed the world of a few months of peace, the Emperor Alexander takes his head in his hands and presents himself before me with the request that I explain its content to him. . . . [He] wants to find his way in a labyrinth and asks his old Ariadne for yarn.[47]

The tsar's most influential advisor, the pro-Greek Count Ioannis Capo d'Istria (or Capodistrias), seemed to agree. After Alexander decided not to intervene, he resigned and said that "with friends like Austria, Russia did not need enemies."[48]

On the question of whether or not Alexander was a norm-driven idealist or a dupe, the truth probably lies somewhere in between. According to Matthew Anderson, Alexander was willing to have his hands tied.[49]

---

[46] *Transformation of European Politics,* 621.

[47] Quoted in Kissinger, *A World Restored,* 304.

[48] Paraphrased by Schroeder in *Transformation of European Politics,* 621.

[49] Matthew Anderson, "Russia and the Eastern Question, 1821–1841," in Sked, ed., *Europe's Balance of Power,* 82. Other sources consulted for this section include René Albrecht-Carrié, *The Concert of Europe: 1815–1914* (New York: Harper Torchbooks, 1968), 99–113; Barbara Jelavich, *Russia's Balkan Entanglements, 1806–1914* (Cambridge, England: Cambridge University Press, 1991), 49–75; Kissinger, *A World Restored,* 286–311; Matthew Tobias Rendall, "Russia, the Concert of Europe, and the Near East, 1821–41: A Status Quo State in the Vienna System," Ph.D. diss., Columbia University, New York, 2000; Schroeder, *Transformation of European Politics,* 614–21, 636–64; Temperley, *Foreign Policy of Canning,* 319–62, 390–409; Webster, *Foreign Policy of Castlereagh,* 349–400.

Assessment

The main turning point in this crisis occurred when Alexander was convinced not to intervene. This episode hints that mechanisms that are supposed to increase transparency may be used to manipulate the truth. As H1′ suggests, it is likely true that anything that either transfers or generates information can also transfer or generate false information. In this case though, the forum was probably not used to spread misinformation, and thus H1′ does not apply. Questions that deserve more research are when, how often, and under what conditions do mechanisms that increase transparency make deception easier?[50]

The example of the Greek crisis alone is not sufficient to answer these questions fully, but Alexander's gullibility suggests that the degree to which transparency helps or hinders deception depends to a large extent on the vigilance of states and their leaders.

FIFTH CRISIS: INDEPENDENCE OF BELGIUM

As with the Poland-Saxony episode, the crises surrounding the independence of Belgium show how Concert diplomacy speeded communications, helped states to communicate threats, and helped avert miscalculation. Because of this, the case provides evidence H3, which contends that transparency can clarify bargaining positions and reduce conflict. Evidence for the contributions of forum diplomacy and transparency is mitigated by the considerable amount of bilateral diplomacy, which also helped resolve problems.

For hundreds of years, the area of the Netherlands/Belgium/Luxemburg had been a source of tension and a flashpoint for European wars. The 1815 Vienna settlement attached Belgium to the Dutch Netherlands to create a stronger buffer against France. In August of 1830, the Belgians, however, began to rebel against Dutch rule. At the end of September, the Dutch had appealed to all the great powers save France for military help in suppressing the revolt. Russia and Prussia, the conservative Eastern powers, were most favorable to intervention. In October, the Belgians declared their independence, and on November 4, all five great powers met in London to discuss the problem.

Remembering Napoleon and aware of France's perennial appetite for Belgium, the rest of Europe feared French intervention. France in turn feared the consequences of a British or Prussian intervention. Russia

---

[50] A good stab at this issue is found in the surprise attack literature, cited in fn. 44 in chap. 2.

mobilized intervention forces but would not act unilaterally, and it was soon distracted by more proximate problems when Poland rebelled against it in November 1830. With everyone fearing intervention more than rebellion, the conference agreed in fairly short order to allow Belgium's separation. By late January 1831, the great powers had issued several joint Protocols specifying Belgium's new borders, guaranteeing its independence (primarily from the French), and providing for freedom of navigation on rivers.

Despite progress in the negotiations over Belgian independence at the London conference, Luxemburg remained occupied by Belgian troops, and this caused a crisis by summer 1831. On August 2, the Dutch attacked Belgium, and this time Belgium appealed to France for help. France quickly entered Belgium and convinced Holland to take its troops home. France then reversed a promise to withdraw its own troops and left its forces in Belgium pending a full settlement between Belgium and Holland and resolution of France's concerns over fortresses on the Belgian border with France.

Alarmed by the French move, the British thought that continued occupation would lead to war. France's King Louis-Philippe, a generally pacific leader, waffled in responding to British concerns. At the urging of Britain's foreign office, Granville Leveson-Gower, 1st Earl Granville, Britain's ambassador in Paris, had a blunt discussion with France and made clear that continued French occupation risked serious consequences. At first, the French did not budge. Britain's foreign minister, Viscount Henry Temple Palmerston, wrote to Granville, "One thing is certain, the French must go out of Belgium, or we shall have a general war, and war in a few days." Prussia threatened to move into the Rhine Provinces, and Russia's threats to intervene regained their credibility as they came nearer to crushing the Polish revolt. Britain's Granville took the diplomatic lead and, with the support of the Austrian, Prussian, and Russian ambassadors to France (in Paris), convinced the French to leave Belgium in early September.[51]

This was a turning point. The others powers were able to clarify and underscore their desire to have France leave. Here we see the regime providing transparency (H1), helping states signal their positions, and reducing conflict (H3). Support for these hypotheses is tempered, however, by the fact that much of the diplomacy seemed to take place in Paris, not at the ongoing London conference. It is hard to discern the relative contributions of forum diplomacy and bilateral diplomacy to the resolution of the crisis in this instance.

---

[51] G.W.T. Omond, "Belgium: 1830–1839," in Sir A. W. Ward and G. P. Gooch, eds., *The Cambridge History of British Foreign Policy: 1783–1919*, vol. 2 (New York: Macmillan, 1923), 144–146, quote on p. 145.

Even though the French occupation had been dealt with, matters between Belgium and Holland were unresolved. On October 15, 1831, the London conference put forward another plan for settling the situation. Among its numerous provisions, the Twenty-four Articles called for Luxemburg to be partitioned between Belgium and Holland.

A year later, the Dutch still rejected the Articles and were hindering shipping on the Scheldt river. Holland still occupied Antwerp; Belgium still occupied Luxemburg. To prevent escalation between Holland and Belgium, the Concert powers agreed to step up pressure on the Dutch. The Eastern powers wanted to apply economic pressure on Holland, but the British and French thought that these measures were insufficient. The French were prepared to remove Holland from Antwerp unilaterally by force. Unilateral French action risked wider war, while inaction risked unilateral Prussian intervention. Omond says this about the possibility of European-wide war, with France poised to move unilaterally against Antwerp:

> One Prussian Corps was at Aix-la-Chapelle, and another was posted in reserve on the Rhine. . . . The danger of an explosion was increased by the temper of the Belgians; for it was quite possible that, if the two Western Powers did not act immediately, they might break loose and attack the Dutch. If so, Prussia would rush in to the help of Holland and, should she be victorious, would take from France Alsace and Lorraine . . . all of which she tried to obtain during the Congress of Vienna. If Prussia was defeated, France would endeavor to annex the Rhine Provinces and . . . Luxemburg. Austria and the other States of the Germanic Confederation would be drawn into the struggle. Russia would intervene. . . . Great Britain, unless she deserted France, would find herself at war with more than one Continental Power; and soon not only Europe, but half the world, would be at war.
>
> With such a prospect, hesitation would have been fatal. If Great Britain and France acted together . . . Prussia, it was known, would not oppose the coercion of Holland.[52]

Prussia made this known in Paris, not at the London conference.

On October 22, the British and French agreed to joint sea and land operations to get the Dutch out of Antwerp, free up shipping, and restore other territories in the low countries to their allotted Belgian or Dutch owners. Russia left the conference, Austria and Prussia protested, but French troops reentered Belgium on November 15 while the British blockaded the Scheldt. According to Schroeder, this affront to the Eastern powers

---

[52] Omond, "Belgium," 153–54.

"caused suspension of the conference and created a war scare more serious than any earlier one."[53] It also resolved the crisis.

It is difficult to judge whether tensions would have been higher or lower without the Concert. Problems in Belgium were problems in the center of Europe, and would have drawn in most of the Great Powers anyway. That said, diplomacy at the London conference, in Paris, and elsewhere did clarify the stakes and stances in the crisis. As this happened, tensions rose, as predicted by H3', but then fell as the crisis broke; this later development supports H3. Depending on the dynamics of a crisis and the interests of the actors, reducing uncertainty about positions and stakes can raise tensions, reduce conflict, or both.

Because the bilateral and multilateral bargaining prevented unilateral action, it is possible (or even likely, given the threats and fears of war) that the bargaining lessened miscalculation and prevented war. This is predicted by H3, which contends that transparency can reduce uncertainty and miscalculation, thereby promoting peaceful outcomes from strategic interaction. Support for these hypotheses, however, exists only to the extent that forum diplomacy helped achieve these results by speeding up the flow of information.

In the face of Franco-British actions, the Dutch quickly withdrew from Antwerp and the French pulled out their troops. This ended the immediate crisis, but the blockade persisted until May 1833. The Belgian situation was not fully resolved until, after nearly a decade of diplomacy, coercion, and seventy Great Power protocols, a treaty was finally signed by Holland and Belgium on April 19, 1839.[54]

Assessment

There were two turning points in this crisis. The first was getting France to leave Belgium on September 9, 1831. This result was certainly aided by concerted diplomacy, but not necessarily by forum diplomacy. Inasmuch

---

[53] Schroeder, *Transformation of European Politics,* 690.

[54] General sources consulted for this section include: Albrecht-Carrié, *Concert of Europe,* 60–98 (which has the text of the final treaty and several of the seventy Great Power protocols—something in between minutes of meetings and a U.N.-type resolution—that document the diplomatic negotiations); Albrecht-Carrié, *Diplomatic History of Europe,* 31–36; J. A. Betley, *Belgium and Poland in International Relations 1830–1831* (The Hague, Netherlands: Mouton, 1960); J. S. Fishman, *Diplomacy and Revolution: The London Conference of 1830 and the Belgian Revolt* (Amsterdam, Netherlands: CHEV, 1988); Fl. de Lannoy, *Histoire Diplomatique de L'Indépendance Belge* (Brussels, Belgium: Librairie Albert Dewit, 1930); Christopher Layne, "Lord Palmerston and the Triumph of Realism: Anglo-French Relations, 1830–1848," in Miriam Fendius Elman, ed., Paths to Peace: Is Democracy the Answer? (Cambridge, MA: MIT Press, 1997), 61–100, esp. 78–81; Omond, "Belgium;" Schroeder, *Transformation of European Politics,* 670–91; Harold Temperley

as it was the European diplomats to Paris who took the lead in convincing France, the key diplomacy therefore took place in Paris and not in London, where the conference was being held. To the extent that the forum was not used to speed the information flow, this undercuts support that would otherwise be generated for H1, which contends that regimes provide transparency.

The second turning point was when Britain and France joined forces to coerce the Dutch on October 22, 1832. Britain and France knew of the impending dangers of war and, calculating correctly, took joint action to prevent it. To calculate the danger of war correctly, the French and British had to know of Belgium's impending threat to attack Holland and of Prussian intentions to support the Dutch in case the French intervention crossed onto Dutch territory. Letters between Prince Talleyrand, the French envoy to the London Conference, and Victor Duc de Broglie, a French foreign ministry official, reveal that the French and British exchanged key information about their own intentions and capabilities and on the dangers of Prussian intervention in London and in Paris. Further, the Prussians had made their intentions clear in direct communications with French government representatives in Paris.[55]

Here, the conference at London (or at least the diplomacy that took place in London) appears to have been helpful, but perhaps not crucial, in clarifying the situation. Thus, there is some modest evidence that forum diplomacy increased transparency (H1). Clarification of dangers and signaling of intentions first raised tensions (H3′), then led to Franco-British cooperation (H3). The most important clarifier in this episode, however, was the fact of joint British and French action, not the diplomacy surrounding it. This action deterred Prussia and/or reduced its incentives to intervene, coerced the Dutch, and obviated Belgian action. Finally, the amount of diplomacy that happened outside of the London forum weakens support for the contention that forum-based diplomacy accelerated communications, as predicted by H1.

It is plausible that war might have resulted had the powers been forced to undertake the time-consuming bilateral dance that characterized the partition of Poland in the eighteenth century. Even though the big picture is that the Belgium crisis persisted for years, some key aspects of it were resolved with relative alacrity, a possible indicator that transparency was increased. The best example is the speed with which the French were

and Lillian M. Penson, eds., *Foundations of British Foreign Policy from Pitt (1792) to Salisbury (1902)* (Cambridge, England: Cambridge University Press, 1938), 88–100; Sir Charles Webster, *The Foreign Policy of Palmerston, 1830–1841: Britain, the Liberal Movement, and the Eastern Question*, vol. 1 (London: G. Bell, 1951), 89–176.

[55] From letters between Talleyrand and the Duc de Broglie in de Broglie, ed., *Memoirs of the Prince de Talleyrand*, 5: 12–15, and fn. 1, p. 12.

persuaded to leave Belgium in the summer of 1831, a major turning point. This crisis shows transparency enhancing realpolitik. The Concert modestly and with limits enabled coercive transparency, which in turn helped reduce miscalculation and helped keep the peace (H3).

CONCLUSION

The Concert increased transparency in varying degrees at turning points in most of the five crises. When it did, the effect was often to facilitate coercive bargaining. The Concert's institutional effects lay not with rules or norms, as the frequent war scares, blunt language, and forceful bargaining make clear. Instead, the Concert sometimes increased transparency, and transparency in turn helped realpolitik lead to peaceful outcomes. Crises often had to get worse as bargaining clarified the differences (H3'), before coercion worked and broke the deadlock (H3). There was little evidence that transparency ever seriously lessened unwarranted fears (H4), a notable finding because this is supposed to be a main peace-promoting benefit of transparency.

Castlereagh, the prime mover behind the Concert, expressed some hope that forum diplomacy would increase transparency and thereby reduce tensions. I am not sure how much this view persuaded others to form the Concert, but Castlereagh at least believed that increased transparency was a reason to form a regime; this evidence supports H2.

The mechanism of the forum diplomacy was used often. States often supplemented Concert diplomacy, however, with meetings in other locations, bilateral contacts, side-meetings, and so forth. These may be valuable supplements to or byproducts of forums, and they may serve to increase transparency. They may also serve to generate private information or diminish the importance of the forum in helping states communicate. While the Concert was clearly helpful in some instances, the Concert did not increase transparency as much as it might at first appear, and so the first hypothesis (H1) receives only modest support.

The Concert helped states conduct power-political diplomacy and in three instances the increased speed of communication helped reduce miscalculation (in the Poland-Saxony crisis and twice in the Belgian crisis). This provides support for H3, but because it is not clear that the states would have miscalculated in the absence of the Concert, I code this support as moderate to moderate/strong, despite the gravity of these three instances.

There is only one bit of evidence that Concert diplomacy reduced fears, and so H4 is only weakly supported. Instead, transparency often reduced uncertainty by helping states learn about the extent of the problems they faced, about new counter-coalitions, or about deadlock. When states clarify their positions and stakes, and it increases conflict, these events support H3. In several instances during the Poland-Saxony and Belgian crises, however, this clarification was just a stage that then led to further action or resolution. When clarification of stakes, stances, and options during bargaining helps resolve a crisis, it supports H3, the contention that transparency promotes peace by reducing incomplete information and helping bargaining and coercion.

Thus, H3 and H3' may help describe different phases of a crisis. For example, in Poland-Saxony, forum diplomacy helped states make threats and for a while this increased the chance of war (H3'). In the end, though, a final coercive threat broke the deadlock, which supports H3.

Table 3-1 summarizes the main findings by hypothesis.

Implications

These findings occupy the middle ground in the debate between Concert optimists who have not fully explored the informational and transparency contributions of the Concert, and Concert pessimists who, in their rush to dismiss institutionalism, have ignored transparency altogether.

According to a number of scholars, the Concert contributed to peace because it fostered and operated according to several norms: states behaved with moderation; they compensated each other when territorial and other adjustments became necessary; they consulted with one another and did not act unilaterally; and they kept the general equilibrium in mind when judging the consequences of their actions. As a result, these scholars give the Concert credit for numerous peace-enhancing accomplishments: creating buffer states, isolating regional conflicts, specifying spheres of influence, suppressing revolutions by multilateral action, and observing the general practice of multilateral conflict resolution.[56]

Paul Schroeder, among others, argues that all these effects amounted to a sweeping transformation, even "revolution," of diplomacy and international relations.[57] Concert optimists make some of the strongest

[56] Elrod, "The Concert of Europe"; Lauren, "Crisis Prevention in Nineteenth-Century Diplomacy"; Paul W. Schroeder, "The 19th-Century International System: Changes in the Structure," *World Politics* 28, no. 2 (January 1986).

[57] Schroeder, *Transformation of European Politics,* 580. For a symposium that largely reaffirms Schroeder's interpretation, see *The International History Review* 16, no. 4 (November 1994) including H. M. Scott, "Paul W. Schroeder's International System: The View from Vienna"; Charles Ingrao, "Paul W. Schroeder's Balance of Power: Stability or Anarchy?" T. C. W. Blanning, "Paul W. Schroeder's Concert of Europe"; and Jack S. Levy, "The Theoretical Foundations of Paul W. Schroeder's International System"; and Schroeder, "Balance of Power and Political Equilibrium: A Response."

TABLE 3-1
Findings by Hypothesis

Hypothesis	Evidence	Strength of evidence	Overall strength of hypothesis
Regimes provide transparency (H1)	Poland-Saxony: forum enabled and quickened many discussions and deal-making, esp. the semi-secret alliance, esp. p. 68	Strong	Moderate
	Naples and Spain: discussion of regime's functions; evidence throughout case	Weak	
	Belgium: communication of threats, discussion of stakes; evidence throughout case	Moderate/Weak	
Regimes spread misinformation (H1')	No evidence found that the disinformation campaign in the Greek case used the forum, p. 73		
Anticipated transparency promotes cooperation (H2)	Castlereagh's statement about the purpose of a Concert, p. 64	Weak	Weak
Anticipated transparency hinders cooperation (H2')	No evidence		
Transparency promotes cooperation and prevents conflict (H3)	Poland-Saxony: quick making and revealing of the crisis-resolving semi-secret alliance, p. 68	Strong	Moderate/ Strong
	Poland-Saxony: Russia and Prussia back down, p. 68	Strong	
	Belgium: France convinced to leave (summer, 1831), p. 76	Moderate/Strong	
	Belgium: Prussia prevented from intervening unilaterally, p. 77	Moderate/Weak	
	Belgium: getting British and French to intervene together, p. 77	Moderate	

Table 3-1 (continued)

Hypothesis	Evidence	Strength of evidence	Overall strength of hypothesis
Transparency hinders cooperation and causes conflict (H3')	Poland-Saxony: increased tensions and threats, p. 67	Strong	Moderate
	Naples and Spain: clarified Britain's objections; evidence throughout case	Moderate/Weak	
	Belgium: war scare prior to joint 1832 intervention, p. 77	Moderate	
Transparency reduces unwarranted fears and worst-case assumptions (H4)	Castlereagh's statement about meeting together reducing prejudice, p. 66	Weak	Weak
Transparency confirms fears (H4')	No evidence		
Transparency reduces cheating, rogue, and spoiler problems (H5)	No evidence (less applicable to an informal regime like a forum)		
Transparency about the regime (or self-transparency) increases its effectiveness (H6)	No evidence (less applicable to an informal regime like a forum)		

Note: Coding: "Strong" means that the phenomenon or effect was clear and very influential if not decisive, producing behavior that would be hard to replicate without the regime. "Moderate" means that the phenomenon played a discernible and somewhat influential role. Other factors help explain the outcome. "Weak" means that the phenomenon was probably but only weakly present. Other factors explain most of the outcome. "Failure" means that the regime tried to do something and failed, or that something that the regime did was counterproductive. The overall ratings are judgments based on the significance of transparency and its effects for each hypothesis within the context of each case.

claims for the effectiveness of institutions and regimes to be found in any issue area.

Realists discard institutional arguments and contend that if the Concert worked at all it was because skilled diplomats knew how to play power politics. Realist interpretations of the Concert go back to Kissinger and others,[58] but only recently have a few Concert pessimists emerged to combine theory and history to challenge the post–Cold War wave of Concert optimism. Matthew Rendall, for one, offers a balance of power interpretation of Russian diplomacy during the Greek rebellion against Turkey in the 1820s, while acknowledging that the great powers were also content with the status quo. Korina Kagan's analysis of the Greek case is more sweeping. She lays out the normative arguments made by the institutionalists, notes the significant amount of realpolitik in the case, and concludes that

> since the Concert of Europe is widely hailed as the major paradigmatic case of an effective security regime, these findings deprive institutionalism of its strongest case in the security area.[59]

I argue that the Concert was neither a normative transformation of politics nor a phenomenon devoid of institutional benefits. Rather, there was an institutional benefit provided by the Concert: that of transparency.

The Concert of Europe is not a good place to find idealism, norms, rules, or even much enlightened self-interest. To this extent, recent realist critiques of the Concert from Kagan and Rendall are valid. The only significant norm evinced, and the only transformation to persist to this day, was the then-new practice of meeting together in a forum. The lack of norms and rules does not, however, destroy the institutionalist argument, because rules and norms are only part of the institutionalist repertoire.

Realist critics have neglected the informational arguments central to institutionalist claims. According to liberal institutionalists, a major benefit of institutions is their ability to provide more and higher-quality information to participants. Chapters and articles by Jervis, Lipson, and Kupchan and Kupchan have looked at transparency and information in the context of the Concert of Europe.[60] While I stand on their shoulders, I grapple with the new arguments of the transparency pessimists, compare Concert

---

[58] Kissinger, *A World Restored;* and W. N. Medlicott, *Bismarck, Gladstone, and the Concert of Europe* (London: University of London/Athlone Press, 1956).

[59] Kagan, "Myth of the European Concert"; and Matthew Rendall, "Russia, the Concert of Europe, and Greece 1821–29: A Test of Hypotheses about the Vienna System," *Security Studies,* 9, no. 4 (Summer 2000). See also Bradley A. Thayer, "An Offensive Realist Examination of the Concert of Europe" presented at the American Political Science Association conference, Boston, MA, August 2002.

[60] See fn. 13 in chap. 1.

diplomacy with prior, non-forum diplomacy, and show more precisely how and when the Concert increased transparency and helped crisis management. Transparency did not prevent serious war scares, but it did help avert escalation to war.

Many scholars and analysts use the Concert as the basis for recommendations that would shape the future of NATO, the U.N., and other regional security organizations from Asia to Africa. Whatever the deductive appeal of a Concert-like Great-Power discussion forum or mechanism for a Great Power condominium, these recommendations lose some of their shine if the Concert's actual paths to peace were in fact more rough-and-tumble and less norm-driven than the optimists assert.

CHAPTER FOUR

The United Nations Force in Cyprus

THE UNITED NATIONS PEACEKEEPING FORCE IN CYPRUS (UNFICYP) went through two phases. In the first, from 1964 to 1974, the adversarial Greek Cypriot and Turkish Cypriot populations were interspersed throughout the island. UNFICYP thus deployed across the island, hoping to avert conflicts wherever they might erupt. In 1974, Turkey invaded Cyprus, dividing it in two with a Turkish Cypriot Northern portion and a Greek Cypriot Southern portion. The U.N. mission changed to monitoring the buffer zone created between the two sides.

I look at both these periods, and answer these main questions: What does UNFICYP monitor and verify? What incidents occur along the buffer zone and what does UNFICYP do to manage them? Do the activities of UNFICYP affect tensions along the buffer zone and between the Greek Cypriots and Turkish Cypriots?

FORMATION OF UNFICYP

To test H2, the contention that the promise of regime-provided transparency promotes cooperation, I begin by examining the formation of UNFICYP to see if anticipated transparency helped the Greek and Turkish Cypriots make peace, or at least accept a peacekeeping operation.

After several years of revolutionary and intercommunal violence, Cyprus was granted independence from Britain in 1960 by agreement of the Guarantor Powers—Britain, Greece, and Turkey. Following a constitutional crisis, fighting broke out in 1963 between the majority Greek Cypriots (80 percent) and minority Turkish Cypriots (18 percent). Britain tried to stop the conflict, but turned to the United States and NATO when it failed. Risking an intra-NATO Greco-Turkish war, Turkey threatened to intervene to prevent Greek Cypriots from uniting the island with Greece and to protect the endangered Turkish Cypriots. While issuing stern warnings that prevented Turkish military action and thus a possible war between Greece and Turkey, Washington proposed sending a NATO force of 10,000 troops. The left-leaning (Greek) Cypriot President Archbishop Makarios III rejected the U.S./NATO proposal, and the Soviets viewed the NATO move with alarm. To reconcile these competing interests, the parties turned to the U.N. The United States and Britain wanted some sort of peacekeeping operation, even if was not run by NATO, while Makarios and the Soviets were willing to accept only a U.N. mission. So a U.N. mission it was, and in March 1964, the U.N. Security Council authorized the establishment of a U.N. peacekeeping operation mandated to "prevent a recurrence of fighting and, as necessary, to contribute to the maintenance and restoration of law and order and a return to normal conditions."[1]

UNFICYP quickly reached its peak strength of 6411 multinational soldiers in June 1964, declining to 4737 by the end of 1967.[2] In contrast, between 1964 and 1967, the Greek Cypriots and Greeks had roughly 33,450 men under arms on Cyprus while the Turkish side had 13,450.

While the forum of the U.N. helped the sides compromise, the peacekeeping force was imposed on Cyprus. The promise of U.N. peacekeeping did little to help the Cypriots to cooperate to achieve peace, and there is no evidence for H2.

THE FIRST YEARS OF UNFICYP: 1964–74

UNFICYP deployed along the Green Line dividing Nicosia, in towns where trouble was expected, and throughout Cyprus more generally. In the early to mid-1960s, the Greek and Turkish communities were spread across the island, although the violence of 1963–64 led most Turkish Cypriots into purely Turkish villages or enclaves adjoining Greek areas.[3] The "Green

[1] Karl Th. Birgisson, "United Nations Peacekeeping Force in Cyprus," in William J. Durch, ed., *The Evolution of UN Peacekeeping: Case Studies and Comparative Analysis* (New York: St. Martin's, 1993), 222.

[2] This section is based on Birgisson, "United Nations Peacekeeping Force in Cyprus," 219–22; U.S. Department of the Army, *U.S. Army Handbook for Cyprus* (Washington, DC: Department of the Army, 1964), 224–25; Eugene K. Keefe, "Historical Setting," in Frederica M. Bunge, ed., *Cyprus: A Country Study,* 3rd ed. (Washington, DC: American University Press, 1980), xiii, 17–53; Franz Georg Maier, *Cyprus: From the Earliest Time to the Present Day,* Peter Gorge, trans. (London: Elek, 1968), 127–63; Richard A. Patrick, *Political Geography and the Cyprus Conflict: 1963–1971* (Waterloo, Canada: Department of Geography, University of Waterloo, 1976), 27–67; H. D. Purcell, *Cyprus* (London: Ernest Benn, 1969); Norma Salem, "The Constitution of 1960 and Its Failure," in Norma Salem, ed., *Cyprus, A Regional Conflict and Its Resolution* (New York: St. Martin's, for the Canadian Institute for International Peace and Security, 1992), 121–22; James A. Stegenga, *The United Nations Force in Cyprus* (Columbus, OH: Ohio State University Press, 1969), 15–72, 82–83; United Nations, *The Blue Helmets: A Review of United Nations Peace-Keeping,* 2 ed. (New York: United Nations, 1990), 281–88.

[3] See J. Jeffrey Hoover, "The Society and its Environment," in Bunge, *Cyprus,* 60–65; Patrick, *Political Geography,* esp. 8–13, 340–348.

Line" dividing Cyprus's capitol, Nicosia, into separate Turkish Cypriot and Greek Cypriot areas was created by the British during their abortive peacekeeping efforts in late 1963/early 1964.

Although violence was frequent between 1964 and 1967, UNFICYP peacekeepers were often successful at interposing themselves between adversaries and deterring or halting conflict, as well as at mediating temporary cease-fires. Because of this, observers agree that in its first decade UNFICYP did a decent job at ameliorating (but not stopping) intercommunal violence.[4]

UNFICYP also used patrolling and observation to prevent violence. By being able to give accurate accountings of incidents, UNFICYP sometimes succeeded in deterring violence by preventing the aggressor from escaping in a fog of denials and mutual recriminations. When UNFICYP succeeded in using transparency about defections to bolster deterrence and compliance, it offers evidence of H5 in action. H5 contends that regimes can detect defection and wield information to coerce more peaceful behavior by cheaters, rogues, and spoilers. Some of UNFICYP's (modest) effectiveness in its early years was due to the provision of transparency. The following text from Fetherston illustrates transparency reducing fear between adversaries, as predicted by H4, and clarifying the purposes of UNFICYP's activities, as predicted by H6:

> Breaches of the ceasefire were dealt with through a liaison system . . . [the system also made] sure that information about any planned activities by UNFICYP (troop movements or removal of fortifications for example) was received by both sides well in advance. The liaison system was meant to reduce tensions by providing both sides with reliable information and in this sense facilitate communication between the antagonists (such liaison systems are employed in all U.N. peacekeeping operations).[5]

Today, the liaison system is still very important, but the post-1974 fixed buffer zone also helps increase transparency. Prior to 1974, the cease-fire lines were fluid—when they existed at all. Violence might occur anywhere. Since 1974, there has been only one cease-fire line, positions of the op-

---

[4] Birgisson, "United Nations Peacekeeping Force in Cyprus," 227–28; Michael Harbottle, *The Impartial Soldier* (London: Oxford University Press, 1970); Michael Harbottle, *The Blue Berets* (London: Leo Cooper, 1975); Rosalyn Higgins, *United Nations Peacekeeping: Documents and Commentary,* vol. 4, *Europe 1946–1979* (Oxford, England: Oxford University Press, 1981), 312–14; Patrick, *Political Geography,* 63–64; James D. Rudolf, "National Security," in Bunge, *Cyprus,* 213–215; Stegenga, *United Nations Force in Cyprus,* 81–156; United Nations, *Blue Helmets,* 2 ed., 285–93.

[5] A. B. Fetherston, *Towards a Theory of United Nations Peacekeeping* (New York: St. Martin's, 1994), 51–52.

posing forces are well known, and violence and rogue behavior is relatively easy to spot and localize. In this way, the buffer zone itself increases transparency, thus potentially reducing unwarranted fears (H4) and incentives to cheat (H5).

Cyprus faced two major crises in 1964 and 1967, and transparency helped a little bit in the latter. In November 1967, the National Guard attacked two Turkish enclaves in Southern Cyprus. As the crisis continued, Turkey mobilized to invade Cyprus and attack Greece. Heavy weather and U.S. pressure on Turkey prevented the invasion and ended the crisis. UNFICYP arranged a cease-fire at one of the enclaves, Ayios Theodhoros, and refuted exaggerated rumors about atrocities.[6] Although it was not a big factor during the 1967 crisis, rumor reduction is transparency in action and this offers mild support for H4, which predicts that transparency can calm fears.

Refuting rumors may have played a bigger, more moderate role on a more routine (noncrisis) basis in the early years of UNFICYP. Its initiatives "acting as mediators on different levels, trying to dissuade the parties from the use of violence or counteracting false propaganda about atrocities and reporting what has actually taken place have served . . . the causes of peace in Cyprus."[7] Reporting the truth, thus increasing transparency and calming unwarranted fears, fulfills the predictions of hypothesis H4.

Following a pro-enosis (unification of Cyprus with Greece) coup on Cyprus, Turkey invaded in July of 1974. The conflict ended in August with a Turkish/Turkish Cypriot area in the North (comprising 37 percent of the island), with the rest of Cyprus left for the Greek Cypriots. The area that existed (3 percent of Cyprus) between the two opposing cease-fire lines at the end of the invasion became the current buffer zone. The buffer zone and de facto partition changed UNFICYP's modus operandi. Instead of trying to keep the peace throughout the interspersed or enclaved communities of Cyprus, UNFICYP now endeavored to maintain the peace and the status quo by protecting the integrity of the new buffer zone.[8] Although the partition lowered inter- and intracommunal violence, UNFICYP continued through 2002 to confront over 1000 incidents a year.

---

[6] See Parker T. Hart, *Two NATO Allies at the Threshold of War; Cyprus: A Firsthand Account of Crisis Management, 1965–1968* (Durham, NC: Duke University Press, 1990); Harbottle, *Impartial Soldier*), 145–67; Higgins, *United Nations Peacekeeping,* 312–14, 343–57; Robert McDonald, "The Cyprus Problem," *Adelphi Paper 234* (London: International Institute for Strategic Studies, 1989), 15; Patrick, *Political Geography,* 63–72; Purcell, *Cyprus,* 350–54, 380–84; Rudolf, "National Security," 213–17; Stegenga, *United Nations Force in Cyprus,* 191–93; and United Nations, *Blue Helmets,* 2nd ed., 294–98.

[7] Andrestinos N. Papadapoulos, "Cyprus: A Case Study, Peace-Making and Peace-Keeping by the United Nations," working paper, Nicosia, Cyprus, 1969.

[8] See Harbottle, *Blue Berets,* 100–107; Higgins, *United Nations Peacekeeping,* 4:370–85; Eleni Meleagrou and Birol Yesilada, "The Society and Its Environment," in Eric Solsten,

PEACEKEEPING IN CYPRUS IN THE 1990S

Here, I assess the role of transparency beginning with an overview of the operation that focuses on two of the main tools that help UNFICYP increase transparency and peacekeep more generally: the liaison system and the status quo. Then I assess the role of transparency when UNFICYP responds to several categories of violations and peacekeeping activities in and along the buffer zone.[9] The role of transparency varies greatly by the type of incident, and this variation provides a number of insights into its effects.

Overview

In 2002, there were roughly 130,000 (18 percent) Turkish Cypriots on Cyprus out of a total population of 760,000.[10] Over 30,000 troops from Turkey joined 4000 Turkish Cypriot soldiers on Cyprus, along with 26,000 Turkish Cypriot reservists. There were two infantry battalions and 1300 officers and noncommissioned officers from Greece on Cyprus. Greek officers also control the 10,000-strong Greek Cypriot National Guard and the 88,000 Greek Cypriot reservists. Because of numbers, training, and proximity to their home country, the Turkish forces enjoy clear superiority on Cyprus.

The Greek and Greek Cypriot governments combined pay about half of UNFICYP's budget.[11] Unfortunately, this payment arrangement reduces UNFICYP's impartiality in the eyes of the Turkish side. This in turn reduces their trust in the operation and limits UNFICYP's ability to increase transparency.[12]

To maintain surveillance of the buffer zone, the U.N. staffs twenty-two permanent observation posts along the buffer zone and uses another 120 observation posts less frequently. Routine patrols within the buffer zone are

---

ed., *Cyprus: A Country Study,* 4th ed. (Washington, D.C.: Government Printing Office, 1993), 56; Rudolf, "National Security," 216–27; United Nations, *Blue Helmets,* 2nd ed., 301–9; United States Senate, Subcommittee to Investigate Problems Connected with Refugees and Escapees, Committee on the Judiciary, *Crisis on Cyprus* (Washington D.C.: Government Printing Office, 1974; reprinted in 1975 by the American Hellenic Institute), 18–30. An estimated 6000 Greek Cypriots and 1500 Turkish Cypriots died, and 214,000 Greek Cypriots and 42,000 Turkish Cypriots were displaced.

[9] Some categories of violations, such as overmanning of positions, overflights, and crossing of the Maritime Security Line, are omitted because they are simultaneously trivial and offer no insights about transparency.

[10] Central Intelligence Agency, *World Factbook,* Cyprus, at www.cia.gov/cia/publications/factbook/geos/cy.html, accessed on January 9, 2002.

[11] United Nations Secretary-General, *Report of the Secretary-General on the United Nations Operation in Cyprus,* S/2001/1122, November 30, 2001, p. 3.

[12] Interview, Aytug Plumer, Under-Secretary, Ministry of Foreign Affairs and Defense, "TRNC," June 5, 1996.

conducted from nineteen patrol bases. Patrols are also sent out to investigate whenever one of the sides complains about the other's construction, overmanning, or harassment—all frequent occurrences. Patrols, investigations, and observation posts are all possible mechanisms UNFICYP can use to increase transparency (H1). The buffer zone is 180 kilometers long, varies in width from five meters in Nicosia to seven kilometers in the countryside.[13] A map is availabe at the U.N. website: www.un.org/Depts/Cartographic/map/dpko/unficyp.pdf.

UNFICYP's liaison system is the network of contacts between UNFICYP officers and soldiers with their counterparts on each side of the buffer zone. UNFICYP uses the liaison system to communicate to each side, and it is the primary vehicle that each side uses to get the U.N. to deal with complaints about the other. The opposing forces also use the liaison system to communicate indirectly with each other. Thus, the liaison system is the primary mechanism with which UNFICYP can provide transparency (H1).

The system follows two guidelines: (1) deal with the problem at the lowest possible level and (2) be "firm, fair, and friendly."[14] The standard operating procedure for dealing with violations and incidents involves discussions with the opposing forces in an attempt to calm things down, to find out the truth about what happened, and/or to cajole, persuade, or coerce proper behavior. Depending on the incident, the talks and investigations that follow may lead to increased transparency and reduced fears, or to disciplining of the violator.[15]

THE STATUS QUO

Hoping to foster the conditions helpful for negotiating a peace settlement, UNFICYP's chief responsibility is to preserve the cease-fire. The main way it does so is to maintain the status quo in and along the buffer zone. Because moving perceptions toward a common or base truth is one hallmark of increased transparency, the status quo's role as the base truth means that it is crucial to UNFICYP's ability to provide transparency. The U.N. explains the status quo:

> [The] cease-fire came into effect at 1800 hours on 16 August 1974. Immediately afterwards, UNFICYP inspected the areas of confrontation and recorded the deployment of the military forces on both sides. Lines

---

[13] United Nations, S/1996/411, pp. 1–3, United Nations, *Blue Helmets,* 2nd ed., pp. 306–7, and interview/briefing, Lt. Colonel Nick Parker, Chief Operations Officer, UNFICYP, May 9, 1996.

[14] Interviews with Colonel Ian Talbot, Chief of Staff, UNFICYP, May 9, 1996, and Lt. Colonel Andrew Snowdon, Commanding Officer Sector 2, May 10, 1996.

[15] Interview, Chief of Staff Talbot, May 9, 1996; and discussions with the Chief Operations Officer, Lt. Colonel Parker.

drawn between the forward defended localities became respectively the National Guard and Turkish Forces cease-fire lines. In the absence of a formal cease-fire agreement, *the military status quo, as recorded by UNFICYP at the time, became the standard by which it was judged whether any changes constituted violations of the cease-fire. . . .*

It is an essential feature of the cease-fire that neither side can exercise authority or jurisdiction or make any military moves beyond its own forward military lines. In the area between the lines, which is known as the U.N. buffer zone, UNFICYP maintains the status quo.[16]

The status quo applies not only to the location of the cease-fire lines but also to every militarily significant feature along the buffer zone. This includes the number of sandbags, the number of soldiers, the number of firing holes, and the quality of the concrete blocks in every observation post and position along the buffer zone. Keeping track of all these details—the base truth—is a daunting task and the knowledge must be passed on to each successive rotation of troops. If UNFICYP does not master the minutiae of the buffer zone, it will lose arguments with the opposing forces, be less able to provide transparency and calm incidents, and will slowly lose control over the buffer zone itself.

With varying degrees of thoroughness, UNFICYP maintains sketches, photos, written records, computerized records, and file folders of various positions, areas, and buildings along the buffer zone. A number of the buildings, barbed wire fences, barrels, and other terrain features in and along the buffer zone are marked with U.N. signs indicating what it is and who owns it.

Despite these efforts, there are numerous problems involved in keeping track of the status quo. There is no unambiguous record of the status quo. Files are often incomplete, and there is no comprehensive and centralized photo or video database of the buffer zone. Fearing espionage, both sides prohibit photographs of the buffer zone, even by the U.N. UNFICYP does have a limited supply of photos, but because it cannot admit to them, UNFICYP must instead use its sketches to try to make its case about the status quo.

Another problem is that when the cease-fire lines were drawn, it was done on a large scale map (1:400,000) with a thick pencil. This invited numerous and continuing disputes about the actual location of the cease-fire lines, because the swath of the pencil covered about 300 meters. Three hundred meters is wider than the buffer zone itself at many points.[17]

---

[16] United Nations, *Blue Helmets,* 2nd ed., 307–308; emphasis added.

[17] Interview with General Vartiainen, Force Commander, May 7, 1996. See also Harbottle, *Impartial Soldier,* 63. The exact same problem occurred on the maps that were drawn between Israel and Syria when the U.N. Disengagement Observer Force (UNDOF) was created.

The consequences of an uncertain base truth are that if UNFICYP cannot tell if a position has been upgraded, or where the exact line of the buffer zone is, it cannot use information to coerce cheaters, rogues, and other violators into backing down (H5) or to reduce unwarranted suspicions (H4). Thus, while UNFICYP generally succeeds at maintaining the integrity of the buffer zone and calming incidents, some of the problems it faces are due to or exacerbated by the difficulties of establishing the base truth. These are problems in the provision of transparency (H1).

Dealing with Violations: Peacekeeping and the Role of Transparency

To provide a complete picture of UNFICYP's activities, the following subsections examine the principal categories of violations confronted by UNFICYP, including antagonism, construction, shooting and weaponry, and moves forward (and local agreements), as well as demonstrations. The importance of transparency varies by type of incident, and I remark on the limits of transparency in a number of places. While I am interested in variation in the successes, failures, and irrelevancies of transparency within and across cases, I do not process-trace incidents that offer no lessons about transparency. In these incidents or categories of violation, I simply note that transparency does not play a role.[18]

ANTAGONISM VIOLATIONS

Antagonisms are among the most common violations, constituting about 30 percent of all violations.[19] They consist of stone-throwing, insult-hurling, slingshotting, gesturing, and so forth between the two sides. Typically, one side antagonizes the other, the offended side calls the local U.N. headquarters, and a patrol is sent out. Less frequently, patrols come across incidents. In either case, UNFICYP talks to one or both sides, and tries to get them to calm down. Incidents end in one of three ways: first, they run their course and die down; second, UNFICYP increases its presence and patrols, and this calms the incident; or third, UNFICYP threatens or actually does report the incident up the chain of command and the

---

[18] For those interested in fine-grained details about peacekeeping on Cyprus, please consult my dissertation, "Transparency and the Effectiveness of Security Regimes: A Study of Concert of Europe Crisis Management and United Nations Peacekeeping," MIT, (Cambridge, MA, 1998). With 200 pages devoted to the Cyprus case, there is considerably more interview material, redacted incident reports, situation reports, and diplomatic records. Of note are the histories of the Roccas Bastion construction, killings in the buffer zone, and the 1996 demonstrations.

[19] I estimated this (and the percentages in the following violations subsection) based on statistics in *Report of the Secretariat Review Team on the United Nations Peace-keeping Force in Cyprus*, S/21982, December 7, 1990, paragraph 13. See Lindley, "Transparency and the Effectiveness of Security Regimes" for more on the estimates.

incident is calmed. This third method, detecting defection and using this information to coerce violators, is fairly common and is an example of H5.

There is little miscalculation or misperception between the adversaries in most antagonism incidents. After all, either you are hit on the head by a rock, or you are not. What each side says to UNFICYP about who started the incident and who did what to whom is, however, a different story. In these cases, the peacekeeper has to conduct an investigation to see who really did what to whom in order to get the right people in trouble. To use information to coerce violators into backing down, as contended by H5, the peacekeepers must cut through opacity and deliberate disinformation. Examples of investigations that ended up resolving false claims by one of the sides include peacekeepers physically climbing around barriers in the buffer zone to see if one side's claims to have seen an enemy soldier might be true, or trying to throw pebbles through a wire mesh to see if the pebbles near a broken window could be what caused the broken window (nope).[20]

The ability of UNFICYP to get violators in trouble often rests on the coercive use of information (H5). This ability provides an operation definition of consent to a peacekeeping operation, a crucial precondition for the success of traditional peacekeeping operations. With consent, each side always has someone of higher rank than the troublemaker who can reprimand the troublemaker and make amends for his/her offenses. Violators ultimately get disciplined because they are going against a policy that the government at the highest levels has agreed to. Consent means that, in the end, a damper can be put on potentially aggravating incidents.

Unfortunately for UNFICYP, both sides' militaries intentionally provoke each other and then rely on UNFICYP to calm things. They are "masters of provocation."[21] Yet, I believe the provocations would continue or escalate without UNFICYP, and thus that the probability of war would be higher without UNFICYP.[22] The violations end up being a combination

[20] The dated Immediate Reports (IMREPs) upon which this section is based are from IMREP folder, Sector 2, West, Kingston, as well as a number of interviews on the line, and in particular with Bombardier Elwyn Jones who gave me a line tour, May 10, 1996, Sector 2, East, Maple House (central Nicosia).

[21] Interview, Spokesman Rokoszewski, May 6, 1996. Several UNFICYP officials suggested that the authorization or planning for some incidents can occur as high up as the battalion or regimental level of the opposing forces.

[22] It is in part for this reason that I disagree with Nicholas Sambanis that UNFICYP is a failure. His pre-1967 history is interesting, but he holds UNFICYP to a very high bar. That said, this analysis supports Sambanis's overall model in that the multifunctional missions in particular reveal a relationship between peacekeeping and peacemaking, and that "peacekeepers can shape the parties' peacemaking preferences." See Nicholas Sambanis, "The United Nations Operation in Cyprus: A New Look at the Peacekeeping-Peacemaking Relationship," *International Peacekeeping* 6, no. 1, (Spring 1999), quote p. 85. See also Dan

of winked-at provocation along the buffer zone, as well as undisciplined roguish behavior by bored or angry soldiers. Either way, they are a threat to the peace, albeit usually minor. Either way, if UNFICYP can find out who did what to whom and when, it can often use this information to restore order (H5).

CONSTRUCTION

Part of UNFICYP's mission to preserve the status quo includes assuring that construction along the buffer zone adds no military advantage to either side.[23] Construction is limited to maintenance of current military positions. New positions may not be built, and repairs may not improve positions. This means that when repairs are made, each brick should be replaced with the same sort of brick, regular concrete should not be replaced by reinforced concrete, and so forth.

UNFICYP deals frequently with construction incidents, which constitute about 20 percent of the violations that it confronts. New construction may be found by a patrol or be reported by one of the opposing forces. UNFICYP can usually calm nerves if it determines that the reported construction is not an improvement, or when it succeeds in telling the violating side to take down the new construction.

Because it can be hard to tell exactly what the other side is constructing or whether it is improving its positions, inspections and transparency can be important in construction incidents. Only UNFICYP is in a position to conduct onsite investigations and determine the nature of constructions. Such inspections are an information-generating activity, an observable implication of H1, which contends that regimes can provide transparency. This information can then be used either to calm fears and de-escalate tensions, as predicted by H4, or help coerce compliance from violators, as predicted by H5. UNFICYP's ability to provide transparency depends on its ability to recognize and make convincing arguments about the status quo/base truth (see previous section). To distill insights about transparency, this section surveys a variety of construction incidents, including the controversial construction of a supposed playground that was built at the Roccas Bastion in Nicosia.

The first incident is a dispute over the base truth, and shows how difficult it can be for UNFICYP to argue about the status quo. In May 1996,

---

Lindley, "Assessing the Role of U.N. Peacekeeping Force in Cyprus," in Oliver P. Richmond and James Ker-Lindsay, eds., *The Work of the U.N. in Cyprus: Promoting Peace and Development* (New York: Palgrave/St. Martins Press, 2001), for a longer version of my argument that UNFICYP helps promote peace.

[23] This section on typical construction incidents is from "Folder 8: OPFOR Character Profiles (CPs) and OPFOR Meeting Notes," Sector 2, West, Kingston, and various interviews, including Lt. Col. Snowdon, May 10, 1996.

the National Guard replaced some barrels in one of their positions with the same number of similar barrels—exactly the way maintenance is supposed to be performed. The Turkish Forces tried to convince UNFICYP that the position had changed, in part by using a photo taken at a different location 100 meters down the line; the Turkish Forces maintained their stance even after walking to this location with UNFICYP officers and after being shown UNFICYP sketches of the various positions. Nothing UNFICYP did moved the Turks closer to the base truth, and the incident subsided.

In the second incident, UNFICYP calms a construction/security spiral. This is a classic tactical demonstration of H2, which contends that the promise of transparency can promote cooperation, and of H4, which contends that transparency reduces security spirals based on unwarranted fears. In early 1996, the Turkish Forces began refurbishing a bunker position. The National Guard claimed it was an improvement, and so on February 2 they responded by building a position of their own on top of a nearby building. The National Guard soldiers cocked their weapons and called in a quick reaction force while the Turkish Forces waited for a meeting with UNFICYP. In the meeting, the UNFICYP captain told the Turkish Forces major that the National Guard undertook their construction believing that the Turkish Forces were improving their position and that the National Guard had been told that the Turkish Forces construction was not an improvement. This information from UNFICYP, however, did not calm the Greeks, and so there is no evidence yet of transparency reducing fears. On February 9, the Turkish Forces responded by building a new wall near their position. Much blaming, meeting, and arguing ensued.

A few days later, transparency resolved the standoff. An UNFICYP lieutenant colonel stood in the buffer zone close enough to the Turkish Forces to talk to them, while talking on the phone to the National Guard, helping each side simultaneously and step-by-step deconstruct their improvements. Resolution of this incident depended on the verifying presence of the lieutenant colonel in the buffer zone to get the opposing forces to despiral and take down their constructions. This is a tactical example of the hypothesis that the promise of transparency can help two sides make peace by allaying fears of cheating, and this supports H2. Once the peacekeeper actively managed the implementation of the agreement and increased transparency, the events supported H3.

The third is a case where UNFICYP recognizes that transparency might confirm fears and aggravate tensions, and opts not to tell the full truth. Here, the Turkish Forces replaced sandbags with a wall outside of an observation post. The Greeks complained to UNFICYP, who spoke to the Turkish Forces, and the Turkish Forces said the wall had been there for years. It was clear, however, that the wall had been put up overnight, and the Turkish Forces promised UNFICYP that they would get rid of the wall. That night, a UNFICYP observation post saw what they thought was the wall being taken down, but later analysis revealed that the Turkish Forces had just covered the wall with sandbags. The National Guard could see only the sandbags and were happy, and so that brought the matter to a close. If UNFICYP had told the truth, transparency would have inflamed the National Guard and confirmed their fears, as predicted by H4'. Transparency is not a blanket good.

"TRNC" construction at Roccas Bastion.   In June 1995, the "Turkish Republic of Northern Cyprus" ("TRNC")[24] began construction of a supposed playground in the strategically sensitive Roccas Bastion in North Nicosia.[25] The playground contained concrete underground tunnels, and its construction raised a furor in the South, which suspected that it was built for military purposes. This story is noteworthy because UNFICYP battled for inspections, a mechanism that could help provide transparency as suggested by H1, in the hope that the information would reduce fears and tensions as predicted by H4. It offers numerous and specific details on what information the inspections revealed and what effects the information had.

The Roccas Bastion is a protrusion from the Venetian walls that surround inner Nicosia. It measures about seventy meters by sixty meters, and overlooks the main node of the Cyprus Telecommunications Authority (CYTA) in the South.

In early June, UNFICYP, having been notified by the "TRNC" of the impending construction, twice relayed this news to the Greek Cypriot National Guard (H1).[25] The Greek Cypriot side nonetheless became enraged when excavation began on June 20. The National Guard Chief of Staff wrote UNFICYP charging that talk of a playground was certain to be a ruse to disguise military construction and asking that the U.N. correct the situation. There were ten to fifteen highly suspicious stories a day in the Greek Cypriot press about the construction as it took place.[26]

Quickly responding to Greek Cypriot fears, UNFICYP requested inspections at the military level on June 21, but were referred to "TRNC" political authorities. UNFICYP tried to gather information (H1), but the

---

[24] In 1983, the North declared itself to be the independent state of the "Turkish Republic of Northern Cyprus." It has been recognized only by Turkey, and because of nonrecognition elsewhere, it is standard convention to put the "TRNC" in quotes.

[25] The majority of this section is based on detailed notes taken from UNFICYP's Roccas Bastion file, as well as numerous interviews. The file contained cables from UNFICYP to U.N. headquarters and vice-versa, inspection reports, notes on meetings, press releases, diagrams, and so forth. I was not allowed to use specific names, addresses, or direct quotes. See my dissertation, Lindley, "Transparency and the Effectiveness of Security Regimes," for many more details on this incident.

[26] Interview, Spokesman Rokoszewski, May 13, 1996.

Turkish side built obstacles to obstruct UNFICYP's view, and burned down an UNFICYP observation post that overlooked the bastion. UNFI-CYP resorted to helicopter overflights.

The effort to get inspections, the sine qua non for UNFICYP to provide transparency in this case (H1), went as high up the diplomatic pecking order as UNFICYP could go: to the U.N. Security Council and the secretary-general.[27] The effort to muster diplomatic leverage worked: the "TRNC" backed down under the international spotlight—thus supporting H5. On July 12, the "TRNC" agreed that UNFICYP's chief of mission could visit the Roccas Bastion the next day, followed by an UNFICYP technical team inspection on the 14th. On July 18, the "TRNC" finally agreed to regular inspections during the construction and to periodic inspections thereafter.

Following the initial inspections, the chief of mission met with the Greek Cypriot president and later with a Greek Cypriot official to explain that, while the construction raised a number of doubts, the materials used were below military specifications and that the design of the construction conformed to no military logic. The chief of mission told the president that UNFICYP was arranging visits in order to keep the construction that way. None of this allayed the fears of the Greek Cypriots, who in fact remained almost hysterical.

A few days later a Greek Cypriot ambassador brought to UNFICYP a Turkish mainland newspaper (*Hurriyet,* July 20) article that included photographs of Turkish fortifications and tunnels, and he fumed that it was about the Roccas Bastion. In short order, the U.N. determined that neither the photographs nor the article's text were about the Roccas Bastion. So far, despite UNFICYP's inspections and meetings with the Greek Cypriot president and others, there is not much sign of transparency reducing fears (H4).

A notable provision of transparency by the U.N. (H1) occurred on July 25 when the secretary-general publicly reported the findings of the technical inspection, including a detailed diagram of the Roccas Bastion and its underground contents (S/1995/618). The secretary-general wrote that "the construction on Roccas Bastion to date, including the material used, does not indicate work carried out to normal military specifications, or to any evident military logic. At the same time, the construction appears unnecessarily elaborate and costly for its stated purpose." He noted that the Turkish Cypriot authorities had promised unhindered regular and periodic access to the bastion and that "these arrangements will enable UNFICYP to satisfy itself that the new infrastructure being built on Roccas Bastion continues to be used exclusively for civilian purposes." By emphasizing

[27] S/1995/561.

continued inspections, the secretary-general was trying hard to reduce the uproar with transparency, an effect predicted by H4.

The Greeks did not believe the calming parts of the report, and this was reinforced by the more dangerous "unnecessarily elaborate and costly" aspects noted by the secretary-general. The information in the report justified a certain amount of fear on the Greek Cypriot side, and thus, there is some evidence for H4' in that transparency confirmed fears. Even if the facts justified it, I doubt that a completely exculpatory report would have overcome the Greek's preformed worst-case assumptions about the Turks. In a meeting with UNFICYP's force commander, the head of the Greek Cypriot National Guard said that he did not believe UNFICYP's assessment about the nonmilitary nature of the trenches. This suggests that transparency has a hard time reducing fears (H4) in the face of strong suspicions or bias.

Transparency is supposed to create common understandings and base truths, yet a year after the construction, divergent views remained. Dr. Leonides Pantelides, a political officer in the Foreign Ministry's Cyprus Problem Division, said that the inspections helped resolve some of the acute aspects of the crisis. He said, however, that the Greek Cypriots still do not believe it is a playground, and think that the deep digging and concrete indicate a possible future military use.[28] Dr. Aytug Plumer, an undersecretary at the "TRNC" Ministry of Foreign Affairs and Defense, said that UNFICYP had clearly reported that the construction was not military in its reports and that these reports show that the Greek Cypriots' big fuss was a big lie.[29] John Koenig, first secretary for political affairs at the U.S. embassy, said that the U.N.'s actions helped reassure each side, but that he was still not entirely satisfied with the situation: the way the Turks handled it was designed to raise doubts, and Greek Cypriots still think it is a military construction.[30]

This raises an interesting issue: what kind of information is needed to reassure a status quo party (H4) if the other party is intent on making provocative bluffs? Perhaps it is impossible. Provocation is provocation, and so even if the Turks ended up constructing a playground on the Roccas Bastion, the nighttime construction and their obstruction of UNFICYP still conveyed hostile intent. Surely a playground beats a minefield and artillery emplacements, but if the goal is to rile the other side, provocations will likely always succeed.

On two visits to the Roccas Bastion, I tried to use the underground bathrooms (and thus see the tunnels) and both times I was not allowed in. The

---

[28] Interview, May 16, 1996.
[29] Interview, June 5, 1996.
[30] Interview, June 4, 1996.

above-ground doors leading to the underground tunnels and bathrooms are clearly marked as bathrooms, yet they are constructed of thick metal, have small peephole windows, and resemble doors on old-fashioned armored cars. I doubt this is an ordinary park. As far as I know, UNFICYP never reported on the armored nature of the doors. Even if this helped calm the situation in the short term, this puts their long-term credibility at risk, and credibility is a key component when using transparency to promote peace.

In sum, transparency was provided by the U.N. inspections, supporting H1. The effects of transparency, however, were mixed, something not unexpected given the mixed reports. Greek alarm without the inspections would have likely been even higher, and this counterfactual suggests that transparency did reduce fears, as predicted by H4. Nonetheless, the inspections also helped justify the suspicions, and when transparency confirms fears, this supports H4'. Despite the conflicting messages in the UNFICYP reports, most Greeks felt that the inspections helped calm the crisis, and so the beneficial effects of transparency in reducing fears (H4) modestly prevail in this case.

Looking at construction incidents overall, UNFICYP's role and the role of transparency should not be overstated. The U.N. *Reports of the Secretary-General on the United Nations Operation in Cyprus* almost always express disapproval about continual construction and military buildups on Cyprus—with no effect. Most of this construction is out in the countryside, which is less inflammatory than in sensitive, strategic, and closed-in areas like downtown Nicosia.

SHOOTING AND WEAPONS VIOLATIONS

Shooting deaths within the buffer zone are rare, but have more potential than other incidents to escalate. From the 1974 cease-fire through 2002, six Greek Cypriot and three Turkish soldiers had been killed in or along the buffer zone, a casualty rate far below that of the 1950s through 1974.[31] The last deaths occurred between June and October of 1996 when a Greek Cypriot National Guard soldier, a Turkish Forces soldier, and three Greek Cypriot civilians were killed in and along the buffer zone.

Nonfatal shootings and weapons discharges are more common; the most dangerous of these are deliberate shots that cause strike marks on an opposing forces position. There were three or four of these types of shooting incidents in the Nicosia area during the first five months of 1996.[32]

---

[31] This information is based in part on figures from Chief Clerk, Operations Branch (UNFICYP), Memorandum to the Chief Operations Officer, "OPFOR Deaths Within the BZ" June 6, 1996. Totals do not include deaths by mines, hunting, or other accidents.

[32] Lt. Col. Snowdon, May 10.

Cocking and pointing of weapons by the opposing forces at each other or at UNFICYP soldiers is frequent, as are accidental shootings and discharges. All told, weapons incidents account for about 10 percent of all violations. Transparency is not a big factor in most weapons violations, although some incidents demonstrate the value of UNFICYP investigations, as well as the ability of rumors to outpace those investigations.

General Vartiainen said that the opposing forces load and cock at each other at least once a week in the Nicosia area (where the density and proximity of opposing forces are highest). Often loading and cocking is the highest rung on the escalatory ladder of insults: others include finger and other gestures ("international signs," said the general), throwing of bottles and stones, and slingshotting.[33] The opposing forces sometimes point their weapons at UNFICYP soldiers, and many peacekeepers told me that loading and cocking was the scariest thing that happened to them on Cyprus.

UNFICYP's ability to investigate and provide information (H1) faces a number of barriers in shooting incidents. For example, shots are so quick that it can be hard to tell where they came from, especially at night. Evidence like bullets and casings is hard to find and easy to conceal. Since many, if not most, shootings are accidents ("negligent discharges" in UNFICYP-speak), soldiers are highly motivated to lie and cover them up. A frequent technique of soldiers in disguising an accident is to fire off a couple of rounds after the accident to make it appear as if a more serious shoot-out occurred.[34] When UNFICYP's investigations succeed and they report their findings to the perpetrator's officers, the shooters are often disciplined. These are instances of H5, which contends that disclosure of information coerces aggressors.

The Shooting of Stelios Panayi.   Killings in the buffer zones are among the most severe challenges faced by UNFICYP. Does transparency play a role? National Guard private Stelios Panayi was shot on June 3, 1996,[35] the first of several killings in and along the buffer zone in the summer of 1996.[36] This killing shows how quickly rumors can spread, and it reveals

[33] Interview, May 7, 1996. Colonel Talbot, the Chief of Staff, thought that loading and cocking incidents occurred somewhat less frequently. Interview, May 8, 1996.

[34] Interviews with Lt. Col. Parker, Lt. Col. Snowdon, and Bombardier Raymond Cowie, May 9, 10, and 24 respectively, and IMREP folder, Sector 2, West, Kingston.

[35] The sources for this section include the "Temporary Hot Spot File," for the incident that included a number of UNFICYP situation reports, cables, memorandums, faxes, incident logs, and so forth. In addition to these and other documents, I arrived at UNFICYP headquarters soon after the shooting, had free range there during the day, and spoke at length about the shooting thereafter. See Lindley, "Transparency and the Effectiveness of Security Regimes," for more details.

[36] Most occurred during Greek demonstrations (see following section).

UNFICYP's limited ability to combat rumors when they outpace its investigations. Over the longer term, UNFICYP's thorough investigation calmed Greek Cypriot anger at UNFICYP. This is modest evidence of self-transparency reducing unwarranted fears and clarifies purpose, predicted by H6.

At roughly 6:15 a.m. in an area just west of central Nicosia, an UNFICYP soldier heard shouting between a National Guard observation post and a Turkish observation post. A Turkish Forces soldier, carrying his rifle, was observed walking into the buffer zone and going down into reedbeds where he would no longer be seen.

At 6:30, the UNFICYP soldier heard a single shot while he was calling his supervisor. A Turkish Forces soldier was then seen running back toward Turkish lines. At some time prior to this, Panayi, unarmed and off-duty, had apparently gone into the buffer zone. Proceeding toward the scene of the shooting at 6:35, the UNFICYP soldier was told by a National Guard soldier that a fellow soldier had been shot. The UNFICYP soldier tried to approach Panayi but was ordered to halt by Turkish Forces who pointed their weapons at him. By 6:40 the UNFICYP soldier had returned to his observation post to report the incident and call an ambulance. When a U.N. captain and another soldier reached the scene, the three UNFICYP personnel tried to approach but were again told to halt. As the peacekeepers continued forward, the Turkish Forces fired a warning shot and UNFICYP backed off. They tried to move forward two more times, but each time backed off after warning shots were fired. The captain's efforts to negotiate with the Turkish Forces were unsuccessful.

Between 7:05 and 7:10, UNFICYP soldiers escorted a civilian ambulance forward to the closest National Guard observation post. Two of the three UNFICYP soldiers who tried found a faint pulse on Panayi but he was pronounced dead at the hospital. A National Guard cap with the name of another National Guard soldier was found near Panayi and another cap was found in his pocket. UNFICYP's investigation later revealed the Panayi had entered the buffer zone intending to trade caps with a Turkish counterpart.

In the meantime, both sides rapidly built up their forces in the immediate area. Up to ninety Turkish Forces soldiers had arrived by the time the body was removed. Machines guns and RPG-7 rocket launchers were brought in by one or both sides. Both sides built down their forces rapidly as well. UNFICYP's chief operations officer noted that the situation was calm at 8:45.

At 11:08, a TV news flash broke the news of the killing to the Greek Cypriots. Before noon, Cyprus President Clerides issued a televised statement expressing sympathy to Panayi's parents and calling the shooting "cold-blooded murder." The parents were shown crying at the hospital.

As the Cypriot press geared up for the story, rumors became mixed with facts,[37] and UNFICYP tried to figure out exactly what happened—how many shots were fired, where the body was found, where the shots came from, how many soldiers from each side were in the buffer zone, why Panayi entered the buffer zone, and so forth. In UNFICYP's operations center, officers sorted through incoming reports that contained conflicting answers to many of these questions. UNFICYP's Spokesman Rokoszewski could not address many of the rumors because UNFICYP had yet to complete its own investigation. Many rumors cast the Turkish Forces in the worst possible light (the light was pretty grim already, but the rumors consisted of false reports of multiple shooters and multiple bullet wounds, making it seem like a slaughter). The rumors outpaced fact-finding activities such as the autopsy as well as UNFICYP's abilities to coordinate the information that it was receiving.

This shows that the provision of transparency (H1) depends on the availability of correct information in the first place. Had UNFICYP had complete information from the start, perhaps some of the rumors could have been dispelled (H4). Instead, it had to wait for its investigations to yield results.

The National Guard and Government of Cyprus vigorously protested the killing.[38] That afternoon, UNFICYP's force commander met with the commander of the Turkish Forces to protest the incident—both the killing and the warning shots. The commander of the Turkish Forces expressed sadness about the death, but said that the soldiers were acting according to standard operating procedures. The force commander followed up with a letter of protest on June 5. On June 7, the Turkish Forces commander counterprotested with a letter claiming that the whole incident took place on "TRNC" territory. He tried to support his claims with photographs and a map, and it was amusing watching the UNFICYP operations staff uncover all the inaccurate and misleading elements. While UNFICYP protested the Turkish story at the highest levels, especially the claims that the shooting was not in the buffer zone, the Greek Cypriots were never told of this letter and its errors. The "TRNC" political authorities continued to insist that although the incident was unfortunate, Panayi was to blame for failing to heed warning shots and for crossing into "TRNC" territory.[39]

---

[37] Jean Christou, "Was Soldier Lured to His Death by Turks?" *Cyprus Mail,* June 7, 1996, p. 3.

[38] From Cyprus News Agency, "Cyprus Protests to UN over Soldier's Murder," June 3, 1996, available at www.hri.org/news/cyprus/cna/.

[39] Statement by Turkish Cypriot leader Rauf Denktash on June 3, Nicosia BRTK Television Network, 16:30 GMT in Foreign Broadcast Information Service (FBIS) *Daily Report,* FBIS-WEU-96–108, June 4, 1996, and interview with Aytug Plumer, Under-Secretary, Ministry Foreign Affairs and Defense, "TRNC."

On the Greek side, there was initial dismay and anger at UNFICYP's slow response. This sentiment changed after UNFICYP made it clear to the Greek Cypriots that repeated warning shots prevented UNFICYP from reaching Panayi. The *Cyprus Mail* wrote "No UNFICYP officer in his right mind would risk walking into the buffer zone after warning shots were fired."[40] Here, UNFICYP's efforts to clarify why it responded as it did to the multiple warning shots reduced anger at the operation. When clarifying the actions of the operation helps calm local perceptions of the operation, this effect of self-transparency is evidence for H6.

The overall reaction of the Greeks was muted, and contrasts with the protests and shootout after Athanasios Kleovoulou's death in 1993. An UNFICYP investigation revealed that Kleovoulou had gone into the buffer zone to trade brandy with the Turks, and this caused the National Guard to crack down on their troops. In 1996, the mood in the Greek Cypriot press and in the streets soon combined a sullen "Turks will be Turks" attitude with a recognition that Panayi had made a fatal mistake. Newspapers and government authorities spoke of the poor training of Greek Cypriot soldiers. The *Cyprus Mail* editorialized, "It may seem insensitive, but in the final analysis, the guardsman died because he disobeyed army orders."[41]

UNFICYP and its investigations can take some credit for this rare level of blunt introspection and learning.[42] UNFICYP's information helped the Greek Cypriots realize the dangers of their own lax discipline along the buffer zone. While not justifying the Turkish shootings of Panayi or Kleovoulou, UNFICYP helped the Greek Cypriots understand their soldiers' unwise actions, calming their reactions to the killings. There is no transparency hypothesis for this effect, but it combines elements of H4 (reducing fears) and H5 (coercing better behavior) because the Greek Cypriots came to place some blame on themselves and thus take responsibility for their own actions.

Finally, the killings illustrate how quickly things can escalate on Cyprus, and shows that UNFICYP's presence is critical in rare circumstances. Immediately following the June 3 killing, for example, both opposing forces quickly built up their forces. What if UNFICYP had not been there? What if the Turkish warning shots had been fired at National Guard soldiers coming into the buffer zone to pick up the body, rather than at the UNFICYP soldiers?

[40] "Murder on the Green Line," *Cyprus Mail*, June 5, 1996, p. 9.

[41] Ibid. See also "Need for tougher discipline," *The Cyprus Weekly*, June 7–13, 1996, p. 4.

[42] *Report of the Secretary-General on the United Nations Operation in Cyprus*, for the period December 11, 1995 to June 10, 1995, S/1996/411, dated June 7, 1996, pp. 3–4 and *Corrigendum*, S/1996/411/Corr.1 dated June 14, 1996.

MOVES FORWARD AND LOCAL AGREEMENTS

Moves forward include instances when the opposing forces enter the buffer zone, and these account for about 20 percent of all violations. As seen in the deaths of Kleovoulou and Panayi, going into the buffer zone sometimes results in shooting. Most moves forward into the buffer zone, however, are minor. UNFICYP's response is usually just to hustle the violators back to their side. Little transparency is needed or used in these instances.

Two quite serious forms of moves forward threaten the status quo and challenge UNFICYP's authority and freedom of movement in the buffer zone. First, the opposing forces may challenge the status quo by trying to move the actual cease-fire lines forward. Second, they may contest UNFICYP's right to patrol in a given area. For example, these sorts of challenges probably explain why the *Reports of the Secretary-General on the United Nations Operation in Cyprus* went from describing the minimum width of the buffer zone as 20 meters in the June 15, 1995, (S/1995/488 report p. 3), to describing it as a "few" meters in the next report on December 10, 1995, (S/1995/1020 p. 1).

Local agreements make these challenges even worse by codifying new borders of the buffer zone. A local agreement is when new lines are drawn or patrol routes adjusted in the buffer zone by lower-level officers. These agreements essentially legitimize a new status quo. Local agreements are very difficult for UNFICYP to deal with, because the local commanders often do not notify their superiors or successor rotations.

According to one of UNFICYP's folders on moves forward, local agreements are due to a "lack of understanding and weakness of UNFICYP at [the] local level" over time. And it is "clear that local agreements and understandings have far-reaching effects when changes are made to activities within the buffer zone without clearance from HQ UNFICYP." UNFICYP's spokesman echoed these concerns, saying that local agreements are "hell in this mission."[43]

Moves forward and local agreements blur the base truth about the status quo and thus reduce UNFICYP's ability to increase transparency (H1). UNFICYP cannot easily facilitate bargaining, reduce misperceptions, or coerce better behavior (H3, H4, H5) if it cannot establish a base truth. Without a base truth, there is no way to refute either side's claims, no way to help move each side closer to the truth and away from miscalculation and misperception, and no way for UNFICYP to press its side with certainty.

---

[43] Folder "Move Forward of TFCFL Nicosia," 20/002–1303, 5/24/89 and interview with Spokesman Rokoszewski, June 6, 1996.

Moves forward are often accompanied by arguments about the true location of the cease-fire lines. UNFICYP should be able to win these arguments hands down, but sometimes it does not, and this is because of ambiguities about the base truth. As mentioned, UNFICYP has no comprehensive database of photographs or videos of the whole buffer zone, and the cease-fire lines were drawn ambiguously. When UNFICYP cannot master the facts, it has a harder time providing transparency.

The extent of the difficulties posed by local agreements are hard to judge because they are a self-concealing phenomenon. Who would admit to making a side-deal that reduced UNFICYP's authority? Yet local agreements and disputes about patrol tracks and the delineation of the cease-fire lines came up in a number of my interviews, and were also covered in several folders that I reviewed.[44]

For example, UNFICYP's Chief Operations Officer, Lt. Colonel Parker, said that different maps revealed three different cease-fire lines in the "4 Minute Walk" area of the buffer zone in central Nicosia. He noted more generally that he had huge files on unresolved cease-fire line interpretations. Parker said that if the cease-fire line problems could be resolved, this would calm both sides and generate much more peace.[45] In other words, establishing and monitoring a base truth (H1) would go a long way toward reducing unwarranted fears (H4), as well as limiting accidental and intentional cheating (H5). It is hard for each side to negotiate agreements to limit these fears and incidents when there is no base truth, and this uncertainty helps cause these fears and incidents in the first place. This implies that transparency would promote cooperation (H3) if the base truth could be established (H1).

Government officials are not fully aware of the tactical rough-and-tumble in and along the buffer zone, and so it would take a fairly drastic change in incidents along the buffer zone for them to view the peacekeeping mission differently. For example, Government of Cyprus officials believe UNFICYP successfully maintains control of the buffer zone, preserves the status quo, and keeps small things small. Dr. Pantelides of the Ministry of Foreign Affairs called UNFICYP "extremely successful." Thalia Petrides, director for European Affairs in the Ministry of Foreign Affairs, thought that UNFICYP helped keep the Turkish side from gaining ground in the buffer zone.[46]

[44] See sources cited as well as "Folder 8: OPFOR Character Profiles (CPs) and OPFOR Meeting Notes," both from Sector 2, West, Kingston, and interview Major Walsh, Sector 2 West battery commander, May 25, 1996. See Lindley, "Transparency and the Effectiveness of Security Regimes" for details on incidents at Bourhan Tan, Wayne's Keep, and the 4 Minute Walk.

[45] Interviews with Bombardier Jones and Lt Colonel Parker, May 10, 1996, and May 9, 1996, respectively.

[46] Interviews, May 16 and 15, 1996, respectively.

On the "TRNC" side, Dr. Plumer, an under-secretary in the Ministry of Foreign Affairs and Defense, was much less supportive. Even though he said that UNFICYP's job had gotten easier since the creation of the buffer zone in 1974, he thought that the Turkish Forces were doing the real peace-keeping on Cyprus and that UNFICYP was not big enough to do its job adequately. He also noted with displeasure the U.N.'s reluctance to rec-ognize the "TRNC" and said that UNFICYP was 70 percent paid for by the Greeks and Greek Cypriots.[47] Thus, he argued that UNFICYP's bene-fits appear to accrue more to the Greek than Turkish side.

DEMONSTRATIONS AND CROWD CONTROL

Although not counted by UNFICYP as "violations," a major problem confronted by UNFICYP is demonstrations. Most demonstrations are held by Greek Cypriots to protest the Turkish invasion and occupation. The demonstrators create havoc for UNFICYP as they frequently try to cross into the buffer zone. Some throw rocks, bottles, and occasional molotov cocktails at Turkish Cypriots or other targets of opportunity, in-cluding UNFICYP personnel. Injuries can result, and as happened in 1996, even death.

UNFICYP's responsibility during the demonstrations is to protect the integrity of the buffer zone. The Cyprus police (CYPOL) are supposed to help control the demonstrators and protect UNFICYP. UNFICYP learns about demonstrations from a variety of sources, including the media and the protesting groups themselves. The Cyprus police are supposed to no-tify UNFICYP of upcoming demonstrations, although the Cyprus police's level of cooperation in this and other ways is spotty at best. Occasionally, UNFICYP is taken by surprise by demonstrations.

The Turkish Cypriots often learn of demonstrations through liaison with UNFICYP. According to Colonel Talbot, UNFICYP tells the Turkish side what they are going to do about the upcoming demonstration and this helps build trust. He said it was very important for him to say "I'm doing this" about the demonstration and ask about their (Turkish) con-cerns and respond to them. He believed that the trust this engendered may help disengagement over the long term.[48] UNFICYP's information-gathering about demonstrations and Colonel Talbot's remarks about using this information and self-transparency to build trust both support H1, which contends that regimes can increase transparency by providing new information, and H6, which predicts that information about the regime's activities can calm fears.

---

[47] Interview, June 5, 1996. The correct figure is 50 percent, suggesting that UNFICYP might benefit from some self-transparency (H6).

[48] Interview, May 9, 1996.

The number of demonstrators can vary from several tens to the low thousands, and demonstrations vary in their level of hostility and danger. Motorcycle protests are the most violent and troublesome for UNFICYP to confront. With belligerence, speed, walkie-talkies, and portable phones, these demonstrators often run around and outwit UNFICYP troops. With UNFICYP's "limited resources, the protestors just entangle you."[49]

In 1996, the demonstrations became lethal. On the morning of August 11, 1996, as many as 7000 motorcyclists were set to cross the buffer zone from the South into the North. The demonstration was in part a deliberate provocation whipped up by escalating rhetoric from the Government of Cyprus.[50] Members of the Turkish mainland militant right-wing group the Grey Wolves came to confront the demonstration, and were joined by many Turkish Cypriot civilians. In the ensuing violence, Greek Cypriot Tasos Isaac was clubbed to death, and fifty or more other Greek Cypriots, about twelve Turkish Cypriots, and twelve UNFICYP personnel were injured. On August 14, Isaac was buried and at his funeral, the "heroic death" of this "symbol of freedom" was eulogized as a "source of inspiration" by the Primate of the Church of Cyprus.[51] Another demonstration followed the funeral. Several hundred Greek Cypriots charged the cease-fire lines and entered the buffer zone. As the protestors threw stones, Solomos Solomos, a cousin of Isaac, began to climb a flagpole to take down a Turkish Cypriot flag. He was killed and four others were wounded (including two UNFICYP personnel) when Turkish Forces opened fire and shot twenty-five to fifty rounds into the crowd.[52] Many protests from the U.N. and Greek Cypriot ensued, culminating in U.N. Security Council Resolution 1092, December 23, 1996, which deplored the deaths.

Transparency played a role in preventing the violence from getting even worse during the August 1996 demonstrations. According to UNFICYP's journal, *The Blue Berets,*

> UNFICYP played a unique role in defusing tension between the two parties. During the height of the crisis, rumours and disinformation were rampant on both sides, which could easily have triggered military

[49] Spokesman Rokoszewski, interview, May 6, 1996.

[50] *Report of the Secretary-General on the United Nations Operation in Cyprus,* December 10, 1996, S/1996/1016, p. 1.

[51] Cyprus News Agency, "Buffer Zone Killing Strengthens Will for Freedom" August 14, 1996, 1345, available at www.hri.org/news/cyprus/cna/.

[52] *Report of the Secretary-General on the United Nations Operation in Cyprus,* December 10, 1996, S/1996/1016, pp. 1–2; Elizabeth Neuffer, "Greek, Turkish Foes Clash on Cyprus," *Boston Globe,* August 11, 1996, p. A2; and Neuffer, "Turkish Troops Kill Protester as Strife Worsens on Cyprus," *Boston Globe,* August 15, 1996, p. A1.

clashes. UNFICYP's liaison officers attached to the police and military headquarters were instrumental in keeping both sides informed of developments and in quickly clarifying any misperceptions.[53]

In tactical terms, UNFICYP appears to have increased transparency by keeping both sides informed, as predicted by H1. By so doing, they reduced misperceptions and miscalculations that were worsening tensions and heightening risks of escalation; these are the effects of transparency predicted by H3 and H4. That said, each side maintains dramatically different interpretations of the August demonstrations. For example, the dead Greek Cypriots are hailed as hero patriots by their side.[54]

Despite UNFICYP's success with near-real time transparency during these exceptionally violent demonstrations, transparency generally does not play a large role in demonstrations. The facts of the case in demonstrations are fairly clear, as are each side's interpretation of them.

The limits of UNFICYP's ability to wield information to coerce the adversaries into more helpful behavior are shown in UNFICYP's repeated scoldings of the Cyprus police who frequently aid the protestors and not UNFICYP. No amount of criticism from the U.N. provokes anything more than temporary improvement in cooperation. This weakens support for H5, which contends that disclosure of information can coerce better behavior.[55]

Humanitarian Activities and Societal Transparency

Part of UNFICYP's mandate is to help Cyprus "return to normal conditions." Accordingly, UNFICYP engages in a number of humanitarian activities on the island designed to bring the two sides together to foster communication and cooperation. These are called bicommunal activities, and they range from concerts to coordination of the electrical, water, and sewer systems (which are still linked between the North and South).

---

[53] *The Blue Berets* 33, no. 8 (August 1996): 3.

[54] For more on these demonstrations, see Dan Lindley, "UNFICYP and a Cyprus Solution: A Strategic Assessment," working paper, Defense and Arms Control Studies Program, MIT, Cambridge, MA, May 1997.

[55] Interviews with Lt. Colonel Parker, May 14, 1996; Colonel Talbot, May 9; and Lt. Colonel Snowdon, May 10 and *Reports of the Secretary-General on the United Nations Operation in Cyprus:* November 30, 1988, S/20310, p. 5, May 31, 1989, S/20663, p. 5, November 22, 1993, S/26777, p. 18, and December 10, 1995, S/1995/1020, pp. 2–3, Various UNFICYP demonstration folders note problems with the Cyprus police, including their complicity in letting schoolchildren through to the South Ledra Checkpoint A scathing 8/9/95 Sector 1 report in a folder on the 8/6/95 Cyprus Motorcycle Organization rally noted that the Cyprus police obstructed U.N. personnel, did not stop demonstrators, and did not arrest anyone, and that the Cyprus police helped the demonstrators remove U.N. obstacles.

Embassies (especially the U.S. and British) and businesses also sponsor and promote bicommunal events, but these often have to be coordinated with UNFICYP since they involve crossing the buffer zone. UNFICYP promotes these exchanges believing that:

> Bicommunal contacts can contribute significantly to facilitating an over-all settlement. It is obvious that the encouragement of tolerance, trust and reconciliation between the two communities through increased contact and improved communication is an essential part of the peace process.[56]

This quotation evokes H1, with its emphasis on communication, and especially H4, as communication is seen to reduce the lack of trust, racism, and enemy-imaging (fears and worst-case assumptions) that hinder peace.

Bicommunal activities are efforts to increase what I dub societal transparency—what societies know about each other. It is important to figure out the provision and effects of societal transparency. For example, the issue is at the center of debates about whether globalization is increasing cross-cultural understanding, and societal transparency informs the hopes of scholarships like the Fulbright and the Rhodes that support international educational exchanges.[57]

Unfortunately, on Cyprus it is hard to tell whether bicommunal activities increase transparency, promote peace, or reduce misperceptions. Organizers of bicommunal activities claim that the various activities do have positive effects on participants' views toward the other side, yet acknowledge that these effects are hard to measure more concretely. Moreover, while thousands of people may attend a concert, far fewer attend more lengthy and intensive workshops. It is hard to discern any changes in behavior or attitude associated with these events and whatever large-scale effects bicommunal activities may have are likely to take place over a very long time. This does not make bicommunal events irrelevant or unworthy of pursuit; they have a lot of intuitive appeal. It just means that there is little hard data with which to measure the impact of bicommunal contacts.

In addition to measurement difficulties, bicommunal activities are often politically manipulated, whether being used for propaganda by the South,

---

[56] *Report of the Secretary-General on the United Nations Operation in Cyprus,* 7 June 1996, S/1996/411, p. 9.

[57] Though not an analysis of transparency per se, one scholarly analysis of these sorts of exchanges is Matthew Evangelista, *Unarmed Forces: The Transnational Movement to End the Cold War* (Ithaca, NY: Cornell University Press, 1999), in which he argues that the transnational arms control community and other societal contacts influenced Soviet/Russian security policy and helped end the Cold War.

or cancelled or attended by plants and plainclothesman by the North.[58] Further, pervasive bias, especially in the press and schools, hinders societal transparency. Much of the press is politically affiliated, highly nationalistic, and one-sided. With twenty-five newspapers for a country the size of Indianapolis, journalists "go off the deep end" and blow small things way out of proportion.[59] General Vartiainen, UNFICYP's force commander, said that "what they know [about each other] is what is in the newspapers and that is bullshit."[60] Initially segregated into separate Greek and Turkish systems by the British, the schools continue to inculcate malignant nationalism. Feissel said it was "education that made things bad" on Cyprus, while Vartiainen said that the schools teach the children to view the other side as "beasts."[61] Teachers often lead their students to the demonstrations. It is hard to expect lasting peace in a situation where, as pithily summed up by General Vartiainen, "the Greeks don't remember what happened before 1974 and the Turks can't forget it."[62]

Even after the opening of the intra-Cypriot border in 2003, the communities remain distant. "There are no results of all those twenty years of citizens being involved. . . . There are no pages on our newspaper on the life of the other side. The Green Line is open physically for us to move but there is an invisible barrier that stops us," says Greek Cypriot Katie Economidou, a bicommunal activist."[63]

CONCLUSION

UNFICYP enjoys considerable success patrolling the buffer zone and keeping small incidents small. A modest amount of UNFICYP's peacekeeping effectiveness depends on transparency, and UNFICYP also relies on

[58] Interviews with UNFICYP Chief Humanitarian Officer, Lt. Colonel Jorges Tereso, May 14, 1996; Asim Altiok, Director/Representative of the Consular and Minority Affairs Department, "TRNC" June 5, 1996; Dr. Pantelides, Cyprus Ministry of Foreign Affairs, May 16, 1996; Petrides, Cyprus Ministry of Foreign Affairs, May 15, 1996. See also *Report of the Secretary-General on the United Nations Operation in Cyprus*, December 10, 1996, S/1996/1016, p. 5.

[59] Quote from Gustave Feissel, UNFICYP Chief of Mission, interview May 8, 1996. Also, interviews with Rokoszewski, May 6, 1996; and Eliza Kimball, Senior Political Affairs Officer, Department of Peacekeeping Operations, April 18, 1996; and see Ellen Laipson, "Government and Politics," in Solsten, ed., *Cyprus: A Country Study,* 188, 197, and 262.

[60] Interview, May 7, 1996. He followed up this point by saying he was "optimistic that [the bullshit] is not the opinion of the people."

[61] Interviews, May 8 and May 7, 1996, respectively; and Meleagrou and Yesilada, "The Society and Its Environment," 72–73, 85–87.

[62] Interview, May 7, 1996.

[63] Tabitha Morgan, "Cyprus keeps its hidden barrier," BBC News, October 5, 2005, available at news.bbc.co.uk/2/hi/europe/4313016.stm.

TABLE 4-1
Findings by Hypothesis

Hypothesis	Evidence	Strength of evidence	Overall strength of hypothesis
Regimes provide transparency (H1)	The liaison system is used in almost every instance	Strong/Weak; depending on incident	Moderate/Weak
	UNFICYP investigations of incidents	Depends on incident	
	Patrols and monitoring are constant	Depends on incident	
	The buffer zone clarifies cease-fire lines, pp. 88, 89	Moderate	
	Bicommunal activities, p. 110	Effects unknown	
	Note: Overall ability to provide transparency weakened by difficulties establishing base truth; buffer zone could work better		
Regimes spread misinformation (H1')	Because it fears exacerbating tensions (H3'), sometimes UNFICYP does not reveal everything it knows or uncovers; pp. 97, 103	Moderate/Weak, depending on incident—but UNFI-CYP is wise to be discreet	Moderate/Weak
Anticipated transparency promotes cooperation (H2)	Some tactical agreements catalyzed by transparency (construction de-spiraling, p. 96)	Moderate/Weak	Weak
Anticipated transparency hinders cooperation (H2')			
Transparency promotes cooperation and prevents conflict (H3)	The buffer zone itself clarifies the status quo and reduces miscalculation, especially compared to pre-1974, p. 88	Moderate/Weak	Weak

(continued)

TABLE 4-1 (continued)

Hypothesis	Evidence	Strength of evidence	Overall strength of hypothesis
	UNFICYP's claim to have prevented clashes by using transparency during 1996 demonstration, p. 109	Moderate	
	Investigations and verification de-spiral some construction incidents, p. 96	Moderate/Weak	
	Note: Local agreements muddy the base truth, hindering bargains that could calm the buffer zone, and increasing uncertainty and miscalculation, pp. 105, 106.		
Transparency hinders cooperation and causes conflict (H3′)	No evidence		
Transparency reduces unwarranted fears and worst-case assumptions (H4)	Sharing information about opposing forces' activities reduced tensions in the early years, p. 89	Moderate	Moderate/Weak
	The buffer zone itself clarifies the status quo and reduces miscalculation, especially compared to pre-1974, p. 88	Moderate/Weak	
	UNFICYP refuted atrocity rumors in 1967 crisis, p. 89	Moderate/Weak	
	Investigations and verification de-spiral some construction incidents, p. 96	Moderate	
	Some aspects of the U.N.'s Roccas Bastion reports and inspections, together with the overall effects of their efforts in this case, pp. 98, 100	Moderate	

(continued)

TABLE 4-1 (continued)

Hypothesis	Evidence	Strength of evidence	Overall strength of hypothesis
	UNFICYP-provided information helps Greek Cypriots accept blame for ill-discipline in lethal shootings, p. 104	Moderate	
	Local agreements cause misperception, pp. 105, 106	Failure	
	UNFICYP defused rumors in 1996 demonstration, p. 109	Moderate	
Transparency confirms fears (H4′)	Some aspects of the U.N.'s Roccas Bastion reports and inspections confirmed fears, while the incomplete or overly optimistic U.N. reports imply that more information would have further angered the Greek Cypriot side, p. 99	Moderate/Weak	Weak
Transparency reduces cheating, rogue, and spoiler problems (H5)	Investigations help get the right people to cease and desist and/or get them in trouble:	Strong/Weak; depending on incident, but overall:	Moderate/Weak
	in antagonism incidents, p. 94	Moderate/Weak	
	in construction incidents, pp. 95, 98	Moderate	
	in non-lethal shootings, p. 101	Weak	

(continued)

TABLE 4-1 *(continued)*

Hypothesis	Evidence	Strength of evidence	Overall strength of hypothesis
	UNFICYP-provided information helps Greek Cypriots take responsibility for ill-discipline in lethal shootings, p. 104	Moderate	
	UNFICYP's ability to get the Cyprus police to contain demonstrations, p. 109	Failure	
	Note: Difficulty establishing base truth also limits ability to coerce cheaters and rogues into better behavior pp. 105, 106		
Transparency about the regime (or self-transparency) increases its effectiveness (H6)	Sharing information about UNFICYP activities reduced tensions in the early years, p. 88	Moderate	Moderate/ Weak
	UNFICYP explaining why it could not get to the wounded Panayi, p. 104	Moderate	

Note: Coding: "Strong" means that the phenomenon or effect was clear and very influential if not decisive, producing behavior that would be hard to replicate without the regime. "Moderate" means that the phenomenon played a discernible and somewhat influential role. Other factors help explain the outcome. "Weak" means that the phenomenon was probably but only weakly present. Other factors explain most of the outcome. "Failure" means that the regime tried to do something and failed, or that something that the regime did was counterproductive. The overall ratings are judgments based on the significance of transparency and its effects for each hypothesis within the context of each case.

cajoling, interposition, deterrence, mediation, and getting violators in trouble. These tools are not mutually exclusive, and many incidents are calmed by some combination of them.

With respect to each side's overall assessment of the other's capabilities and intentions, UNFICYP adds very little.[64] It is possible, but hard to prove, that UNFICYP's general presence on the island helps deter aggression by increasing the probability that the initiating aggressor would be identified.

This chapter offers four main lessons about transparency. First, the variation in the importance of transparency by category of violation and by incident within categories of violations underscores a simple but fundamental point: that transparency cannot be of use unless there is some underlying uncertainty or lack of information to begin with. For example, construction may create more suspicion than slingshotting, because the uncertainties surrounding construction are likely to be larger. Likewise, transparency may be of help combating rumors during crises. Second, it is hard to move adversaries toward a common truth if the base truth itself is not well-identifiable by the regime. As transparency is fundamentally about reducing misperceptions and moving parties toward a base truth, the inadequately established base truth hinders UNFICYP's ability to provide transparency (H1). This in turn hurts UNFICYP's ability to help the sides make bargains to reduce tensions (H3), to reduce unwarranted fears, and to coerce the opposing forces into compliance (H5).

Implications

A number of policy recommendations for UNFICYP result from this observation, and are applicable to many other peacekeeping operations. Local agreements should not be recognized and should be prohibited unless signed by the UNFICYP force commander and the opposing forces' counterparts. UNFICYP should set up a commission that would work with the opposing forces to identify and resolve different interpretations of the cease-fire lines and the status quo. Video and photographic records could help establish the agreed-upon status quo, the location of patrol tracks, and so forth. UNFICYP should also delineate the cease-fire lines more clearly with rocks, barrels, barbed wire, and so forth. They should use the global positioning system (GPS) to indicate positions of these markers on the markers themselves and in record books. This would deter the opposing forces from trying to move the markers, and help accurately replace those that do get moved. Finally, to increase UNFICYP's ability to investigate and gather facts, audio triangulators could help UNFICYP fig-

---

[64] Interview General Vartiainen, May 7, 1996.

ure out where shots came from, how many were fired, and so forth. Remote video and sensor monitoring could leverage UNFICYP's stressed resources. UNFICYP's night vision capability should be augmented and upgraded.[65]

Third, the provision of transparency faces barriers when there are large amounts of ingrained bias, or when adversaries already know much about each other.

Finally, this chapter confirmed the necessity of including H5 in this study, the hypothesis that contends that information can be used to deter and coerces cheaters, rogues, and spoilers.

[65] Reynolds M. Salerno, et al., "Enhanced Peacekeeping with Monitoring Technologies," SAND2000-1400 (Albuquerque, NM: Sandia National Laboratories, June 2000), and Dorn, "Blue Sensors," argue that advanced monitoring technology is not often used in peace-keeping operations.

CHAPTER FIVE

The United Nations Disengagement Observer Force in the Golan Heights

THE UNITED NATIONS DISENGAGEMENT OBSERVER FORCE (UNDOF) operates a formal and elaborate inspection and arms control regime in the Golan Heights. The numbers of Israeli and Syrian troops, tanks, artillery, and anti-aircraft missiles are sharply and explicitly limited in the Areas of Separation and Limitation (AOS/AOLs) dividing the two sides. In addition to regular patrols and monitoring from observation posts, U.N. troops in the Golan inspect 500 Israeli and Syrian military locations on a biweekly basis. In theory, these mechanisms should greatly increase transparency. In reality, they do not.

This chapter answers two sets of questions: First, was UNDOF put into place because verification was needed to help seal the cease-fire agreement? This question bears on H2, the hypothesis that contends that the promise of regime-provided transparency can promote cooperation and help adversaries reach peace agreements. I argue that transparency did not help each side agree to the cease-fire. Instead, the buffer zone blurred the endstate of the war because it was land that neither side possessed; this helped end haggling over the last square inch of land. This blurring, or figleaf, over the endstate—not transparency—promoted peace.

Second, what does UNDOF monitor and verify, and how well does it do so? What incidents does UNDOF confront, and how does it deal with them? Do these activities affect relations and help keep the peace between Israel and Syria? Answering these operational questions not only identifies a number of barriers to the provision of transparency, but also calls into question the oft-heard claim that UNDOF is a model peacekeeping operation.[1]

This chapter makes two main arguments about transparency. The first is that mechanisms designed to increase transparency might look good on

---

[1] See for example, UNDOF's *The Golan Journal*, no. 65 (March-April 1996): 4; and Alan James, *Peacekeeping in International Politics* (New York: St. Martin's, 1990), 333–34. I also heard this claim many times in my interviews. For the record, Syria objects to the term "peacekeeping" because they view the Golan Heights as their land. As the Syrians do not want to admit to having lost any land, UNDOF is an observer force overseeing a cease-fire, not a peacekeeping force overseeing a peace agreement. On this, see John Mackinlay's very instructive *The Peacekeepers*, 131–32.

paper, but might not work well in practice. U.N. troops cannot in fact conduct thorough inspections. This provides a cautionary note to a number of arms control agreements currently on the table. Can agreements like the chemical or biological weapons conventions really tell us what we need to know?

The second argument is that a regime cannot add value to the information flow when both sides already know more than the regime. The ability of regimes to provide transparency (H1) runs into difficulties when information is hard to gather, and when the regime is operating in an information-rich environment. In contrast, the relatively poor information environments in Namibia and Cambodia help explain the U.N.'s successes with information in those operations.

THE FORMATION OF UNDOF: ASSESSING THE ROLE OF TRANSPARENCY IN THE SYRIA–ISRAEL DISENGAGEMENT AGREEMENTS

In the spring of 1974, U.S. Secretary of State Henry Kissinger negotiated a disengagement between Israel and Syria in the Golan Heights, bringing an end to the October 1973 Arab-Israeli War.[2] The settlement included the creation of UNDOF. This operation was supposed to monitor the phased disengagement of forces and withdrawal from the lines of confrontation, observe the cease-fire, and conduct inspections throughout the AOS/AOLs to make sure the terms of the cease-fire and disengagement were being respected.[3]

If either side—or better, both sides—needed an UNDOF to be assured of compliance with the cease-fire before they would be willing to sign it, this would provide evidence that the promise of transparency promoted cooperation (H2). This was not the case. Instead, Kissinger's filtering of information helped the negotiations, offering implicit support of H3′, which contends that transparency hinders cooperation.

On October 25, a U.N. force was created to help bring peace to the Sinai front of the October War.[4] This provided something of a model for calming the situation in the Golan Heights, where Syria and Israel were still in conflict. In addition, the United Nations Truce Supervision Organization (UNTSO) had been monitoring a buffer zone in the Golan since

---

[2] Technically, there had been a cease-fire in the Golan since October 25, 1973. The intensity of the fighting calmed markedly, but there were still a number of artillery duels in the months that followed.

[3] Ensio Siilasvuo, *In the Service of Peace in the Middle East, 1967–1979* (London: Hurst, 1992), 255–261.

[4] Mona Ghali, "United Nations Emergency Force II, 1973–1979" in Durch, ed., *Evolution of UN Peacekeeping*, 133–36.

the 1967 war. From the start then, the idea for a U.N. force in the Golan may have been in the air. It appears, however, that Syria's first proposal for a disengagement on January 20, 1974, did not mention the U.N. or a buffer zone.[5]

On the other hand, when the Israelis tendered a counter-offer on February 27, their idea was modeled on the Egypt-Israel accord and included a U.N.-monitored AOS/AOLs.[6] The Area of Separation (AOS) is a buffer zone that separates the two sides. Areas of Limitation (AOLs) flank the two sides of the buffer zone and are where the forces of each side are limited to fixed numbers.

At this point, both sides had proposed forward lines that the other would not accept. Indeed, Kissinger thought that the distance between the two proposals was so great that he did not communicate all the details of each plan to each side, for fear that the agitation that this would provoke might be enough to break off the negotiations. Even though Israel made some concessions on its original position by March 29, Kissinger continued to filter the information given to each side: "My usual report to all interested parties—a procedure designed to minimize the dangers of suspicions fed by rumors—would be pretty skimpy this time."[7] Kissinger revealed "*no*" aspects of Israel's plans to Syria—skimpy indeed.[8]

Kissinger said in discussing the Egyptian-Israeli disengagement, "In mediation I almost invariably transmitted any proposal about which either side felt strongly, thus reassuring the parties that their viewpoint would receive a fair hearing." In the Israel-Syrian negotiations, however, Kissinger clearly believed that too much transparency would be a bad thing. In maintaining ambiguity, Kissinger was trying to avoid a situation where clearer information would harden positions and hinder bargaining (H3').

According to Kissinger, the Syrians had embraced a U.N. buffer zone and AOLs by April 13.[9] But mutual embrace of these U.N. confidence-building measures did not break the deadlock. Acceptance of steps to in-

---

[5] Henry A. Kissinger, *Years of Upheaval* (Boston, MA: Little, Brown, 1982), 937–39. This account is not definitive proof that the Syrians had no U.N. role in mind.

[6] Kissinger, *Years of Upheaval*, 964; and William B. Quandt, *Peace Process: American Diplomacy and the Arab-Israeli Conflict since 1967* (Washington, DC: Brookings Institution, and Berkeley, CA: University of California Press, 1993), 208.

[7] Kissinger, *Years of Upheaval*, 1043.

[8] Ibid., 965, emphasis in original. I noted this finesse and nuance in manipulating information at several points in the UNFICYP chapter when UNFICYP personnel withheld telling everything to the opposing forces.

[9] Ibid., 1044. It is possible that my time line is not accurate. None of the accounts cited in this chapter explicitly examines the role of UNDOF in the negotiations. For example, UNDOF could have appeared earlier in Syria's proposals and simply not been mentioned by Kissinger or the other scholars.

crease transparency did not create a turning point, and so there is no evidence as yet of anticipated transparency promoting cooperation (H2).

Exacerbated by the fact that each side was governed by relatively weak leaders or coalitions who could not afford the image of giving into the other side, there were serious and difficult disputes that hindered the disengagement agreement. The two sides debated the disposition of a hotly contested town in the Golan called Quneitra, Palestinian terrorism, and prisoner of war issues. In general, Mackinlay notes,

> From Kissinger's point of view, the negotiations took the form of an endless series of haggles, and central to every exchange was the question of the Golan. Each village and field, every ridge line and watercourse, was contested step by step; such was the significance of this watershed between the two nations.[10]

There were also disputes about what type of U.N. force would be put into place. The Syrians wanted a small unarmed observer group that would not stand out amidst the 20,000 or so Syrian civilians that would return to the Golan. These civilians would likely think Syria gained more (or lost less) in the negotiations if the observer group were small. A small group would appear less threatening to the sovereignty that Syria claimed over the Golan. On the other hand, Israel wanted as large a force as possible and proposed an armed force of up to 3000 U.N. troops. Many observers believed that a large force would help Israel solidify its gains in the Golan.[11] Aronson says, however, that the Israelis wanted a large U.N. force so that it could actually help deter Syria and so that it could do its monitoring effectively.[12]

If Aronson's interpretation is correct, then the part of Israel's argument about monitoring provides evidence that the promise of regime-provided transparency helped bring at least Israel to the peace table (H2). Israel also appears to have believed that this transparency would continue to promote peace, perhaps by lessening unwarranted fears (H4) or by deterring the Syrians from provocations if it could not afford being identified as an

[10] Mackinlay, *The Peacekeepers*, 126–27. Mackinlay notes that even when the two sides went to Geneva to cut the final cease-fire deal, they would not sit at the same table or take part in ritual handshakes and photographs.

[11] See Shlomo Aronson, *Conflict and Bargaining in the Middle East: An Israeli Perspective* (Baltimore, MD: Johns Hopkins University Press 1978), 242; James, *Peacekeeping in International Politics*, 328; Kissinger, *Years of Upheaval*, 1089–90; Mackinlay, *The Peacekeepers*, 130–32; Quandt, *Peace Process*, 213; Bernard Reich, *Quest for Peace: United States-Israel Relations and the Arab-Israeli Conflict* (New Brunswick, NJ: Transaction Books, 1977), 266–67; and Siilasvuo, *In the Service of Peace*, 260.

[12] Aronson, *Conflict and Bargaining in the Middle East*, 242. Aronson also says that the Israelis wanted between 3000 and 5000 U.N. troops.

aggressor in a new conflict, a contention dependent on the power of information to deter aggression (H5).

By May 31, 1974, these various disputes had been sufficiently resolved for a cease-fire and disengagement agreement to be signed. In most of the cited accounts, there is surprisingly scant indication of why each side wanted UNDOF or what benefits they really thought it would bring. Reich offers the most detail on UNDOF's strategic and transparency-related significance (see also Aronson's foregoing interpretation). He says that Israel's generals and strategic planners thought the new lines of defense were as good as the previous, pre-1973 war lines and that the buffer zone and AOLs "would act as additional inhibiting factors (albeit minor ones) to the outbreak of hostilities." In addition, Reich says that the disengagement agreements, which established UNDOF and specified the exact mechanics of disengagement,

> significantly diminished the prospects for war by reducing the tension resulting from the unstable postwar troop movements, while setting in motion a possible movement toward further negotiations for a settlement. . . . The general feeling was that the consummation of the two technical agreements improved the prospects for a broader settlement involving the political concepts and attitudes of the parties involved.[13]

It certainly seems likely that UNDOF's establishment helped each side make peace and that the provision of transparency played a role. Reich's argument that UNDOF's monitoring helped reduce tension during the disengagement, and that these agreements fostered further movement toward a settlement, reinforces support for H2, supports H3 as it shows that transparency promotes peaceful outcomes, and indicates that transparency reduced fears (H4). Adrian Verheul, a political affairs officer in the U.N. Department of Peacekeeping Operations, said that transparency is useful only when it is useful and that the 1974 disengagement was one of those times. He said that UNDOF provided information only to the two sides and to the secretary-general.[14]

At the strategic level, neither side wanted war. The promise of these benefits, especially the monitoring (as anticipated by Israel, according to Aronson), in turn supports H2 because it helped promote peace.

In a backhanded way, Lieutenant General Siilasvuo, Chairman of the U.N. Military Working Group, which determined the technical aspects of UNDOF's deployment, supports the argument that the anticipation of transparency promotes peace (H2). He says,

[13] Reich, *Quest for Peace*, 267–268.
[14] Interview, April 23, 1996.

In everything one could see the deep distrust between the parties and the illusion that security would increase if only the limitations were defined in great detail and UNDOF had the task of verifying them. It was hard for me to understand such endless distrust and I could hardly bear the continual hair-splitting. A detailed scheme of limitations would not resolve the situation on the Golan or ensure the success of UNDOF. Only increasing trust between Israel and Syria would calm the tension, while UNDOF would succeed only if the parties had the political will, based on mutual interests, to maintain the peace.[15]

While he chides Syria and Israel for not seeking a more durable and profound peace, he nonetheless confirms the existence of their fears and their belief (however illusory in his view) that UNDOF's verification would promote peace.

Complementary Explanations

Three other factors contributed to the eventual success of the negotiations and thus vitiate support for H2: Transparency promotes cooperation. First, it is clear that the United States used significant leverage to make these negotiations succeed. Kissinger put a large amount of personal and U.S. prestige on the line with his exhaustive shuttle diplomacy. In addition, the United States combined carrots and sticks by threatening to reassess its relationship with Israel if the Israelis did not make reasonable compromises, while hoping to foster compromise by waiving $1 billion out of $2.2 billion that Israel owed the United States for arms purchases. President Nixon was prepared to make even larger adjustments in aid to help get both sides to make concessions.[16] Kissinger and Nixon applied pressure with threats of public embarrassment if Israel blocked an accord and subsequent loss of the U.S. public's support as well as with threats to suspend the negotiations after having promised Quneitra to Syria (thus giving Syria real reason to want to continue the negotiations and gain this prize).[17]

Second, the disengagement agreement had benefits for both sides, independent of UNDOF's inclusion in the agreement. The agreement pushed Israel back from the 1973 war's Saassa salient, only twenty-five miles from Damascus. Syria also gained back some of the land it had lost in 1967, especially Quneitra—a key bargaining goal for Syria. Aronson

[15] *In the Service of Peace,* 265.

[16] Kissinger, *Years of Upheaval,* 1056–57; Quandt, *Peace Process,* 210–12; and Siilasvuo, *In the Service of Peace,* 261.

[17] Saadia Touval, *The Peace Brokers: Mediators in the Arab-Israeli Conflict, 1948–1979* (Princeton, NJ: Princeton University Press, 1982), 255–57.

argues that the turning point in the disengagement negotiation was on May 16 when Israel agreed to cede Quneitra and let it become part of the Syrian-administered U.N. demilitarized zone (Syria accepted on May 18).[18] This concession also allowed Syria to paint the agreement as a success and a step toward further concessions. For Israel, the agreement put an end to a costly war while it still retained very good positions in the Golan.[19] Finally, the United States made various security guarantees to each side that reduced the risks of the agreement. This included supporting Israel's right to retaliate for any terrorism staged from Syrian territory against Israel and U.S. promises to Syria that Israel would place no heavy weapons on the hills surrounding Quneitra.[20]

Third, UNDOF's most important role in the negotiations may have resulted from putting a figleaf over the final territorial disposition, not transparency. UNDOF's areas of responsibility were adjusted several times in the course of negotiations, and I argue that both sides were able to make territorial concessions to UNDOF that they could not make to each other. They could allow UNDOF to control and patrol land (i.e., have the land become part of the AOS/AOLs) that they could not give to the other side. Kissinger makes this point at several junctures. In *Years of Upheaval*, Kissinger says,

> Having let [his aide] Shihabi agree to a UN buffer zone, [President Hafiz al-]Asad now informed me it was unnecessary to have zones of limited armaments as well—to which Shihabi had also agreed. But it was inconceivable that Israel would tolerate having the main force of the Syrian army follow it into territories evacuated as a result of the agreement. I was thus faced with two conditions certain to blow up the negotiations: If Israel maintained its view about the location of the line of separation, the negotiation would collapse in Damascus. If Asad insisted on his second thought about zones of limited armaments, the shuttle would come to a halt in Jerusalem.[21]

In the end, Israel did agree to move the line of separation, but it could do so only because Syria agreed to have Areas of Limitation. UNDOF's AOS/AOLs meant that Syrian troops would not follow Israel's withdrawal and occupy all the territory that Israel gave up. UNDOF's impending existence seems to have facilitated compromise by creating a figleaf effect that took the edge off an otherwise tightly zero-sum negotiation. The figleaf meant that each side did not have to end the negotiation

---

[18] Aronson, *Conflict and Bargaining in the Middle East*, 242. See also Kissinger, *Years of Upheaval*, 1079–89.

[19] Kissinger, *Years of Upheaval*, 1079–10; and Reich, *Quest for Peace*, 266–67.

[20] Kissinger, *Years of Upheaval*, 1088; and Touval, *The Peace Brokers*, 258–59.

[21] Kissinger, *Years of Upheaval*, 1047.

with a bargain that explicitly gave every square inch in the Golan Heights to one side or the other. The figleaf created by UNDOF's zone enlarged each side's apparent win-set while reducing apparent losses, allowing each side to make territorial "compromises" to the zone that they could not to each other. It also made the agreement easier to sell domestically. A pretty neat trick when there is haggling over each meter—an apparent indivisible zero-sum game if there ever was one.

Similarly, the whole point of Kissinger's use of the "United States Proposal" was that each side could seem to be agreeing with the United States, and not with each other.[22] In addition, the reason Kissinger had to engage in shuttle diplomacy in the first place was that the two sides refused to talk face to face. The negotiation itself necessitated a third party.[23]

The Quneitra issue was central in the disengagement negotiations and resolving it was the main turning point.[24] Discussion of UNDOF's role was an integral part of the Quneitra negotiations that preceded the turning point. For example, on May 2, Israel's Moshe Dayan formulated a proposal in which "the Israeli line of separation be pulled west a bit (by broadening the UN buffer zone) so that the eastern part of Quneitra could be given to Syria." On May 14, Assad counter-proposed "to divide the hills west of Quneitra between Israel (on the western slopes) and Syria (on the eastern slopes), with the ridge under UN control."[25] These proposals underscore the importance of the U.N.'s lines and the placement of the buffer zone in the negotiations over Quneitra.

The evidence about this third point shows that when each side considered compromises in the Golan and in particular around Quneitra, they considered UNDOF's future lines and zones of control. Further, it is clear that contrivances were necessary to help each side compromise and even negotiate. Thus, I argue that UNDOF's Areas of Separation and Limitation lines facilitated compromise because, when they were manipulated, each side could appear to be making way for something other than its enemy's border. This does not mean that the positions of the lines were not taken seriously, just that having UNDOF lines to negotiate over made

---

[22] Ibid., 1079–99. The obviousness of the purpose behind this proposal is shown by Kissinger putting the term in quotes to help indicate that it is being used as a figleaf term to help the negotiations. A "United States Proposal" was also used in the Sinai negotiations.

[23] One area for further transparency research is the role of third-party mediators. In contrast with the Concert, which was a passive forum, third-party mediators can be seen as active forums that make sure information is exchanged. While not a one-man security regime, Kissinger and his shuttle diplomacy can be viewed as an active forum whose effectiveness was due in part to the provision of transparency and in part to the withholding of information.

[24] Aronson, *Conflict and Bargaining in the Middle East*, 242.

[25] Kissinger, *Years of Upheaval*, first quote, p. 1057; second, p. 1075, emphasis in the original. See also 1090.

moving the lines seem like less of a zero-sum game. I. William Zartman and Jeffrey Z. Rubin argue that ambiguity is "usually" the key to agreements because it allows both sides to claim some degree of victory.[26] This does not necessarily support the contention that anticipated transparency hinders cooperation (H2′), but it is another way in which transparency and uncertainty reduction can have downsides.

In conclusion, there is some evidence that the strategic and transparency benefits promised by UNDOF's creation encouraged the successful disengagement negotiations. The negotiations were also successful, however, because of U.S. leverage and because the agreements were mutually beneficial. The strategic and transparency benefits are not mutually exclusive, but the number of complementary factors certainly dilutes support for H2, which contends that the promise of transparency can help adversaries cooperate.

Finally, deliberate opacity and ambiguity—not transparency—also played a significant role in UNDOF's creation. The first example is Kissinger's filtered reporting during the negotiations. The second is the figleaf effect created by the AOS/AOLs that lessened the zero-sum nature of the bargaining over territory. Without these steps, clarity would have increased tensions. When transparency increases tensions during bargaining, this supports H3′.

UNDOF's Mandate and Operations

UNDOF's creation and mandate was part of the May 31, 1974, separation of forces agreement and protocol between Israel and Syria. Its name, the United Nations Disengagement Observer Force, and the strength of its 1250 troops reflected elements of Israeli and Syrian demands.[27] UNDOF was tasked to maintain and observe the cease-fire and to supervise and inspect the AOS/AOLs. The exact details of the disengagement and specific limitations in the AOLs were determined by the U.N. Military Working Group and signed on June 5 in Geneva.

No Syrian or Israeli armed forces were allowed in the 80-km-long and 15-km-to-300-m-wide AOS (buffer zone). Syrian civilians, however, were permitted to return to towns and land in the AOS/AOLs, and Syrian police were allowed to help provide law and order in this Syrian admin-

---

[26] I. William Zartman and Jeffrey Z. Rubin, "Symmetry and Asymmetry in Negotiation," in I. William Zartman and Jeffrey Z. Rubin, eds., *Power and Negotiation* (Ann Arbor, MI: University of Michigan Press, 2000), 286–87.

[27] UNDOF is supplemented by eighty to ninety observers from UNTSO. While I go into some of the details of the operational and organizational relationship between UNDOF and UNTSO, the reader can refer to the subsequent citations in this chapter for more information on this somewhat baroque arrangement.

istered area. Three layers of AOLs were established on each side. In the AOLs closest to the AOS, two brigades' worth of armed forces were allowed on each side, with specific limits set on tanks (75), short-range (122mm or less) artillery (36), and total troops (6000). In the middle AOLs, 162 artillery pieces were allowed with a maximum range of 20 kilometers; 450 tanks were allowed; and there were no limits on personnel. Finally, from the AOS to the outer AOLs, no surface-to-air missiles were allowed.[28] Table 5-1 summarizes this agreement.

From June 14 to 27, 1974, UNDOF monitored and verified the phased withdrawal that took the forces on each side down to the specified levels in the AOS/AOLs. The disengagement was successful and peaceful. Siilasvuo notes no problems, save for a mine accident that killed four Austrian peacekeepers.[29]

After overseeing the initial disengagement, UNDOF turned to delineating the AOS/AOLs. Clarity about these areas would provide a base or commonly accepted truth, similar to the buffer zone on Cyprus. UNDOF had some difficulties measuring and marking the lines for the AOS, in part because there were no map experts among the U.N.'s military observers (Siilasvuo hoped that, in the future, professional surveyors could do the job). The ambiguities led only to minor disputes, even though some persist. This contrasts with Cyprus, where the same difficulties in the same year, 1974, led to various, more severe incidents and continued disputes in and along the buffer zone.[30] Cease-fire lines created in the summer of 1974 appear

---

[28] This section has so far drawn from: Ghali "United Nations Disengagement Observer Force," 152–55; Siilasvuo, *In the Service of Peace*, 260–69; as well as its appendix 8a "Separation of Forces Agreement," May 31, 1974, appendix 8b, "Protocol concerning the United Nations Disengagement Observer Force," and appendix 9, "Statement by the Chairman as Agreed by the Parties [operational plan for UNDOF]," 369–374; and United Nations, *Blue Helmets*, 3rd ed., 73–75.

[29] Ghali, "United Nations Disengagement Observer Force," 159; James, *Peacekeeping in International Politics*, 331; Mackinlay, *The Peacekeepers*, 136; Siilasvuo, *In the Service of Peace*, 269–71, 371–74; and United Nations, *Blue Helmets*, 3rd ed., 77. UNDOF helped as well with the sensitive issue of repatriation of POWs and war-dead. Unfortunately, according to Mackinlay, there is no official record of how UNDOF contributed on the ground to the success of the disengagement, and Siilasvuo's account—the next most likely source— says little about the operation as well. One can imagine that this was a time when UNDOF's ability to provide transparency could have been quite important to calming tensions and preventing miscalculation (H3 and H4). The peaceful disengagement could either indicate UNDOF's success or show that UNDOF was unnecessary. Reich takes the former view, p. 122.

[30] When I visited, UNDOF was trying to fix these problems with what they called pinpointing operations in conjunction with U.N. Military Observers (UNMOs) from UNTSO. They were re-measuring the lines and trying to put numbered barrels (which mark these lines precisely) where they should be. The barrels are often moved or removed by locals, but this is not too serious because UNDOF has photographs showing the locations of the barrels.

The story of the lines is in Mackinlay, *The Peacekeepers*, p. 137. Because of its similarities with what happened on Cyprus, it is worth summarizing. Mackinlay notes that the Military

TABLE 5-1
Summary of the Areas of Separation and Limitation

⟵ Israeli side/Syrian side ⟶

	Outer Area of Limitation	Middle Area of Limitation	Inner Area of Limitation	Area of Separation (a.k.a. buffer zone)	Inner Area of Limitation	Middle Area of Limitation	Outer Area of Limitation
Width of Zone	20 to 25 km from AOS	10 to 20 km from AOS	First 10 km from AOS	Width varies	First 10 km from AOS	10 to 20 km from AOS	20 to 25 km from AOS
Limits	no surface-to-air missiles; no limits on soldiers, tanks, or artillery.	450 tanks; 162 short-range artillery pieces; no surface-to-air missiles; no limits on soldiers.	6000 soldiers; 75 tanks; 36 short-range artillery pieces; no surface-to-air missiles.		6000 soldiers; 75 tanks; 36 short-range artillery pieces; no surface-to-air missiles.	450 tanks; 162 short-range artillery pieces; no surface-to-air missiles; no limits on soldiers.	No surface-to-air missiles; no limits on soldiers, tanks, or artillery.

Note: Adapted from Mackinlay, *Peacekeepers*, p. 129

to be of poor quality. Uncertainty about the base truth leads to disputes and hinders the ability of peacekeepers to provide transparency.

Monitoring and Verification

To monitor the AOS and verify the absence of troops within it (the heart of H1: Regimes provide transparency), UNDOF used to staff some thirty permanent positions and seventeen other observation posts, but it is currently shrinking the number of permanent positions to seventeen. It will use the freed-up forces to boost foot and vehicular patrols in the AOS.[31] These armed observer forces are supplemented by unarmed UNTSO observers who permanently staff eleven observation posts along the AOS lines.[32] A map of these deployments is available at the U.N. website: www .un.org/Depts/Cartographic/map/dpko/undof.pdf.[33]

Working Group (MWG) in Geneva had only been able to negotiate the boundary lines down to at best 100 meters and that every terrain feature in the Golan was bitterly fought over in the war and in Geneva. To finalize the exact locations and lines agreed on in the negotiation, the MWG worked with four 1:100,000 maps and thick pencils. The lines subtended several hundred (often at least 300) meters. The four maps were from different series or editions, and so they did not align well, and their inaccuracies made them inadequate for field use. Later, on June 9, 1974, the Israelis provided 1:50,000 maps with their own version of the AOS lines marked. These were agreed to by nonspecialized UNDOF staff, but rejected by the Syrians. On July 20, 1974, an American DMATL 1:50,000 map was provided, and this was agreed to by the Syrians. It is now the official UNDOF map and is regarded by the Israelis as accurate. Minor disputes over line locations nevertheless continued, but generally led to compromises between UNDOF and the Israeli defense forces. I have supplemented Mackinlay's information with that taken primarily from UNDOF's standard operating procedures (SOPs), dated January 1994 (copy made January 1995), p. 3–10; and also from interviews with UNDOF personnel on May 22, 1996; a briefing by UNTSO Captain Richard Deschambault, Military Public Information Officer (MPIO), May 20, 1996; and a briefing by UNTSO Captain Sander Luijten, May 20, 1996.

[31] Interview, Susan Allee, Senior Political Affairs Officer and desk officer for UNDOF, U.N. Department of Peacekeeping Operations, July 16, 2003.

[32] United Nations, *Blue Helmets,* 3rd ed., 76–78; and United Nations, *Report of the Secretary-General on the United Nations Disengagement Observer Force,* S/2003/655. UNDOF now numbers 1060, including 372 Austrian, 357 Polish, 191 Canadian and 94 Slovakian troops. Japan contributes 45 soldiers, which for them marks a significant foray into peacekeeping. UNTSO observer officers number 78, and because each of the eleven UNTSO OPs is supposed to be staffed by two officers from different countries, the UNTSO force is made up of 20+ nationalities. UNDOF cost $41 million from July 2002 through June 2003.

[33] Thanks to the hospitality of UNDOF, UNTSO, and their host countries, I was able to spend ten days in Syria and Israel visiting U.N. offices in Jerusalem, Damascus, and Tiberias as well as Camp Faouar and Camp Ziouani in the Golan Heights, and positions 10, 71, 16, 60, 52, and 55 (in north-south order). These positions cover the entire length of the AOS, except for the heights of Mt. Hermon.

One must examine the details of UNDOF's inspection system to assess how well UNDOF is able to gather information and provide transparency. To verify the Areas of Limitation, UNDOF, using UNTSO observers, conducts biweekly inspections of at least 500 Syrian and Israeli positions. The U.N. observers are accompanied by liaison officers from whichever side they are inspecting. According to UNDOF's standard operating procedures (SOPs), inspectors are not supposed to actually count the troops at each base in the first ten-kilometer AOL. Instead, they ask for headcounts from the local commander. In the first and second ten-kilometer zones, tanks are supposed to be counted by the inspectors, and they are supposed to distinguish among combat tanks, fixed tanks, and support tanks. APCs are ignored. Artillery pieces are counted, and these are to be distinguished by range or caliber. MLRS systems count as one artillery piece. In all zones, surface-to-air missiles are automatic violations to be reported. Inspectors are not allowed to be intrusive during inspections, meaning that they cannot go into buildings. They can count only what they can see out in the open.[34]

After inspections, UNDOF reports the results to both sides. To the violators, it gives fairly specific information: the exact type and number of the offending weapon(s) and personnel and their location down to 1000 yards. The other side receives more general information about the category of the violation (although UNDOF can apparently threaten to release more specific information if the violator does not comply with the agreed limits). For political reasons, even if reports of violations are made public, the identity of the violating side is never released. Even though violators remain cloaked, this shaded reporting system shows that UNDOF understands that it can use information to coerce potential violators into backing down, and it thus offers modest support for H5.

With their clear zones and limitations on capabilities, the AOS/AOLs should greatly increase transparency and offer strong support for H1. There are, however, five operational problems with the inspection system, the first three of which are built into the non-intrusive and rigid SOPs for the inspections. These problems offer lessons for improvement of UNDOF and other operations.

First, the inspectors have to trust the troop figures that the local Israeli and Syrian commanders give them. Second, inspectors can count only weapons that are visible. Combined, these points indicate that the inspections are less thorough and precise than carefully calibrated AOS and AOL limits imply. On paper, the limitations are clear and specific. In practice, the inspections cannot ensure compliance.

Third, there are no surprise inspections, and the routinization of the biweekly inspections allows for exploitation of the SOPs by the Israelis in particular. Several sources mentioned that the Israelis sometimes take ad-

[34] UNDOF SOPs, p. 3–37.

vantage of the rigid biweekly inspection schedule to move weapons up for exercises and then move them back to avoid the inspections. Despite several high-level UNDOF and UNTSO officials being aware of this problem, the "fortnightly inspections of equipment and force levels in the areas of limitation" continue with the same routine.[35]

The Israelis' habit of moving equipment forward to conduct exercises in between inspections indicates disrespect for the AOL limits and shows that they ultimately choose military readiness over compliance as their fundamental priority. It seems probable that if UNDOF tried to be more intrusive, or if they randomized their inspections to catch the Israelis, then the Israelis would restrict UNDOF's freedom of movement and would conduct exercises anyway. This point is reinforced by the Israeli response to violence in the Shab'a farms area near Mount Hermon, just above the northern perimeter of UNDOF's area of operations. In late 2000 and into 2001, conflict erupted between Israel and Hizbollah. Israel shut down UNDOF's freedom of movement in its northern area (Area 6), even though the Shab'a farms are technically in the U.N. Interim Force in Lebanon's (UNIFIL) area of operations. When the violence lessened after a number of months, UNDOF's freedom of movement was restored.[36] When push comes to shove, UNDOF gets shoved out of the way.

Fourth, both sides routinely deny the inspectors freedom of movement in the AOL and access to areas that should be inspected (the intelligence-gathering stations, in particular). This difficulty is routinely reported in the *Reports of the Secretary-General* on UNDOF. Denial of access reveals the physical limits of UNDOF's ability to gather information and provide transparency (H1). Fifth, both sides commit "permanent violations," which refer to the forward locations of some of the early-warning and surveillance posts.

There are several problems with the monitoring/OP system as well. Although UNDOF's buffer zone is fairly short at eighty kilometers, there are still not enough troops or technology to provide round-the-clock, all-weather, very high-confidence monitoring. Several factors bear this out. According to UNDOF's force commander, Major-General Johannes C. Kosters, the night vision equipment is inadequate. In his 1989 book, Mackinlay wrote that there was no night vision equipment at all, and it is uncertain whether better night vision gear was included in the 2002–05 three-year modernization plan.[37] Even if they were better equipped,

---

[35] S/2003/655, para. 3.

[36] S/2001/499, para 2; S/22001/1079; and *Report of the Secretary-General on the United Nations Interim Force in Lebanon,* January 22, 2001, S/2001/66.

[37] Kosters, interview, May 21, 1996. Major R. H. Chase (U.S. Marines) said that the AN/PVS-5/7s that were available have limited depth perception, conversation, May 30, 1996. Susan Allee, interview, July 16, 2003.

the OPs are not sufficiently staffed to provide complete surveillance. This is in particular true of the two officers in the UNTSO OPs who can scarcely be expected (and they are not) to maintain a constant watch during their lengthy shifts. Several peacekeepers told me that at night and/or in the fog, smugglers often come quite close to UNDOF/UNTSO OPs (as they must because of the OPs' locations and/or the locations of mine fields). Mackinlay also wrote of "reports" claiming that neither side wants to see the surveillance equipment of UNDOF updated. This would seem to downgrade the stock that they place in UNDOF's provision of transparency.[38] Advanced monitoring technology, however, is rarely used in any peacekeeping operation, and so UNDOF's experience may simply be par for the course.[39]

Given UNDOF's political constraints, it might be hard for it to be more intrusive or to upgrade its information-gathering capabilities. UNDOF (and the U.N. more generally) is too politically weak relative to Syria and Israel to bargain its way to a new deal or status of forces agreement (SOFA). U.N. operations deploying to other locations, as in the developing world, may be able to wield greater leverage and be able to arrange better inspection regimes.

Some of UNDOF's inspection and monitoring problems are not as severe as appearances suggest. First, both sides generally keep so far below the agreed limits that there is virtually no question about compliance. Typical personnel counts are about 2000, where 6000 are permitted. Equipment is generally at 40 to 60 percent of allowed levels.[40] Even if the counts are off by 50 percent, the troops would still be one-third below the limit, equipment one-quarter below. Second, one would predict that if either side thought the other was committing a violation (or cared about it), then they would report it to UNDOF and request a special inspection—however, this almost never happens. According to Major-General Kosters, in the one and a half years that he had led UNDOF, there had not been a single request for a special inspection and this was because both sides trusted that UNDOF was doing its work. "They never argue our verification."[41]

[38] Mackinlay, *The Peacekeepers,* 141, 151.
[39] Salerno et al., "Enhanced Peacekeeping with Monitoring Technologies"; and Dorn, "Blue Sensors."
[40] Captain Deschambault, May 20, 1996.
[41] Interview, May 21, 1996. It was difficult evoking any stories at any level of UNDOF or UNTSO about problems in the Golan that were serious enough for either side to call on UNDOF to go solve or investigate (quite a contrast with Cyprus, where UNFICYP intervenes on a daily basis). Still, at lower levels of authority, a few such stories emerged. One UNDOF company commander thought that perhaps one or two times a month one side would complain about some suspected military problem on the other side. For example, on the night before this interview, the Golan Israel Defense Force Liaison Officer (GILO) reported about twenty mysterious searchlights to UNDOF, which in turn sent out a ready re-

Had any of the afore-mentioned operational problems caused serious disputes, UNDOF's ability to provide transparency (H1) would be clearly called into question, and its operational flaws might increase tensions in the Golan. But they do not cause disputes. That UNDOF's inspection reports are accepted unchallenged could mean that UNDOF is sufficiently accurate with its monitoring, does provide some level of transparency, and that H1 receives some support. After all, if UNDOF were inaccurate, or if one side committed unacceptable violations that the other side detected and UNDOF did not, then we would likely see more calls for special inspections. The counterargument is that unchallenged acceptance of UNDOF's inspection reports could mean that the inspections do not matter very much. I think the latter is more true, given how often I heard about Israeli violations during exercises and given the frequent comments that neither side protests. This contrasts with Cyprus, where both sides protest every minor violation.

Things do not change much in the Golan Heights. There was only one publicly revealed protest from the mid-1990s to 2003 in the biannual *Reports of the Secretary-General* on UNDOF. In late 1997 to early 1998, Israel protested that the way the Syrians were rearranging rocks in an agricultural project might have military benefits. In response to the protest, Syria removed some of the new stone walls. No other such incidents were reported in the fourteen Secretary-General reports from May 1996 to June 2003.[42] Even during a period of tension that raised the possibility of armed conflict in fall of 1996, the U.N. reported that forces and armaments remained "well below" their respective ceilings in the AOLs.[43] Overall, since my field research in 1996, "pretty much nothing" has changed for UNDOF.[44]

On the positive side, the fact that personnel and equipment levels are always below allowed limits and that the opposing forces never refute or question the inspection reports and verification indicates a fairly low level of tension in the Golan Heights.[45] While it is good for the Golan that

---

action patrol. The problem turned out to be the headlights on a farmer's tractor. And so it goes in the Golan. These examples are on the local or field level. They are not examples of either side calling the AOL inspections into question.

[42] See S/1998/391. The reports I surveyed are S/1996/959; S/1997/372; S/1997/884; S/1998/391; S/1998/1073; S/1999/575; S/1999/1175; S/2000/459; S/2000/1103; S/2001/499; S/2001/1079; S/2002/542; S/2002/1328; and S/2003/655.

[43] S/1996/959.

[44] Interview, Susan Allee, July 16, 2003.

[45] To underscore further the lack of tension in the Golan, while the Israelis conduct real exercises on the Golan, one UNTSO official said that Syrian exercises consist of forty men, one rifle, and half a bullet. I heard several other tales of woe about the state of Syrian forces in the Golan. Syria sends its best troops to Lebanon and also harbors significant fears

miscalculation and fear (H3 and H4) do not seem to be much in play, this makes it is hard to judge the effects of UNDOF's activities by examining variance in the levels of tensions.

In sum, although there are a number of reasons why doubt is cast on the ability of UNDOF to provide transparency (H1), these problems turn out not to affect UNDOF's operations substantially. It is possible that transparency may not be all that important to UNDOF.

Violations

There are a number of categories of possible violations that UNDOF confronts, including military entry into the AOS, overflights, firing into or across the AOS, military construction in the AOS, and civilian crossings of the wrong A and B lines (the A line is the Israeli side of the AOS; the B line is the Syrian side). Military entry into the AOS does occur from time to time, but these incidents are of little consequence. The same is true of overflights. For example, sometimes Syrian vehicles take shortcuts through the AOS. Unlike on Cyprus, violators usually have a practical excuse for these minor violations (or they are lazy), and they are not trying to annoy UNDOF or Israel. Israel commits less of these violations because a mildly electrified touch-sensitive, alert-sending technical fence runs the length of their side of the buffer zone (actually, the fence is a short distance in from the A line, often as close as 200 to 300 meters, but also sometimes kilometers away).[46]

According to UNTSO Lt. Colonel Ray Martin, the head of Observer Group Golan—Tiberias, there had not been a major violation in twenty-two years. He attributed this to a clear mandate, to a system that was "very transparent" in that everyone knows where everything is, to the co-operation of both sides, and to UNDOF's deterrent effect. He made an analogy that UNDOF was like a police car on a highway. If people see the police car, they will slow down. When asked if the U.N. had made peace work in the Golan, he said it was a chicken and egg problem: "Who can tell?"[47]

This brings us to sheep. By far the largest problem UNDOF faces, at least in numerical terms, is sheep and shepherd violations. Shepherds become violators if they go beyond the grazing line, which runs between the

---

toward Turkey. Some suggested that one reason that the Golan is so peaceful is that Syria is (was) able to harass Israel through Lebanon.

[46] Israeli patrols generally arrive within five minutes after the fence is touched.

[47] In this May 30, 1996, briefing and interview, Martin also noted that things could change very quickly in the Golan Heights. During Israel's Grapes of Wrath Operation in Lebanon (only twenty kilometers from the Golan), some Syrian military forces crossed the B line and within ninety seconds, two Israeli F-16s came flying along the A line.

Israeli A line and the Israeli technical fence. They are often motivated to do so, because this forbidden zone often contains good grazing land. Sheep are technically not violations, but as shepherds often follow their sheep, errant sheep are often good indicators of soon-to-be errant humans. At least two sources said that sheep and shepherds constituted 99 percent of all violations (the other 1 percent are unidentified civilians, sometimes defectors, according to one of these sources). Another source indicated that there were 100 to 130 sheep and shepherd violations a week. At the UNTSO morning briefing that I went to in Tiberias (May 30, 1996), the briefer said that there had been six civilian and twenty-one shepherd violations in the past day.

UNDOF's response to these violators is to send out a patrol and persuade the shepherds to return to their side of the line. UNDOF's patrols use various placards with appropriate messages in local languages to help them with this and other tasks. These incidents are reported to UNDOF, but typically not to the U.N. in New York.

These incidents can be serious, especially for the sheep and shepherds involved. Often, they move into a heavily mined area, and the sheep or shepherds become "purple clouds" (in the words of UNDOF soldiers). Sometimes the shepherds move the mines onto UNDOF patrol paths. In other cases, Israeli soldiers will send warning shots to shoo away the approaching sheep and shepherds. Sheep are shot on a fairly regular basis by Israelis wary of terrorists and bombs, which can appear in any guise. When UNDOF sends out a ready reaction patrol to reign in shepherds, it is more of a humanitarian than peacekeeping gesture.[48]

The reason that there are so few problems on the Golan is that neither side wants problems. This point was underscored when Israel fought Syria in Lebanon in 1982: while Israel built up its forces in the Golan, Syria actually drew down its Golan forces. It is implausible to believe that Syria did this because UNDOF's 1200 troops provided a shield or affected Syria's threat assessments. Instead, war itself in the Golan appeared implausible to Syria, despite the heavy fighting only a short distance away.[49] Likewise, both sides seemed to gloss over a shooting incident on January 8, 2003. Israeli Defense Forces (IDF) shot two Syrian soldiers in civilian clothing who had passed beyond the AOS and were approaching the Israeli technical fence. One died and one was wounded. UNDOF recovered

[48] The source for these last paragraphs is briefing, Captain Deschambault, May 20, 1996; interview, Captain Ken-Ichi Kawazu, Deputy MPIO, May 20, 1996; interview, Lt. Colonel Mats Torping, Chief, Observer Group Golan, May 21, 1996, and other interviews. See also Mackinlay, *The Peacekeepers*, 144.

[49] Ze'ev Schiff and Ehud Ya'ari, Ina Friedman ed. and trans., *Israel's Lebanon War* (New York: Simon and Schuster, 1984), 117–18 and 155; and Yair Evron, *War and Intervention in Lebanon: The Israeli-Syrian Deterrence Dialogue* (London: Croom Helm, 1987), 190.

the body from the IDF the next day; and Israel returned the wounded Syrian to Syria via UNDOF. The two Syrians apparently had been in a wadi that they had used for washing clothes for years, so something went wrong somewhere. There were perfunctory protests, but both sides cooperated readily with the U.N., and a U.N. official noted that neither side allowed the incident to escalate.[50]

Finally, it may be that the fact of physical distance provided by the AOS/AOLs promotes peace. Physical distance, coupled with the UNDOF-monitored arms control agreement of the AOL, offers some assurance to each side that the other side was not building up for an attack. Crossing the AOLs' lines could signal an impending attack, and avoiding sending off that signal complicates attack planning. Seen this way, monitored physical distance offers stability in part because transparency is helping each side calculate more clearly (H3) and is calming fears (H4), while helping deter attacks as UNDOF might identify the aggressor (H5). Distance also shifts the offense/defense balance toward the defense by making it easier for the defense to anticipate and plan. The case of Cyprus demonstrates that physical proximity allows the opposing forces a number of ways to harass each other, methods that would not be available if the buffer zone were wider (slingshotting, stone throwing, verbal insults, etc.). Incidents are most frequent where the buffer zone is narrow (as in Nicosia), and they diminish where it is thicker. The two-and-a-half-mile-wide buffer zone in Korea certainly does not prevent all antagonisms and more severe incidents, but things would likely be worse if it were narrower.

Scholar and Practitioner Assessments of UNDOF and the Role of Transparency

If UNDOF is supposed to provide transparency, it must be able to add value to each side's own threat assessments. Thus, a central question is how much transparency UNDOF can add to what each side already knows or can learn. Mackinlay argues that when UNDOF was deployed in 1974, its monitoring ability may have been "as effective as that of the Syrian and Israeli armies." This situation has changed as both sides have rebuilt and improved their intelligence-gathering capabilities, while those of UNDOF remained largely stagnant. Mackinlay says that this means that neither side relies much on UNDOF's monitoring, except to the ex-

---

[50] Report of a briefing from Kieran Prendergast, United Nations Security Council, S/PV.4685 January 16, 2003; David Rudge, "Captured Soldier, Body of Second Returned to Syria," Jerusalem Post, January 10, 2003; and Hua Jiang, "Highlights of the Noon Briefing; UN: Situation Returns to Normal Following Shooting in Golan Area," January 10, 2003. Also, interview, Susan Allee, July 16, 2003.

tent that it serves as a backup.[51] He adds, however, that the two sides can communicate through UNDOF if there are problems in the Areas of Separation and Limitation (as shown earlier, this does not happen much). Mackinlay and UNDOF's force commander (and several other UNDOF and UNTSO officers in interviews) agree that, even though both sides have adequate intelligence, the Israelis have a much better picture of what goes on in the Golan than the Syrians.[52] This discussion suggests that, in terms of strategic threat assessment, there is little that UNDOF can add to each side's unilateral capabilities, especially to the Israelis.

One high-ranking UNDOF officer said that "UNDOF clarifies all real or supposed violations, but we don't have many serious violations here." He added that both sides are aware that serious violations would threaten the peace process.[53] Lieutenant Colonel Torping, whose experience with UNDOF spanned eleven years, said that Syria and Israel "want a guarantee that the other side won't take unexpected steps and they know that neither side has tried anything for twenty years." He also said that the U.N. has been doing its job in a good way, but that it was more important that both sides want peace and trust the U.N.[54] Major-General Kosters cautioned not to make too much of the confidence-building effects of UNDOF; the chance of conflict is very low and UNDOF's force is only "barbed wire and nothing more."[55] Zenon Carnapas, UNTSO's Senior Advisor, said that with UNDOF/UNTSO the two sides get an objective opinion about each other in regard to the Geneva agreement. He thought that if UNTSO were withdrawn it might serve as a political trigger.[56] With the exception of Force Commander Kosters, the general sense I got from high-level U.N. staff was that they believed they were increasing transparency (H1), and thereby lowering already low levels of fear about supposed violations and unexpected steps (H4).

---

[51] On the argument that UNDOF serves as intelligence backup, the Deputy Chief of Staff of UNTSO, Colonel Jaako Oksanen made something of a counterpoint by suggesting that, because each side knows pretty much what the numbers are (especially on its own side, of course), UNDOF's inspections can be seen as tests of UNDOF. Interview, May 28, 1996. UNDOF reports only specifics to the inspected side.

[52] Mackinlay, *The Peacekeepers,* 151. Interview, Major-General Kosters, May 21, 1996. Mackinlay says that the Syrians and Israelis both have huge surveillance towers in the Golan. From what I could tell, they are not equivalent. The Israeli observation stations are much more prominent, and there are at least two huge stations atop the dominant point of Mt. Hermon, as well as several others on top of hills throughout the Golan. Mackinlay also noted that it is a "popular joke among the UN troops that with these [surveillance] devices the Syrians and Israelis cannot only pick out individual soldiers in the Area of Separation but read the nametags on their shirts," 150.

[53] Interview, May 21, 1996.

[54] Ibid.

[55] Ibid.

[56] Interview, May 27, 1996.

TABLE 5-2
Findings by Hypothesis

Hypothesis	Evidence	Strength of evidence	Overall strength of hypothesis
Regimes provide transparency (H1)	Monitoring during disengagement, pp. 122, 127	Moderate	Moderate/Weak
	Sophisticated monitoring mechanisms (on paper), pp. 130, 133	Moderate/Weak	
	Existence of AOS/AOLs, p. 136	Moderate	
	Liaison between Israel and Syria, p. 140	Weak	
	Others' assertions that transparency is provided, pp. 136, 137, 140	Moderate/Weak	
Regimes spread misinformation (H1')	No evidence		
Anticipated transparency promotes cooperation (H2)	Israel wanted a large UNDOF in part to monitor effectively, p. 121	Weak	Moderate/Weak
	Assessments by scholars and practitioners, pp. 136, 137, 140	Moderate	
Anticipated transparency hinders cooperation (H2')	No evidence		
Transparency promotes cooperation and prevents conflict (H3)	Significantly, but only during the disengagement and only on a tactical/incident level, pp. 122, 127	Moderate	Weak
	Physical distance, p. 136	Weak	
Transparency hinders cooperation and causes conflict (H3')	Kissinger filters information during negotiations to prevent breakoff and deadlock, p. 120	Strong	Moderate

(continued)

TABLE 5-2 (continued)

Hypothesis	Evidence	Strength of evidence	Overall strength of hypothesis
Transparency reduces unwarranted fears and worst-case assumptions (H4)	The "figleaf effect" provided by the AOS/AOLs during the negotiations implies support for H3', because greater clarity would have increased the chance of deadlock, pp. 124, 125	Moderate/Weak	Moderate/Weak
	Significantly, but only during the disengagement, pp. 122, 127	Moderate	
	Yes, according to assertions by others that this is UNDOF's effect, pp. 137, 140	Moderate/Weak	
	Physical distance, p. 136	Moderate/Weak	
Transparency confirms fears (H4')	No evidence		
Transparency reduces cheating, rogue, and spoiler problems (H5)	Reporting system, p. 130	Moderate in theory, Weak in practice	Weak
	Could sound alarm and identify aggressor, pp. 137, 140	Weak	
Transparency about the regime (or self-transparency) increases its effectiveness (H6)	No evidence		

Note: Coding: "Strong" means that the phenomenon or effect was clear and very influential if not decisive, producing behavior that would be hard to replicate without the regime. "Moderate" means that the phenomenon played a discernible and somewhat influential role. Other factors help explain the outcome. "Weak" means that the phenomenon was probably but only weakly present. Other factors explain most of the outcome. "Failure" means that the regime tried to do something and failed, or that something that the regime did was counterproductive. The overall ratings are judgments based on the significance of transparency and its effects for each hypothesis within the context of each case.

Alan James says that the inspections "are a means of helping to keep anxiety at a somewhat lower level than it would otherwise reach and as such are of value" (H4).[57] Mackinlay argues that UNDOF's liaison system provides a "limited but important diplomatic link between the Syrians and the Israelis." By facilitating communication, this may be another way in which UNDOF increases transparency (H1). He notes that UNDOF "will certainly cry the alarm to the whole world if either opponent force attempts to maneuver to regain the Golan." If fears of the alarm deterred the attempt, it would support H6 as an example of information deterring or coercing aggressors.[58]

Something like this happened in the case of the U.N. Emergency Force I. When Egypt asked UNEF I to leave the Sinai/Gaza armistice line with Israel in 1967, it helped signal impending conflict and helped identify the aggressor.[59]

CONCLUSION

UNDOF is the most formal arms control and verification mission in this study, and it offers a number of insights about transparency. First, the promise of transparency was not crucial to each side's willingness to accept U.N. forces in the Golan, and it mostly seemed a factor only for Israel. Thus, the hypothesis that the anticipation of transparency promotes cooperation, H2, receives modest to weak support. Superpower leverage was the biggest factor that led to the U.N. monitoring of the cease-fire.

Second, there was evidence that the management and selective communication of information promoted peace. Kissinger edited and withheld information as he shuttled between Israel and Syria. Indeed, these adversaries might have deadlocked had they known how far apart their respective positions were at certain points. This supports H3', because here incomplete information promotes cooperation. One way to view Kissinger's diplomacy is as an active forum where the information between states is transmitted and manipulated by an outside actor; he also had the leverage and power of the United States at his disposal.

Third, even though H2 receives little support, the buffer zone created by UNDOF's deployment helped each side make territorial compromises.

---

[57] James, *Peacekeeping in International Politics*, 332.

[58] Mackinlay, *The Peacekeepers*, 150, 152.

[59] Mona Ghali, "United Nations Emergency Force I," 124–25; James, *Peacekeeping in International Politics*, 220–23; Indar Jit Rikhye, Michael Harbottle, and Bjorn Egge, The *Thin Blue Line: International Peacekeeping and Its Future* (New Haven, CT: Yale University Press, 1974), 58–70; and Stein, "Detection and Defection," 620.

Because of what I called the figleaf effect, they could give up territory to the U.N. zone that they would not be willing to concede to each other.

Fourth, UNDOF's day-to-day operations in the Golan do not increase transparency very much. Both sides, but especially the Israelis, know a lot from their own sources about the other side's forces. Information from UNDOF can add little. While UNDOF's elaborate monitoring and verification mechanisms in the AOS/AOLs would seem to be able to increase transparency considerably, they in fact do not. There are numerous manpower, equipment, and procedural difficulties. Both Syria and Israel have taken steps to block and limit UNDOF's capabilities. The relative power and capabilities of UNDOF compared to the OPFORs is limited, and this in turn reduces its effectiveness. Despite appearances, UNDOF is unable to add much information, and its ability to provide transparency is less than meets the eye; H1 therefore receives only moderate/weak support.

Fifth, there are virtually no tension-raising incidents in the Golan, and the sides never dispute UNDOF's observations. These tranquil conditions preclude much of a role for transparency to reduce fears, as contended by H4. After the initial disengagement, H4 receives only moderate/weak support, and this strength is less due to evidence that I found than to the arguments of other scholars that UNDOF exerts a calming effect.

Sixth, the distances and limitations created by the AOS/AOLs may alter the offense/defense balance somewhat in favor of the defense, and this may reduce miscalculation. If true, this means that distance rivals or perhaps surpasses transparency in reducing miscalculation. Further, as war has so far been virtually off the table in the Golan, there has been little opportunity for calculation or miscalculation. For these reasons, after the disengagement, only very weak support is offered for H3, which suggests that transparency can reduce miscalculation, reduce uncertainty, and promote cooperation.

Seventh, the last two points reinforce important preconditions for regime-provided transparency to be effective. The sides have to have incomplete information, uncertainty, or harbor unwarranted fears in order for regime-provided transparency to have a shot at reducing miscalculation (H3) or lowering misperceptions (H4).

Eighth, despite all these caveats, analysts tend to concur that UNDOF's presence promotes peace. Although the peace-promoting effects of transparency may be less than all the AOS/AOLs and monitoring imply, physical distance and the presence of the U.N. and international community likely add some marginal increment toward peace.

The basis for these findings are summarized in table 5-2.

CHAPTER SIX

The United Nations Transition Assistance Group for Namibia

MEDIA EFFORTS by the United Nations Transistion Assistance Group (UNTAG) clarified the operation's purpose and defused rumors and fears that would have otherwise threatened the successful execution of the mandate. This provides support for the hypotheses that regimes provide transparency (H1), and that transparency and self-transparency reduce unwarranted fears (H4 and H6). After discussing the conditions that led to UNTAG's deployment, I then assess UNTAG's mandate, operations, and the extent to which its considerable success relied on transparency. Information operations and the provision of transparency greatly assisted UNTAG, and without them, the hurdles it faced would have been much greater.

ORIGINS OF UNTAG

UNTAG helped free Namibia from South African rule, marking the end of one of the world's longest processes of decolonization. From 1884 to 1914, Namibia was a German colony, then known as South West Africa. Under the League of Nations' mandate system, South West Africa was turned over to South Africa following World War I. When World War II ended and the League of Nations dissolved into the U.N., South Africa refused the U.N.'s requests to place South West Africa under trusteeship—direct administration by the U.N. In 1966, the U.N. General Assembly voted to end South Africa's mandate, but this changed little on the ground.

Formed in 1960, the South West Africa People's Organization (SWAPO) aimed to gain independence for the country, and resorted to violence in 1966. SWAPO became a full-fledged guerilla rebel group, operating out of Zambia and then Angola when the latter became independent in 1975. SWAPO's reliance on Angolan bases swept it into Cold War–politics as superpower support for various Angolan factions made Angola one of the central battlegrounds for influence in sub-Saharan Africa. Conflict between SWAPO and South Africa smoldered for years. The U.N. General Assembly recognized SWAPO as the sole representative of the Namibian people in 1976. This recognition fueled South Africa's perception that the U.N. was biased in favor of SWAPO and prompted some of its efforts to undermine the Namibian election. During the 1989 transition period, however, SWAPO was supposed to forgo its U.N.- granted special privileges, and it was to be treated as just "one political party among others."[1]

South Africa offered a plan for Namibian independence in 1975. The plan was flawed because it preserved apartheid in Namibia. In response, the West (the U.S., France, Britain, Canada, and West Germany) formed a Contact Group to try to help manage a peaceful transition to independence, while avoiding apartheid, civil war, and Soviet influence. By 1978, the Contact Group had come up with a plan to grant Namibia independence. As specified in U.N. Security Council Resolution 435 of 1978, a key element in Namibia's move to self-determination and self-governance was to be free elections, assisted by the U.N., and a United Nations Transition Assistance Group in particular.[2] It took a decade, though, before South Africa decided to leave Namibia and UNTAG could be activated.

The reason for the delay was that South Africa viewed Namibia as a buffer between itself and the 50,000-strong Cuban military contingent in Angola. Because of this, South Africa insisted that the Cubans withdraw from Angola before they would grant independence to Namibia. Thus, the main reason why South Africa left Namibia was Cuba's late-1988 decision to leave Angola.

Cuba's departure from Angola relied in part on transparency provided by the U.N. According to Virginia Page Fortna,

> South Africa was capable of verifying the Cuban withdrawal with its own technology, but charges of Cuban noncompliance would carry little weight coming from South Africa alone. South Africa was uncomfortable about the UN's impartiality but trusted UN monitors to report what they saw. Angola and Cuba wanted verification of their compliance with the peace plan to be indisputable to ensure they were not blamed for any attempt by South Africa to back away from the plan.[3]

This passage offers support for H2 because the promise of transparency is helping the peace process. It also shows various parties using transparency instrumentally, albeit still in the service of peace.

The influence of transparency is diminished, however, by several factors. First, by 1988 the international political climate started to shift. Soviet political and economic support for its clients was shrinking, and this was a major trigger for the Cuban departure from Africa. As the United

---

[1] "UNTAG: What It Will Do and How," *United Nations Chronicle* 26, no. 2 (June 1989): 13.

[2] *Report of the Secretary-General* submitted pursuant to paragraph 2 of Security Council Resolution 431 (1978) concerning the situation in Namibia (U.N. Document S/12827 of 29 August 1978).

[3] Virginia Page Fortna, "The United Nations Angola Verification Mission I," in Durch, ed., *Evolution of UN Peacekeeping*, 379.

States and Soviets began to cooperate to bring peace and independence to Namibia, the stage was set for effective U.S. mediation by Assistant Secretary of State Chester Crocker.

Second, domestic politics in South Africa had become more liberal and South Africa was increasingly unwilling to bear the cost of conflict in Namibia. In Crocker's words, "the right alignment—the proper constellation—of local, regional, and international events" necessary to create peace in Namibia (and Angola) had come about.[4]

Finally, the basic plans for UNTAG had been sitting on the shelf for years. The promise of transparency (including monitoring) had been on offer for a decade, but had been ignored. This suggests that factors other than transparency, such as international and domestic politics, caused the turning point toward peace in Namibia.[5]

UNTAG's Mandate, Operations, and Transparency

UNTAG's mandate had two main components and each depended to some degree on transparency for its effectiveness. The mission of the military and police component was to supervise the cease-fire and verify the withdrawal of South African forces. By so doing, this first component was supposed to create the necessary preconditions for the election. In addition, SWAPO forces, named the "People's Liberation Army of Namibia" (PLAN), were to be demobilized or cantoned while U.N. Civilian Police (UNCIVPOL) monitored the remaining South African–controlled South West African Police (SWAPOL).

The civil component's mission was to sponsor free and fair elections. This was the most important part of the mandate, as elections were the sine qua non of independence and self-governance.

---

[4] Chester Crocker, cited in Daniel S. Papp, "The Angolan Civil War and Namibia," in David R. Smock, ed., *Making War and Waging Peace: Foreign Intervention in Africa* (Washington, DC: United States Institute of Peace Press, 1993), 186.

[5] This section was based on Fetherston, *Towards a Theory of United Nations Peacekeeping*, pp. 59–62; Virginia Page Fortna, "United Nations Transition Assistance Group," in Durch, *Evolution of UN Peacekeeping*; Vivienne Jabri, *Mediating Conflict: Decisionmaking and Western Intervention in Namibia* (Manchester, England: Manchester University Press, 1990); Robert B. Oakley, "A Diplomatic Perspective on African Conflict Resolution," in David R. Smock and Chester A. Crocker, eds., *African Conflict Resolution: The U.S. Role in Peacemaking* (Washington, DC: United States Institute of Peace Press, 1993), 61–66; United Nations, *Blue Helmets*, 3rd ed., 203–9; United States Department of State, "Background Notes: Namibia, April 1995," available at gopher://gopher.state.gov; "What the Two Agreements Say," United Nations Chronicle 26, no. 1 (March 1989): 36; and I. William Zartman, *Ripe for Resolution: Conflict and Prevention in Africa,* updated edition (New York: Oxford University Press, 1989).

UNTAG started formal operations on April 1, 1989, when it began to deploy its forces of 300 military monitors, 2550 troops (one battalion each from Kenya, Malaysia, and Finland), 1500 civilian police from twenty-five states, a number of logistics and other units, and various support and political personnel. UNTAG numbered about 8000 when the November 1989 elections began. UNTAG lasted until March 1990 and cost about $370 million, not including voluntary contributions to the operation.[6]

Military Component

SWAPO launched a major incursion south from Angola into Namibia on April 1, 1989, the day the cease-fire began. UNTAG was just beginning to deploy, had only 100 staff and 921 troops in Namibia, and could do little to stop the 1500-strong incursion. In fairly short order, the U.N. agreed to let South Africa repel the SWAPO forces. Although the South African forces were supposed to be confined to base, the agreement with the U.N. was eased in part because they had already been beating SWAPO. Facing disproportionate losses, SWAPO agreed to the Mount Ejo Declaration, which stipulated that they would withdraw ninety miles into Angola under UNTAG supervision. Even though the deal to end the incursion was reached in little over a week, SWAPO's actions threatened UNTAG's whole mission at its outset, delayed the mission, cost UNTAG and SWAPO some credibility, and was a "bitter experience" that "revived the mistrust and division which had begun to be assuaged during the seven months of de facto cease-fire."[7]

Several of UNTAG's early radio programs (and parts of other information efforts) were devoted to covering the events of early April and subsequent monitoring of the cease-fire. Fortunately, after early April, there was good news to report, and UNTAG's monitoring and information efforts worked to help calm fears, as predicted by H4. More details about these efforts are offered in the next section, on the civilian component.

Except for the SWAPO incursion, UNTAG enjoyed nearly complete cooperation and consent from the parties. UNTAG even demobilized most of the armed elements in Namibia, including the almost 12,000-strong South Africa–trained militia named the South West Africa Territorial Force. Consent was the major reason for UNTAG's success, and it became a virtuous circle as UNTAG's information efforts spread what became calming news. There was very little pre-election violence.

[6] United Nations, *Blue Helmets*, 3rd ed., 210–214, 228.

[7] Quotes from interview, Ayman El-Amir, Chief, Radio Section, United Nations, Department of Public Information, April 26, 1996; and United Nations, *Blue Helmets*, 3rd ed., 219, respectively. See also, "Namibia Independence Back on Track," and "The Crisis Unfolds," in *United Nations Chronicle*, 26, no. 2, (June 1989).

Civilian Component

The civilian component educated Namibians about democracy and elections. Namibians knew little about self-governance, and many did not believe the U.N. was impartial or did not even know what it was supposed to do. According to the U.N.,

> UNTAG personnel found that the Namibian people were, in many cases, perplexed about what was happening and what UNTAG actually was. As a result of many years of colonialism and apartheid, Namibia had a public information system which was geared to maintain this situation, with deeply partisan newspapers and a public broadcasting system prone to disinformation. UNTAG had to neutralize these processes and to provide Namibians with relevant and objective information.
>
> The effort was led by UNTAG's information service which used radio, television, all kinds of visual materials, and print, as well as the traditional word of mouth. . . . Information proved to be one of the key elements in UNTAG's operation; by the end, more than 200 radio broadcasts (usually translated into the country's many [13] languages), 32 television programmes, and more than 590,000 separate information items had been produced.[8]

According to Cedric Thornberry, director of the Office of the Special Representative of the Secretary-General in Namibia, "[I]gnorance has been generated by deliberate misinformation, and by rather unprofessional print media, sapping the capacity for independent judgement."[9]

Because of these background uncertainties and fears, and because of the poor and biased information environment, the situation was ripe for UNTAG to calm Namibians about the security situation in two ways. If UNTAG could use information to calm peoples' fears about their own security, this would support H4, which contends that transparency can lessen unwarranted fears. Also, if UNTAG could explain its mission to a skeptical populace, this would support H6, which predicts that self-transparency improves mission effectiveness by reducing unwarranted fears and uncertainty about the purpose of the operation.

Yet the idea of mounting an information operation to help with elections was new for the U.N. Indeed, the information component was left out of the mandate, and received a budget only at the last moment. Thornberry, responsible for day-to-day political operations, initially sat with fif-

---

[8] United Nations, *Blue Helmets*, 3rd ed., 220.

[9] Quoted in Fetherston, *Towards a Theory*, 67. See also, Jane Madden, "Namibia: A Lesson for Success," in Kevin Clements and Robin Ward, eds., *Building International Community: Cooperating for Peace Case Studies* (St. Leonards, Australia: Allen Unwin, 1994), 258.

teen of his staff trying to figure out, "What is an information campaign? Video, brochures, pamphlets for elections. . . ."[10]

Radio, television, print, and other such tools are mechanisms for providing transparency, and they are observable implications of hypothesis H1. Of these, the level of education in Namibia was too low for newspapers to be of great use, and television broadcast coverage was too limited. Many areas lacked telephone service. Thus, radio, simpler print products such as pamphlets, buttons, and stickers as well as direct people-to-people contact became the main mechanisms for the information campaign.[11] Over a hundred mobile teams were sent into the rural areas (home to 75 percent of the population) and forty-two regional or district offices were established to help educate people about the elections. The district centers were also tasked to gather information and help the information teams fine-tune their messages.[12]

The main topics and themes for the information campaign were voter registration, the code of conduct for the elections, secrecy of ballots, the process of voting repatriation of refugees, explaining the role of U.N. civilian police (UNCIVPOL) units, and explaining the disarming and removal of South African units. So much emphasis was placed on voter education because Namibia lacked a history of free and fair elections, and the election was the capstone of UNTAG's mandate. To help target its messages and keep up with current events in Namibia, the UNTAG information officers received weekly briefings from the Special Representative's office. UNTAG tried to enhance its messages by relying on professionalism, repetition of key themes, and avoidance of overt controversy. UNTAG's explanations about its mission and activities, or self-transparency (H6), successfully overcame much of the initial distrust and helped calm Namibians' suspicions about UNTAG, including worries about what UNTAG was doing in the country, or fears that UNTAG was not impartial.

An example of using the media on the issue of impartiality occurred when Thornberry took to the radio to respond to allegations from some that UNTAG was partial to SWAPO and from others that it was partial to South Africa: "I think if you are being criticized by both sides for being

[10] Interview, Fred Eckhard, Senior Liaison Officer, United Nations, Department of Peacekeeping Operations, April 19, 1996; and Lehmann, *Peacekeeping and Public Information,* 33.

[11] Interview, Ayman El-Amir, April 26, 1996. UNTAG itself had to rely on radios and satellite phones for much of its internal communications. Fortna, "United Nations Transition Assistance Group," 366. See also Lehmann, *Peacekeeping and Public Information,* 37–38 and 42, for more details on the poor media infrastructure in Namibia.

[12] Transcript of Programme No. 17, UNTAG Information Service (airdate is listed as July 3, 1989 on the transcript, but as July 4 on the index); and Lehmann, *Peacekeeping and Public Information,* 43–44.

partial to the other, then the likelihood is that you must be getting some of it right, some of the time . . . impartiality is an extremely important concept within 435 [the UN resolution authorizing UNTAG]."[13]

Related to educating Namibians about its mission and activities (H6) was UNTAG's "identity program" in which it tried to build up a positive "brand" image with its uniforms, as well as with posters, decals, sales of UNTAG clothing, and so forth. Catchy on-message slogans reminded Namibians that "It's your time to Choose for Namibia," "Free and Fair Elections mean . . . Your Vote is Secret," and "UNTAG Supervises and Controls the Voting Process." Giving schoolchildren UNTAG stickers and buttons was a "great tool" for gaining sympathy.[14]

UNTAG built credibility by being honest and not glossing over obvious problems. For example, on September 21, 1989, UNTAG reported on the radio that political intimidation was rife and increasing in the North as the political campaigning got more serious.[15] Intimidation in the North subsided and did not threaten the elections.[16]

Namibians harbored a number of specific, but often unwarranted, fears. The U.N. used information and the media as it worked to reduce them. For example, many refugees were fearful of returning home. In response, the U.N. told stories of successful repatriation in all the media. Others feared the return of South African forces. In response, the U.N. reported on the agreements that South Africa had signed, on the departure of tanks, on the monitoring of former trouble spots along border, and so forth, as well as on the attention being paid to the problem by the international community. Some worried that there would be no jobs when the U.N. left (these U.N. jobs were helpful in winning over the hearts, minds, and wallets of Namibians). In response, the U.N. announced all the agencies that would remain to help after UNTAG left: UNDP, UNICEF, WHO, UNFP, and UNESCO, among others.[17] Radio was used to defuse unwarranted fears and rumors about vigilantes, or hostile incidents between blacks and whites, as well as to channel rivalries between political parties into "honest confrontations."[18] Rumors that National Union for

---

[13] Transcript of Programme No. 6, UNTAG Information Service, airdate: June 19, 1989. Another program specifically addressing impartiality was No. 89, October 12, 1989.

[14] Lehmann, *Peacekeeping and Public Information,* 39–41, 36.

[15] Transcript of Programme No. 74, UNTAG Information Service, airdate: September 21, 1989.

[16] United Nations, *Blue Helmets,* 3rd ed., 224.

[17] Interview, Lena Yacoumopoulou, Film/Video Archives, United Nations Department of Public Information, April 23–24, 1996; sample radio broadcasts addressing some of these issues include nos. 42, 49, 54, 176, and 177.

[18] Interview, Ayman El-Amir, April 26, 1996.

the Total Independence of Angola (UNITA) members were coming into Namibia and registering to vote were addressed and refuted.[19]

Techniques for calming fears and rumors are revealed by looking at the transcripts of the radio programs.[20] The U.N. did not run its own station but had to use the state radio facilities. The broadcasts were only five minutes long and, to ensure tight control over content, none was performed live. The broadcasts' reputation and audience grew, in part because of the dearth of other media outlets, and also because of the Namibians' need for reliable information about UNTAG. Here are excerpts from a radio program that dealt with the fears of returnees:

> *Yacoumopoulou (host):* Today, more on the situation of the returnees. Returnees are naturally concerned about their future in Namibia. . . . Jeff Crisp, Information Officer for UNHCR [U.N. High Commissioner for Refugees], has recently returned from a visit to the reception centers—with this report.
>
> *Crisp:* Now of course UNHCR's primary responsibility is to ensure that refugees can come back to their homeland in conditions of safety . . . it's quite certain at the moment that there will be severe problems for some of the returnees in finding shelter . . . employment . . . medical care. . . . So there is a growing effort amongst the UN agencies . . . to see how [these problems] can be tackled.
>
> *Yacoumopoulou:* Another element that Jeff Crisp feels has been exaggerated in the press is that returnees are overwhelmed with fear.
>
> *Crisp:* Of course there's a degree of caution amongst people and it's totally understandable that if you've been out of your country for 10 or 12 years, you're not really sure where you're going back to . . . what reception you are going to get. . . . It is quite understandable that people should be cautious and perhaps even a little bit apprehensive. But I wouldn't say there was any genuine atmosphere of fear in the reception centres.
>
> *Yacoumopoulou:* On the whole, though, Jeff Crisp reports that the mood in the reception centres in the North is one of excitement and liveliness.

---

[19] Transcript of Programme No. 17, UNTAG Information Service, airdate: July 4, 1989 (transcript is misdated as July 3).

[20] I am grateful for the help of Lena Yacoumopoulou, who was a U.N. radio information officer in Namibia, for allowing me to review these transcripts and for talking with me at length about the U.N.'s operations in Namibia and elsewhere. Almost everyone I talked to at the U.N. was helpful, but she went beyond the call of duty. According to Fred Eckhard, then in the Department of Peacekeeping Operations (DPKO) and now the secretary-general's spokesperson, Yacoumopoulou single-handedly produced the radio programs in Namibia—something confirmed by the radio show transcripts, which show she was the interviewer for the vast majority of programs.

Crisp: As soon as they jump off the buses, they are looking around to see people they may not have seen for several years. Often there's spontaneous singing . . . and various forms of jubilation.[21]

In this excerpt, UNTAG is using information to calm the refugees' unwarranted fears for their safety, to refute overblown rumors about the extent of these fears, as well as to clarify its own actions. The U.N. is being honest about the fears, but it is also reporting that things are not as bad as rumored in the local press and that the U.N. is working hard to fix whatever problems remain. This is evidence of UNTAG using information mechanisms to provide transparency, an observable implication of H1. The effects of these transparency-increasing efforts to reduce fears and clarify the operation's purpose were confirmed in interviews, and this provides evidence for H4, which contends that transparency reduces fears, and H6, which predicts that self-transparency can help parties understand the actions of the regime.[22] Forty-three thousand refugees were successfully repatriated.[23]

There were many similar broadcasts explaining the election process, assuring voters about the secrecy of ballots, giving details about how UNTAG was monitoring South African forces, and so forth.[24]

A dramatic example of the power of information and investigations occurred in the days just prior to the elections. South Africa escalated its longtime claims that SWAPO, operating from bases in Angola, was about to invade Namibia. South Africa cited intercepted messages between UNTAG military units who had supposedly been monitoring pre-invasion activities. UNTAG's special representative, Martti Ahtissari, investigated the charges, reviewed the transcripts, quickly proved them to be fraudulent, and the South African foreign minister publicly withdrew the charges two days later. This was the last event "in what had appeared to be a campaign by certain quarters to disrupt the independence process through disinformation and other, more direct, means, including an attack on UNTAG's regional office in Outjo." This episode is clear evidence in support of H5, which contends that regimes can conduct investigations and

---

[21] Transcript of Programme No. 22, UNTAG Information Service, airdate: July 11, 1989. Most of the radio programs were of this short interview format where an expert or responsible official was asked to comment on various topics of concern.

[22] Interviews with Lena Yacoumopoulou, April 23–24, 1996; and Fred Eckhard, April 19, 1996.

[23] United Nations, *Blue Helmets,* 3rd ed., 225. A story, "UNTAG Goes Home," in the *United Nations Chronicle* 27, no. 2 (June 1990), claims that 433,000 exiles were repatriated, but *Blue Helmets* is authoritative.

[24] See, for example, transcripts of UNTAG Information Service Programmes nos. 11–19, 93–94, and 100–104, among many.

use the resulting information to coerce more lawful or peaceful behavior from aggressors and troublemakers.[25]

Overall, "the ability of the United Nations to overcome the suspicions and hostility it faced . . . was also a key to its success" and UNTAG's information program "was probably the best that the United Nations is capable of mustering in the field."[26] Why were UNTAG's media, liaison, and outreach efforts so effective? In good part because they increased transparency and thereby reduced rumors and fears.

In the end, UNTAG succeeded in holding the pivotal elections. UNTAG registered 701,000 voters out of the total Namibian population of 1.3–1.5 million people. Ninety-six percent of eligible voters voted between November 7 and 11, 1989. A scant 1.4 percent of the ballots were rejected. SWAPO received 57 percent of the vote and the U.N. declared the elections free and fair on the 14th. The new Constituent Assembly quickly set about the task of writing a constitution. Thanks primarily to the overall cooperation and consent of relevant local, regional, and international actors, Namibia's conflict was over. While cooperation and consent were crucial, UNTAG's information operation and its efforts to increase transparency played a clear role in helping create the conditions necessary for a free and fair election.[27]

CONCLUSION: UNTAG AND TRANSPARENCY

UNTAG came into being largely because of political changes at international and domestic levels. Transparency involved with the Cuban departure from Angola helped trigger peace in Namibia, and this offers support for H2, the hypothesis that transparency promotes cooperation. On the other hand, the promise of transparency was not a factor in UNTAG's actual deployment. Thus, overall, H2 is at best only moderately supported.

Fortunately, UNTAG's military component faced largely consensual adversaries (after an initial debacle). Thus, the information division could report mostly good and calming news about the durability of the cease-fire

---

[25] United Nations, *Blue Helmets,* 3rd ed., 222; see also *Reports of the Secretary-General* S/20943, November 3, 1989, and S/20947, November 4, 1989.

[26] Fen Osler Hampson, *Nurturing Peace: Why Peace Settlements Succeed or Fail* (Washington, DC: United States Institute of Peace Press, 1996), 54 and Lehmann, *Peacekeeping and Public Information,* 46.

[27] In addition to specific references, general sources for this chapter include Paul F. Diehl and Sonia R. Jurado, "United Nations Election Supervision in South Africa: Lessons from the Namibian Peacekeeping Experience," *Terrorism* 16 (January/March 1993); James, *Peacekeeping in International Politics,* part IV, section K; Fetherston, *Towards a Theory,* 62–78; Fortna, "United Nations Transition Assistance Group"; Lehmann, *Peacekeeping and Public Information,* chap. 3; and United Nations, *Blue Helmets,* 3rd ed., chap. 11.

TABLE 6-1
Findings by Hypothesis

Hypothesis	Evidence	Strength of evidence	Overall strength of hypothesis
Regimes provide transparency (H1)	Monitoring, radio, and other information tools used in military component, pp. 144, 145	Moderate	Moderate/ Strong
	Radio, television, print, and other tools used in civil component, pp. 146, 147	Strong	
Regimes spread misinformation (H1′)	No evidence		
Anticipated transparency promotes cooperation (H2)	Monitoring Cuban withdrawal from Angola helped spur Namibia accord, p. 143	Moderate/ Weak	Moderate/ Weak
Anticipated transparency hinders cooperation (H2′)	No evidence		
Transparency promotes cooperation and prevents conflict (H3)	No evidence		
Transparency hinders cooperation and causes conflict (H3′)	No evidence		

(continued)

TABLE 6-1 (continued)

Hypothesis	Evidence	Strength of evidence	Overall strength of hypothesis
Transparency reduces unwarranted fears and worst-case assumptions (H4)	After initial setback, information used to calm fears about possible violence during cease-fire, p. 145	Moderate/Strong	Moderate/Strong
	UNTAG calmed fears about repatriation, South African forces, and even jobs, pp. 146, 150	Strong	
Transparency confirms fears (H4')	No evidence		
Transparency reduces cheating, rogue, and spoiler problems (H5)	Investigating claims of a SWAPO pre-election incursion, and getting South Africa to withdraw those claims, p. 150	Strong	Moderate
Transparency about the regime (or self-transparency) increases its effectiveness (H6)	UNTAG used information to tell suspicious Namibians about its mission and about how elections worked, pp. 146, 148, 150	Strong	Strong

Note: Coding: "Strong" means that the phenomenon or effect was clear and very influential if not decisive, producing behavior that would be hard to replicate without the regime. "Moderate" means that the phenomenon played a discernible and somewhat influential role. Other factors help explain the outcome. "Weak" means that the phenomenon was probably but only weakly present. Other factors explain most of the outcome. "Failure" means that the regime tried to do something and failed, or that something that the regime did was counterproductive. The overall ratings are judgments based on the significance of transparency and its effects for each hypothesis within the context of each case.

and departure of foreign troops. This information helped reduce fears, which supports H4: Transparency can reduce unwarranted fears.

Transparency was a larger factor in the civilian aspects of the mandate, and UNTAG reduced rumors and fears in a number of areas, including the electoral process and repatriation of refugees. These efforts provided much clear evidence for H4. UNTAG also expended considerable effort clarifying the purposes of its mission and calming fears that it was partial to one side or the other. Success here provided evidence for H6, which predicts that self-transparency reduces unwarranted fears and clarifies purpose. Table 6-1 summarizes these findings.

Why did UNTAG succeed with information and transparency? The country had a poor media infrastructure, and the media that did exist lacked credibility. This made it relatively easy for the U.N. to provide credible, authoritative, transparency-increasing information. These themes are reinforced in the next chapter on Cambodia.

According to Yacoumopoulou, another key variable was that there was no government in place opposing UNTAG's broadcasting. She noted that government opposition explained why the U.N. radio in Rwanda never worked and that the refugees there were still in fear, and she pointed out the troubles that Slobodan Milosevic caused for independent Yugoslav broadcaster Studio B92.

CHAPTER SEVEN

The United Nations Transitional Authority in Cambodia

THIS CHAPTER begins by describing the negotiations leading to the creation of the United Nations Transitional Authority in Cambodia (UNTAC). The promise of transparency played a small part in getting the Cambodian parties to agree to peace (H2), but the biggest factor behind UNTAC's formation was shifts in regional and great power politics. I then assess UNTAC's extensive operations on the ground, which included everything from refugee repatriation to holding elections. Although many aspects of UNTAC's activities did not involve much transparency, a number of analysts laud UNTAC's effective use of the media to promote its message and reduce fears and rumors. UNTAC helped Cambodians understand its mission, taught people how to vote and not to fear elections, and refuted rumors of polling place violence during the election. This chapter provides vivid evidence supporting H4, which contends that transparency reduces unwarranted fears and worst-case assumptions, and H6, which predicts that self-transparency reduces unwarranted fears and clarifies purpose. In the history of U.N. peacekeeping, UNTAC provides the exemplar of information operations and the effectiveness of transparency in promoting peace.

PEACE NEGOTIATIONS AND THE ROLE OF TRANSPARENCY (H2)

UNTAC was created in 1991 after two decades of murderous turmoil in Cambodia. Cambodia gained independence from France in 1954. In 1970, the U.S.-backed General Lon Nol overthrew the French-installed Prince Norodom Sihanouk. The China-backed Khmer Rouge under Pol Pot quickly began an insurgency against Lon Nol that succeeded in toppling him in 1975. During their short rule, the Khmer Rouge killed at least one million Cambodians (one in eight), targeting the educated elites in particular. Vietnam invaded Cambodia in late 1978, in part to put an end to border skirmishes with the Khmer Rouge. With Soviet support, Vietnam installed its own puppet party under Heng Samrin and Hun Sen. A counter-coalition of rebel factions involving Sihanouk and Khmer Rouge, and backed by China and the United States, then formed against the new but internationally unrecognized government in Phnom Penh.

The civil war continued along for years until April 1989, when Vietnam announced that its troops would leave the country. This announcement coincided with a number of developments that led the major outside powers to rethink their commitments to their clients and that helped make the end of the conflict possible. The end of the Cold War made strange bedfellows less necessary. The United States stopped backing China's support of the Khmer Rouge, which in the Cold War context had fought against the Soviet-backed, Vietnam-installed Hun Sen government. Perhaps more importantly, China backed off, because the Soviets pulled away from Vietnam and began to warm up ties with China (and of course with the United States) as the Cold War ended. Finally, within Cambodia, the civil war had "reached something of a 'mutually hurting stalemate.'"[1]

Earlier peace conferences sponsored by Indonesia in 1988 and 1989 brought all the Cambodian factions together but did not bring peace. Vietnam's announced withdrawal, however, prompted the French and Indonesians to rededicate themselves to the peace process, and the first Paris Conference was held in July 1989. The negotiations bogged down over power-sharing arrangements during the interim period before elections. Hun Sen rejected power-sharing in general and sharing with the Khmer Rouge in particular.

The idea that broke the deadlock was to transfer most political power in Cambodia to the U.N. during the interim period. A weak Supreme National Council (SNC) made up of members from each of the factions would hold or symbolize national unity and sovereignty, but real administrative power would lie with what became UNTAC. Under the accords, the SNC granted the U.N. all powers necessary to assure the peace agreement's implementation. The U.N. was mandated to

> organize and conduct free and fair elections; coordinate the repatriation of Cambodian refugees and displaced persons; coordinate a major programme of economic and financial support for rehabilitation and reconstruction; supervise, monitor and verify the withdrawal of foreign forces, the cease-fire, the cessation of outside military assistance to all Cambodian factions, and the demobilization of at least 70 percent of the military forces of the factions; coordinate, with the International Committee of the Red Cross, the release of all prisoners of war and civilian internees; and foster an environment of peace and stability in

[1] Trevor Findlay, *Cambodia: The Legacy and Lessons of UNTAC*, SIPRI Research Report No. 9 (Oxford, England: Oxford University Press, 1995), 3, quoting I. W. Zartman's well-known phrase.

which all Cambodians could enjoy the rights and freedoms embodied in the Universal Declaration of Human Rights."[2]

One reason that the U.N. was given such an unprecedented degree of authority was that the "parties could not trust each other enough to rule together [so the U.N. had to] take over the administration of Cambodia during the period between a political settlement and the installment of freely, democratically elected leaders."[3] Such a need for a security regime confirms H2, which hypothesizes that the anticipation of regime-provided transparency promotes cooperation.

Setting the stage for the provision of transparency, Article 6 of the Paris Agreements paid special attention to several areas, one of which was information. The U.N. secretary-general's implementation plan for UNTAC also gave a role for information including the establishment of radio broadcasting capabilities. The new Advisor on Information to the Special Representative of the Secretary-General (a brand new post) Tim Carney said that the parties to the Paris Peace Accords acknowledged early on "the vital, central role of information," and these various encouragements let him "treat information imaginatively."[4]

Two specific areas of the U.N.'s mandate required significant monitoring and verification by the U.N. for them to work: (1) the elections and (2) the cease-fire and other limits on forces and arms. Here again, the prospect of increased transparency assuaged the fears of participants and helped lead them to sign the accord (H2). For example, Hun Sen's State of Cambodia party (SOC) during the negotiation said they felt endangered by the prospect of military demobilization.[5] Seeking reassurance in the form of U.N. monitors, Sihanouk in his role as president of the Supreme National Council requested to have "200 UN personnel sent to Cambodia as 'observers' in September 1991 in order to assist the SNC in controlling the cease-fire and the cessation of foreign military assistance, as a first step within the framework of a comprehensive political settlement."[6] For their part, the U.N. Permanent Five and

---

[2] United Nations, Department of Public Information, *The United Nations and Cambodia: 1991–1995*, United Nations Blue Book Series, vol. 2 (New York: United Nations, 1995), 9.

[3] Doyle, *UN Peacekeeping in Cambodia*, 23.

[4] Lehmann, *Peacekeeping and Public Information*, 60–61, quoting Carney on p. 60.

[5] Carlyle A. Thayer, "The United Nations Transitional Authority in Cambodia: The Restoration of Sovereignty," in Tom Woodhouse, Robert Bruce, and Malcolm Dando, eds., *Peacekeeping and Peacemaking: Towards Effective Intervention in Post–Cold War Conflicts* (New York: St. Martin's, 1998), 150.

[6] Letter to the U.N. Secretary-General, transmitting the final communique of the SNC's meeting in Pattaya, August 26–29, 1991. A/46/494-S/23066, September 24, 1991, Document 15, in United Nations, *The United Nations and Cambodia*, 122.

Indonesia insisted on U.N. verification for the military aspects of the accord.[7]

It appears that the anticipation of transparency played some role in helping bring the leaders of the factions to sign the Paris Accords in October 1991, and H2 receives some support.

Two other factors, however, were more important than transparency in bringing about the peace accords. First, most of what became the peace accords was worked out ahead of time by the U.N. Permanent Five and other outside players, including Australia, Indonesia, and Japan. The draft framework reached by these players was then sold to or forced on the Cambodian factions. Findlay notes, "To a great extent the Accords were pressed on a mostly reluctant Cambodian political elite by an international community eager to be rid of the Cambodian problem."[8] Of particular importance appears to be a secret agreement between Vietnam and China to pressure their clients (Hun Sen and the coalition that included Sihanouk for Vietnam, and the Khmer Rouge for China) into compliance.[9] This agreement was in turn made possible by the political shifts occurring as the Cold War ended and because China wanted to repair its image after the bloody suppression of the uprising at Tiananmen square. Power politics played the greatest role in getting the war-weary factions to accept the draft framework for peace.

Second, even if the promise of transparency played a role in getting the factions to accept the peace accord, the promise of the U.N.'s physical presence probably played an even larger role as an anticipated deterrent to their adversaries' aggression or trouble-making. Physical deterrence likely outweighed transparency in calming fears of adversaries. That said, deterrence and transparency are not mutually exclusive products of UNTAC because the same peacekeepers provide both functions.

Finally, fights over transparency-related issues also bogged down negotiations—further undercutting the role of transparency in promoting agreement (H2). For example, Hun Sen and the SOC tried to maintain their leadership and political advantages by lobbying to limit the size of U.N. monitoring during the negotiations. On the other hand, most of the op-

[7] Letter dated August 1, 1991 to the U.N. Secretary-General, from China, France, Indonesia, the USSR, the United Kingdom, and the United States transmitting communique of the Co-Chairmen of the Paris Conference on Cambodia and the five permanent members of the Security Council issued in Beijing, July 18, 1991. A/46/340-S/22889, 5 August 1991, Document 12, in United Nations, *The United Nations and Cambodia,* 118.

[8] Findlay, *Cambodia,* 16. See also Tali Levy, "The 1991 Cambodia Settlement Agreements," in *Words Over War: Mediation and Arbitration to Prevent Deadly Conflict* (Lanham, MD: Rowman and Littlefield, for the Carnegie Corporation of New York, 2000), 148–56; and James A. Schear, "Riding the Tiger: The United Nations and Cambodia's Struggle for Peace," in Durch, ed., *UN Peacekeeping,* 139.

[9] Janet E. Heininger, *Peacekeeping in Transition: The United Nations in Cambodia* (New York: Twentieth Century Fund, 1994), 23.

position groups tried to counter these advantages by pushing to increase the size of any monitoring force that would deploy subsequent to a peace deal.[10] A twist on this was the Khmer Rouge's position that it wanted maximum disarmament, knowing the Phnom Penh-based SOC's forces would be easier to monitor than its more far-flung troops.[11]

Although the factions accepted the draft framework in September 1990, it took months of wrangling over still more demobilization and election issues until the final Paris Peace Accords were signed in October 1991. During these negotiations, the civil war raged until being tempered by a cease-fire in May 1991.[12]

The U.N. Advance Mission in Cambodia

The U.N. sent the Advance Mission in Cambodia (UNAMIC) in November 1991 to pave the way for UNTAC's March 1992 deployment. UNAMIC's primary mission was to maintain the cease-fire until the arrival of UNTAC. It also began de-mining the country.

To maintain the cease-fire, the plan for UNAMIC "called for a team of 50 military liaison officers who would, in a good-offices role, aim to facilitate communications between the military headquarters of the four Cambodian factions by, for example, passing messages between the factions and arranging meetings between them."[13] UNAMIC was also supposed to work with the Mixed Military Working Group (MMWG), a forum

[10] Sorpong Peou, *Conflict Neutralization in the Cambodia War: From Battlefield to Ballot Box* (Oxford, England: Oxford University Press, 1997), 40, 45.

[11] Jin Song, "The Political Dynamics of the Peacemaking Process in Cambodia," in Michael W. Doyle, Ian Johnstone, and Robert C. Orr, eds., *Keeping the Peace: Multidimensional UN Operations in Cambodia and El Salvador* (Cambridge, England: Cambridge University Press, 1997), 75.

[12] The general sources for the preceding text include Mats Berdal and Michael Leifer, "Cambodia," in James Mayall, ed., *The New Interventionism 1991–1994: United Nations Experience in Cambodia, former Yugoslavia and Somalia* (Cambridge, England: Cambridge University Press, 1996), 25–36; MacAlister Brown and Joseph J. Zasloff, *Cambodia Confounds the Peacemakers: 1979–1998* (Ithaca, NY: Cornell University Press, 1998), chap. 2; Doyle, *UN Peacekeeping in Cambodia*, 13–31; Findlay, *Cambodia*, 1–20; Heininger, *Peacekeeping in Transition*, 9–31; Peou, *Conflict Neutralization*, chaps. 1, 2, and 4; Steven R. Ratner, "The United Nations in Cambodia: A Model for the Resolution of Internal Conflicts?" in Lori Fisler Damrosch, ed., *Enforcing Restraint: Collective Intervention in Internal Conflicts* (New York: Council on Foreign Relations Press, 1993), 241–52; Schear, "Riding the Tiger," 136–51; Song, "Political Dynamics"; United Nations, *The United Nations and Cambodia*, 5–9; United Nations, *Blue Helmets*, 3rd ed., 449–58; and United States, Department of State, "Background Notes: Cambodia, January 1996," available at gopher://gopher.state.gov.

[13] United Nations, *The United Nations and Cambodia*, 10.

established by the Paris Accords to bring together military representatives of the Cambodian factions.

One could not ask for a clearer plan to increase transparency. From liaison officers to forums to a commitment to facilitating communication, many mechanisms and intentions to increase transparency are evident (H1). Yet the evidence raises doubts about UNAMIC's performance as a liaison. For example, Sihanouk said that UNTAC's absence during the early phases of the peace left the factions without a neutral mediator to deal with political and military tensions. This was said despite UNAMIC's presence, and thus serves as a critique of its service as liaison. Second, the Khmer Rouge repeatedly violated the cease-fire and boycotted a meeting of the MMWG during UNAMIC's tenure. Third, UNAMIC lacked investigative rigor. Finally, UNAMIC personnel also had trouble communicating with the Cambodians due to language difficulties.[14] Communication is a prerequisite for providing transparency.

Because of these difficulties, the U.N.'s initial involvement reflects a failure for H1, which contends that regimes can provide transparency. There is thus no need to search for the effects of transparency.

Further, UNAMIC's overall effectiveness in maintaining the cease-fire was poor. The entire Cambodian settlement was on the verge of unraveling by the time UNTAC began its deployment four months later, in March of 1992 (by the end of April, only 3,700 UNTAC troops and personnel had arrived out of a planned full strength of 22,000). UNTAC was not fully operational until September 1992. UNTAC's late arrival and slow start combined with UNAMICs small size to create a crisis in Cambodians' faith that the U.N. could keep the peace and fulfill its ambitious mandate.

In February of 1992, four months after the accords had been signed, the U.N. Security Council passed resolution 745 establishing UNTAC. The deployment began in March, and UNTAC's size grew to 22,000 staff, including 16,000 peacekeepers from more than thirty countries. The operation cost $1.9 billion, and peacekeepers had just eighteen months to accomplish their wide array of mandated tasks. These tasks ranged from disarming and cantoning 200,000 regular troops and disarming 250,000 militia to repatriating 360,000–370,000 refugees and holding a nationwide election. UNTAC did not achieve its full strength and was not fully operational until about a third of the way through its mandate. Cambodia is a country of 181,000 square kilometers, about the size of Oklahoma, and its population in the early 1990s was around nine million.[15]

[14] Findlay, *Cambodia*, 24–26, 119; Peou, *Conflict Neutralization*, 177–84.
[15] Schear, "Riding the Tiger," 144–45; United States CIA, *World Factbook*, available at www.cia.gov/cia/publications/factbook/index.html; 1990 population figures from World Health Organization, *Tobacco or Health: A Global Status Report, Country Profiles by Region, 1997*, available at: www.cdc.gov/tobacco/who/cambodia.htm.

UNTAC: Mandate, Activities, and Transparency

UNTAC's mandate falls into two broad categories: a military component and a civilian component. I review these two areas and assess the role that transparency played in UNTAC's performance.

UNTAC's Military Component

In military affairs, UNTAC was mandated to do the following:[16]

1. monitor the cease-fire and disengagement of forces
2. monitor withdrawal of foreign forces (Vietnamese forces) from Cambodia
3. facilitate and monitor the demobilization and disarming of 70 percent of each factions' forces
4. facilitate and monitor the cantonment of the remaining 30 percent of each factions' forces
5. conduct mine clearance

In theory, transparency should have contributed significantly to UNTAC's military missions. From the cease-fire and disarming to cantonment, UNTAC's monitoring and verification could have given each side the assurance that others were indeed adhering to the accords, which could have further increased compliance and helped build peace. Unfortunately, obstructionist policies implemented primarily by the Khmer Rouge (but also by Hun Sen's party, the State of Cambodia or SOC) torpedoed most of UNTAC's military mandate and made efforts to increase transparency in this area irrelevant. A transparency lesson here is that regimes cannot provide transparency (H1) when adversaries reject the regime and do not want to cooperate in the first place.

UNTAC's military mission fell apart in several ways. First of all, fighting continued sporadically throughout UNTAC's tenure, albeit at a lower level than before. No one needed UNTAC to tell the factions that fighting and violence continued. A major exception to this was during the election, discussed in the next section. UNTAC's ability to tell the people that there was no electoral violence greatly increased the turnout and the overall success of the elections.

Second, UNTAC lacked the power to enforce or effectively coerce demobilization, disarming, and cantonment. As James A. Schear points out, UNTAC was between a rock and a hard place. UNTAC would look bad

---

[16] The following is drawn largely from Schear, "Riding the Tiger," 146–49.

if it tried to coerce the parties, because UNTAC's relative weakness and inability to resort to force meant that it would inevitably fail. On the other hand, voluntary compliance was likely to fail as well because the Khmer Rouge resisted the military aspects of UNTAC's mandate almost from the start.[17] Seeing the writing on the wall, UNTAC made cantonment voluntary and partial. By November 1992, UNTAC had completely suspended its efforts to disarm, demobilize, and canton the factions.[18]

Because of these failures, there was little to verify with respect to demobilization, disarming, and cantonment, and so transparency was not relevant. Again, the factions did not need the U.N. to tell them the agreements had been violated.

Related to this problem were deficiencies in gathering military intelligence. The U.N. is wary of intelligence-gathering, fearing for its image of peaceful impartiality. Because of this, much of whatever intelligence that U.N. operations do collect comes from the press and information components of the operations. UNTAC could not determine the real strength of the Khmer Rouge, definitively refute Khmer Rouge claims that Vietnamese forces were still in Cambodia, or even adequately monitor its own operation. Within the military component, there were many ways in which UNTAC failed to obtain information, making it impossible to provide transparency (H1).[19]

Third, there were a number of ways in which UNTAC's specific efforts to increase transparency failed. For example, the Khmer Rouge simply did not believe potentially calming reports (H4) from UNTAC's Strategic Investigation Teams that monitored the presence of foreign forces and cease-fire violations. Although its intelligence capabilities were weak, UNTAC found almost no evidence of Vietnamese or Vietnam-controlled forces in country. The Khmer Rouge disputed these findings, disagreed with the definition of foreign forces, and never provided to UNTAC the required information on the manpower and materiel of its own forces. Willful disbelief, preformed judgements, resistance to UNTAC, and UNTAC's inadequate intelligence capabilities all undermined the peacekeepers' ability to provide transparency (H1) and exploit transparency to reduce fears and lessen tensions (H4).

Fourth, some 50,000 troops were sent into cantonment and as many weapons were turned over to the U.N. Most of these were from the SOC. Many of the weapons were not operable, however, and the troops (if they were soldiers at all) were of such poor quality that the SOC actually im-

---

[17] Schear, "Riding the Tiger," 154.

[18] United Nations, *Blue Helmets*, 3rd ed., 476; Heininger, *Peacekeeping in Transition*, 70–72.

[19] Berdal and Leifer, "Cambodia," 48–49.

proved its army by getting rid of them. Many of these soldiers left the cantons on agricultural leave.[20] Hence, even here, there was little calming news for the U.N. to spread.

On the plus side, UNTAC made serious efforts to start de-mining Cambodia. It trained 2,300 Cambodians and disposed of 37,000 out of six to ten million mines. Admirable as this was, this meant that only one-half of one percent of the mines were removed (de-mining continues to this day). Also, de-mining's success has little to do with transparency.[21]

In sum, where UNTAC could have increased transparency in the military mission, noncompliance meant that there was little to verify or monitor. Investigative and monitoring capabilities were weak with respect to military intelligence. For this reason, and bias, the Khmer Rouge dismissed UNTAC's reports that foreign forces had left Cambodia. Failures in the military mission and weakness in transparency mechanisms (H1) left no hope that fears could be assuaged (H4). Given this, the peaceful elections seem remarkable and the later failure of democracy predictable.

UNTAC's Civil Components

In civil affairs, UNTAC was given this mandate:

1. repatriate approximately 360,000–370,000 refugees
2. restore and rehabilitate aspects of Cambodia's infrastructure in areas including housing, transport, utilities, and education
3. control most major aspects of civil administration (defense, foreign affairs, finance, public security, and information) and supervise those other aspects of governance that could influence the elections
4. promote human rights with an education campaign, monitoring, investigations, and supervision of local law enforcement
5. organize and conduct free and fair elections, including civic education and election monitoring
6. conduct an information program to support UNTAC's activities and educate Cambodians about the Peace Accords and UNTAC's missions

UNTAC's civil mandate was complex, had mixed results, and each element depended in varying degrees on transparency for its success. In the order outlined, I assess UNTAC's effectiveness with its civil mandate and the role of transparency in whatever was achieved. Information/education

---

[20] Heininger, *Peacekeeping in Transition*, 71.

[21] The preceding section was based on Berdal and Leifer, "Cambodia," 36–43; Findlay, *Cambodia*, 36–51, 72; Schear, "Riding the Tiger," 156–58; United Nations, *Blue Helmets*, 3rd ed., 476–77; Jianwei Wang, *Managing Arms in Peace Processes: Cambodia*, UNIDIR/96/17 (New York: United Nations, 1996).

was explicitly part of several aspects of UNTAC's civil mandate: in human rights and especially in preparing Cambodians for the election—the sine qua non of UNTAC's mandate. In contrast to the military component, transparency played a large role in UNTAC's success in sponsoring the elections.

REFUGEE REPATRIATION

Refugee repatriation worked well. Slightly more than the estimated 360,000–370,000 refugees returned to Cambodia. There were many reasons for this success. The refugees wanted to return. Thailand, where most refugees were located, wished to get them out. The Cambodian factions cooperated with their return. And the U.N. offered cash, jobs, food, and/or land to returning refugees. The U.N. High Commissioner for Refugees helped logistically, and this engendered cooperation from the Khmer Rouge, who were much more willing to cooperate with the UNHCR than with UNTAC. In addition, Cambodia's factions all saw the refugees as returning members or as potential new members. There was not a single deliberately disruptive incident in the whole endeavor.[22]

Despite all these interest- and incentive-based reasons for the success of repatriation, transparency played a modest role. "Making certain that all factions were apprized of developments in the repatriation process, which entailed endless dialogue and negotiation, helped allay their suspicions and gain their cooperation."[23] In other words, UNTAC increased transparency (H1) and reduced apprehensions (H4).

REHABILITATION AND RECONSTRUCTION

Rehabilitation and reconstruction did not work out as well as planned, and the results had little to do with transparency. Although the international community ended up pledging $880 million for Cambodia's reconstruction, well over the $593 million planned, disbursement of funds was slow. Only $100 million had been spent prior to the election.[24] Logistical and political difficulties plagued planned projects.

Long-term, large-scale projects were difficult to start, much less complete, during UNTAC's short tenure. Much of the aid ended up being focused on the Phnom Penh area simply because that was where it was easier to get things done. This helped the SOC, which was dominant in that region and angered the rural Khmer Rouge. The Khmer Rouge blocked some rehabilitation projects, even though considerable funds would have

[22] Findlay, *Cambodia*, 52–54; Heininger, *Peacekeeping in Transition*, 48–54; and Schear, "Riding the Tiger," 163.

[23] Heininger, *Peacekeeping in Transition*, 54.

[24] Brown and Zasloff, *Cambodia Confounds the Peacemakers*, 124–25.

been spent in areas it controlled. On the positive side, jobs were created, and the basis was laid for further reconstruction of war-torn Cambodia.[25]

CIVIL CONTROL

UNTAC's mandate for civil control called for supervision of the five main branches of government (defense, foreign affairs, finance, public security, and information, as well as any other branch that could affect the elections). This in turn required monitoring and gathering large amounts of information. To do this, UNTAC attached teams to all major sectors of government and maintained a separate investigations division. The purpose of such massive oversight was to maintain a neutral political environment during the pre-election interim period. According to its mandate, UNTAC should have been in a good position to gather information, correct abuses, introduce transparency in government, and reassure all factions that the interim government was working fairly, effectively, and impartially. Because of these roles and intended effects, any success that UNTAC enjoyed with its civil control mandate should have depended to a significant degree on transparency (H1) for reassurance (H4), and to deter (or catch) spoilers (H5).

As it turned out, UNTAC faced numerous difficulties in civil control, many of which affected its ability to provide transparency (H1), calm the factions (H4), and stop spoilers (H5). First, the parties varied in their cooperation with UNTAC. The Khmer Rouge, as usual, resisted UNTAC's efforts. The smaller factions, including Sihanouk's FUNCINPEC (Front Uni National pour un Cambodge Independent, Neutre, Pacifique, et Cooperatif),[26] had very little structure to monitor at all. As a result, UNTAC focused its monitoring on the SOC in Phnom Penh. The SOC viewed this disproportionate attention as discriminatory and it became uncooperative. UNTAC's greatest failure in this respect was its inability to reign in the SOC's security forces and secret police. The continued activity of SOC's forces endangered the neutral political environment that UNTAC was trying to create.[27] The SOC's resistance to UNTAC's monitoring supports H2', which contends that anticipated transparency hinders cooperation.[28]

---

[25] Findlay, *Cambodia*, 69–72; Heininger, *Peacekeeping in Transition*, 54–64; United Nations, *Blue Helmets*, 3rd ed., 480–81.

[26] United National Front for an Independent, Neutral, Peaceful, and Cooperative Cambodia.

[27] Findlay, *Cambodia*, 60.

[28] This situation supports H2': Anticipated transparency hinders cooperation, rather than H3': Transparency hinders cooperation, because the SOC resisted UNTAC's attempts to monitor it and this hurt the operation. H3' is supported when the actual, rather than anticipated, effects of transparency hurt cooperation.

Second, despite its relatively elaborate and formalized organization, the SOC did not govern in ways that could be effectively monitored. Power often resided with army officers, provincial governors, local officials, relatives of bureaucrats, and so forth. Many decisions were made informally and without written record.

Finally, UNTAC was simply overwhelmed by this very sophisticated task. UNTAC was slow to assert its authority and never caught up. The quality of its personnel varied and was sometimes poor.

All of these factors meant that UNTAC did not do very well at civil control, had difficulty monitoring government functions, and therefore could not provide much transparency. While these problems caused a near failure for H1, UNTAC did introduce "a fair amount of transparency into Cambodia's institutions," and this might in turn have deterred abuses by helping identify fraud or partisan use of government power or facilities. Had this worked, institutional transparency would have provided evidence that information disclosure deters or coerces cheaters and spoilers (H5).[29] It did not work very well, however, because the SOC in particular "evaded UN controls" and often prevented information from being gathered in the first place.[30] Thwarting of monitoring by the U.N. Civilian Administration Component included creative use of wireless phones by government officials and switching of government functions to agencies not under U.N. supervision.[31]

Despite such resistance, analysts agree that without UNTAC's attempts at civil control, the situation would have been worse. Even more abuses, violence, and political harassment would have occurred. Some analysts suggest that UNTAC planted a seed for further maturation of Cambodia's political institutions.[32] Nonetheless, the litany of problems lead me to code this as "weak/failure" for H5, because U.N. efforts to monitor cheating, rogues, and spoilers were so frequently thwarted, and the U.N. could not use information to coerce better behavior.

PROMOTION AND PROTECTION OF HUMAN RIGHTS

UNTAC had limited success with its mandate to promote and protect human rights. Although information and education were central to UNTAC's efforts to promote human rights, transparency appears not to have played much of a part.

Human rights abuses continued throughout UNTAC's tenure, though

---

[29] Schear, "Riding the Tiger," 159.

[30] Thayer, "United Nations Transitional Authority in Cambodia," 158.

[31] Brown and Zasloff, *Cambodia Confounds the Peacemakers*, 105–6.

[32] Ibid., 107–8; Findlay, *Cambodia*, 59–63; Heininger, *Peacekeeping in Transition*, 83–90; Schear, "Riding the Tiger," 158–61.

nowhere near the level of those committed during Pol Pot's murderous regime. UNTAC's small human rights staff documented a number of abuses, but it could not arrest violators or fire them from government posts. Although the secretary-general's Special Representative could transfer personnel found to be hindering the peace agreements,[33] UNTAC mainly had to rely on the SOC to police and judge the human rights violators whom it had identified. This often amounted to the bad guys watching the bad guys, and so enforcement was rare.[34] Asia Watch harshly criticized UNTAC for failing to take concrete actions to defend human rights and punish abusers. This represents a failure for H5, because UNTAC did not even try to stop cheaters, rogues, and spoilers even though it knew violations were occurring.

Further, UNTAC often had to work with violators in other areas of its operations, and so antagonizing these officials (or others) on the basis of human rights violations jeopardized other aspects of the mandate. UNTAC therefore focused more on human rights education, than on accusing human rights violators.[35] While UNTAC tried to train judges and lawyers, it did not have the resources to conduct a more sweeping overhaul of Cambodia's judicial system. Most lawyers and judges and others with any sort of higher education and training had been killed by Pol Pot's regime, leaving Cambodia ill-prepared to govern itself.

On the positive side, all four major factions, including the Khmer Rouge, signed onto major international human rights agreements. UNTAC helped gain the release of several hundred political prisoners. UNTAC undertook a large-scale, countrywide human rights education campaign. Using a wide range of information tools from radio to puppets and cartoon flyers, UNTAC raised awareness in Cambodia about human rights. About 150,000 Cambodians joined human rights groups. Cambodia also gained what Michael Doyle called the freest press in Southeast Asia, and the citizens enjoyed what was for them unprecedented freedom of movement and association.[36] UNTAC's ability to teach Cambodians peace-promoting ideas, such as human rights, supports H6, which says that regimes can use information to promote the purposes of their missions and increase effectiveness.

---

[33] Thayer, "United Nations Transitional Authority in Cambodia," 152.

[34] These same failings plagued the civilian police efforts more generally. See Brown and Zasloff, *Cambodia Confounds the Peacemakers,* 108–12.

[35] Interview, Adriaan Verheul, Political Affairs Officer, United Nations Department of Peacekeeping Operations, April 23, 1996.

[36] Doyle, *UN Peacekeeping in Cambodia,* 45–47; Findlay, *Cambodia,* 63–68; Heininger, *Peacekeeping in Transition,* 91–100; Schear, "Riding the Tiger," 163–64; Thayer, "United Nations Transitional Authority in Cambodia," 158; United Nations, *Blue Helmets,* 3rd ed., 474–76.

ELECTIONS

Organizing and conducting free and fair elections was the centerpiece of UNTAC's mandate, and it was here that UNTAC enjoyed its most prominent success. This success depended to a large degree on the provision of transparency. I will discuss UNTAC's effectiveness with the elections in this section and leave most of the discussion of transparency for the next section on information and education.

Ninety-six percent of all eligible voters were registered before the May 23–28, 1993, elections. Ninety percent of Cambodia's eligible voters then voted. Despite considerable violence and intimidation prior to the election, Cambodia was surprisingly peaceful during the actual voting. Since March 1, there had been 200 deaths, 338 injuries, and 144 abductions attributed to politically motivated pre-election violence. The Khmer Rouge committed most of the violence. The Khmer Rouge, for reasons still unknown, did not disrupt the elections, however, and the polling period was one of the "least violent in Cambodia for years."[37]

UNTAC operated and monitored some 1400 fixed polling stations and 200 mobile stations. U.N. peacekeepers guarded most of these stations and the collected ballots were even more heavily guarded.

Sihanouk's FUNCINPEC won the election with 45.47 percent of the vote. Hun Sen's SOC party, called the Cambodian People's Party (CPP), won 38.23 percent. The Buddhist party got 3.81 percent of the vote, and seventeen other parties split the remaining 12.56 percent. As a result, FUNCINPEC won fifty-eight seats in the new Constituent Assembly, while the CPP won fifty-one. There was some post-election bickering about vote-counting and so forth. Control of the executive was disputed. In the end, Sihanouk's son, Prince Norodom Ranariddh, and Hun Sen shared the executive and became co-prime ministers, the former as "first" prime minister and the latter as "second" prime minister.

The election calmed the civil war, lessened the power of the Khmer Rouge, and brought, at least temporarily, a multiparty system into a traditionally one-party ruled state.[38]

INFORMATION/EDUCATION AND TRANSPARENCY

The Information/Education Division of UNTAC had a number of diverse tasks and is widely recognized by analysts as being extremely successful in its support role. Among these tasks were educating Cambodian

---

[37] Findlay, *Cambodia*, 81–83.

[38] Doyle, *UN Peacekeeping in Cambodia,* 55–58; Findlay, *Cambodia,* 75–90; Heininger, *Peacekeeping in Transition,* 100–116; Schear, "Riding the Tiger," 168–72; United Nations, *Blue Helmets,* 3rd ed., 470–71.

journalists on establishing a free press, helping political candidates get out their messages, educating Cambodians about what UNTAC was doing and how elections worked, countering propaganda and rumors, and addressing unwarranted fears.[39] The Information/Education Division served other aspects of UNTAC's mandate, including promoting human rights, repatriation, and so forth.

Information conditions prior to the start of Radio UNTAC and other UNTAC information efforts were poor. The media in Cambodia had been controlled by the political parties and factions. The SOC dominated with a wide-ranging but sporadically broadcasting radio and television network out of Phnom Penh, and with an established newspaper. The opposition parties of FUNCINPEC, the Khmer Rouge, and the Khmer People's National Liberation Front (KPNLF) began the UNTAC period with radio facilities in Thailand or near the Thai border. By mid-1992, some opposition bulletins and newsletters began to be published out of Phnom Penh, but radio and television were particularly important because 52 percent of the men and 78 percent of the women in Cambodia were illiterate.[40] The broadcast range of television reached only seventy-five kilometers out of Phnom Penh, making radio key for reaching the countryside.[41]

It took until July 1992 for more independent sources such as the English-language *Phnom Penh Post* to begin to appear. Newspapers and newsstands proliferated in early 1993, although many newspapers folded quickly, were intimidated or bribed into partisanship, and/or were biased from the outset. In February 1993, FUNCINPEC began broadcasting radio from Phnom Penh; their TV programs began in April.

More generally, Cambodia had suffered from years of isolation and inadequate education. It was a "traditional society dominated by rumors."[42] Cambodians knew little of the outside world, or of how the elections and campaigning of democracy were supposed to work. UNTAC was a novelty, and many Cambodians did not know why it was there and were suspicious of the new operation.

Given the dearth of quality information, the considerable level of uncertainties as well as long-standing suspicions among the various factions, the need for information and education was critical, and the situation was

---

[39] UNTAC also conducted educational activities in support of its human rights efforts as well. Please see the human rights section presented earlier.

[40] Findlay, *Cambodia*, 82–83.

[41] Lehmann, *Peacekeeping and Public Information*, 61. See also John Marston, "Neutrality and the Negotiation of an Information Order in Cambodia," in Price and Thompson, eds., *Forging Peace*, 177–79, 190.

[42] Interview, Takahisa Kawakami, Principal Officer, Asia and Middle East Division, United Nations Department of Peacekeeping Operations, April 25, 1996.

ripe for the provision of transparency. As it turned out, UNTAC success-fully calmed many fears about itself, taught Cambodians about elections, and calmed fears of election-period violence.

The initial paucity of competing media outlets, and their technical backwardness, limited reach, partisanship, and limited credibility, made it relatively easy for UNTAC to dominate the news flow. People were eager to hear credible, frank, and well-presented news and information. UNTAC became "the one source of news and information they [Cambo-dians] felt they could rely on."[43]

These points about the poor quality of information in Cambodia sug-gest two preconditions for similar information efforts. First, the U.N. (or other information source) has to be able to compete with the in-formation flow in the target area. This is partly a technical and quantita-tive issue: it is better to be one radio station among five than among 100, and it is better to have more area coverage than less. Second, the value added and credibility of the new information has to be high. A security regime whose message is implausible and has no impact cannot provide transparency.

Overall, the ability to be an "information competitor" is a prerequisite for a regime to provide transparency (H1). For example, the U.N. could not hope to make much of a dent in a developed state's dense news flow. In Namibia and especially Cambodia, however, the U.N. became quite influential. These factors offer some hope that the U.N. (or any other in-formation producer) might become influential when there is a media mo-nopoly, as long as it could penetrate the target area.

To accomplish its information missions, UNTAC availed itself of radio, television, video, puppet shows, billboards, singers, local artists, cartoon flyers, banners, leaflets, and other resources. It published guidelines and directives and ran discussion groups. UNTAC brought the candidates to-gether for round-table discussions and gave them access to its television, video, radio, and other facilities to help them spread their messages. UNTAC even ended up running its own radio station, Radio UNTAC, a first for a U.N. operation. All of these are transparency-increasing mecha-nisms, and they are observable implications of H1, which contends that regimes provide transparency.

At its peak, Radio UNTAC broadcast fifteen hours a day and was the most popular station in the country. To give some sense of the scale and penetration of UNTAC's information efforts, Japanese NGOs and politi-

---

[43] Quote from interview, Frederick Schottler, Information Officer, Peace and Security Sec-tion, United Nations Department of Public Information, April 25, 1996. See also John Marston, "Cambodian News Media in the UNTAC Period and After," in Steve Heder and Judy Underwood, eds., *Propaganda, Politics, and Violence in Cambodia: Democratic Tran-sition under United Nations Peace-keeping* (Armonk, NY: M.E. Sharpe, 1996), 212–27.

cal parties contributed 347,804 hand-held radios for distribution through-out Cambodia (along with 849,400 batteries and 1000 radio-cassette recorders).[44] Crowds would gather in marketplaces to listen to U.N. broad-casts. Relay stations were installed by UNTAC so that its broadcasts would reach the whole country, because in-country facilities were unable to do so. Before installation of the relays, UNTAC had to rely on borrowed transmitter time from the VOA to broadcast throughout Cambodia. UNTAC's estimates for its radio station's audience ranged from almost the entire population to even more than the population (by including lis-teners in neighboring countries).

To see if UNTAC's messages were getting through, a six-person Analysis/Assessment Unit of the Info/Ed Division conducted public opinion polls, traveled throughout the country, and monitored Cambodia's newspapers, radio and television programs, and political newsletters. It synthesized the information that it gathered for distribution throughout UNTAC, helping UNTAC prepare its political reports and respond to emerging problems. The unit's data helped UNTAC improve its image and credi-bility, prepare its information programs, and even vet the factions' public statements.[45] Gathering information is crucial for UNTAC to be able to provide transparency (H1), while tracking rumors and propaganda are necessary for UNTAC to be able to reduce fears among parties and about itself (H4 and H6).

The main message and function of the Information/Education cam-paign was to teach Cambodians about the elections, and a major theme was convincing Cambodians that their ballots were indeed secret. Many feared retaliation if they did not vote for one party or another. In re-sponse, UNTAC instructed Cambodians about the mechanics of elections and the procedures for insuring ballot secrecy. In doing so, UNTAC made its own system transparent (H6) and also reduced unwarranted fears (H4). Another message involving self-transparency (H6) was UNTAC's promise to Cambodians that it was not there to take over the country, and that it would eventually leave.[46]

Sometimes potential voters' fears were wildly unfounded. Some feared that the pencils for marking ballots contained radio beacons that linked up to satellites and would reveal who had voted for whom.[47] Others feared secret electronic eyes in the polling places. These and other concerns about ballot secrecy and fears of retribution were expressed by Cambodians in letters to the station and in frank discussions on talk shows. UNTAC officials could then respond appropriately with necessary information.

---

[44] Marston, "Neutrality," 191.

[45] Lehmann, *Peacekeeping and Public Information*, 64.

[46] Interview, Michael Doyle, Senior Fellow, International Peace Academy, April 19, 1996.

[47] Ibid.

Thanks to repeated messages over Radio UNTAC that their ballots would be secret, "People started to whisper around the assurances that the UNTAC had given, such that there was no such thing as a secret electronic eye to detect who they were voting for."[48] The success of UNTAC in reducing these rumors and unfounded fears about retribution and its election again offers strong evidence in support of H4 and H6.

A second function of UNTAC and especially Radio UNTAC was to help all the parties get out their messages. Radio UNTAC gave free air time weekly to all the political parties. In a transparency-related assist to the parties, it also gave a right of response to parties that felt particularly aggrieved by misstatements or lies in others' broadcasts. These efforts helped defeat the SOC's media near-monopoly and increased the fairness of the election. Unfortunately, one downside to opening up the process was that it antagonized the SOC.

Another division of UNTAC, the Control Unit, liaised with the local media, trying to promote higher and more neutral standards of journalism, promulgating media guidelines, and arm-twisting to prevent the broadcasting of false and defamatory news stories that were not conducive to the elections and UNTAC's mission. They also surveyed other campaign materials and helped enforce the four-day post-campaign cooling-off period before the elections. Unfortunately, the unit did not have enough speakers of Khmer to monitor adequately the Cambodian media.[49]

A third function of the Information/Education Division and Radio UNTAC was to reduce Cambodians' fears and combat hostile propaganda and rumors, especially about UNTAC, its mission, and the U.N. In accomplishing these various tasks, Radio UNTAC became a "powerful tool."[50]

The SOC and Khmer Rouge often propagandized against UNTAC, the U.N., and the elections.[51] One of the main messages of the SOC was that UNTAC could not protect the Cambodians and that only the SOC could do so. The SOC accused U.N. soldiers of coming to Cambodia to sleep with "Vietnamese bitches."[52] The SOC also tried to confuse Cambodians

---

[48] Tan Lian Choo, "The Cambodian Election: Whither the Future?" in Timothy Carney and Tan Lian Choo, *Whither Cambodia? Beyond the Election* (Singapore: Institute of Southeast Asian Studies, 1993), 23.

[49] Marston, "Neutrality," 180–86; and interview, Joao Lins de Albuquerque, Media Division (and former chief of information control in Cambodia), United Nations Department of Public Information, April 24, 1996.

[50] Findlay, *Cambodia*, 152.

[51] Steve Heder and Judy Ledgerwood point out that sometimes the SOC propagandized that UNTAC and the SOC were cooperating closely. This hurt UNTAC's image of impartiality, especially with the Khmer Rouge. They do not make clear the SOC's motive for doing this. See "Politics of Violence: An Introduction," in Heder and Underwood, eds., *Propaganda, Politics, and Violence in Cambodia*, 32–33.

[52] Interview, Joao Lins de Albuquerque, April 24, 1996.

about UNTAC's role in Cambodia. For example, the SOC claimed to be able to register people to vote, even though this was solely UNTAC's responsibility. UNTAC successfully combated this sort of propaganda, using self-transparency to help the mission (H6).

Similarly, the SOC tried to confiscate people's voter registration cards in an attempt to intimidate nonsupporters. UNTAC used its media resources to convince people that this was against electoral law and the SOC's efforts blew up in its face. This embarrassment shows how information can be used to punish those who misbehave, an example of H5 in action. The SOC also coerced people to join their party, then falsely told these people that they had to vote for the party to which they belonged. This intimidating misinformation was largely defeated by UNTAC information efforts, offering evidence of how transparency reduces fears (H4). Another SOC propaganda message was to try to tie FUNCINPEC and other opposition parties to the Khmer Rouge.

Although UNTAC was forced to confront a number of specific SOC transgressions, one item of craft knowledge for those dealing with media issues in the U.N. is that it is often unwise to combat propaganda with tit-for-tat counterpropaganda.[53] Doing so often degenerates into a war of words and adds credibility to the hostile propaganda.[54] Instead, the strategy is to stick to one's own message, repeat it a lot, and subtly change the focus as needed to combat whatever rumors are the most pernicious. This is why UNTAC Force Commander General Sanderson remarked that the U.N.'s information campaign allowed UNTAC to "bypass the propaganda of the Cambodian factions."[55] This is an operational aspect of using information to reduce fears and misperceptions (H4 and H6).

The Khmer Rouge waged a serious information campaign against the elections, with the main message being, Do not vote because not all parties are participating (i.e., the Khmer Rouge was not participating). Some of its physical attacks before the elections were conducted with the express purpose of expanding the areas over which they could propagandize.[56] Despite these efforts, which ranged from print to radio, Khmer

[53] Lehmann believes that the topic of counterpropaganda is a subject particularly ripe for future research; see Lehmann, *Peacekeeping and Public Information,* 151.

[54] Interviews Steve Whitehouse, Video Section, United Nations Department of Public Information, April 24, 1996; Joao Lins de Albuquerque, April 24, 1996; Frederick Schottler, April 25, 1996; and Takahisa Kawakami, Principal Officer, Asia and Middle East Division, United Nations Department of Peacekeeping Operations, April 25, 1996.

[55] Quoted in Michael W. Doyle, "Authority and Elections in Cambodia," in Doyle, Johnstone, and Orr, eds., *Keeping the Peace,* 152.

[56] Steve Heder, "The Resumption of Armed Struggle by the Party of Democratic Kampuchea: Evidence from National Army of Democratic Kampuchea 'Self-Demobilizers,'" in Heder and Underwood, eds., *Propaganda, Politics, and Violence in Cambodia,* 101.

Rouge propaganda was generally unsuccessful in convincing people not to vote. UNTAC's inability to shut down the Khmer Rouge disinformation campaign was mostly due to the peacekeepers' inability to move freely in Khmer Rouge–controlled areas and to escalating authorizations from Khmer Rouge leaders to attack UNTAC personnel. Yet, because UNTAC's own information also failed to stop Khmer Rouge propaganda, the evidence indicates a weak failure for H5.

Sometimes, Radio UNTAC combated fears generated by pre-election violence and rumors of election-time disruption. When the Khmer Rouge captured the symbolic town of Siem Reap near Angkor Wat three weeks before the election, Radio UNTAC sent a reporter and broadcasts from the town helped convince Cambodians not to be intimidated and to continue with plans for the elections. Radio UNTAC assured voters that the Khmer Rouge was not tearing up their voting cards.[57]

One source claims that the jamming of Khmer Rouge radio (Voice of Democratic Kampuchea) by UNTAC information officers prevented codes from getting to Khmer Rouge operatives and was crucial in preventing election-time violence. This was done apparently without the consent or knowledge of the heads of UNTAC's Info/Ed division. Timothy Carney, director of Info/Ed and Stephen Heder, deputy director, countered that the jamming had no effect, and called this claim "fanciful" and "fanciful nonsense," respectively.[58]

At other times, though, news of violence encouraged more fear. When the Khmer Rouge attacked Vietnamese targets in Phnom Penh, news of these attacks, reported by Radio UNTAC, greatly increased fears in Cambodia. Even though it may have hurt the mission in the short term, UNTAC strove to tell the truth and remain impartial. In the end, Radio UNTAC built up considerable credibility going into the election. This was crucial because fears of election violence ran high.

When the voting began on May 23, Radio UNTAC reporters were stationed around the country. Many Cambodians (as well as UNTAC) anticipated Khmer Rouge attacks on polling places, and many hesitated to vote, fearing for their safety. Radio UNTAC's reports that voting was being conducted safely throughout the country are widely credited with helping bring Cambodians to the polls. Thus, during the crucial election period, Radio UNTAC and other UNTAC information efforts successfully lessened unwarranted fears, helped generate the 90 percent turnout, and thus provided clear evidence for H4. The election might have been severely impaired without these information efforts. Of course,

[57] Interview, Ayman El-Amir, Chief, Radio Section, United Nations, Department of Public Information, April 26, 1996.

[58] Not for attribution telephone interview; email correspondence Timothy Carney, November 10, 2003, and Stephen Heder, November 10, 2003; see also Marston, "Neutrality," 184.

the physical presence of the 16,000 peacekeepers also helped calm these fears.

After the elections, Radio UNTAC continued to play transparency-related roles and helped protect the election results from attacks launched by the political parties.

On 31 May 1993, Chea Sim, President of the CPP [Cambodian People's Party], who controlled the Interior Ministry (and its 40,000 police force) demanded that Radio UNTAC should stop broadcasting the results. Radio UNTAC was accused of misleading and confusing the public. UNTAC rejected the allegations. UNTAC's stand was broadcast over Radio UNTAC that day:

"The decision to make the progressive results of the counting available to the media, and through the media to the people of Cambodia and of the World, flows from UNTAC's commitment to the principle of openness and transparency in the administration and conduct of the election. In addition, it reflects the fact that since progressive results are made available to all registered political parties (whose agents have the right to be present at the counting and to observe every aspect of that process), they are in effect already in the public domain."[59]

The SOC had expected to win the election and became bitter as the results came in showing FUNCINPEC in the lead. Had the SOC gotten away with its anti-election message, the election might have failed amidst recriminations and disagreements about the election's fairness. Again, Radio UNTAC told the truth, dispelled rumors and lies, and thereby helped consolidate the election results. This is evidence of self-transparency and transparency reducing suspicions (H6 and H4).[60]

[59] Zhou Mei, *Radio UNTAC of Cambodia: Winning Ears, Hearts, and Minds* (Bangkok, Thailand: White Lotus Press, 1994), 57. Mei was chief of production for Radio UNTAC.

[60] This section on the Information/Education Division was based on the following sources: Brown and Zasloff, *Cambodia Confounds the Peacemakers*, 127–29; Doyle, *UN Peacekeeping in Cambodia*, 30–31, 34, 54–55; Findlay, *Cambodia*, 40–43, 75–76, 152; Kate Freison, "The Politics of Getting out the Vote in Cambodia," in Heder and Underwood, eds., *Propaganda, Politics, and Violence in Cambodia*, 184–201; Steve Heder and Judy Legerwood, "Politics of Violence: An Introduction"; Heininger, *Peacekeeping in Transition*, 84, 109–11; Jeffrey Heyman, "The Story of Radio UNTAC: The United Nations First Peace-Keeping Radio Station," in a fax from Heyman to a U.N. official, a version of which appears in *Monitoring Times* 13, no. 10 (1994); Judy Legerwood, "Patterns of CPP Political Repression and Violence during the UNTAC Period," in Heder and Underwood, eds., *Propaganda, Politics, and Violence in Cambodia*, 122–130; Lehmann, *Peacekeeping and Public Information*, chap. 4; Marston, "Cambodian News Media," 209–27; Marston, "Neutrality;" Mei, *Radio UNTAC of Cambodia*; Peou, *Conflict Neutralization*, 207–11; Schear, "Riding the Tiger," 169; United Nations, *Blue Helmets*, 3rd ed., 479–80; United Nations Secretary-General, *Third Progress Report of the Secretary-General on UNTAC,*

TABLE 7-1
Findings by Hypothesis

Hypothesis	Evidence	Strength of evidence	Overall strength of hypothesis
Regimes provide transparency (H1)	UNAMIC failed in many attempts to communicate, liaison, monitor, and investigate, p. 160	Failure	Moderate
	Inadequate military intelligence gathering capabilities, p. 162	Failure	
	Dialogue with factions about refugee repatriation, p. 164	Moderate	
	Had difficulty monitoring government functions as part of civil control mandate, p. 166	Failure	
	Radio, television, video, puppet shows, singers, local artists, cartoon flyers, banners, leaflets and other tools used by Information/Education Division, p. 170	Strong	
Regimes spread misinformation (H1')	No evidence		
Anticipated transparency promotes cooperation (H2)	Promise of transparency helped factions overcome fears and agree to Paris Accords, but great power coercion/persuasion and transparency-related disputes undercut support, pp. 157, 158	Moderate/Weak	Moderate/Weak
Anticipated transparency hinders cooperation (H2')	SOC's successful resistance of UNTAC civil control monitoring, pp. 158, 165	Moderate	Moderate
Transparency promotes cooperation and prevents conflict (H3)	No evidence		
Transparency hinders cooperation and causes conflict (H3')	No evidence		

(continued)

Hypothesis	Evidence	Strength of evidence	Overall strength of hypothesis
Transparency reduces unwarranted fears and worst-case assumptions (H4)	Khmer Rouge did not believe UNTAC reports that Vietnamese forces had left Cambodia, p. 162	Failure	Moderate/Strong
	Allayed suspicions about refugee repatriation, p. 164	Moderate	
	Reduced fears of election violence, helping turnout, p. 174	Strong	
	Stopped SOC from coercing people to vote for it, p. 173	Strong	
	Defeated rumors that the election was rigged and that UNTAC was manipulating the results, p. 175	Strong	
Transparency confirms fears (H4')	No evidence		
Transparency reduces cheating, rogue, and spoiler problems (H5)	Could not adequately monitor or control SOC; poor civil control, p. 166	Weak/Failure	Weak/Failure
	Inability to stop SOC human rights abuses, p. 167	Failure	
Transparency about the regime (or self-transparency) increases its effectiveness (H6)	Khmer Rouge did not believe UNTAC reports that Vietnamese forces had left Cambodia, p. 162	Failure	Moderate/Strong
	Allayed suspicions about refugee repatriation, p. 164	Moderate	
	UNTAC taught about human rights, p. 167	Moderate	
	Stopped SOC from coercing people to vote for it, p. 173	Strong	
	Reduced fears of election violence, helping turnout, p. 174	Strong	
	Defeated rumors that the election was rigged and that UNTAC was manipulating the results; helped to consolidate the results, p. 175	Strong	

Note: Coding: "Strong" means that the phenomenon or effect was clear and very influential if not decisive, producing behavior that would be hard to replicate without the regime. "Moderate" means that the phenomenon played a discernible and somewhat influential role. Other factors help explain the outcome. "Weak" means that the phenomenon was probably but only weakly present. Other factors explain most of the outcome. "Failure" means that the regime tried to do something and failed, or that something that the regime did was counterproductive. The overall ratings are judgments based on the significance of transparency and its effects for each hypothesis within the context of each case.

CONCLUSION: CAMBODIA AND TRANSPARENCY

UNTAC had several failings and shortcomings, but the core of its man-date—the holding of free elections—was a success. In achieving this suc-cess, transparency was not a sufficient tool, but it was a necessary tool. UNTAC's experience offers clear and unambiguous support for the ability of regimes to provide transparency (H1), to reduce fears (H4), and espe-cially to clarify the purposes of its own operation (H6).

The promise of transparency (H2) was mildly helpful in getting the Cambodian parties to agree to the Paris Accords. Power politics and his-torical circumstances were far more important. Hence, H2 receives very modest support.

The Cambodian factions resisted many of the military aspects of the Paris Accords. There was little for UNTAC to monitor and verify. When it reported what it did successfully verify—the departure and subsequent absence of Vietnamese forces—the Khmer Rouge did not believe UNTAC. As with Cyprus, we see the ability of transparency to reduce suspicions (H4) undercut by willful disbelief and bias.

Turning to the civil part of the mandate, UNTAC failed at civil control. This effort could have depended to a large degree on transparency for its success. Like the military aspects of UNTAC's mandate, however, resist-ance by the factions torpedoed UNTAC before transparency could help.

Information and education played a large role in UNTAC's human rights campaign, although transparency was not much of an issue. UNTAC had difficulty in this area because of its very limited capabilities for coer-cion and enforcement.

UNTAC's greatest success was the election, and here transparency played a large role. Through information and education, with Radio UNTAC in particular (H1), UNTAC defused many rumors, calmed many fears (H4),

---

S/25154, (New York: United Nations, January 25, 1993); United Nations Secretary-General, *Report of the Secretary-General on the Implementation of Security Council Resolution 792 (1992), S/25289*, (New York: United Nations, February 13, 1993); United Nations Secretary-General, *Fourth Progress Report of the Secretary-General on UNTAC, S/25719* (New York: United Nations, May 3, 1993).

In addition to places where they are specifically cited, the following interviews were help-ful, particularly for the UNTAC and UNTAG chapters. I interviewed these U.N. officials at the U.N. in New York over the period April 12–28, 1996: Joao Lins de Albuquerque, Media Division, Department of Public Information; Henry Breed, Political Affairs Officer, Department of Peacekeeping Operations; Ayman El-Amir, Chief, Radio Section, Department of Public Information; Fred Eckhard, Senior Liaison Officer, Department of Peacekeeping Operations; Kevin Kennedy, Chief, Peace and Security Section, Department of Public Infor-mation; Frederick Schottler, Information Officer, Peace and Security Section, Department of Public Information; Steve Whitehouse, Video Section, Department of Public Information; Lena Yacoumopoulou, Film/Video Archives, Department of Public Information.

clarified UNTAC's role (H6), stopped interference with electoral procedures, and helped end disputes about the election's results. Without information/education and transparency, the elections might been marred or ruined. Ingrid Lehmann, citing five scholars and UNTAC officials, says that "Radio UNTAC was, according to most observers, one of the prime success stories of the U.N. operation in Cambodia."[61] Kevin Kennedy, chief of the Peace and Security section of the U.N. Department of Public Information, said that Radio UNTAC was "extremely useful" and "critical."[62]

Table 7-1 summarizes these findings.

The U.N.'s successes in Namibia and Cambodia suggest conditions under which an security regime can promote peace with transparency. Transparency is about information. Making information provided by the U.N. (or others) count is easier to do in areas where information is otherwise hard to come by or the current sources are blatantly biased and/or are under monopoly control. This is more likely to be the case where poverty, underdevelopment, and/or dictators reign. Before the U.N.'s arrival in each country, the existing media were extremely biased, had limited coverage, and were based on relatively outmoded technologies. There was considerable room for improvement, and this helped the U.N. step in and increase transparency. The information provided by these U.N. operations added value by being credible, by covering wide areas, and by using a range of methods from radio relays to town meetings and puppet shows.

Epilogue

In the summer of 1997, Hun Sen staged a coup and took over Cambodia's government. However ominous a development, he still allowed elections in 1998. The turnout was 93 percent; Hun Sen's CPP received 41 percent of the vote while FUNCINPEC came in second with 32 percent. The election was largely free and fair, even though only 500 international observers were on hand to monitor the voting.

This turn of events suggests that Cambodia took a step forward with UNTAC's help. Having tasted a multiparty election, a free press, and progress in human rights, Cambodians did not let their country take too many steps backward. Indeed, the training and socialization resulting from the 1993 election helped Cambodians prepare for the 1998 election.[63]

[61] Lehmann, *Peacekeeping and Public Information*, 65.

[62] Interview, Kevin Kennedy, Chief, Peace and Security Section, Department of Public Information, April 24, 1996.

[63] Brown and Zasloff, *Cambodia Confounds the Peacemakers*, epilogue, esp. 307.

CHAPTER EIGHT

Conclusion

THIS BOOK examines the provision and effects of transparency to help us understand when transparency can best be used to promote peace. Here I offer the lessons learned from looking at diverse cases, from forums to different kinds of peacekeeping, and at a number of incidents in each case.

My findings about transparency ranged from dramatic success to modest usefulness to outright failure. The variance in results across the cases raises such questions as, Why is the strongest evidence of success for transparency located in the multifunctional, democracy-promoting peacekeeping operations? Why is transparency limited to moderate and weak success in the traditional buffer zone monitoring operations? Why is transparency's role in bargaining in the Concert of Europe case found to be consistent with realpolitik? What do the answers to these questions tell us about when security regimes can best use transparency to promote peace?

To address these issues, I first review the findings about the hypotheses on transparency. I then offer the implications of these findings for international relations theorists and policymakers. An appendix describes the current status of U.N. information operations to further the policy relevance of the book's findings.

FINDINGS

As shown here in table 8-1, the strength of each hypothesis varied widely by case. To explain the table, I will now summarize the findings by hypothesis.

Do security regimes provide transparency (H1)? Yes, they sometimes can. For informal regimes like forums, which do not actively generate or exchange information, a primary benefit is increased speed of communication. Multilateral communication can be faster than bilateral communication, and face-to-face communication can be faster than communication from a distance. The effects of increasing the pace of diplomacy on fears, miscalculation, and bargaining are discussed shortly, but the bottom line is that forums facilitate bargaining. In the case of the Concert, the bargaining reflected many of the same realpolitik elements seen in the pre-Concert era. Coercive arrangements were made and coercive threats were communicated more quickly than before.

The ability of more formal security regimes to generate and add value to information depends on a number of factors, but a key variable is the quality of information already available to the adversaries. Active attempts by security regimes to provide and increase transparency will work only if they can generate and exchange information over and above the independent information-gathering capabilities of the adversaries. This means that efforts to increase transparency by security regimes will work best when there is poor unilateral (intelligence) and ambient (press, trade, travel) transparency. The United Nations Peacekeeping Force in Cyprus (UNFICYP) and the United Nations Disengagement Observer Force (UNDOF) in the Golan Heights operate in fairly developed areas of the world where the adversaries can themselves gather high-quality information, especially about matters concerning the strategic military balance. The level of background information available to the adversaries is already high, and uncertainty tends to be low.

In contrast, the United Nations Transition Assistance Group (UNTAG) in Namibia and the United Nations Transitional Authority in Cambodia (UNTAC) operated in the developing world where the information quality was relatively poor: lack of media outlets, biased media outlets, rampant illiteracy, and lack of education. These conditions create a greater need for information and transparency, which makes it easier for the U.N. to add value to the existing flow of information. The ability to provide transparency also depends on the relative information power of the regime compared to the adversaries. As the U.N. is relatively weak compared to developed states, the U.N. is likely to fare better with transparency in the developing world. U.N. information may also be more likely to be accepted as credible in the developing world.

A sad case is UNMEE, where peacekeeping could be quite helpful, in part because a border dispute creates considerable uncertainty and tension, and because unilateral and ambient transparency is low. Thanks to these background conditions, U.N. monitoring and provision of transparency could help calm tensions, but each side has imposed restrictions on the peacekeepers. In December 2005, Eritrea ordered Western peacekeepers to leave the country.[1] Even when UNMEE had more opportunity to do so, it made little effort to exploit information operations and use transparency to create peace (see n. 15 in this chapter).

Table 8-2 (p. 184) summarizes these arguments about how background information conditions are likely to influence the effectiveness of transparency.

---

[1] Susannah Price, "UN Pulls Out Eritrea Peacekeepers," BBC News, December 15, 2005, available at news.bbc.co.uk/1/hi/world/africa/4530410.stm.

TABLE 8-1
Summary of Findings by Case and Hypothesis

Hypothesis	Concert of Europe
Regimes provide transparency (H1)	Moderate
Regimes spread misinformation (H1′)	
Anticipated transparency promotes cooperation (H2)	Weak
Anticipated transparency hinders cooperation (H2′)	
Transparency promotes cooperation and prevents conflict (H3)	Moderate/Strong
Transparency hinders cooperation and causes conflict (H3′)	Moderate
Transparency reduces unwarranted fears and worst-case assumptions (H4)	Weak
Transparency confirms fears (H4′)	
Transparency reduces cheating, rogue, and spoiler problems (H5)	
Transparency about the regime (or self-transparency) increases its effectiveness (H6)	
For more information, see each chapter's summary table	p. 82

These arguments also apply to information operations and public diplomacy more broadly. It is a truism that if transparency is already high, then efforts to increase transparency are not so helpful. It is worth noting, however, that the level of information competition is a key variable in making transparency and information operations work.

Note that strong information competitors may also be a factor in creating low uncertainty and opacity, because these information sources may increase ambient or unilateral transparency. The link is not tight however, because one can have strong information competitors and high uncertainty and opacity at the same time when the competitors are biased or untruthful. As noted during the UNFICYP case study, for example, South Cyprus had many newspapers, but almost all of them had a strong Greek Cypriot tilt in addition to their often-explicit political party affiliations and leanings. In this case, box 2 of table 8-2, UNFICYP had to compete

United Nations Peacekeeping Force in Cyprus (UNFICYP)	United Nations Disengagement Observer Force (UNDOF) in the Golan Heights	United Nations Transition Assistance Group (UNTAG) in Namibia	United Nations Transitional Authority in Cambodia (UNTAC)
Moderate/Weak	Moderate/Weak	Moderate/Strong	Moderate
Moderate/Weak			
Weak	Moderate/Weak	Moderate/Weak	Moderate/Weak
			Moderate
Weak	Weak		
	Moderate		
Moderate/Weak	Moderate/Weak	Moderate/Strong	Moderate/Strong
Weak			
Moderate/Weak	Weak	Moderate	Weak/Failure
Moderate/Weak	Moderate/Strong	Strong	
p. 112	p. 138	p. 152	p. 176

not just against a high baud rate generated by the Cypriot press and political opportunists, but also against the biases that these influences helped build and sustain. On the other hand, UNDOF's inspections contributed less transparency than they otherwise might have, due to the intelligence services of each side. It is not axiomatic, however, that a strong press presence automatically increases ambient transparency, or that intelligence efforts necessarily yield credible unilateral transparency.

In addition to information competitors, the cases revealed other barriers to the provision of transparency (H1), ranging from procedural issues such as inadequate forces and faulty standard operating procedures to operational failures and political resistance. From areas held off-limits to the U.N. in the Golan Heights to Khmer Rouge intransigence on disarmament and cantonment, these failures often reflected the power imbalance between the U.N. and the local parties.

TABLE 8-2

Information Conditions and Likely Operational Effectiveness of Transparency in U.N. Peacekeeping Operations

	Low Uncertainty and Opacity	High Uncertainty and Opacity
Strong Information Competitors (well-equipped news outlets, well-organized political parties, and powerful intelligence services—all potential sources of ambient and unilateral transparency, if accurate and unbiased)	1. Transparency not likely to be relevant to mission effectiveness as there are few information-related problems to solve. (cases of UNDOF and UNFICYP offer evidence for this contention, especially with issues related to strategic military balances)	2. Transparency could help mission, but the U.N. faces uphill battle making it work. (UNFICYP offers evidence for this, in instances when political opportunists and the abundant press play on biases and blow things out of proportion)
Weak Information Competitors (fewer and less credible media outlets, disorganized political parties, weak intelligence services)	3. Transparency not likely to help as there are few problems to solve, however, U.N. can fairly easily provide its own mission-aiding information.	4. U.N.-provided transparency stands a good chance at working, and providing meaningful help to the operation. (cases of UNTAG and UNTAC offer evidence for this, in many instances)

There was little evidence that security regimes spread misinformation (H1′), although there were instances of shading the truth or withholding information in the case of the UNFICYP.

Finally, if active peacekeeping operations face the challenge of adding value to existing information, this hurdle is even higher for forums. A forum is most useful when states have few other means of communication. Given the number of forums and other means of communication available in the late twentieth century, this condition is increasingly rare—at least among the more powerful states. The policy part of the conclusion argues, however, that forums may still be useful particularly in parts of Asia and Africa.

Does the promise of security regime–provided transparency help adversaries make peace, as per the contention of hypothesis H2? Although this is an intuitively appealing proposition, there was only modest or weak evidence for this in the cases. Castlereagh, the Concert's prime architect, looked forward to better communications with the forum, but there was no evidence that he tried to sell others with this argument. Coercion and persuasion by outside powers was the primary explanation for the deployment of U.N. peacekeeping operations, though the promise of monitoring and providing transparency was mildly helpful in three of the four peacekeeping operations. There was moderate support for the contrary hypothesis that anticipated transparency can hinder cooperation (H2'), and this was found when the SOC in Cambodia resisted and thwarted UNTAC's attempts to monitor its governance.

Does transparency promote cooperation by reducing uncertainties and miscalculations that hinder bargaining, as H3 contends? There was solid evidence that forum diplomacy reduced miscalculation during the Concert period, but there was little evidence for H3 in the peacekeeping operations.

Because the Concert period was permeated by war scares and hard bargaining, I do not offer the most enthusiastically optimistic interpretation of the Concert's effects, and I do not believe the Concert period represented a transformation of diplomatic and international relations. Yet it is precisely because war was possible, and the stakes were high, that the effects of forum diplomacy and transparency are worth noting. It is natural that H3 was more prominent during the Concert than during the peacekeeping operations, however, because the conditions under which each come into play were different. Crisis management forums are convened because war is in the air. Peacekeeping operations are not normally put in place until there is a peace to consolidate. On Cyprus, the peacekeepers could help with tactical bargains about rock throwing or construction. During the Concert, the forum helped states avoid war on several occasions. The fact that there were several war scares during the Concert's crises may also explain why the Concert facilitated hardball diplomacy, reduced uncertainty and miscalculation (H3), and also clarified the existence of deadlock or conflict (H3 and H3').

Bargaining helps establish each side's stakes and positions, and it can clarify the existence of deadlock. Does this reduce conflict, as contended by H3, or increase conflict, as suggested by H3'· Does transparency help resolve the crisis, or cause it to escalate? The answer is both. The Concert's crises often showed H3 and H3' operating in the same case or incident. This is because they described the dynamics of a crisis: escalation and de-escalation. Crises can of course escalate to war, but this did not happen in my cases. Even when conflict initially spiked, the Concert powers in the end were able to avoid war. In the most serious crises (Poland-Saxony and Belgium), this was due to coercion, restraint, and the reconfiguring of alliances.

Ultimately, these findings tended to support a modest but generally optimistic view of transparency. On the whole, transparency was moderately helpful in a number of instances across the cases and was rarely harmful. There were a few home runs for transparency during the Concert and UNTAG and UNTAC, but there were also a number of instances where its effects were weak or where attempts to increase transparency failed. While the great majority of observations about the provision and effects of transparency were positive, their magnitude was on the whole moderate. Although more research needs to be done across different domains, these findings suggest that added transparency entails few risks, and many possible benefits, but that expectations for gains should not be overblown.

An interesting counterpoint to this optimistic view is found during the peace negotiations between Syria and Israel when Kissinger filtered, limited, and slowed information exchange and almost certainly helped prevent deadlock or worse. This evidence supports H3', because it clearly implies that more transparency would have hindered cooperation (H3'). How and when to filter information in mediation is worthy of more study.[2]

Does transparency reduce fears and worst-case assumptions, as suggested by H4? UNDOF could not reduce fears because there were none, while UNFICYP had trouble because of deeply ingrained biases. In contrast to UNDOF and UNFICYP, UNTAG and UNTAC did a great job in reducing fears. Fears about violence and retribution were widespread yet not deeply ingrained. Some fears, like the idea of Khmer Rouge radio transmitters in voting pencils, were so outlandish that they could be easily calmed. These missions were able to dominate the information flow and provide some of the most credible information in the country.

This range of outcomes suggests that there is a fairly narrow band—a Goldilocks zone—where transparency can help allay fears. On the one hand, if transparency is to reduce fears, there have to be unwarranted fears for the regime to address. On the other, these fears and suspicions (and tensions more generally) cannot be so great that nothing the regime

---

[2] For example, there appears to be no consensus in the field of mediation on how to deal with information asymmetries between disputants. See Alexis Gensberg, "Mediating Inequality: Mediators' Perspectives on Power Imbalances in Public Disputes," Program on Negotiation, Harvard Law School, Cambridge, MA, 2003; and Zartman and Rubin, "Symmetry and Asymmetry in Negotiation," 286. Nor there does there appear to be consensus on when filtering in general is wise or unwise, a point confirmed by John Darby, Professor of Comparative Ethnic Studies, Joan B. Kroc Institute for International Peace Studies at the University of Notre Dame, in a conversation on November 2, 2005. See also Christopher W. Moore, *The Mediation Process: Practical Strategies for Resolving Conflict*, 2nd ed. (San Francisco, CA: Jossey-Bass, 1996), 182–86, 217–23, 329, who discusses all sorts of variables involving framing and information flow, but does not specify the effects of those variables or how they work in different conditions (except to say that reframing disputes over values is harder than in disputes over interests, 219).

does can reduce them. In addition, the foregoing discussion argues that the ability of regimes to use transparency is also helped when ambient and unilateral transparency is low, when the regime can compete with the local information competitors.

There was little evidence that security regime–provided transparency confirmed or justified what might have been unwarranted fears or worst-case assumptions (H4'). In contrast, however, appendix B has cases where IAEA inspections confirmed fears or revealed that things were worse than previously assumed.

Were security regimes able to prevent or stop cheaters, rogues, or spoilers by using information to deter or coerce them, the contention of hypothesis H5? This happened at moderate or weak levels in all of the peacekeeping cases. The lesson here is that the same information-gathering and -disseminating mechanisms that can be used for transparency—such as patrols, monitoring, and liaison systems—can also coerce. They constitute instruments of power for peacekeeping operations. Regimes with more elaborate rules, benchmarks of behavior, and reporting procedures are more likely to be able to avail themselves of this tool (although UNDOF shows some limits to this). It is more difficult to define cheating, identify defection, and coerce behavior in the absence of rules.

Did transparency and the use of information help regimes reduce fears about their own operations, as contended by H6?[3] Clearly yes. UNTAG and UNTAC faced suspicions and doubts about their missions and mandates. For the same reasons they succeeded with H4, UNTAG and UNTAC also strongly succeeded using transparency to clarify their roles and practices and thereby helped their missions achieve their mandates (H6). This reinforces a prior insight about the provision of transparency: where U.N. presence and activities like elections, voting, and campaigning are novel, much more attention has to be paid to explaining the mission. Fortunately, the U.N. is most likely to succeed with information campaigns and transparency precisely where the need for self-explanation is highest (see table 8-2). In the developed world the mission itself is less likely to need explanation.

IMPLICATIONS FOR SCHOLARS

The key issue in the study of transparency is to figure out how and under what conditions it will promote peace or conflict. To summarize my main contributions to this effort, I show that in the context of forums,

[3] This hypothesis is less relevant for informal and passive regimes like the Concert that have no mission or institutional capacity to gather and disseminate information actively, and the same applies to H5.

transparency can facilitate hard bargaining, but that crises may be made worse by transparency before they are made better. In the context of peacekeeping operations, transparency works best when the regime can dominate the information flow and when information competitors such as other media or intelligence are limited. Transparency needs some prior level of uncertainty, incomplete information, and misperception to work, otherwise it is irrelevant. Transparency hits hurdles, however, when biases and misperceptions run so deep that new information cannot affect attitudes or refute rumors. Transparency therefore operates best in a Goldilocks zone defined by few information competitors and by some—but not too much—bias, misperception, and incomplete information. This Goldilocks zone is likely generalizable to efforts like public diplomacy which that actively try to shape information environments.

The first and most important observation that generates the need for more research is that transparency has conflicting effects. Although this book ends up being modestly optimistic about transparency, it does not resolve the optimist versus pessimist debate. This is because, although I hope I have furthered the study of transparency, more work remains to be done to figure out how the positive and negative effects of transparency work in additional cases and circumstances. That said, my findings suggest that transparency optimists, those who believe that transparency almost always has benevolent effects, have to rethink their arguments. Transparency is often helpful, but it falls short of being an elixir of peace.

Second, because transparency can both exacerbate and calm conflict, more analysis also needs to be done to figure out the relationship between the two effects—especially in the context of bargaining. Models need to be constructed that depict transparency at first causing a rise in tensions while clarifying stakes, capabilities, and resolve, and then helping to reduce tensions, redefine win-sets, and seal a bargain (or helping coercion work). The reverse may also be true in some situations, with initial calming giving way to increased tension. The models must also depict increased transparency ending in conflict, depending on the circumstances. Empirical work on transparency and incomplete information is scanty. More process-tracing needs to chart these multiple effects to help determine when rising tensions are a precursor to a bargain, or part of the path to war. Process-tracing can test the competing contentions, in particular the numerous ones generated by the rationalists. As I hope this book shows, these rationalist and qualitative efforts should be mutually reinforcing in providing new insights into the workings of transparency.

The cross-cutting effects of transparency also apply to anticipated transparency as it can help seal a deal or make states resist cooperation. The Soviets in particular felt threatened by transparency and arms control in the earlier days of the Cold War (and throughout, really). Despite this rather prominent—though not unique—example, the distributional consequences of transparency are underappreciated by most political scientists. As seen in appendix B, such concerns are often evident in historical accounts about arms control, but it may be that arms control became largely passé for political scientists just as these analysts became more interested in the influence of incomplete and asymmetric information on outcomes.

Third, another issue that deserves more research is: the question of when, how often, and under what conditions do mechanisms that increase transparency make deception easier? A common critique of arms control by its critics is that it can create a lulling effect. Is this true? How easy is it to dupe a regime or misuse its mechanisms?

A fourth area for more research is the role of mediators and how they control information flow. Kissinger's mediation between Syria and Israel suggests that filtering information can be beneficial. As is, this is a counterargument against the transparency optimists. It is only one case, however, and its generalizability has yet to be determined. From what I can tell, there is no consensus or in-depth analysis on the opposing effects of transparency or information provision in the literature on mediation, and so this suggests a research program for scholars in this area.[4] Andrew Kydd and Barbara Walter note that the "role of third-party information provision" in providing reassurance is a worthy topic for future research.[5]

Fifth, I have yet to see an article or book that could be titled "When Does Familiarity Breed Contempt?"[6] The cases here revealed some instances where transparency hindered bargaining, and even rarer instances of transparency confirming fears. There are surely more cases out there, however, and the conditions under which transparency breeds contempt (leads parties to confirm their worst fears and to break off negotiations H4' and H3') need more exploration. Appendix B has mini-cases where IAEA and UNSCOM inspections had this effect.

Sixth, a major area for more research lies in tying together the multiple expertises that bear on transparency. Among others, the institutionalist, qualitative, and rationalist causes of war, misperception/cognition/political psychology, media/propaganda/advertising, and negotiation/mediation literatures all offer insights on the influence of transparency. Yet crossover studies (much less in-depth crossover citations) are rare. Significant cross-disciplinary borrowing remains to be done among political scientists (and

---

[4] See fn. 2 in this chapter.

[5] Kydd and Walter, "Sabotaging the Peace," 290.

[6] Gaddis in *Long Peace* says that history is replete with examples of this on p. 225, but his examples such as Greece and Turkey need examination to make sure that familiarity is not the same as proximity leading to geopolitical contests over narrow waterways, for example.

those in our subfields), psychologists, sociologists, historians, and others. I have tried to touch on and integrate several literatures, but I have only kicked the can down the road.

A final subject for more research is the tactical use of transparency and its relationship to strategic goals. The cases here suggest that tactical interventions in specific places or about specific rumors can make a difference in helping strategic goals such as elections (UNTAC and UNTAG). Walter is surely correct to argue that security guarantees are a key to peaceful settlements; but she undervalues the role of transparency and information operations, especially in light of the relatively high cost of providing security guarantees.[7] Transparency and information operations will not make as much of a difference as boots on the ground, but they are easier and cheaper to bring to bear.

IMPLICATIONS FOR POLICYMAKERS

Concert and Forums

My findings about the Concert and transparency have three main implications. First, scholars continue to advocate Concerts for everything from replacing NATO to helping deal with terrorism. There would be much wisdom in a working Concert of great powers to confront terrorism and achieve other political goals, and indeed when the U.N. Security Council works well, it resembles an effective Concert. There is, however, only mixed historical justification for using the Concert of Europe as a precedent to justify policy recommendations. The Concert period shows more realpolitik than rule-guided or norm-driven behavior. I argue that when the Concert worked to dampen conflict, it did so by facilitating hard bargaining. This is a worthy contribution, but, it is not a transformation of international politics in the direction of rules, norms, or enlightened self-interest. The Concert did establish the norm of meeting together to try to manage crises, and in this way, the Concert of Europe was a milestone in international relations. Yet the meetings themselves evinced much power-politics, and their chief benefit was to increase transparency.

Second, expectations about what forums can achieve should be modest. Simply put, forums make power politics easier. Forums bring leaders together, making it easier to engage in confrontation as well as to find common ground. Forums do not actively defuse crises or actively help adversaries overcome fears of cooperation or of each other in the way more formal methods of increasing transparency (such as peacekeeping operations) do. That said, forums do help states communicate, which often

---

[7] Walter, *Committing to Peace.*

reduces miscalculation and clarifies bargaining positions, stakes, and relative power. This in turn can spur agreement, successful coercion, or acceptance of deadlock. Even modest results for security forums are to be welcomed, because effective tools to promote peace are hard to come by.[8] Moreover, modest results for security forums do not necessarily indict other regimes which have been much more effective and beneficial, especially in the realm of international political economy.[9]

Do forums necessarily improve transparency and facilitate power politics across space and time? To extrapolate from the findings on the Concert, it is probable that forums generally increase transparency, though it follows from my peacekeeping findings that they would do so most in areas where communications are minimal. While I find that forum-provided transparency facilitates power politics, it seems reasonable to conclude that forums act as conveyor belts for the predominant political tone of their members, whether it be power politics, a politics of enlightened self-interest, or perhaps something more altruistic. There is no evidence in the cases, however, that increased transparency causes enlightened self-interest or altruism. This point is underscored by the high level of coercion and war scares that prevailed during the Concert.

Third, Concert-like forums, periodic summits, or hot lines may be useful when states and other adversaries lack the means to communicate on a regular basis, or at all. Using transparency as a tool depends on boosting the availability of information, and so the utility of forums in adding information depends on the level of preexisting mechanisms to exchange information. A plethora of Concert-like forums already exist—especially for the great powers, including the U.N. Security Council, the G-8, the OSCE, the E.U., and ASEAN.

Nonetheless, when communication is minimal, summits or forums may be desirable and may be the only way to get adversaries to communicate. U.S. Army General Gary Luck, commander of U.S. and U.N. forces in Korea, said, "They [North Korea] refuse to meet us at Panmunjom on armistice-related issues, and they refuse to talk to us on the telephone when we've called to protest armistice violations." He believes that "the lack of communication is dangerous because it would inhibit efforts to defuse a border situation."[10] There are no regular meetings and not even a hotline between North and South Korea. Contact between India and Pakistan is better, but still sporadic.

[8] Lipson, "International Cooperation in Economic and Security Affairs."

[9] See, for example, Ikenberry, *After Victory,* which depicts the striking growth of international institutions over time.

[10] Bill Gertz, "U.S. Commander in Korea Sees North Near Disintegration," *Washington Times,* March 16, 1996, p. 7. The first statement quotes Luck's testimony before the U.S. House Appropriations Subcommittee on National Security; the second is Gertz's paraphrase of what Luck said. See more generally "Mistrust and the Korean Peninsula: Dangers of Mis-

Despite ASEAN, more forums may be useful in Asia. The *Economist* reported in June 2002 that ASEAN has "floundered" as a regional forum for discussing security issues. It recommended that a recent conference of defense ministers from across East Asia become an annual event, because it was "needed in order to increase transparency" in a region "riven by mutual suspicions," rivalries, and arms races.[11]

Finally, forums may be especially helpful in areas of the developing world, particularly Africa, where networks of communication between states and adversaries are less well established. For example, the U.N. notes the use of forums to reduce tensions between adversaries in Congo:

> In view of the pervasive fear and mistrust that characterize relations between the Lendu and the Hema [in the Ituri district of Congo], it is essential that a dialogue between the two groups . . . be initiated and maintained. In the past, the organization of forums and round tables involving community leaders and traditional chiefs has helped defuse tensions.[12]

Local conflict resolution initiatives involving U.N.-facilitated meetings have helped calm parts of Congo, thus confirming the success of forum diplomacy and the effects of transparency. Forums and meetings have had less success, however, in the Ituri district. As part of the Luanda Agreement of September 2002, the U.N. did subsequently establish a formal forum, the Ituri Pacification Committee, to bring the parties in the area together. Unfortunately, the conflict continues between the Hema and Lendu and serves as a reminder of the limits of forums.[13]

Peacekeeping

My findings about peacekeeping and transparency result in three policy recommendations. First, policymakers and U.N. officials should recognize the value of increasing transparency to the success of their peacekeeping operations. A tool will be correctly used only if its effects are well studied and its potential is appreciated. Although it is no elixir of peace,

---

calculation," United States Institute of Peace Special Report, October 1998, which notes that reliable information about North Korea is "sparse" and that its decision-making process is "opaque."

[11] "China Feels Encircled," *Economist,* June 6, 2002.

[12] United Nations Security Council, *Special Report of the Secretary-General on the United Nations Organization Mission in the Democratic of the Congo,* S/2002/1005 (September 10, 2002), para. 59, 10.

[13] United Nations Security Council, *Fourteenth Report of the Secretary-General on the United Nations Organization Mission in the Democratic of the Congo,* S/2003/1098, (November 17, 2002). Frank Nyakairu, Kefa Atibuni, and Tabu Butagira, "Hema, Lendu Peace Deal Flops in Arua," *Monitor,* Kampala, Uganda, January 1, 2003, posted to the web January 2, 2003 at allafrica.com/stories/200301020580.html.

transparency and information operations have proven potential for reducing tension and defusing crises and hostile incidents.

This recommendation is surprisingly necessary: during my research interviews when I explained that I was researching whether and how peacekeeping operations increase transparency, the person I was interviewing often did not understand transparency or assumed I meant that I was investigating whether or not the operation itself was transparent to others. While increasing self-transparency is important, whether and how peacekeeping operations could increase transparency among adversaries appeared not to have crossed many practitioners' minds until I explained further. Even those who realize the need to use information to educate local parties about the role of the U.N. often do not grasp the other roles of information and transparency examined in this study: reducing fears among adversaries, reducing miscalculation, or making violators back down. Information is a crucial tool in helping peacekeepers become peacemakers by shaping the interests and preferences of adversaries.[14] The major argument of appendix A is that the U.N. continues to avoid exploiting information and transparency to help their missions.[15] Unfortunately, the same is largely true of the United States where public diplomacy receives little respect within the State Department, despite the media profile of Under-Secretary for Public Diplomacy and Public Affairs Karen Hughes and several new broadcasting efforts into the Middle East.[16]

Once aware of the importance of the informational aspects of their missions, peacekeepers might be more willing to devote adequate personnel and resources to information-gathering and -dissemination. Five-minute or one-hour-a-week broadcasts are inadequate. For peacekeepers to provide information that mitigates fears, they must be able to learn about whatever rumors and misperceptions are circulating. Greater use of information technologies must be accompanied by the development and deployment of experts on the area of operations for each peacekeeping operation. Peacekeeping operations often do not have enough in-house expertise or information-gathering capability to help them adequately separate myth from fact or provide tension-reducing information.[17]

[14] Sambanis in "The United Nations Operation in Cyprus" offers a general model in which peacekeeping can have positive or negative effects on peacemaking, pp. 83–85.

[15] This remains true as of September 26, 2005, when I received an email from an UNMEE official stating, "I'm writing to commend you on your excellent article 'Untapped Power?' I currently work with UNMEE and sadly agree with your analysis of the lost opportunities." See Lindley, "Untapped Power? The Status of U.N. Information Operations," *International Peacekeeping*, 11, no. 4 (Winter 2004): 608–24.

[16] Stephen Johnson, "Public Diplomacy Needs a Commander, Not a Spokesman," Web-Memo no. 869, Heritage Foundation, September 30, 2005, available at www.heritage.org/Research/NationalSecurity/wm869.cfm.

[17] For the U.N.'s difficulties in intelligence gathering, see Hugh Smith, "Intelligence and UN Peacekeeping," *Survival* 36, no. 3 (Autumn 1994); for details on how the U.N. can

A greater emphasis is needed on up-to-date monitoring technologies from audio-triangulators to motion-sensors and night vision goggles. Much of this equipment would end up saving money by increasing the effectiveness of each peacekeeper.[18]

Second, if peacekeepers become more aware of their transparency-increasing roles, this could lead them to a number of new roles and missions. For example, peacekeepers could go beyond often-passive border patrols and post-hoc incident reports and take the initiative to try to increase transparency. They could monitor each sides' policies and statements and try to supplement these with relevant facts to help get the adversaries operating with more common and accurate information. While U.N. peacekeeping operations may have resources devoted to media monitoring, this usually amounts to a news-clipping service, not the purposeful collection of data for later analysis. There appears to be no formal procedures for using media monitoring as part of more active information operations.

U.N.-flagged aerial surveillance planes could help track rebel and government forces in internal conflicts, which would allow for the possibility of subjecting them to the international spotlight and international condemnation. Refugees in these conflicts occasionally become literally lost, making aid deliveries impossible. An ancillary but nontrivial benefit of the aerial surveillance would be to help locate refugees.[19]

Peacekeepers could set up truth squads and seek to quash or defuse myths and rumors before they get out of hand. To do this, doctrines, procedures, and capabilities would have to be provided to the in-house information and media departments organic to most peacekeeping operations. In cases where a full-scale peacekeeping operation is not possible or desirable, the U.N. could experiment with limited information operations that seek only to increase transparency. A U.N. news radio located near a troubled area might do some good if it helped quash rumors and deflate myths held by each side. In general, among the peacekeepers' jobs is to talk to both sides. This means that even the lowest-ranked peacekeepers on the line should be educated about the conflict that their mission is trying to defuse.

Third, this research, combined with the recognition that hate-mongering is a major cause of ethnic conflict, suggests that information and anti-

---

successfully gather information and direct media campaigns to address specific problems and defuse tensions, see chap. 7 on the U.N. mission in Cambodia, especially discussion of Radio UNTAC.

[18] For more, see Salerno et. al., "Enhanced Peacekeeping with Monitoring Technologies"; and Dorn, "Blue Sensors."

[19] This benefit was suggested to me in a November 9, 2005, email from Francis X. Stenger, Deputy Division Chief for implementation of the Open Skies Treaty at the Defense Threat Reduction Agency (DTRA) within the Department of Defense.

propaganda campaigns might be effective tools against ethnic conflict. My research shows that the U.N.'s information campaigns, by substituting facts for rumors, helped defuse tensions in Cambodia and Namibia. The U.N.'s radio station in Cambodia became the most popular in the country and competed with stations run by the rival political parties. Research indicates that many ethnic conflicts are started by ethno-nationalist political entrepreneurs who are quick to grab control of the media and use hate-mongering to come to power and/or cause harm to others.[20] These two observations provide the logic for the recommendation that the U.N. and other actors should launch information and anti-propaganda campaigns to try to defang the hate-mongers, whose propaganda manipulates ethnic histories and politics and thus fuels many deadly conflicts.

These three sets of recommendations are more likely to apply to smaller and less well-developed states. The active provision of transparency—such as that achieved in peacekeeping operations—will be most helpful to states whose own unilateral abilities to gather intelligence are limited. Similarly, information and anti-propaganda campaigns are more workable and are more likely to succeed in areas with relatively undeveloped media infrastructures.

[20] See Gagnon, "Ethnic Nationalism and International Conflict"; Misha Glenny, "Yugoslavia: The Revenger's Tragedy," *New York Review of Books,* August 13, 1992; and Michael Brown, *The International Dimensions of Internal Conflict* (Cambridge, MA: MIT Press, 1996).

Information Operations in Recent
U.N. Peacekeeping Missions

EXPERIENCE FROM the peacekeeping cases discussed previously shows that information operations can achieve a number of objectives, including the following:

- Reducing false rumors that adversaries may have about each other (examples: reducing fears of election-day violence, rumors of troop movements or military construction). This effect is expressed by hypothesis H4, which contends that transparency reduces unwarranted fears and worst-case assumptions.
- Confirming or reinforcing positive developments (example: confirming troop withdrawals or disarmament). This effect is also conveyed by H4.
- Disclosing violations by local parties (and the threat of disclosure), which can help spur compliance (example: disclosure reducing pre-election fraud and dirty tricks). This outcome reflects H5, which contends that disclosure coerces aggressors.
- Reducing false rumors that local parties may have about the U.N. operation (example: informing locals that the U.N. is not there to displace people or support one side or another). This result is captured by H6, which contends that transparency about the regime and its mission increases its effectiveness.
- Helping local parties understand why and how to vote, or how to fulfill other functions helpful to society (example: instructions on how to use ballot boxes and explaining why votes are secret). This is also H6.

Information is power, and UNTAC and UNTAG show that information in the hands of the U.N. is power to help promote peace. Yet the U.N. remains reluctant or unable to use this form of power. There has been no sustained program to experiment with information operations, and the U.N.'s information capabilities and expertise are getting better but remain inadequate. Why do these problems persist more than a decade after the recognized information successes of UNTAC and UNTAG? How can these problems be fixed?

In this appendix, I examine why the U.N. does not use information to maximum advantage, and I note a few positive trends. I begin by reviewing a number of recent U.N. reports and show that information is underappreciated at the leadership level of the U.N., but that the U.N. is taking steps in the right direction.

Then, to understand recent trends in the use of information at the field level, I survey three of the most recently launched peacekeeping operations. These operations are the United Nations Mission in Ethiopia and Eritrea (UNMEE), the United Nations Organization Mission in the Democratic Republic of Congo (MONUC), and the United Nations Interim Administration Mission in Kosovo (UNMIK). Without doing field research, and without the time for scholarship to develop on these missions, I cannot tell too many stories about the provision and effects of transparency. I do not have enough details to answer the question, Who said what to whom and what effects did it have? I can, however, assess the U.N.'s overall commitment to information operations from U.N. documents and interviews. The overall picture is mixed, with some signs of hesitancy and inadequacy, and other signs of innovative uses of information.

Finally, I show how problems ranging from hardware and training to bureaucratic inertia stand in the way of the U.N.'s more aggressive use of information.

The Status of Information Operations at the Headquarters Level

The August 2000 *Report of the Panel on United Nations Peace Operations,* better known as the Brahimi report, remains a keystone for assessing and critiquing peacekeeping operations.[1] The report reveals the U.N.'s inadequate appreciation of information operations in peacekeeping operations. The report's assessment of the causes of conflict does not recognize the information environment as a factor that can affect the difficulty of coming to or implementing a peace accord. The report ignores issues of whether the media in the conflict area is independent or partisan, sparse or dense, or whether the adversaries are illiterate, or besieged by rumors, fears, and misinformation.[2] If information-related factors are not recognized as parts of the problem, they are less likely to be recognized as parts of the solution. Information tools such as radio and television broadcasting are mentioned only once in a laundry list of expertises that have proven hard to deploy on short notice.[3] The report does not mention broadcasting or print hardware.

[1] United Nations, A/55/305-S/2000/809 (New York: August 2000). Lakhdar Brahimi chaired the panel that wrote the report.
[2] S/2000/809, p. 4.
[3] S/2000/809, p. 22.

The report strongly recommends an Executive Committee on Peace and Security Information and Strategic Analysis Secretariat (EISAS). This sounds promising for information operations, but the focus of this ultimately unsuccessful recommendation was instead to gather and coordinate information about operations and world events.

Only five of the report's 280 paragraphs are devoted to public information (PI). One is a summary paragraph, and two relate to strengthening internal communications within operations. Only two paragraphs relate to the external face of operations. This is .7 percent of the report, coincidentally in line with paragraph 149's observation that public information rarely exceeds 1 percent of an operation's budget.[4]

The most encouraging paragraph for information operations is number 146:

An effective public information and communications capacity in mission areas is an operational necessity for virtually all United Nations peace operations. Effective communication helps to dispel rumour, to counter disinformation and to secure the cooperation of local populations. It can provide leverage in dealing with leaders of rival groups, enhance security of United Nations personnel and serve as a force multiplier. It is thus essential that every peace operation formulate public information campaign strategies, particularly for key aspects of a mission's mandate, and that such strategies and the personnel required to implement them be included in the very first elements deployed to help start up a new mission.[5]

While the report is to be commended for recognizing the role of information in dispelling rumors and acting as a force multiplier, the following paragraphs describe how the report led to only one "relatively minor" recommendation for improving information operations.[6]

The Brahimi report's most critical information-related finding was that "no unit at [U.N.] Headquarters has specific line responsibility for the operational requirements of public information components in peace operations." They note that the small, but soon expanding, team of four in the Peace and Security Section of the Department of Public Information (DPI) "has had little capacity to create doctrine, strategy or standard operating procedures for public information functions in the field."[7]

To address this concern, an August 2001 implementation report proposed setting up a team of four information specialists within the

---

[4] S/2000/809, p. 26.

[5] S/2000/809, pp. 25–26, quote on p. 25.

[6] David Wimhurst, "Preparing a Plebiscite under Fire: The United Nations and Public Information in East Timor," in Price and Thompson, eds., *Forging Peace*, 307.

[7] S/2000/809, p. 40. The team now numbers five.

Department of Peacekeeping Operations (DPKO).[8] The Advisory Committee on Administrative and Budgetary Questions soon blocked this worthy initiative:

> The Committee is of the opinion, however, that the Department of Public Information should have a dedicated technical unit to perform the functions described. The operational activities and related programmes should be requested in the context of each peacekeeping mission. Accordingly, the Committee does not agree to the establishment of this functional capacity in the Department of Peacekeeping Operations.[9]

This assessment implies the improbable: that the DPI is more likely to consider the context of each mission than the DPKO. While the DPI does much good work, an information unit within the Department of Peacekeeping Operations is more likely to think creatively about using information in ways that go beyond self-promotion or clarification of an operation's purposes (valuable as those functions are). A subsequent implementation report avoids the issue of the technical unit, perhaps because of the bureaucratic politics issues hinted at earlier.[10] As is, there is currently only one information specialist, David Wimhurst, within the DPKO. I argue below that the U.N. should greatly expand this capacity.

A source close to the initial Brahimi report and subsequent implementation reports thinks that the foregoing critique is too strong. He noted that the short mention of information operations was meant to "tee up" the issue and give reformers license to reform. In this way, a few paragraphs helped lead to the attempted initiative to put an information unit in the Department of Peacekeeping Operations. Moreover, he said that the few paragraphs on information should be put into context. Many other important issues received few or even no words at all, including gender, medical support, HIV/AIDS, transitions, and safety of personnel. In the end, though, he said that it was still "hand to mouth" with information operations.[11] A response to this comment is that perhaps the information initiative failed because it was not teed up more prominently.

An outside report, "Refashioning the Dialogue," which gathered international reaction to the Brahimi report, suggests why the Brahimi report

---

[8] See United Nations, *Comprehensive Review of the Whole Question of Peacekeeping Operations in All Their Aspects: Programme Budget Implications of Draft Resolution* A/C. 4/55/L.23 (New York: United Nations, August 8, 2001), A/C.5/55/46/Add.1, p. 13, para 5.12.

[9] See United Nations, *Implementation of the Report of the Panel on United Nations Peace Operations* (New York: United Nations, October 16, 2001), A/56/478, p. 7.

[10] United Nations, *Implementation of the Recommendations of the Special Committee on Peacekeeping Operations and the Panel on United Nations Peace Operations: Report of the Secretary-General* (New York: United Nations, December 21, 2001), A/56/732.

[11] Not for attribution.

may have shied away from the discussion of information operations: governments fear spying or any impingement of their sovereign control. For example, the report relayed that some member states were "alarmed" by the plan for an Information and Strategic Analysis Secretariat (EISAS), even though the EISAS is primarily intended to improve the flow of information from the field to headquarters and vice-versa. Many governments in Africa resist even fact-finding missions, and so some hostility to EISAS is not surprising.[12] On a general level, information operations and radio stations are "threatening and provoke caution in an organization where sovereignty is king."[13]

On the other hand, peacekeeping operations are routinely preceded by survey missions and other analysis. It is a bit contradictory that member states fear better information-gathering and analysis (as well as active information dissemination) by the U.N., when the executive summary of "Refashioning the Dialogue" said that many simultaneously argued that "Impartiality should be seen in terms of the fair application of a mandate, not as an excuse for moral equivocation. In Africa in particular, there was strong support for more robust mandates for peacekeepers to deal with spoilers."[14] Why are information operations so sensitive when there are calls for the U.N. to be strong enough to take on spoilers?

THE STATUS OF INFORMATION OPERATIONS IN THE FIELD

A survey of three recently launched operations presents a complex picture, with successes in areas where missions undertake local initiative and innovation, and room for improvement where information operations are underappreciated. The reason that there is so much variation among missions is lack of leadership and innovation from U.N. headquarters.

UNMEE operates between Ethiopia and Eritrea, where misperceptions about the other side run high, and where both sides misperceive the U.N. The current chief of mission, however, does not value information, and so information efforts are scant. In Kosovo, UNMIK started out with very high UNTAC-like ambitions, but peaked with moderate print and broadcast operations, which were then scaled back. UNMIK appreciates the role of information and is leveraging its limited resources in part by coordinating with and urging stories upon the local media. In Congo,

---

[12] International Peace Academy and Center on International Cooperation, "Refashioning the Dialogue: Regional Perspectives on the Brahimi Report on UN Peace Operations," International Peace Academy, New York, April 2001, p. 9, quote on p. 16.

[13] Interview, Frederick Schottler, April 25, 1996.

[14] International Peace Academy, "Refashioning the Dialogue," 5.

MONUC helps run the most ambitious radio operation in the U.N.'s history, Radio Okapi, developed by an innovative partnership between the U.N. and a Swiss NGO, the Fondation Hirondelle. The use of other media by MONUC, however, seems wholly inadequate to the scale of the mission. On the whole, recognition of the potential of information operations is uneven, and information resources are generally insufficient.

United Nations Mission in Ethiopia and Eritrea (UNMEE)

Following a successful and bloody thirty-year liberation struggle, Eritrea gained its independence from Ethiopia in a referendum in April of 1993. Despite the prior conflict and pervasive insecurity in the Horn of Africa, hopes for a more permanent peace between Ethiopia and Eritrea grew through the mid-1990s. Optimism peaked when President Clinton viewed Ethiopia and Eritrea as exemplars of the African Renaissance. A border dispute reopened conflict in May of 1998, and the war waxed and waned until December 2000.[15]

In July 1999, the two sides accepted a Framework Agreement mediated by the Organization for African Unity (OAU). Although fighting continued, the agreement called for the separation of forces, demilitarization and delimitation of the border areas, and monitoring of the new temporary security zone (buffer zone) by international observers. In mid-June 2000, Ethiopia and Eritrea signed an OAU-brokered cease-fire, and on July 31, the U.N. Security Council established UNMEE with resolution 1312. Ethiopia and Eritrea signed a permanent peace agreement on December 12, which required "establishment of a neutral Boundary Commission to 'delimit and demarcate the colonial treaty border.'" UNMEE quickly deployed, reaching and then exceeding its mandated strength of 4,200 troops (including 220 observers) in early 2001. It costs about $231 million per year. The core of UNMEE's mandate is to monitor the cease-fire, the redeployments of the Ethiopian and Eritrean forces, and the subsequent buffer zone, as well as to assist the Boundary Commission and to help with demining and with humanitarian activities.[16]

---

[15] Paul B. Henze, "Ethiopia and Eritrea in Transition: The Impact of Ethnicity on Politics and Development," Rand publication number P-7937 (Santa Monica, CA: Rand Corporation, 1995); Terrence Lyons, "Great Powers and Conflict Resolution in the Horn of Africa," in I. William Zartmann and Victor A. Kremenyuk, *Cooperative Security: Reducing Third World Wars* (Syracuse, NY: Syracuse University Press, 1995); Jane Perlez, "U.S. Did Little to Deter Buildup as Ethiopia and Eritrea Prepared for War," *New York Times,* May 22, 2000; John Prendergast and Mark Duffield, "Liberation Politics in Ethiopia and Eritrea," in Taiser M. Ali and Robert O. Matthews, eds., *Civil Wars in Africa: Roots and Resolution* (Montreal, Canada: McGill-Queens University Press, 1999).

[16] See "Ethiopia and Eritrea—UNMEE—Background," United Nations, New York, 2002, available at www.un.org/Depts/dpko/missions/unmee/background.html; "Ethiopia

Information operations started slowly, suffered setbacks, and remain inadequate. UNMEE radio first broadcast from Eritrea in January 2001. The broadcasts lasted for one hour, and were repeated twice a week. Eritrea suspended broadcasts in October 2001, and permitted resumption of the one-hour shows in June 2002. Ethiopia does not want to cede control of its airwaves, and it refuses to give UNMEE free air time. To help circumvent these local difficulties, UNMEE began shortwave broadcasts from the United Arab Emirates, with one-hour shows on Tuesdays and Fridays. Considerably reducing the effective length of its shows, UNMEE divides each hour into English and anywhere between three to five local languages.

The central purpose of the broadcasts, and the two outreach centers originally put in each country, is to explain and publicize the mission's mandate and work. These goals are on the modest end of the information operations continuum, but UNMEE's means remain insufficient for the task. For example, the information centers have staff and documentation to help citizens understand the U.N. and the peace process, and to increase mine awareness. Before the Eritrean government shut down its two centers in mid-summer 2003, the center in the Eritrean capital of Asmara (population: 435,000) served only several hundred people a week. UNMEE's weekly press briefings are still the "key instrument for disseminating news about the Mission's activities."[17] A weekly press briefing does not a meaningful information operation make.

This is unfortunate because, according to Chris Coleman, team leader for UNMEE at the DPKO, there are still many misperceptions and misunderstandings to clear up. A March 2002 U.N. report noted that there remains tensions and suspicions between the two sides' forces. Coleman stressed that the biggest need was for the proactive use of information to clarify the role of UNMEE and especially that of the Boundary Commission.

Both Eritrea and especially Ethiopia resist U.N. information efforts. Another U.N. official (not Coleman), however, placed the blame for inadequate use of information by UNMEE on the current chief of mission: he "does not subscribe to the importance of public information on a regular basis."[18]

---

and Eritrea—UNMEE—Facts and Figures," United Nations, New York 2003, available at www.un.org/Depts/dpko/missions/unmee/facts.html; and "Ethiopia and Eritrea—UNMEE-Mandate," United Nations, New York 2002, available at www.un.org/Depts/dpko/missions/unmee/mandate.html.

[17] United Nations, *Progress Report of the Secretary-General on Ethiopia and Eritrea,* S/2003/665 (New York, NY: United Nations, June 23, 2003), 7.

[18] This section is based on: UNMEE, "Near-Verbatim Transcription of Press Briefing," 06 September 2002, available at www.waltainfo.com/Conflict/Articles/2002/September/

U.N. Interim Administration Mission in Kosovo (UNMIK)

On June 10, 1999, Security Council Resolution 1244 created the U.N. Interim Administration Mission in Kosovo (UNMIK). UNMIK was to help Kosovo move toward autonomy from Serbian-led Yugoslavia. This followed years of tension and sometimes conflict with Belgrade, culminating in the U.S.-led NATO military campaign against Serbia and its leader Slobodan Milosevic in Spring 1999. More specifically, UNMIK was mandated to help with civilian administration and promote self-government in Kosovo, help coordinate the humanitarian efforts of international agencies, help maintain law and order, promote human rights, and assist with refugee repatriation.

The broad range of the mandate requires education of the populace on a range of issues, from the operation of a free market economy and political development to the creation of a new Constitutional Framework. To service these needs, UNMIK produces a weekly twenty-five-minute television broadcast on issues from human rights to health, including "themes that are still too sensitive for local media to cover."[19] UNMIK also produces a monthly program on crime and another on the economy.

On radio, UNMIK broadcasts a five-minute daily program in Albanian, Serbian, and English, and a six-minute weekly roundup. UNMIK borrows station time for its TV and radio programs from Radio Television Kosovo (RTK). RTK is the national public broadcaster in Kosovo, supervised by the Organization for Security and Cooperation in Europe (OSCE) and managed by the European Broadcasting Union. UNMIK's print unit produces a number of items covering a similar range of topics as the broadcast division: a bimonthly magazine, fact sheets, booklets and leaflets, and UNMIK newsletters; and they used to produce weekly inserts for the local newspapers.

---

article1.htm; UNMEE Public Information, "Edited Transcript of 2 November 2001 Press Briefings, available at www.un.org/Depts/dpko/unmee/pc021101.htm; United Nations, *Progress Report of the Secretary-General on Ethiopia and Eritrea,* S/2002/977 (New York: United Nations, August 30, 2002), 5; United Nations, *Report of the Secretary-General on Ethiopia and Eritrea,* S/2002/744 (New York: United Nations, July 10, 2002), United Nations, *Progress Report of the Secretary-General on Ethiopia and Eritrea,* S/2002/245 (New York: United Nations, March 8, 2002), 1–2, 7; Dr. Hansjoerg Biener, "Radio for Peace, Democracy and Human Rights: Eritrea," at www.evrel.ewf.uni-erlangen.de/pesc/peaceradio-ERI.html; telephone interview with Chris Coleman, January 29, 2003; email correspondence with Dr. Hansjoerg Biener, Universität Erlangen-Nürnberg, Nürnberg, Denmark, January 2003; and email correspondence and a telephone interview with a U.N. official (not for attribution).

[19] "UNMIK: Television," (UNMIK-DPI, 2001) available at www.unmikonline.org/tv/tv.htm.

The print effort is more substantial than the broadcast activities, but all seem to pale before the scope of the mandate, before the number of other information sources in the area (some ninety-two radio stations, twenty-four television stations, and seven daily newspapers), and before the precedent set by UNTAC and its variety of information operations—especially Radio UNTAC. This is not an indictment per se; it is difficult for the U.N. to compete in a dense media environment.

Nonetheless, some in UNMIK went in hoping to replicate the UNTAC model—but the resources and political support were not there. For example, the Organization for Security and Cooperation in Europe (OSCE) and UNMIK divided media responsibilities, but cooperation between the two soon soured. Instead of sharing the information burden, OSCE and UNMIK policies often conflicted and/or their initiatives were redundant.[20]

There are three notable positives about the use of information in Kosovo. The first is UNMIK's Temporary Media Commissioner, who monitors the media and ensures adherence to print and broadcast codes. The aim is to prevent libel, overtly hostile hate radio broadcasts, and the like. The commissioner has the authority to fine violators, and this appears to be an aggressive effort by the U.N. to control the information flow and reduce tensions.[21]

The second was the cooperation between UNMIK and the Fondation Hirondelle to set up the Blue Sky radio station. Funded by the Swiss government, the station was a step toward increasing the amount of independent journalism in Kosovo. Independent media efforts have been opposed by everything from organized crime to political parties. Blue Sky started up in October 1999, but was folded into RTK in July 2000. Blue Sky covered UNMIK's activities and other developments in Kosovo, thus the station was an information-multiplier for UNMIK, and it demonstrated productive collaboration between the U.N. and an NGO to meet common goals. UNMIK, however, does not coordinate routinely with NGOs about information issues.

Finally, UNMIK officials influence the information flow in a number of peace-promoting ways that are more subtle than direct UNMIK broadcasting. According to UNMIK press officer Eleanor Beardsley, in one instance in August 2002, UNMIK began arresting major Kosovo Liberation Army (KLA) heroes for war crimes. As the anti-Serb KLA enjoys considerable support in Kosovo, there were huge and violent protests in the street involving 10,000 Kosovars. UNMIK got the top police people

---

[20] Julie Mertus and Mark Thompson, "The Learning Curve: Media Development in Kosovo," in Price and Thompson, eds., *Forging Peace*, 261–64, 270, 272.

[21] United Nations, *Report of the Secretary-General on the United Nations Interim Administration Mission in Kosovo*, S/2001/926 (New York: United Nations, October 2, 2001), 10–11.

on the TV that night and showed that those arrested had tortured Albanians (Kosovars and Albanians are cultural brethren or even co-nationals in the minds of many). The protests "stopped on a dime." UNMIK also hosts dinners for editors and intellectuals to talk on background, and they bring journalists along for police operations. This sort of relationship-building gets good stories out. Having locals help produce UNMIK's print and broadcast output helps build credibility. Beardsley said, "We are in the business of changing society and hearts and minds here. . . . There is so much twisting of information and misinformation out there, especially in the Balkans. So we don't try to counter all of it. But we do fight back."[22]

UNMIK's intentions are good, and they are doing what they can with limited resources.[23]

United Nations Organization Mission in the Democratic Republic of Congo (MONUC)

Supported by Rwanda and Uganda, Zaire was taken over by Laurent Kabila in 1997 and renamed the Democratic Republic of Congo. A schism developed between Kabila and his backers, however, causing a rebellion in 1998. Angola, Namibia, and Zimbabwe sided with Kabila against Rwanda and Uganda, turning Congo into a multinational war zone. A peace agreement was signed by most of the parties in December 2002. Some foreign forces have withdrawn, but Uganda and Rwanda still ap-

---

[22] Email correspondence, Eleanor Beardsley, Press Officer, UNMIK, and Senior Editor, Focus Kosovo, Kosovo, January 2003.

[23] Other sources for this section include the following: Ivo H. Daalder and Michael E. O'Hanlon: *Winning Ugly: NATO's War to Save Kosovo* (Washington, D.C.: Brookings Institution, 2000); Mertus and Thompson, "The Learning Curve"; United Nations, *Report of the Secretary-General on the United Nations Interim Administration Mission in Kosovo*, S/2002/62 (New York: United Nations, January 15, 2002); United Nations, *Report of the Secretary-General on the United Nations Interim Administration Mission in Kosovo*, S/2002/1126 (New York: United Nations, October 9, 2002); and Larry Wentz, contributing editor, *Lessons for Kosovo: The KFOR Experience* (Washington, DC: Department of Defense Command and Control Research Program, 2002) as well as Radio Netherlands Media Network Dossier: Peace Radio: Outside Africa, updated September 25, 2002, at: www.rnw.nl/realoradio/dossiers/html/peaceradiorest.html; Dr. Hansjoerg Biener, "Radio for Peace, Democracy and Human Rights: Yugoslavia (Kosovo)," available at www.evrel.ewf.uni-erlangen.de/pesc/peaceradio-YU.html; "UNMIK: Radio," (UNMIK-DPI, 2001), available at www.unmikonline.org/radio/radio.htm; "UNMIK: Publications" (UNMIK-DPI, 2001), available at www.unmikonline.org/pub/pub.htm; "UNMIK: At a Glance" (UNMIK-DPI, 2001), available at www.unmikonline.org/intro.htm; BBC News, "Country Profile: Yugoslavia," January 29, 2003, available at news.bbc.co.uk/2/hi/europe/country_profiles/1039269.stm; "Blue Sky—Fact Sheet" and "Communiqué de Presse, 3 Août 2000," both available at the website of Fondation Hirondelle at www.hirondelle.org.

pear to control much of Eastern Congo, and there is still conflict among various ethnic groups within Congo.

U.N. involvement in the Congo conflict began to increase in July 1999 when U.N. Security Council Resolution 1258 authorized the deployment of up to ninety military liaison personnel to the region. In November, the U.N. formed the United Nations Organization Mission in the Democratic Republic of Congo (MONUC) at a strength of about 600 (500 observers plus the previous 90 liaison and survey personnel) with Resolution 1279. Then in February 2000, Resolution 1291 expanded MONUC to more than 5,500 military personnel. The deployed strength as of December 31, 2002, was 4,420 military personnel, 49 civilian police, and 559 international and 675 local civilian personnel.

According to Resolution 1291, MONUC was mandated to monitor the cease-fire, establish liaison with all parties, collect information on the parties' forces, help to disarm and demobilize those forces, supervise and verify the disengagement of forces, monitor the disengagement line, as well as to assist with humanitarian activities and demining.

MONUC deployed into a violent and complicated ongoing conflict. The situation is still fluid, and it is hard to gather data on the information-related activities of MONUC.

There are, however, some transparency-related stories and facts: for example, in September–October 2002, MONUC verified that 20,941 Rwandan forces had withdrawn from Congo, but the Rwandan forces claimed a withdrawal of 23,760. This discrepancy prompted MONUC to investigate. There are ninety military observer teams at fifty sites, but the bulk of MONUC's force (3,590 out of 4,258) is assigned to protect MONUC headquarters and other facilities.[24] Overall though, it is hard to discern what MONUC has verified or what effects monitoring and verification have had in prompting the adversaries to trust and cooperate with the peace process. This is not a major indictment of MONUC, for it is hard to imagine a peace operation facing a more difficult environment.

Turning to its public information efforts, MONUC produced some 60,000 posters and 50,000 bumper stickers from June to October 2002. It puts out a monthly magazine in French with a circulation of 5,000, a weekly newsletter, and a biweekly bulletin, as well as compiling a daily press review with news clippings. MONUC is using information to encourage combatants to disarm and repatriate, and to achieve this end, they are trying to obtain three mobile FM transmitters.[25] The population

[24] United Nations, *Twelfth Report of the Secretary-General on the United Nations Organization Mission in the Democratic Republic of Congo*, S/2002/1180 (New York: United Nations, October 18, 2002), 2–3, 5.

[25] Ibid., 9–10.

of Congo is about fifty million, and the country covers an area almost equal to one-fourth the size of the United States.

There is one significant exception to this otherwise typical and modest information effort, and that is Radio Okapi. Radio Okapi is the most extensive U.N. radio project ever, broadcasting twenty-four hours a day, seven days a week, and reaching the whole Congo on FM via eight relay stations and on shortwave via three transmitters. Launched in February 2002, Radio Okapi's content ranges from music to news, and includes material provided by the U.N. or interviews with MONUC officials. The main topics that aim to promote peace are: disarmament, demobilization, repatriation, resettlement, and reintegration. According to David Smith, MONUC's chief of information,

> There is no single voice that unites all the Congolese people. This radio project will allow people in the rebel-held territories to speak to people in government-controlled territories for the first time since the war broke out. A big role of the radio will be to convince people that it's in their interest to lay down their arms and either be repatriated to their home country, if they come from somewhere else, or to find ways to join civil society and leave the war behind.[26]

Radio Okapi is a joint project between MONUC and the Swiss-based NGO Fondation Hirondelle. Smith and David Wimhurst of the U.N. and the Fondation Hirondelle began planning the station in June 2001. The Fondation Hirondelle raised the funds, bought the equipment, and donated it to the U.N. which then deployed it out of Brindisi, Italy (the location of the U.N.'s rapid deployment logistics base, UNLB). The NGO currently pays about 85 percent of the operating expenses. The main station is located in MONUC's Kinshasa headquarters, but Radio Okapi is sufficiently independent that, says Smith, it might even criticize the U.N.'s role in the country.[27]

Beyond sheer ambition, Radio Okapi innovated in a number of ways: bypassing the U.N. procurement system, establishing direct ties between the U.N. and an NGO (including legal agreements between them), and deploying rapidly: going from concept to broadcast in seven months. According to Wimhurst, "The U.N. can't do this by itself. The partnership model is successful for the audience, the donors, the mission, and it will leave behind a well-funded independent radio for Congo."[28]

---

[26] Radio Netherlands Media Network Dossier: Peace Radio: Democratic Republic of Congo, updated December 10, 2002, available at www.rnw.nl/realoradio/dossiers/html/congo-p.html.

[27] Telephone interview, January 2003.

[28] Joan B. Kroc Institute for Peace and Justice, "Peace and Justice Update," newsletter, vol. 3, no. 6 (San Diego, CA: University of San Diego, March 8, 2002); telephone interview, David Wimhurst, October 24, 2003.

Asked what effect the radio had in Congo, an official at the Fondation Hirondelle said it was hard to judge as yet, but that in-country polling revealed that it had become the most popular station in the country within six months of its launch.[29]

CONCLUSION: IMPEDIMENTS TO U.N. INFORMATION OPERATIONS

Despite some areas of progress, there are many hurdles to overcome before the U.N. can use information operations to maximum advantage. These include difficulties with personnel, planning, hardware, and bureaucratic resistance. There are also concerns about keeping information operations impartial, and fears harbored by some populations that information operations are tantamount to spying by the U.N. or member states. The fundamental problem for information operations at the U.N. is that they remain ad hoc, with little institutionalized support, and without sufficient planning and resources coming from the highest levels.

Personnel: Problems with Recruitment, Staffing, and Training

The major personnel problem is that there is insufficient training for information operations. As a result, it takes too much time to assemble an information team. There is still a long way to go toward developing a useful rapid deployment roster and some of the reported progress in the years-long effort is "just PR [public relations]."[30]

The DPI and the DPKO have organized some public information–related workshops and training exercises, including one in Dakar in late 2003, to train public information officers in Africa how to handle issues that come up with demobilization, disarmament, and reintegration (DDR).

---

[29] Telephone interview, Dario Baroni, Desk Officer, Fondation Hirondelle, Geneva, Switzerland, January 28, 2003. Other sources consulted for this section include: U.S. Department of State, "Background Note: Democratic Republic of Congo," available at www.state.gov/r/pa/ei/bgn/2823.htm; BBC News, "Country Profile: Democratic Republic of Congo," December 18, 2002, at news.bbc.co.uk/2/hi/europe/country_profiles/1076399.stm; United Nations, "Democratic Republic of Congo—MONUC—Background," United Nations, New York 2002, at www.un.org/Depts/dpko/missions/monuc/background.html; United Nations, "Democratic Republic of Congo—MONUC—Facts and Figures," United Nations, New York 2002, at www.un.org/Depts/dpko/missions/monuc/facts.html; United Nations, "Democratic Republic of Congo—MONUC—Mandate," United Nations, New York, 2002, at www.un.org/Depts/dpko/missions/monuc/mandate.html; Dr. Hansjoerg Biener, "Radio for Peace, Democracy and Human Rights: Kongo (Kinshasa)," at www.evrel.ewf.uni-erlangen.de/pesc/peaceradio-ZAI.html; Juakali Kambale, "Ondes Pacifiques," *Journal Decouverte*, April 3, 2002, at www.afrik.com/journal/decourverte/dec-487–6.htm; Radio Okapi.net, "Programmation de Radio Okapi a l'heure de Kinshasa, Mis à jour le 19/12/2002," at www.monuc.org/radio/programmation.asp.

[30] Telephone interview, David Wimhurst, October 24, 2003.

Unfortunately, the DPKO resisted this effort and sent a lower-level staffer than the DPI had wished for.

The U.N. received a grant from the British government's Department for International Development to train information officers, but it has yet to find a teacher.[31] Unfortunately, the few people who could teach the course are too busy helping in the field. Finally, training for public information issues related to tasks such as DDR is a worthy idea, but there is no training for the nuts and bolts of public information: how to set up an office when deployed, and how to deal with logistics, budgeting, procurement, and so forth. Some "50 percent of staff are not adequately trained or prepared for missions in the field. This is major . . . the single greatest weakness in public information."[32] Recruitment is another problem, in part because there are no hiring and recruitment staff with a background in public information.

Information Planning is Becoming a Higher Priority, but Problems with Doctrine and Procedures Remain

Planners must fully integrate information operations when preparing peacekeeping missions. On the positive side, on July 23, 2003, the secretary-general sent out a publication, "Guidance to Special Representatives of the Secretary-General: public information and Media Relations in United Nations Peace Operations," giving general guidance on how heads of mission should work with their respective spokespersons and public information officers and what kinds of information they should be gathering and disseminating. Another positive is a chapter on public information in a forthcoming U.N. handbook on multidimensional operations. The book leaves specific operational instructions aside, but goes into admirable depth on the need for information operations to confront hate media, to explain the purpose of the mission to the local population, to develop independent media capabilities in-country, to play a proactive role in countering misperceptions, and to engage in counter-propaganda.[33]

Despite these developments, there seem to be perpetual delays in formulating information standard operating procedures (SOPs), and public information staff face hurdles trying to communicate their needs to the planners.[34] According to one source, the SOPs were in draft form in Oc-

---

[31] Telephone interview, Susan Manuel, Chief of Section, Peace and Security Programs, U.N. Department of Public Information, November 24, 2003.

[32] Telephone interview, Simon Davies, December 19, 2003.

[33] U.N., *Handbook on UN Multidimensional Peacekeeping Operations* (New York: United Nations, 2004), chap. 4, pp. 45–54, available at pbpu.unlb.org/pbpu/handbook.aspx.

[34] United Nations, "Meeting of Information Chiefs," report of a conference held December 11–13, 2001, pp. 21–23, and telephone interview, Susan Manuel, November 24, 2003.

tober 2001, and have been almost done for two years, but the DPI's Peace and Security Section has been too overwhelmed to finalize them. Another problem in designing information missions and tailoring them once they are in place is that there are no metrics (polling, surveys, etc.) for measuring the impact of various media efforts. The U.N. can get messages out, but it cannot assess their effects.

Hardware Capabilities: Considerable Progress and Potential

The U.N. has made considerable progress with hardware in two ways. The first is the pioneering cooperative effort between the Fondation Hirondelle and the U.N. in MONUC to provide radio coverage across Congo (see earlier discussion). This is a real hardware (and expertise) multiplier for the U.N., and it provides a model for future innovation. Increasing numbers of NGOs such as Search for Common Ground, Clandestine Radio, and the Open Society Institute have joined the information fray and are trying to combat hate radio and promote peace in various areas.[35] Many governments recognize the value of positive information and the necessity of combating hate radio; the British, Swiss, and U.S. governments are the three largest funders of Radio Okapi, and they channel the funds through their support of the Fondation Hirondelle.

The second area of progress is the acquisition of Public Information Strategic Deployment Stocks (SDS) for rapid deployment of media operations, located at the UNLB in Brindisi. The U.N. has procured about $1.5 million in equipment, mostly for radio broadcasting, along with materiel for print and video media. The procurement and deployment mechanisms, however, are convoluted and inefficient. Information materiel is procured through two different U.N. entities (supply and communications), and it arrives in Brindisi in a haphazard way with no asssurance of compatibility. From there, materiel is stored in different locations, and in part because different departments must release the equipment, it gets sent out from Brindisi in different packages.

The U.N. first used the SDS in its recent deployment to Liberia. The information team barely got a minimal broadcast out the first day. The information officers could not find their main transmitter for seven weeks, and they personally had to unload and search through hundreds of tons of equipment looking for the information materiel. Instead of being rapidly deployable, poor shipping procedures and inventory management meant that equipment languished on the docks.[36]

[35] For more on this issue, see Helen Darbishire, "Non-Governmental Perspectives: Media Freedom versus Information Intervention?" in Price and Thompson, eds., *Forging Peace.*

[36] Telephone interview, Simon Davies, December 19, 2003, and telephone interview, David Wimhurst, October 24, 2003.

Bureaucratic Problems

Bureaucratic problems exacerbate several of the afore-mentioned hurdles facing information operations at the U.N. First, coordination will remain hampered so long as the DPKO continues to have only one information officer in its 600-person-strong department. Second, physical distance between the DPI and the DPKO within U.N. headquarters limits cooperation. Third, the DPKO still does not pay enough attention to information operations.

Fourth, the DPI focuses almost entirely on producing content, and the DPI has no one who focuses on technical issues (the technical people are outside contractors). The DPI also has no specialists in the logistics chain necessary to support information operations.[37] Finally, many sources lamented that the DPI is over-centralized, lacks innovation, is self-absorbed, is insufficiently focused on peacekeeping (and other) missions in the field, and lacks respect from member nations and other units within the U.N.

One way to ameliorate these problems is to create a strong, dedicated information unit within the DPKO. Such a unit is more likely to think creatively about using information in ways that go beyond self-promotion or clarification of an operation's purposes (valuable as those functions are). The DPKO focuses solely on the mandates of its missions, while the DPI has responsibilities throughout the U.N. Hence, from a bureaucratic politics perspective, the DPKO is more likely to use information aggressively and creatively to serve the mission, and to have less institutional incentive or momentum to divert information resources away from the mandate. There are staffers with DPKO experience in the Peace and Security Section of the DPI. This kind of cross-pollinization helps both the DPI and the DPKO, and should be increased, as should rotations between the field and the U.N. in New York.

An information unit within the DPKO would be the kind of bureaucratic shakeup that would lead both units to innovate. For example, if the DPKO gained more control of information operations, the DPI might feel increased competitive incentives to help more aggressively in the field. As is, information operations face greater structural hurdles than they should because most of the DPI is innovation-averse. Likewise, those in the DPKO who undervalue information operations might reassess them if the DPKO contained more information advocates. A final argument for more information-resources going to the DPKO is that for each civilian component in the field (finance, personnel, and so forth), the DPKO has a corresponding support unit in house—except in the area of public information.[38]

---

[37] Telephone interview, Simon Davies, December 19, 2003.
[38] Wimhurst, "East Timor," 307.

Some may fear that increased information operations will cause re-source loss from their own divisions. Luckily, information operations are cheap. For example, MONUC cost 608 million dollars from July 2002 through June 2003. Yet Radio Okapi, the most ambitious radio operation in the history of the U.N., costs about four million dollars a year—about two-thirds of 1 percent of MONUC's expenses.[39]

Fears of Losing Impartiality and Fears of Spying

A source of resistance for information operations is that member states fear spying by the U.N. and are suspicious of activities with the word "in-formation" in their titles. In addition, many in the U.N. fear that the more active use of information would jeopardize its impartiality. I address these concerns in turn.

First, fears of spying cannot be waved away; it will take time and ex-perience with information operations. Those who fear can be reminded that survey missions and strategic analysis routinely precede peacekeep-ing operations, and all peacekeeping operations collect information (on such topics as the sources and nature of rumors, and the location and ar-mament of adversaries), just to be effective. Despite this, some govern-ments, particularly in Africa, resist even fact-finding missions. In this con-text, it is understandable that information operations and radio stations are "threatening and provoke caution in an organization where sovereignty is king."[40]

Second, fears that information operations will impair the U.N.'s im-partiality are off base. Consider the Brahimi report's sage advice about operations that may find themselves in violent situations:

> Impartiality for such operations must therefore mean adherence to the principles of the Charter and the objectives of a mandate that is rooted in those principles. Such impartiality is not the same as neutrality or equal treatment of all parties in all cases for all time, which can amount to a policy of appeasement. In some cases, local parties consist not of

---

[39] MONUC's budget is from the U.N. Department of Peacekeeping Operations fact sheet: "Democratic Republic of Congo—MONUC—Facts and Figures (U.N., 2003), at www .un.org/Depts/dpko/missions/monuc/facts.html. The budget for Radio Okapi was about four million dollars total from all sources in its first year, and so this figure might include some start-up costs. See Radio Netherlands Media Network Dossier: Peace Radio: Demo-cratic Republic of Congo, updated December 10, 2002, at www.rnw.nl/realradio/dossiers/ html/congo-p.html and European Broadcasting Union, Radio Department, "'Newsletter' No. 12 Des Radios Internationales," April 22, 2002, DR/10093, AS/AD-nll.

[40] International Peace Academy, "Refashioning the Dialogue"; and quote from interview, Frederick Schottler, April 25, 1996.

moral equals but of obvious aggressors and victims, and peacekeepers may not only be operationally justified in using force but morally compelled to do so.[41]

The U.N. will not lose impartiality by using truthful information. In any operation that deploys thousands of peacekeepers, it strains credulity to think that radio broadcasts will be the determining factor that makes the mission seem biased or partial. Indeed, information operations are often necessary to help combat misperceptions of bias.

Where aggressors are determined, little will stop them—including information. Where peace and war hang in the balance, however, there is evidence that information operations can coerce violators into better behavior. Combined with the clear benefits of explaining the mission, teaching about elections, and defusing rumors and misperceptions, there are few if any sound reasons not to proceed with more robust information operations.

This book examined whether information can be used to promote peace. I found that it can, and that it is most likely to be successful in areas such as Congo or the Horn of Africa where U.N. missions are deployed and are likely to be deployed in the future. In this appendix, I showed that the U.N. does not adequately understand the power of information or use information as aggressively as it should. While the U.N. continues to face barriers and problems as it plans for the future of information operations, this book should strengthen the arguments of those who wish to overcome these barriers and use information to promote peace more actively.

---

[41] S/2000/809, p. 9. Uncited background sources for this appendix are telephone interviews with: Tory Holt, Senior Associate, Henry L. Stimson Center, Washington, DC, January 28, 2003; Caroline Earle, Research Analyst, Henry L. Stimson Center, Washington, DC, January 28, 2003; Susan Manuel, January 29, 30, 2003; Colonel Mike Dooley, Joint Logistics Officer, U.S. Army Peacekeeping Institute, Carlisle Barracks, PA, January 29, 2003; William Durch, Senior Associate, Henry L. Stimson Center and former Project Director for the Panel on U.N. Peace Operations, May 16, 2003; and Frederick M. Schottler, Information Officer, Peace and Security Section, Department of Public Information, November 10, 2003.

Insights on Transparency from the Open Skies, Strategic Arms Control, and Non-Proliferation Regimes

THIS APPENDIX SURVEYS other regimes to explore how transparency is provided and what effects it has under different conditions. The aims are to reinforce or weaken my findings, to suggest areas for more research, and to get a sense of how my findings might have been different with different cases. The section on Open Skies is about a treaty that epitomizes transparency, but the effects of which are hard to discern in most cases. A bilateral version of Open Skies was, however, signed and implemented between Hungary and Romania. None of my main cases has anything near this clear an example of anticipated transparency motivating cooperation. The section on the Strategic Arms Limitation Talks (SALT) and Anti-Ballistic Missile Treaty (ABMT) shows how transparency-related technologies (especially satellites) enabled arms control, but that arms control itself was buffeted by the larger political forces of the Cold War. I argue that the greatest transparency-related benefit of superpower strategic arms control was to make the future more certain and predictable. Finally, the section on the International Atomic Energy Agency (IAEA) and Nuclear Non-Proliferation Treaty (NPT) shows the nonproliferation regime confirming fears (or worse), illustrates how hard it is to monitor evasive parties, and shows that transparency cannot calm fears when conditions justify the fears.

This appendix helps demonstrate the trade-offs in my case selection. My cases let me say much about forums and about the abilities of peacekeepers to monitor buffer zones, arms control agreements, and elections. I examined how multifunctional operations tried to shape their information environments, and explained why they need to explain themselves in difficult environments. This analysis helped me shed light on public diplomacy and information operations more generally because I showed transparency working better when there are relatively few information competitors and when biases are not so high that new information cannot penetrate.

Had I focused more on superpower arms control, or arms control and confidence-building more generally, I probably would have been able to make stronger arguments about the distributional issues involved with transparency. The reason is that the negotiation and ratification of many arms control agreements are more often accompanied by debates about operational security versus verification, and about security seeking through transparency versus security seeking through secrecy. These issues are less prominent for informal regimes like the Concert, or in the deployment of peacekeeping operations where, at least in my cases, great power politics played a large role in setting up or imposing missions.

Another argument that the arms control cases open up is the extent to which surveillance and verification technology must precede arms control. To the extent that technology is a prerequisite, it may diminish the transparency contribution of arms control. Technology and transparency may also be mutually reinforcing, and so this is a question for further research.

The IAEA/NPT cases in particular contain examples in which bargaining (and transparency, no less) sometimes did lead to hostile deadlock or war. This contrasts with the successful bargaining during the Concert, and again I note that more study needs to be done on when transparency helps or hurts bargaining.

Despite these opportunities suggested by the mini-cases in this appendix, focusing more on these cases would have presented opportunity costs compared to my main cases. I am not sure I would have been able to document as many effects of transparency as well had I used these as main cases, and the other contributions that I made would have been diminished by a focus on arms control. With space and time constraints, there are trade-offs when picking among cases. This is true in terms of target audiences and of the kinds of arguments explored and foreclosed. From what I can tell, and with the exception of the IAEA/NPT case, the transparency-related effects of arms control agreements are often harder to measure than the effects of forums (at least the Concert, thanks to the comparison with pre-forum diplomacy) and peacekeeping operations.

Open Skies

Perhaps nothing symbolizes transparency as much as the concept of Open Skies, which is agreed-upon surveillance overflights between countries. Analysis of Open Skies regimes highlights several themes. First, negotiations over Open Skies and information-sharing reinforce the argument that transparency has severe distributional consequences. This is not a value judgment, but it is clear that there are legitimate security-seeking arguments held by those who value secrecy and those who value transparency. How can one tell under which circumstances which viewpoint is the more wise? In negotiations over regimes that increase transparency, these distributional questions seem much more severe in arms control agreements between rough equals, than in peacekeeping operations where a major factor for their deployments were shifts in superpower relations and/or great power pressure. While this is logical, the point is that even though I highlighted distributional issues earlier, in the main text, there are circumstances when they cut even more deeply.

Second, a factor that influences distributional consequences is the extent of prior means of intelligence collection. The less one has, the more valuable Open Skies becomes. This is similar to the argument that transparency in the context of information operations works best when information competitors are scarce. Redundant sources of information make new sources less valuable. The third theme in this analysis is that the relationships between transparency, intelligence, and Open Skies include some subtle aspects. For example, Open Skies benefits the United States in multiple ways, despite its intelligence advantages. Open Skies allows the United States to devote other intelligence assets such as satellites to hot spots, while letting Open Skies flights compensate, and it establishes a bar of openness for the Russians to meet. That bar is itself a transparency-increasing device.

All told, it is very hard to find documentable examples of threat assessments being altered on the basis of Open Skies overflights. There is one clear case though, and that is the bilateral Open Skies agreement between Hungary and Romania, which I examine at the end of the section.

The idea for Open Skies became public with President Dwight Eisenhower's July 1955 proposal to the Soviet Union to allow mutual overflights of each other's territory, and thus reduce fears of surprise attack. Eisenhower's proposal was generally welcomed on Capitol Hill, and apparently the few conservative senators who dissented did so because they were not consulted. Some, such as Eisenhower, supported the proposal as a move to calm tensions and promote peace. Others including General Arthur Radford, however, envisioned a net intelligence gain for the open United States, which had more difficulty penetrating the closed Russian security apparatus than vice-versa.[1] While the Soviets publicly professed that the proposal did not go far enough to promote peace, they in fact rejected it as a "Western espionage plot."[2] Eisenhower was motivated by mutual gains, but the Soviets were gripped by fears about relative gains.

---

[1] W. W. Rostow, *Open Skies: Eisenhower's Proposal of July 21, 1955* (Austin, TX: University of Texas Press, 1982), 57–62. Rostow is firmly convinced of Eisenhower's sincerity, p. xii. Jonathan B. Tucker, however, sees the Open Skies proposal as a "public relations maneuver," in "Negotiating Open Skies: A Diplomatic History," in Michael Krepon and Amy E. Smithson, eds., *Open Skies, Arms Control, and Cooperative Security* (New York: St. Martin's, 1992), 6. Gaddis seems to side with Rostow in *Long Peace*, 198–99.

[2] Tucker, "Negotiating Open Skies," 5. See also Staff Sergeant Kirk W. Clear, USAF, and Steven E. Block, *The Treaty on Open Skies* (Dulles, VA: Defense Threat Reduction Agency, U.S. Department of Defense, April 1999), 2; and Rostow, *Open Skies*, 63–64.

The Open Skies proposal lay dormant until May 1989 when President George H. W. Bush rekindled the idea in a speech. In the intervening three decades, however, the United States had opened the Soviet's skies with U-2 and SR-71 spy plane overflights and both sides deployed a series of increasingly sophisticated spy satellites. While this may have limited the amount of transparency derived from new aerial photography, the Bush proposal did aim to increase transparency in that the president was testing Russia's commitment to greater openness. He was also countering the good publicity created by Mikhail Gorbachev's many initiatives.[3] The Canadians subsequently prodded Bush into making Open Skies a multilateral agreement, and it came to encompass the twenty-seven NATO and former Warsaw Pact members. Even if Russia and the United States could rely mostly on their satellites, the multilateral version of Open Skies would diffuse the transparency benefits of the aerial flights more broadly.

The State and Defense Departments and the intelligence community had to figure out what kind of sensors the surveillance aircraft would use, what kind of restrictions would be placed on flight plans, who would have access to gathered data, and so forth. As these agencies moved to make the proposal concrete and firm up the U.S. bargaining position, factions split between those who wanted intrusive inspections and were willing to give up some secrecy in return, and those who placed a higher priority on secrecy. This conflict of priorities is "central" to aerial surveillance negotiations, and it applies to bureaucracies within countries as well.[4]

In the end, the United States aimed for an agreement in which flight plans had to be announced in advance, SIGINT sensors were banned, and four types of other sensors were allowed: two cameras, one infrared, and one radar, all with specifically limited resolutions. This proposal went through some intra-NATO discussion and modifications, and the two sides opened negotiations in February 1990.

The Soviets rejected the U.S./NATO proposal because of U.S. sensor superiority, and countered by proposing a common aerial fleet with a central data-processing facility. On a number of points, NATO wanted to use its sensors to its advantage, while the Soviets sought to prevent spying. Moreover, the Soviets thought that the confidence-building aspects of Open Skies could be accomplished with sensors adequate to detect large-scale movements of troops and materiel, while NATO, which maintained low day-to-day readiness and depended on fine-grained advance warning

---

[3] Tucker, "Negotiating Open Skies," 6–8. See also James J. Marquardt, "Open Skies: Not a Moment Too Soon," *Bulletin of the Atomic Scientists* 58, no. 1 (January/February 2002): 18–20.

[4] U.S. Congress, OTA, *Verification Technologies,* 22.

to mobilize reserves and prevent surprise attack, wanted better sensors. As turbulence gripped the Baltics and the Soviet "near-abroad," the Russian military gained a greater voice in the negotiations, and their position hardened. A key sticking point was Soviet resistence to unrestricted territorial access. By late 1991, however, the Soviets acceded to phased-in but more intrusive inspections with no territorial limits. In March 1992, the Open Skies Treaty was signed.[5]

The treaty was quickly ratified by the United States and most of the NATO and former Warsaw Pact countries. It did not, however, come into force until January 1, 2002, after the Russians finally ratified the treaty. Despite participating in a number of trial flights in the 1990s, the Russians delayed ratification because the Duma was hawkishly suspicious of the treaty, the Russians did not want any Open Skies scheme in place during the troubles in Chechnya, and they did not want to reveal the depth of their implosion. A number of factors from the election of Vladimir Putin to diplomacy by the United States and its allies, and the decline in Russian satellite capabilities turned the Russians around.[6]

The aims of the treaty are well expressed here:

According to the agreement of 24 March 1992, twenty-five states from the North Atlantic Treaty Organization (NATO), the former Warsaw Pact, and the former Soviet Union will conduct unarmed overflights of one another's territories to assess the disposition, strength, and preparedness of opposing military forces.

These flights will allow states to evaluate the nature of security threats—based on facts collected independently or collaboratively, not on unfounded suspicions or worst case analyses. They will permit nations

---

[5] Marquardt, "Open Skies"; and Tucker, "Negotiating Open Skies." U.S. Congress, OTA, *Verification Technologies* has a table depicting the trade-offs of Open Skies for each superpower, and its allies (p. 55).

[6] Ernst Britting and Hartwig Spitzer, "The Open Skies Treaty," in Trevor Findlay and Oliver Meier, eds., *VERTIC Verification Yearbook* (London: Verification Research, Training and Information Centre [VERTIC] 2002), chap. 13, 223–38, esp. 226; Zdzislaw Lachowski, *Confidence and Security-Building Measures in the New Europe,* SIPRI Research Report No. 18 (Oxford, England: Oxford University Press, 2004), 177–86; and telephone interview with Francis X. Stenger, Deputy Division Chief for Implementation of the Open Skies Treaty at Defense Threat Reduction Agency (DTRA), Department of Defense, November 3, 2005.

As the Russians feared Open Skies overflights of Chechnya, NATO feared a Ukranian request for a practice overflight of Italy when its bases were being used to help bomb Serbia during the Kosovo conflict. For discussion of the military/security implications of Open Skies, see Jeffrey D. McCausland, "'Squaring the Circle': Cooperative Security and Military Operations," INSS Occasional Paper 45 (USAFA, CO: USAF Institute for National Security Studies, July 2002).

to survey the status of events in countries of interest, gleaning early indications and warning of troubling developments or reassurance of a neighbor's peaceful intent. Thus, the possibility of wars caused by accident, or by a buildup of tensions based on rumor and suspicion can be significantly reduced.[7]

Like almost all the literature on Open Skies, this passage echoes my hypotheses that contend that transparency promotes cooperation by reducing uncertainty and miscalculation (H3) and that transparency reduces unwarranted fears and worst-case assumptions (H4).

With the exception of the Hungary/Romania case, it is unfortunately hard to tell from the sparse Open Skies literature what concrete effects Open Skies flights have had on international politics and levels of tension. Tension levels between the United States and Russia are now so low that the two countries signed a strategic nuclear arms control agreement with no verification provisions at all (p. 227). In addition, the growth of civil remote-sensing satellites and the diffusion of military surveillance satellites have threatened to make aerial surveillance, and therefore Open Skies, redundant.[8] Another critique of Open Skies is that because flights and flight plans are preannounced, important secrets can be sheltered from view (or ruses can be set up).

Arguably however, the Open Skies Treaty succeeded in one of its major political goals, which was to test and demonstrate Russia's commitment to transparency and openness. Officials who negotiated Open Skies, implementing agencies, and other proponents argue that Open Skies still offers a number of transparency and other benefits. Its symbolic importance is said to fuel further cooperation and trust. It helps level the intelligence playing field for participating countries, as all sides have access to the data gathered. Even though satellites have proliferated, most NATO and former Warsaw Pact countries do not operate them. Finally, like most arms control agreements, if the time does come when the treaty is violated (flights denied in this case), then that sends a signal of malign intent. Such signals are less obvious when there are no agreements to break.[9]

[7] Michael Krepon and Amy E. Smithson, "Introduction," in Krepon and Smithson, eds., *Open Skies, Arms Control, and Cooperative Security*, 1.

[8] Johan Swahn, "International Survellance Satellites: Open Skies for All?" *Journal of Peace Research* 25, no. 3 (September 1988): 229–44. See also Marquardt, "Open Skies," 20.

[9] Defense Threat Reduction Agency (DTRA) Fact Sheet, "Treaty on Open Skies" (November 2005), available at www.dtra.mil/press_resources/fact_sheets/display.cfm?fs=os; Hartwig Spitzer and Raael Wiemker, "Perspectives for Open Skies: Technical, Operational, and Political Aspects," presented at the Fourth International Airborne Remote Sensing Conference and Exhibition, 21st Canadian Symposium on Remote Sensing, Ottawa, Ontario, June 21–24, 1999; and Ambassador John Hawes, U.S. representative to the Open Skies Conference, "Open Skies: From Ideas to Negotiation," NATO Review, web edition, vol. 38, no. 2 (April 1990): 6–9, updated March 5, 2002, available at www.nato.int/docu/review/1990/9002–02.htm.

Francis Stenger, Deputy Division Chief for implementation of the Open Skies Treaty at the Defense Threat Reduction Agency (DTRA) within the U.S. Department of Defense, revealed a number of more specific details. He reinforced the argument that the decline in Russian intelligence assets meant that Open Skies gave them real, hard intelligence. Even though the United States has much greater capabilities, Open Skies lets the United States keep more expensive and hard-to-maneuver assets (satellites) focused on hotspots, while overflights help monitor the Eurasian areas within the treaty zone. For states that lack overhead reconnaissance platforms, the Open Skies Treaty affords access to otherwise impossible-to-get data about neighbors.

Stenger noted that no one trusted commercial satellites because images can be manipulated, are hard to read, and do not have as good a resolution as Open Skies platforms. Further, commercial satellites can be extremely expensive and/or impossible to direct where you want them and when. Because Open Skies planes are staffed by the inspecting side, there is a verifiable chain of custody of the images that contrasts with commercial sources, providing insurance of accuracy. For specific instances of tensions calmed and suspicions assuaged, Stenger said that the conflict-ridden history of the central-European region fueled a near-perpetual level of fear. He noted that the Russians take particular care to overfly Poland to make sure they are not threatened by its turn toward the West. Stenger said that the point of Open Skies was to reveal national intentions, such as fleet or mass army movements, not national secrets; it is "Open Skies not Open Spies." For this reason, the seventy-two-hour warning before flights does not corrupt the purpose of Open Skies, because national secrets may be cloaked in that time, but not signals of national intent. Stenger would not discuss any instances of countries trying to use Open Skies flights to perpetrate ruses and spread misinformation.[10]

Finally, Stenger mentioned a number of places where Open Skies overflights might be of use, including the border areas between India and Pakistan where, for starters, the withdrawal of forces beyond mutual firing ranges could be monitored.[11] Other areas of tension that could profit from Open Skies and confidence-building measures include the Middle East and the Koreas. He also noted that overflights could be used in the "three borders" area between Brazil, Argentina, and Paraguay to monitor smuggling, and could be used worldwide to monitor environmental problems such as flooding and deforestation. Indeed, a number Open Skies flights have been sent over the Balkans, and flights also helped assess the damage from

[10] Telephone interview, November 3, 2005.

[11] See also Air Marshal Mohammed Arshad Chaudry (PAF) and Air Marshal K. C. Cariappa (IAF), "How Cooperative Aerial Monitoring Can Contribute to Reducing Tensions between India and Pakistan," SAND-98–0505/22 (Albuquerque, NM: Sandia National Laboratories, December 2001).

Hurricane Mitch to Central America in 1998 and from the flooding of the Oder River in 1997. Numerous proposals exist to expand Open Skies flights to regions ranging from Central Asia to Africa, for purposes ranging from environmental monitoring to verification of arms control agreements such as the NPT.[12]

Hungary/Romania: Bilateral Open Skies

The area of Transylvania has grown and shrunk and gone back and forth between Hungary and Romania several times during the war-torn history of the Balkans. At the end of World War II, Romania gained control of the territory. With the end of the Cold War, hardliners in both Hungary and Romania used the substantial Hungarian population in Transylvania to stir up tensions. The withdrawal of Russia's heavy hand and fall of Romanian dictator Nicolae Ceausescu raised the specter of malignant ethnonationalism in Transylvania.[13] This threat was underscored by the disastrous experience in neighboring Yugoslavia following the rule of Josip Tito. Hungary and Romania had rich historical ties to Transylvania, and there was a long tradition of Transylvania's "owners" reframing history to suit their own glorious past, renaming places and monuments, and making other attempts at cultural and political domination.

So it was no surprise when tensions rose and violence broke out, most notably at Tirgu Mures in March 1990 when almost 20,000 ethnic Romanians and ethnic Hungarians fought in a bloody clash.[14] Fortunately,

[12] Britting and Spitzer, "The Open Skies Treaty," 223–38; Clear and Block, *Treaty on Open Skies,* 49; John Hawes, "Open Skies: Beyond 'Vancouver to Vladivostok'" Stimson Center Occasional Paper, No. 10 (December 1992); and Spitzer and Wiemker, "Perspectives for Open Skies."

[13] George W. White, "Transylvania: Hungarian, Romanian, or Neither?" in Guntram H. Herb and David H. Kaplan, eds., *Nested Identities: Nationalism, Territory, and Scale* (Lanham, MD: Roman and Littlefield, 1999), 267–88, esp. 273; White, *Nationalism and Territory: Constructing Group Identity in Southeastern Europe* (Lanham, MD: Roman and Littlefield, 2000): 67–178; Marton Krasznai, "Cooperative Bilateral Aerial Inspections: The Hungarian-Romanian Experience," in Krepon and Smithson, *Open Skies, Arms Control, and Cooperative Security,* 135–46; and Krasznai, "Scenarios for Co-operative Aerial Observations in Support of Crisis Prevention and Post-conflict Settlement: Lessons from the Bosnia Experience," comments prepared for a seminar "Perspectives for Co-operative Aerial Observation and the Treaty on Open Skies," at the Stockholm International Peace Research Institute (SIPRI), Stockholm, Sweden November 30–December 1, 2004, available at www.sipri.org/contents/director/esdp/KrasznaiOS.html.

[14] Section "ROMANIA, Human Rights Developments" from *Human Rights Watch World Report 1990* available at, www.hrw.org/reports/1990/WR90/HELSINKI.BOU-02 .htm; and George W. White, *Nationalism and Territory: Constructing Group Identity in Southeastern Europe.* Lanham, MD: Rowman and Littlefield, 2000), 93–107, 147–53. Tirgu is spelled Targu in some sources.

cooler heads began to prevail, and both sides sought to calm tensions and to demonstrate to the outside world that the region was stable and worthy of investment. As part of this process, Romania proposed a bilateral Open Skies agreement with Hungary in July of 1990. Hungary, though, was more interested in the multilateral version of Open Skies as proposed by Bush. With the Bush proposal stalled, however, Hungary agreed to talk, and bilateral negotiations began in February 1991. This was a textbook case of anticipated transparency promoting cooperation (H2), as "the perception by both sides of the immediate need for greater transparency led to rapid negotiation and implementation of an agreement."[15]

The main points were hammered out in three days, and a treaty was signed on May 11, 1991. The treaty allowed for four eight-hour flights per year for each country, with a seven-day advance notice (and any flights taken under the multilateral Open Skies Treaty would add to this number). A demonstration flight with a multinational crew went up in June 1991, and media coverage helped boost popular support for the program. Observers from seventeen of the states participating in the multilateral Open Skies negotiations were on hand "to get the message through to their governments: Hungarian-Romania[n] relations were stable."[16]

One analyst cites personal communication with the Hungarian treaty negotiator Marton Krasznai who claimed "enormous" impacts from the bilateral Open Skies Treaty. As of 1996, the overflights still got glowing press coverage; the flights reassured politicians and people on the street about each side's peaceful intentions, and helped them in "overcoming or reframing enemy images."[17] Stenger agreed that the flights had calming effects. If true, this is transparency in action, reducing unwarranted fears and worst-case assumptions (H4).

In the end, although it appears that both sides were interested in increasing transparency, what they got from their four yearly flights was probably as much the appearance of transparency as a real increase in it. The symbolic importance, however, was a real and significant factor in convincing the respective publics in each country that peace should prevail, in contributing to the overall bilateral peace process, and in helping outsiders to perceive the situation as stable.

[15] Arian L. Pregenzer, Michael Vannoni, and Kent L. Biringer, "Cooperative Monitoring of Regional Security Agreements," SAND96–1121 (Albuquerque, NM: Sandia National Laboratories, November 1996), 23

[16] Quote in Krasznai, "Scenarios for Co-operative Aerial Observations." See also Pregenzer et al., "Cooperative Monitoring of Regional Security Agreements"; and Hartwig Spitzer "The Open-Skies Treaty as a Tool for Confidence Building and Arms Control Verification," expanded version of a paper for the 18th ISODARCO Summer Course, Siena, Italy, July 29–August 8, 1996.

[17] Spitzer "The Open-Skies Treaty," 15. See also Krasznai, "Cooperative Bilateral Aerial Inspections."

STRATEGIC ARMS LIMITATION TALKS (SALT)

Arms control has a number of goals, some of which are aided by transparency. The most important goal of arms control is to reduce the probability of war. Secondary goals are to reduce the costs of preparation for war and to reduce the consequences of war if it occurs. Arms control can lessen the probability of war by reducing the production of offensive weapons and thus increasing crisis stability, by limiting arms races and the tensions that they produce, and by embodying or symbolizing the improvement of relations between adversaries and thus prompting better relations.

Transparency can play a role at several junctures to promote peace in the context of arms control. First, no agreement to limit offensive weapons is likely to be signed unless it can be mutually verified (Strategic Offensive Reduction Treaty—SORT—excepted). Further, an agreement that limits specific types of weapons will require far more intrusive verification than Open Skies–type agreements, which seek only to monitor broad indicators of national intent. The sensitivity of these inspections sharply escalates the trade-offs between security-seeking through transparency versus security-seeking through secrecy. Second, agreements can themselves send signals that an adversary is willing to be open or make compromises. Third, a major benefit of arms control (and about regimes in the literature on cooperation more generally) is that it extends the shadow of the future. In this context, proponents argue that strategic arms control, and the Anti-Ballistic Missile Treaty (ABMT) in particular, limited arms racing not only by the obvious fact that it limited arms, but also by its reduction of worst-case assumptions by making the future more predictable.[18] Finally, an ongoing arms control negotiating process serves as a de facto forum for involved parties—though with hard-to-measure effects.[19]

In this space, I cannot hope to provide a detailed account of transparency and its effects within the context of strategic arms control. I do, however, survey the negotiations and effects of the Strategic Arms Limitation Talks (SALT I and II) and the associated ABMT. By 1968, the Soviets and the United States came to broad agreement to pursue arms control. After being delayed by the 1968 uprisings in Eastern Europe, formal negotiations started in late 1969. Catalysts included the need to restrain the resources devoted to the strategic arms race, as well as growing perceptions that an arms race involving missile defenses would be particularly costly and destabilizing.

[18] Overviews of arms control arguments can be found in fn. 1 in chapter 2.
[19] Raymond L. Garthoff, *Detente and Confrontation: American-Soviet Relations from Nixon to Reagan* (Washington, DC: Brookings Institution Press, 1985), 191.

Two background factors enabled strategic arms control. First, the United States recognized that the Soviets had essentially achieved strategic parity, meaning that arms control would not result in disproportional gains for the Soviets. Likewise, once the Soviets gained parity, arms control would not lock them into perpetual inferiority. The second was advances in satellite and remote sensing technologies. Arms control could not take place in the absence of capabilities for verification. This raises the question: What increment of cooperative transparency was added by arms control, or were they mutually reinforcing? It seems clear that unilateral transparency came first and provided perhaps the lion's share of Cold War transparency, at least up until near the end of the Cold War. Even legitimation of satellite reconnaissance preceded strategic arms control. John Lewis Gaddis argues that through mid-1963 the Soviets had insisted that satellite reconnaissance was illegal, but they tacitly accepted it by the end of the year—perhaps because of their own growing capabilities.[20] The SALT agreements, however, made tacit acceptance more explicit, and built in a few relatively minor provisions to make verification easier. Some argue that it was arms control that led to the "overcoming [of] long-standing Soviet resistance to satellite reconnaissance," but Gaddis's history is convincing. If Gaddis is right that 1963 was a turning point for Cold War transparency, then the contribution of arms control to transparency is less than some believe.[21] It took almost twenty years for arms control to provide transparency breakthroughs on its own, with the onsite inspection provisions of the December 1987 Intermediate-Range Nuclear Forces Treaty (INF) being the most notable. By this time, though, Gorbachev was at the helm in Russia and the tectonic plates of Cold War politics were shifting. The INF Treaty reflected and helped cause this shift.

Congress overwhelmingly approved SALT I with votes of 88 to 2 in the Senate and 307 to 4 in the House, and it entered into force in October 1972.[22] It limited the number of delivery vehicles and launchers on each side, while allowing a variety of modernization options. The United States insisted that MIRV (multiple warheads per missile) technology not be capped, as it was in the lead and wanted to exploit this advantage—even though many critics saw MIRVs as destabilizing.

Much more significant was the ABMT, signed alongside SALT I in May 1972. The ABMT limited deployment of missile defenses to one hundred defensive missiles at two sites. This capped a defensive and offensive arms

[20] Gaddis, *Long Peace*, 200–206.

[21] See, for example, Jane M. O. Sharp, "Restructuring the SALT Dialogue." *International Security* 6, no. 3 (Winter 1981–82): 144–76, quote on 145. Gaddis is supported by Herbert Scoville, Jr., "A Leap Forward in Verification," in Mason Willrich and John B. Rhinelander, eds., *SALT: The Moscow Agreements and Beyond* (New York: Free Press, 1974): 160–84, esp. 165.

[22] SALT I was an executive agreement, not a formal treaty.

race, the latter because ABMs hinder each side's offense. For both SALT and the ABMT, verification was provided by two main clauses: one that permitted the use of national technical means (NTMs—satellites) and another that prohibited attempts to interfere with verification. SALT II added a provision that each side not encrypt the radio signals (telemetry) sent by test missiles, and it required satellite-observable differences among different aircraft and cruise missile designs. In a sense, SALT II also incorporated some worst-case assumptions in that once a missile type was tested with MIRVs, deployments of that missile were assumed to all be equipped with MIRVs.

Surprisingly, questions about verification did not plague the SALT I talks, at least on the U.S. side. In the midst of the Vietnam War, the Nixon administration was anxious to the point of "hyperbolic . . . overselling" of SALT I to appear as a peacemaker. And as the Congressional votes noted earlier indicate, the Congress and public were eager for good news as well.[23] Public concerns about SALT I compliance were not raised until 1975. The organization created to work out compliance issues, the Standing Consultative Commission (SCC), was able to resolve six of eight issues raised by the U.S. side in 1978.[24]

SALT II was signed in June of 1979. It reduced the number of launchers slightly, capped warheads on ICBMs to ten, and placed some limits on modernization. SALT II disappointed liberals because it did so little, while it infuriated hawks who were concerned about disproportional limits that they believed favored the Soviets and about anticipated difficulties with verification. In contrast to SALT I, verification issues were among the "most intractable" in debates about SALT II ratification.[25] During the Senate debate, the Carter administration claimed that every compliance issue raised about SALT I had been successfully resolved.[26] Many disagreed. Moreover, the backdrop for these rising concerns about compliance problems was a general worsening of Cold War tensions. There were Soviet-backed Cubans in Angola and a Soviet brigade reported in Cuba. Hope for ratification of SALT II died with Soviet invasion of Afghanistan in December 1979. SALT II was never ratified, though both countries generally abided by its terms.

During the Reagan administration, concern grew over Soviet compli-

[23] Garthoff, *Detente and Confrontation*, 192–93.

[24] Mark M. Lowenthal and Joel S. Wit, "The Politics of Verification," in William C. Potter, *Verification and Arms Control* (Lexington, MA: Lexington Books, 1985), 153–68, esp. 154–57. "Very little is known about the SCC," but because its major task was to reduce uncertainty, a study of its workings would likely shed considerable light on transparency. Sidney Graybeal and Michael Krepon, "Making Better Use of the Standing Consultative Commission," *International Security*, 10, no. 2 (Fall 1985): 183–99, quote on 183.

[25] Strobe Talbott, "Scrambling and Spying in SALT II," *International Security* 4, no. 2 (Autumn 1979): 3–21, quote on 3.

[26] Arms Control Association, *Arms Control and National Security: An Introduction* (Washington, DC: Arms Control Association, 1899), 146.

ance with both SALT I and II and the ABMT. The administration accused the Soviets of building an ABM radar at Krasnoyarsk, far away from permitted locations. The United States also accused the Soviets of building too many new intercontinental ballistic missiles and of encrypting their missile telemetry. In 1983, when the Cold War seemed to be about as tension-filled as it had been prior to the Cuban Missile Crisis, the U.S. Senate passed a resolution 93 to 0 requiring the Reagan administration to submit a report on Soviet compliance with existing agreements.[27] In 1986, the United States said that it would no longer adhere by the SALT structure, and broke out later in 1986 by converting too many B-52s into cruise-missile launching platforms. Just as successful agreements and veri-fied compliance can signal good will, and help good will to grow, suspi-cions about compliance can poison relations. While debates about com-pliance and verification are about transparency, the successes and failures and ultimate influence of transparency are all hard to discern in the greater ebb and flow of superpower relations during the Cold War.

The subsequent Strategic Arms Reduction Treaties (START I and II in 1991 and 1993, respectively) did succeed in substantially reducing strate-gic weapons. Both treaties were made possible by the end of the Cold War. With regard to transparency, however, neither surpassed the INF Treaty's onsite verification provisions.

Perhaps the most remarkable evidence for the argument that arms con-trol agreements are symptoms as much as causes of political relations is the SORT of May 2002. It cuts nuclear warheads significantly by about one half from START II levels. Yet instead of the minutiae about each weapons system found in previous treaties, the text reads instead, "Each Party shall determine for itself the composition and structure of its strate-gic offensive arms, based on the established aggregate limit for the num-ber of such warheads." For implementation and verification, all SORT has is Article III, which reads in its entirety: "For purposes of implement-ing this Treaty, the Parties shall hold meetings at least twice a year of a Bilateral Implementation Commission." In other words, SORT had no verification provisions at all, another symptom of the low levels of U.S.-Russian tensions.[28]

[27] Lowenthal and Wit, "Politics of Verification," 154.

[28] The text of SORT can be found at the Arms Control Association website: www .armscontrol.org/documents/sort.asp.

Other sources consulted for this section include Dan Caldwell, "The SALT II Treaty," in Michael Krepon and Dan Caldwell, eds., *The Politics of Arms Control Verification* (New York: St. Martin's, for the Henry L. Stimson Center, 1991); Steven E. Miller, "Politics over Promise: Domestic Impediments to Arms Control," *International Security* 8, no. 4 (Spring 1984): 67–90; John Newhouse, *Cold Dawn: The Story of SALT* (Washington, DC: Pergamon-Brassey's, 1989); William C. Potter, ed., *Verification and SALT: The Challenge of Strategic Deception* (Boulder, CO: Westview, 1980); and Strobe Talbott, *Endgame: The In-side Story of SALT II* (New York: Harper and Row, 1979).

While arms control was made possible by the confluence of technology, political will, and parity in capabilities, its fortunes were clearly tied to overall superpower politics. Yet the counterfactual seems fairly chilling. In the absence of arms control, it is easy to imagine a world of much greater instability, of greater offensive and defensive arms racing, and of greater fear. Arms control put a lid on this possibility. Perhaps the greatest transparency-related contribution of arms control was to make the future more certain and more predictable.

IAEA/NPT: Iran, Iraq, North Korea

This section offers an overview of how the International Atomic Energy Agency (IAEA) and Nuclear Non-Proliferation Treaty (NPT) have performed in monitoring and constraining the nuclear weapons activities of Iran, Iraq, and North Korea—from the perspective of transparency.

A theme that runs through all three cases in this section is that no level of inspections, onsite and other, can fully assuage the suspicions of skeptical countries. There are two reasons for this. First and obviously, Iran, Iraq, and North Korea all give countries who would be threatened by them ample reason to feel threatened. Covert programs, lies, and deception all provide sound bases for suspicions. Second, the Iraq case shows that even with onsite inspections, it is very hard to verify to an adequate level of assurance when the inspected country resists inspections.

Iran's recent experience with the IAEA includes a private arms control group using commercial satellite photography to help discover and publicize illicit proliferation activities.

Israel and the United States attacked Iraq in part because of the IAEA's inability to provide sufficient transparency. The 1991 Gulf War ended with a major coercive transparency regime—but one that failed in the face of determined resistance. The case of North Korea (and Iraq) shows that breaking agreements can send signals, and that regimes can increase transparency, even in their death throes. It is also possible that North Korea is using the regime precisely to send dangerous signals and increase its leverage at the bargaining table.

Background on the IAEA and NPT

The NPT entered into force in March 1970, with two main provisions known as the "grand bargain." First, the non-nuclear weapons states (NNWS) pledged not to obtain nuclear weapons, while the five original nuclear weapons states (NWS) of the United States, Russia, China, France, and the United Kingdom were allowed to keep their weapons, on condition that they would pursue complete nuclear disarmament. In exchange for forgoing nuclear weapons, the second provision under Article IV gave the NNWS the "inalienable right" to acquire and use nuclear energy for peaceful purposes.[29] In 1995, the NPT was extended indefinitely, putting an end to periodic review conferences.[30]

Under Article III, signatories had to establish a safeguards inspection agreement with the IAEA. Almost every state has signed and ratified the NPT, with three notable exceptions: Israel, India, and Pakistan. In January 2003, North Korea withdrew from the NPT.

Right from the beginning, several transparency-related points emerge. First, a deal that prohibits weapons while allowing nuclear power and research is inherently murky. Even though the IAEA is supposed to monitor the civilian programs, civilian programs are a precursor to weapons development for states who so desire. States can go to the brink of a weapons capability and still be members in good standing of the NPT.[31] Second, as each state negotiates its own safeguards agreement, each agreement is idosyncratic. While this tailoring may be effective, it is also somewhat opaque and uneven. As we saw with UNDOF, inspection agreements that look good on paper may not necessarily work well in practice.

Third, the IAEA is usually limited to monitoring civilian nuclear programs, leaving any illicit programs essentially in the clear. This led to the rather stunningly obvious insight by Jan Lodding that "[e]xperience with *Iraq, DPRK* [North Korea] and *South Africa* underlined the need to focus more on the possibility that States have *undeclared nuclear material and activities.*"[32] Fourth, the fact that the newer nuclear weapons states of Israel, India, and Pakistan never signed is an indication that at least some countries take obligations seriously and are honest proliferators.[33] As I argued earlier, making and breaking agreements sends signals, and here we see that not signing is also a signal. Likewise, North Korea's withdrawal from the IAEA and threat to withdraw from the NPT in 1993–94

---

[29] The text of the treaty can be found at the IAEA website: www.iaea.org/Publications/Documents/Infcircs/Others/infcirc140.pdf.

[30] John Simpson and Darryl Howlett, "The NPT Renewal Conference: Stumbling toward 1995," *International Security* 19, no. 1 (Summer 1994): 41–71; and Raju G. C. Thomas, ed., *The Nuclear Non-Proliferation Regime: Prospects for the 21st Century* (New York: St. Martin's, 1998).

[31] Leonard Spector, "How to Be Weapon-Ready NPT Members," August 16, 2005, Yale Global Online at yaleglobal.yale.edu/display.article?id=6153. If the aim is a dirty bomb, then almost any nuclear research provides for a nearly instant weapon capability.

[32] Jan Lodding, "Verification Pursuant to the NPT: Concluding Safeguards Agreements and Additional Protocols," 2005 NPT Review Conference Briefing, May 2005 at www.iaea.org/NewsCenter/Focus/Npt/npt2005_ppt_020505.pdf; emphases in original.

[33] This statement echoes Sartori's argument in *Deterrence by Diplomacy* that honesty is indeed a powerful commodity in international relations.

helped to signal its intentions to the world and to galvanize a response.[34] Finally, in response to problems with the safeguards that have appeared over time, the safeguards have been progressively strengthened by the international community. Most notably, in 1997, an Additional Protocol to the NPT allowed IAEA inspectors greater access to states' facilities.[35]

Iran

Iran ratified the NPT in 1970, and it has developed a fairly extensive civilian nuclear infrastructure in a program that it accelerated during the Iran-Iraq war and then again after the 1991 Gulf War. Russia has been the main supplier, but Iran also purchased equipment and sought aid from China, Pakistan, and elsewhere. Due to the fall of the Shah and hostage crisis under President Carter, the United States has long been suspicious of Iran. Relations deteriorated further after President Bush's January 2002 State of the Union speech, where he labeled Iran as a member of the "axis of evil."[36]

Later that year, secret Iranian nuclear facilities were discovered, in part by an analysis of commercial satellite photography done by the private arms control group Institute for Science and International Security (ISIS), whose mission is in part to bring "about greater transparency of nuclear activities worldwide."[37] U.S. intelligence satellites and Iranian expatriates also helped reveal parts of the Iranian nuclear program. The pioneering use of commercial satellites by ISIS brings what I have called "ambient transparency" to a new level, and it makes it harder for governments to keep secrets. The proliferation of satellites is why, when I teach about the Gulf War, one of my points is that General Schwartzkopf's surprise left hook might not be possible in today's world.

Iran acknowledged these facilities in December 2002. In early 2003, the IAEA inspected the newly discovered enrichment facility at Natanz,

[34] Jean de Preez and William Potter, "North Korea's Withdrawal from the NPT: A Reality Check," Center for Nonproliferation Studies (CNS) Research Story of the Week, April 9, 2003, at cns.miis.edu/pubs/week/030409.htm.

[35] Other sources consulted for this section include United Nations, Department for Disarmament Affairs, "Review Conference of the Parties to the Treaty on the Non-Proliferation of Nuclear Weapons, 2–27 May, New York," 05–24713-April 2005–2,735. Presskit at un.org/events/npt2005/presskit.pdf.

[36] The text of the speech is available on the White House website at www.whitehouse.gov/news/releases/2002/01/20020129–11.html.

[37] On the discoveries, see David Albright and Corey Hinderstein, "Iran Building Nuclear Fuel Cycle Facilities: International Transparency Needed," ISIS Issue Brief, December 12, 2002, at www.isis-online.org/publications/iran/iranimages.html; and Global Security Newswire Story, "Iran: Photos Show Building at Nuclear Sites, Group Says" December 13, 2002, at www.nti.org/d_newswire/issues/2002/12/13/5s.html. On the mission of ISIS, see www.isis-online.org/about/about.html.

found that it was much more extensive than anyone had thought, and learned of Iranian plans to expand the operation. Iran then admitted to having additional facilities, some of which were elaborately concealed.[38] This added to suspicions, already grounded in the puzzle of why oil- and gas-rich Iran needed any nuclear facilities at all. From a transparency point of view, one interesting observation is that here we see private groups, national intelligence services, and the IAEA all working together to shed light on what the Iranians were up to.

These revelations helped catalyze a European effort to cap the Iranian programs. In late 2003, Germany, France, and the United Kingdom worked together to put pressure on Iran to address IAEA concerns in their entirety. Russia has been slow to sporadic in wanting to hinder the Iranians, while the United States has supported the Europeans, but not with much vigor. As I write, a complicated diplomatic dance continues, with the Europeans and the United States threatening to push harder unless Iran opens up, and Iran periodically threatening to withdraw any cooperation unless the West backs off.

The endgame remains hard to predict. Muhammad el-Baradei, head of the IAEA, recently said that the Iranians have made some progress and yet "[t]here are still some important issues about the extent of the enrichment program, but we are moving in the right direction; and the earlier Iran would allow us through transparency measures to do all that we need the better, of course, for everybody, including Iran." In response, the U.S. State Department's head non-proliferation official, Robert Joseph, "told yesterday's conference that Iran has provided a 'dizzying array of cover stories and false statements' about its nuclear program. He said the best way to assure its compliance with the IAEA is through UN Security Council pressure."[39] Although the IAEA has strengthened its safeguards procedures, it seems unlikely that any conceivable level of inspections would satisfy a suspicious U.S. and allies. For example, in late 2003, the U.S. Central Intelligence Agency told Congress that "even with intrusive IAEA safeguards inspections in Natanz, there is a serious risk that Iran could use its enrichment technology in covert activities."[40] In response,

[38] Roger Howard, *Iran in Crisis? Nuclear Ambitions and the American Response* (London and New York: Zed Books, 2004; distributed in the United States by Palgrave Macmillan), 98–100; and Brenda Shaffer, "Iran at the Nuclear Threshold," Arms Control Association (November 2003) at www.armscontrol.org/act/2003_11/Shaffer.asp.

[39] Robert McMahon, "Iran: Nuclear Agency's Chief Urges Greater Iranian Transparency," Radio Free Europe/Radio Liberty (November 8, 2005) at www.globalsecurity.org/wmd/library/news/iran/2005/iran-051108-rferl02.htm.

[40] Howard, *Iran in Crisis?*, 7. For additional summaries of developments, see Nuclear Threat Initiative, Country Profile Iran at www.nti.org/e_research/profiles/Iran/1788_1772.html; and NTI's Nuclear Profile Iran at www.nti.org/e_research/profiles/Iran/1819.html. Other sources consulted for this section include Leonard S. Spector with Jacqueline R. Smith, *Nuclear Ambitions, The Spread of Nuclear Weapons 1989–1990* (Boulder, CO: Westview, 1990).

Iran makes a few good points, noting, for example, that its nuclear programs began under the Shah. Treaty obligations aside, Iran—like Iraq, Israel, India, and Pakistan—lives in a tough neighborhood.

Iraq

Iraq ratified the NPT in 1969, and in the 1970s it began to build the Osiraq nuclear reactor at the Al Tuwaitha Nuclear Center with French help. Israel destroyed the reactor with an airstrike on June 7, 1981. Israel acted in part because it was "not convinced" by the ability of IAEA safeguards and inspections to prevent diversion of nuclear material and to prevent Iraq from building nuclear weapons.[41] Put another way, distrust in the transparency provided by the IAEA helped spark the bombing. As the world later learned, that distrust was well placed, because Iraq engaged in a long-term and systematic effort to deceive the IAEA.[42]

Following the Gulf War, the U.N. Security Council passed Resolution 687 on April 3, 1991. The resolution ordered Iraq to declare and eliminate its weapons of mass destruction, and to do so under international supervision and onsite inspections by the IAEA for nuclear programs, and by a special commission, UNSCOM, for biological, chemical, and missile programs. Iraq accepted—it had no choice—the resolution within days. An exchange of letters granted UNSCOM and the IAEA unrestricted access to all records and all facility above or below ground, with no advance warning.[43] This is perhaps the clearest example of coerced transparency.

From almost the very beginning, UNSCOM and the IAEA were obstructed and lied to. For example, in June 1991, Iraqi forces fired warning shots at an inspection team, and inspectors found plutonium and a uranium enrichment program, neither of which had been declared. To make a long story short, much of the 1990s were filled with cat and mouse games in which Iraq would try to obstruct inspectors, and the United States and the U.N. would try to pressure Iraq into cooperating. In August 1998, Scott Ritter resigned as head UNSCOM inspector, saying that

[41] Anthony D'Amato, "Israel's Air Strike upon the Iraqi Nuclear Reactor," *American Journal of International Law* 77, no. 3. (July 1983): 584–88, quote on p. 587. For a counterpoint, see Richard Wilson, "Nuclear Proliferation and the Case of Iraq," *Journal of Palestine Studies* 20, no. 3 (Spring 1991): 5–15. See also Federation of American Scientists, fact sheet: "Osiraq / Tammuz I 33°12'30"N 44°31'30"E," at www.fas.org/nuke/guide/iraq/facility/osiraq.htm.

[42] Khidhir Hamza, "Inside Saddam's Secret Nuclear Program," *Bulletin of the Atomic Scientists* 54, no. 5 (September/October 1998): 26–33.

[43] United Nations, Department of Public Information, *The United Nations and the Iraq-Kuwait Conflict, 1990–1996*, United Nations Blue Book Series, vol. 9 (New York: United Nations, 1996).

Iraq "is not disarmed anywhere near the level required by Security Council resolutions," that Iraq had lied since "day one," that significant capabilities remained, and that the "illusion of arms control is more dangerous than no arms control at all."[44] By late 1998, Iraq had made it impossible for the UNSCOM and the IAEA to be effective. The inspectors were withdrawn, and the U.S. and Britain launched a punitive bombing campaign, Desert Fox.

During the 1990s, inspectors nonetheless ended up finding and destroying dozens of missiles and hundreds of tons of chemical weapons agents, and they dismantled extensive biological and nuclear weapons programs.[45] Despite this, there were large gaps between the quantities of WMD materials indicated in Iraqi documents and what was known to have been destroyed. Hence, the consensus of weapons inspectors, and the assessment of many intelligence services around the world, was that Iraq retained significant WMD research and weapon capabilities.[46] Inspectors with boots on the ground, aided by U.S. intelligence, could not seem to find sizable portions of Iraq's WMD programs. This suggests that even under the most favorable circumstances, it is hard to coerce transparency from a resistant party.

After September 11, 2001, the United States became increasingly concerned with WMD terrorism, and looked to confront threats from what President George Bush called the "Axis of Evil": Iraq, Iran, and North Korea. Of these, Iraq became the target of particular concern and the United States threatened war unless Iraq accepted a new inspection regime and proved that it had disarmed. Although it became apparent after the ensuing war that Iraq did not possess WMD, it was not forthcoming in helping prove that it had no more WMD. For example, it produced a 12,000-page collection of documents to show what it had done to its WMD materials and programs, but these documents were unsatisfying, often recycled from years before.[47] Whether or not the new inspection regime would be able to conclude anything decisive, and how long it would take, was a matter of debate between proponents and opponents

[44] William S. Ritter, resignation letter to UNSCOM Executive Chairman Richard Butler, August 26, 1998.

[45] Colin Norman, "Iraq's Bomb Program: A Smoking Gun Emerges," *Science*, November 1, 1991, pp. 644–45; and United Nations fact sheet, "Unscom Main Achievements," March 1998, at www.un.org/Depts/unscom/Achievements/achievements.html.

[46] David Albright, "Masters of Deception," *Bulletin of the Atomic Scientists* 54, no. 3 (May/June 1998): 44–50; Richard Butler, "Letter dated 15 December 1998 from the Executive Chairman of the Special Commission established by the Secretary-General pursuant to paragraph 9 (b) (i) of Security Council resolution 687 (1991) addressed to the Secretary - General," S/1998/1172 (December 15, 1998).

[47] Hans Blix, *Disarming Iraq* (New York: Pantheon, 2004), 104–8.

of the war. My opinion is that for all the important players, their position on the possible war seemed to dictate their position on the prospects for the new verification regime. Reasonable arguments existed on all sides, but in the end, nothing that the U.N. Monitoring, Verification, and Inspection Commission (UNMOVIC) could do seemed likely to change the course of the Bush administration. Without meaning to open up a debate on the war, the point is that a major motivation for war professed by the Bush administration was the inability to make Iraq transparent. There were indeed plenty of reasons to believe that Iraq still had WMD, but I also think that later evidence about Bush's determination for war highlights a theme from Cyprus: transparency has a hard time influencing those whose minds are already firmly locked into a way of thinking.[48]

North Korea

The Democratic People's Republic of Korea (North Korea or DPRK) ratified the NPT in December 1985 but did not follow through with IAEA inspections until January 1992. Shortly thereafter, North Korea refused to allow the IAEA to inspect two nuclear waste facilities, while continuing to operate a reprocessing unit. With inspections blocked, tensions rose. As the IAEA was preparing its report to cite North Korea for noncompliance, North Korea announced that it would withdraw from the NPT in March 1993 (the report came out in April). The withdrawal threat galvanized a global response with relative alacrity. The U.N. passed a resolution urging North Korea to cooperate with the IAEA in May, and the United States began high-level talks with North Korea in June and the North Koreans suspended the threat to withdraw. The talks soon deadlocked, and a crisis erupted in May 1994 when North Korea began to take fuel out of a reactor, presumably for reprocessing into weapons-grade fissile material. The IAEA began to take a tougher line, and North Korea withdrew from the IAEA. This shows that breaking agreements can send signals, but, of course, so do actions like removing fuel.

A visit by former President Carter to North Korea rekindled the talks, and the United States and North and South Korea made a deal called the Agreed Framework, in which North Korea agreed to abandon its weapons programs and cooperate with the IAEA in exchange for the construction of two proliferation-resistant light-water nuclear reactors. This achieved a "quasi–'cease-fire'" between North Korea and the outside parties. There

[48] Bob Woodward, *Plan of Attack* (New York: Simon and Schuster, 2004). See also Kenneth M. Pollack, *The Threatening Storm: The Case for Invading Iraq* (New York: Random House, 2002); and Spector, *Nuclear Ambitions*.

were no major crises until 2002, but no real progress was made by either side in implementing the Agreed Framework. Between 1994 and 2001, seventeen rounds of technical talks were held to try to resolve outstanding issues, but "no progress has been achieved on key issues."[49]

In October 2002, the DPRK revealed to a U.S. diplomat that it had a program to enrich uranium, the purpose of which was to build nuclear weapons. The IAEA passed a resolution condemning North Korea, North Korea rejected the resolution, the United States cut off heavy oil shipments due North Korea as part of the Agreed Framework, and North Korea responded by cutting safeguard seals, disabling surveillance cameras, kicking IAEA inspectors out of the country, and finally withdrawing from the NPT in January 2003. Later in 2003, North Korea said that it had produced enough plutonium to make six nuclear weapons, and in February 2005, the North Korea Foreign Ministry declared that North Korea possessed nuclear weapons.

Alongside these developments were on-and-off diplomatic efforts by the United States, South Korea, Japan, Russia, and China to reengage North Korea and try to get back on track toward disarmament. The negotiations, known as the six-nation talks, have been going one step forward one step back since they began in August 2003. In a September 2005 joint statement, however, North Korea pledged to give up its nuclear weapons program and rejoin the NPT, while the United States promised not to attack. The pledges left many details, including verification, for the future, and the next day, North Korea said it would not give up its weapons program until it had received a civilian nuclear reactor.

Regarding transparency, the continued ups and downs in the bargaining with North Korea are worth more fine-grained study to see how transparency, institutions, uncertainty, bluffing, and posturing affect outcomes. I do not know enough to address these issues confidently. I am in good company, however, because no one really knows what the North Koreans are up to, or what their true capabilities are. The main debate about North Korean intent is whether they are trying to bargain/extort for maximum economic gain or whether they are motivated by insecurity or both. Another debate is whether North Korea is really an irrational

[49] Quote from IAEA, "In Focus : IAEA and DPRK. Fact sheet on DPRK Nuclear Safeguards," at www.iaea.org/NewsCenter/Focus/IaeaDprk/fact_sheet_may2003.shtml. The sheet is undated. The URL implies May 2003, but the last event on the sheet is March 2005. For more on the Agreed Framework and surrounding events, see Federation of American Scientists fact sheet at www.fas.org/nuke/guide/dprk/nuke/index.html; Mel Gurtof, "South Korea's Foreign Policy and Future Security: Implications of the Nuclear Standoff, *Pacific Affairs* 69, no. 1 (Spring 1996): 8–31; Samuel S. Kim, "North Korea in 1994: Brinksmanship, Breakdown, and Breakthrough," *Asian Survey* 35, no. 1, (January 1995): 13–27.

rogue state or not. North Korea is one of the world's most closed societies, and so answers are nearly impossible to come by.[50] Even U.S. foreign policy was oddly and inexplicably low key for a number of years.

That said, certain transparency arguments may be worth illuminating. It is possible that the North Koreans are playing an exquisite bargaining game and are using the IAEA inspectors, IAEA safeguards, and the NPT to send dramatic signals, to create tension, and to offer carrots. Hypothesis H5 contends that transparency can reduce cheating, rogue, and spoiler problems in part because regimes can shine the international spotlight on cheaters and coerce better behavior. It is possible that North Korea is playing jujitsu with the spotlight effect and using the regime to send its own messages to the wider world. To what ends, we do not know, but as the 1998 missile test over Japan showed, North Korea does have a flair for signals.[51]

[50] David C. Kang, in "Rethinking North Korea," *Asian Survey,* 35, no. 3 (March 1995): 253–67, gives a good rundown of myths and "stylized facts" about North Korea.

[51] In 1998, the first stage of the rocket landed to the west of Japan, the second stage to the east, while the final pieces landed near Alaska. See Taewoo Kim, "South Korea's Missile Dilemma," *Asian Survey* 39, no. 3 (May–June 1999): 486–503.

Other sources consulted for this section include Michael J. Mazarr, "Going Just a Little Nuclear: Nonproliferation Lessons from North Korea," *International Security* 20, no. 2 (Autumn 1995): 92–122; and Spector, *Nuclear Ambitions.*

Bibliography

Abbott, Kenneth W. "'Trust but Verify': The Production of Information in Arms Control Treaties and Other International Agreements." *Cornell Journal of International Law* 26, no. 1 (Winter 1993): 1–58.

Abbott, Kenneth W., and Duncan Snidal. "Why States Act through Formal International Organizations." *The Journal Of Conflict Resolution* 42, no. 1 (February 1998): 3–32.

Acharya, Amitav. "A Concert of Asia?" *Survival* 41, no. 3 (Autumn in 1999): 84–101.

Achen, Christopher H., and Duncan Snidal, "Rational Deterrence Theory and Comparative Case Studies." *World Politics* 41, no. 2 (January 1989): 143–69.

Adejo, Armstrong Matiu. "From OAU to AU: New Wine in Old Bottle?" Paper prepared for CODESRIA's 10th General Assembly on "Africa in the New Millennium," Kampala, Uganda, December 8–12, 2002.

Alberts, David S., and Richard Hayes. "Command Arrangements for Peace Operations." Washington, DC: National Defense University Press, 1995.

Albrecht-Carrié, Rene. *The Concert of Europe: 1815–1914.* New York: Harper Torchbooks, 1968.

———. *A Diplomatic History of Europe since the Congress of Vienna.* Rev. ed. New York: Harper and Row, 1973.

Albright, David. "Masters of Deception." *Bulletin of the Atomic Scientists* 54, no. 3 (May/June 1998): 44–50.

Alexandroff, Alan, Richard Rosecrance, and Arthur Stein. "History, Quantitative Analysis, and the Balance of Power." *Journal of Conflict Resolution* 21, no. 1 (March 1977): 35–56.

Allison, Graham. *Essence of Decision: Explaining the Cuban Missile Crisis.* Boston, MA: Little, Brown, 1971.

Anderson, M. S. "Eighteenth-Century Theories of the Balance of Power." In *Studies in Diplomatic History,* edited by Ragnild Hatton and M. S. Anderson. London: Longman Group, 1970.

———. *Europe in the Eighteenth Century: 1713–1783.* 2nd ed. London: Longman, 1976.

Anderson, Matthew, "Russia and the Eastern Question, 1821–1841." In *Europe's Balance of Power: 1815–1848,* edited by Alan Sked. London: Macmillan, 1979.

Arms Control Association. *Arms Control and National Security: An Introduction.* Washington, DC: Arms Control Association, 1989.

Aronson, Shlomo. *Conflict and Bargaining in the Middle East: An Israeli Perspective.* Baltimore, MD: Johns Hopkins University Press, 1978.

Aspen Institute. *Managing Conflict in the Post–Cold War World: The Role of Intervention,* Report of the Aspen Institute Conference, August 2–6, 1995. Washington, DC: Aspen Institute, 1996.

Axelrod, Robert. *The Evolution of Cooperation.* New York: Basic Books, 1984.

Axelrod, Robert, and Robert O. Keohane. "Achieving Cooperation under Anarchy: Strategies and Institutions." In *Cooperation under Anarchy,* edited by Kenneth Oye. Princeton, NJ: Princeton University Press, 1986.

Baker, John C., Kevin M. O'Donnell, and Ray A. Williamson. *Commercial Observation Satellites: At the Leading Edge of Global Transparency.* Santa Monica, CA: RAND Corporation, 2001.

Baldwin, David A. *Neorealism and Neoliberalism: The Contemporary Debate.* New York: Columbia University Press, 1993.

Bandow, Doug. "Avoiding War." *Foreign Policy* 89 (Winter 1992–93): 156–74.

Bartlett, C. J. *Castlereagh.* New York: Scribner's, 1966.

Bates, Robert, et al. *Analytic Narratives.* Princeton, NJ: Princeton University Press, 1998.

BBC News. "Country Profile: Yugoslavia." January 29, 2003. Available at news.bbc.co.uk/2/hi/europe/country_profiles/1039269.stm.

Bellamy, Alex J., and Paul D. Williams. "Who's Keeping the Peace? Regionalization and Contemporary Peace Operations." *International Security* 29, no. 4 (Spring 2005): 157–95.

Bendor, Jonathon. "Uncertainty and the Evolution of Cooperation." *The Journal of Conflict Resolution* 37, no. 4 (December 1993): 709–34.

Bendor, Jonathon, Roderick M. Kramer, and Suzanne Stout. "When in Doubt . . . Cooperation in a Noisy Prisoner's Dilemma." *The Journal of Conflict Resolution* 35, no. 4 (December 1991): 691–719.

Bennett, Andrew, and Joseph Lepgold. "Reinventing Collective Security after the Cold War and Gulf Conflict." *Political Science Quarterly* 108, no. 2 (Summer 1993): 213–37.

Berdal, Mats, and Michael Leifer. "Cambodia." In *The New Interventionism 1991–1994: United Nations Experience in Cambodia, former Yugoslavia and Somalia,* edited by James Mayall. Cambridge, England: Cambridge University Press, 1996.

Bernstein, Richard. "Sniping Is Gnawing at U.N.'s Weakness as a Peacekeeper: The Optimism Has Faded." *New York Times,* June 21, 1993.

Betley, J. A. *Belgium and Poland in International Relations 1830–1831.* The Hague, Netherlands: Mouton 1960.

Betts, Richard. *Surprise Attack: Lessons for Defense Planning.* Washington, DC: Brookings Institution, 1982.

———. "Systems for Peace or Causes of War? Collective Security, Arms Control, and the New Europe." *International Security* 17, no. 1 (Summer 1992): 5–43.

———. "The Delusion of Impartial Intervention." *Foreign Affairs* 73, no. 6 (November/December 1994): 20–33.

Biener, Hansjoerg. "Radio for Peace, Democracy and Human Rights: Yugoslavia (Kosovo)." At www.evrel.ewf.uni-erlangen.de/pesc/peaceradio-YU.html.

Birgisson, Karl Th. "The United Nations Peacekeeping Force in Cyprus." In *The Evolution of UN Peacekeeping: Case Studies and Comparative Analysis,* edited by William Durch. New York: St. Martin's, 1993.

Blacker, Coit D., and Gloria Duffy. *International Arms Control: Issues and Agree-*

ments. Stanford Arms Control Group. Stanford, CA: Stanford University Press, 1984.

Bladen, Christopher. "Alliance and Integration." In *Alliance in International Politics,* edited by Julian Friedman, Christopher Bladen, and Steven Rosen. Boston, MA: Allyn and Bacon, 1970.

Blainey, Geoffrey. *The Causes of War.* 3rd ed. New York: Free Press, 1988.

Blanning, T. C. W. "Paul W. Schroeder's Concert of Europe." *International History Review.* 16, no. 4 (November 1994): 702–14.

Blanton, Thomas. "The World's Right to Know." *Foreign Policy* (July/August 2002): 50–58.

Bleicher, Samuel A. "Intergovernmental Organization and the Preservation of Peace: A Comment on the Abuse of Methodology." *International Organization* 25, no. 2 (Spring 1971).

Blix, Hans. *Disarming Iraq.* New York: Pantheon, 2004.

Bob, Clifford. "Beyond Transparency: Visibility and Fit in the Internationalization of Internal Conflict." In *Power and Conflict in the Age of Transparency,* edited by Bernard I Finel and Kristin Lord. New York: Palgrave, 2000.

Boggs, Marion William. *Attempts to Define and Limit "Aggressive" Armament in Diplomacy and Strategy.* Columbia, MO: University of Missouri Studies, 1941.

Bohlen, Celestine. "Fresh Tension for Cyprus: Counting the Newcomers." *New York Times,* January 23, 1997, p. A10.

Boston Globe. "Turkish Envoy Visits Cyprus." August 16, 1996, p. A7.

Brady, Henry E., and David Collier. *Rethinking Social Inquiry, Diverse Tools, Shared Standards.* Lanham, MD: Rowman and Littlefield, 2004.

Braudel, Fernand. *Civilization and Capitalism, 15th–18th Centuries: The Structures of Everyday Life, The Limits of the Possible.* Vol. I. New York: Harper and Row, 1979.

Bridge, Roy. "Allied Diplomacy in Peacetime: The Failure of Congress 'System,' 1815–1823." In *Europe's Balance of Power: 1815–1848,* edited by Alan Sked. London: Macmillan, 1979.

Britting, Ernst, and Hartwig Spitzer. "The Open Skies Treaty." In *VERTIC Verification Yearbook,* edited by Trevor Findlay and Oliver Meier. London: Verification Research, Training and Information Centre (VERTIC), 2002.

Brodie, Bernard. "On the Objectives of Arms Control." In *The Use of Force,* 3rd ed., edited by Robert J. Art and Kenneth N. Waltz. Lanham, MD: University Press of America, 1988.

Brown, MacAlister, and Joseph J. Zasloff. *Cambodia Confounds the Peacemakers: 1979–1998.* Ithaca, NY: Cornell University Press, 1998.

Brown, Michael. *The International Dimensions of Internal Conflict.* Cambridge, MA: MIT Press, 1996.

Bueno de Mesquita, Bruce. "Toward a Scientific Understanding of International Conflict: A Personal View." *International Studies Quarterly* 29, no. 2 (1985): 121–36.

Bullen, Roger. "The Great Powers and the Iberian Peninsula, 1815–1848." In *Europe's Balance of Power: 1815–1848,* edited by Alan Sked. London: Macmillan, 1979.

Butterfield, Sir Herbert. "Diplomacy." In *Studies in Diplomatic History,* edited by Ragnild Hatton and M. S. Anderson. London: Longman, 1970.

Caldwell, Dan. "The SALT II Treaty." In *The Politics of Arms Control Verification,* edited by Michael Krepon and Dan Caldwell. New York: St. Martin's, for the Henry L. Stimson Center, 1991.

Camdessus, Michel. "From Crisis to a New Recovery: Excerpts from Selected Addresses." Washington, DC: International Monetary Fund, 1999.

Campbell, Thomas M. "Nationalism in America's UN Policy, 1944–1945." *International Organization* 27, no. 1 (Winter 1973): 25–44.

Camus, Albert. *The Myth of Sisyphus and Other Essays.* Translated by Justin O'Brien. New York: Vintage, 1955.

Caporaso, James A. "International Relations Theory and Multilateralism: The Search for Foundations." *International Organization* 46, no. 3 (Summer 1992): 599–632.

Caron, David D. "The Legitimacy of the Collective Authority of the Security Council." *American Journal of International Law* 87, no. 4 (October 1993): 552–588.

Carr, Edward Hallett. *The Twenty Years' Crisis: 1919–1939.* New York: Harper Torchbooks, 1964. Originally published in 1939.

Carter, Ashton B., William Perry, and John D. Steinbruner. *A New Concept of Cooperative Security.* Washington, DC: Brookings Institution, 1992.

Charalambous, Charlie. "Turkish War Planes Fly Over Nicosia: Anger and Fear in Capital as Turkish Jets Violate Cyprus Air Space." *Cyprus Mail,* June 22, 1995, p. 1.

Chatfield, Charles, and Ruzanna Ilukhina. *Peace/Mir, An Anthology of Historic Alternatives to War.* Syracuse, NY: Syracuse University Press, 1994.

Chaudry, Air Marshal Mohammed Arshad, (PAF), and Air Marshal K. C. Cariappa (IAF). "How Cooperative Aerial Monitoring Can Contribute to Reducing Tensions between India and Pakistan." SAND-98-0505/22. Albuquerque, NM: Sandia National Laboratories, December 2001.

Chayes, Abram and Antonia Handler Chayes. "Regime Architecture: Elements and Principles." Pages 65–130 in *Global Engagement: Cooperation and Engagement in the 21st Century,* edited by Janne E. Nolan. Washington, DC: Brookings Institution Press, 1994.

———. *The New Sovereignty: Compliance with International Regulatory Agreements.* Cambridge, MA: Harvard University Press, 1995.

Choo, Tan Lian. "The Cambodian Election: Whither the Future?" In *Whither Cambodia? Beyond the Election,* edited by Timothy Carney and Tan Lian Choo. Singapore: Institute of Southeast Asian Studies, 1993.

Christou, Jean. "Was Soldier Lured to His Death by Turks?" *Cyprus Mail,* June 7, 1996.

Clarke, John. *British Diplomacy and Foreign Policy, 1782–1865: The National Interest.* London: Unwin-Hyman, 1989.

Claude, Inis. *Power and International Relations.* New York: Random House, 1962.

———. *Swords into Plowshares: The Problems and Progress of International Organization.* 4th ed. New York: McGraw-Hill, 1984.

Claude, Inis L., Jr. "Collective Legitimization as a Political Function of the United Nations." *International Organization* 20, no. 3 (Summer 1966): 367–79.

Clear, Sgt. Kirk W., and Steven E. Block. *The Treaty on Open Skies*. Dulles, VA: Defense Threat Reduction Agency, U.S. Dept. of Defense, 1999.

Cohen, Raymond. *Threat Perception in International Crisis*. Madison, WI: University of Wisconsin Press, 1979.

Collier, David, and James Mahoney. "Insights and Pitfalls: Selection Bias in Qualitative Research." Research Note. *World Politics* 49, no. 1 (October 1996): 56–91.

Copeland, Dale C. *The Origins of Major War*. Ithaca, NY: Cornell University Press, 2000.

Cowhey, Peter F. "Domestic Institutions and the Credibility of International Commitments: Japan and the United States." *International Organization* 47, no. 2 (Spring 1993): 292–326.

Coy, Patrick G., and Lynne M. Woehrle, eds. *Social Conflicts and Collective Identities*. Lanham, MD: Rowman and Littlefield, 2000.

Craig, Gordon A., and Alexander A. George. *Force and Statecraft: Diplomatic Problems of Our Time*. 2nd ed. New York: Oxford University Press, 1990.

Cramer, Jane Kellett. *National Security Panics*. Ph.D. diss., MIT, Cambridge, MA, 2000.

Cresson, W. P. *The Holy Alliance: The European Background of the Monroe Doctrine*. New York: Oxford University Press, 1922.

Cyprus Mail. "Murder on the Green Line." June 5, 1996, p. 9.

Cyprus News Agency. "Cyprus Protests to UN Over Soldier's Murder." June 3, 1996, at www.hri.org/news/cyprus/cna/.

Cyprus News Agency. "Bikers Ready to Start Anti-Occupation Ride." August 11, 1996, at www.hri.org/news/cyprus/cna/.

———. "Buffer Zone Killing Strengthens Will for Freedom." August 14, 1996, at www.hri.org/news/cyprus/cna/.

Cyprus Weekly. "Need for Tougher Discipline." June 7–13, 1996, p. 4.

Daalder, Ivo H. "Review of John S. Duffield, 'Power Rules: The Evolution of NATO's Conventional Force Posture.'" *American Political Science Review* 89, no. 4 (December 1995): 1071.

Daalder, Ivo H., and Michael E. O'Hanlon. *Winning Ugly: NATO's War to Save Kosovo*. Washington, DC: Brookings Institution, 2000.

D'Amato, Anthony. "Israel's Air Strike upon the Iraqi Nuclear Reactor." *American Journal of International Law* 77, no. 3 (July 1983): 584–88.

Damrosch, Lori Fisler. *Enforcing Restraint: Collective Intervention in Internal Conflicts*. New York: Council on Foreign Relations Press, 1993.

Daniel, Donald C. F., and Bradd C. Hayes. *Beyond Traditional Peacekeeping*. New York: St. Martin's, 1995.

Daniel, Donald C. F., Bradd C. Hayes, and Chantal de Jonge Oudraat. *Coercive Inducement and the Containment of International Crises*. Washington, DC: United States Institute of Peace Press, 1999.

Darbishire, Helen. "Non-Governmental Perspectives: Media Freedom versus Information Intervention?" In *Forging Peace: Intervention, Human Rights and the Management of Media Space,* edited by Monroe E. Price and Mark Thompson. Bloomington, IN: Indiana University Press, 2002.

de Broglie, Duc, ed. *Memoirs of the Prince de Talleyrand.* vol. 2. Translated by Raphael de Beaufort. New York: Putnam, 1891.

de Figueiredo Jr., Rui J. P., and Barry R. Weingast. "The Rationality of Fear: Political Opportunism and Ethnic Conflict." Pp. 261–302 in *Civil Wars, Insecurity, and Intervention,* edited by Barbara F. Walter and Jack Snyder. New York: Columbia University Press, 1999.

de Lannoy, Fl. *Histoire Diplomatique de L'Indépendance Belge.* Brussels, Belgium: Librairie Albert Dewit, 1930.

Denktash, Rauf. Nicosia BRTK Television Network, in *Foreign Broadcast Information Service (FBIS) Daily Report,* FBIS-WEU-96–108, 16:30 GMT. June 4, 1996.

Deutsch, Karl W., et al. *Political Community and the North Atlantic Area: International Organization in the Light of Historical Experience.* Westport, CT: Greenwood, 1969. Originally published by Princeton University Press, 1957.

Diehl, Paul. *International Peacekeeping.* Baltimore, MD: Johns Hopkins University Press, 1993.

Diehl, Paul F., and Sonia R. Jurado. "United Nations Election Supervision in South Africa: Lessons from the Namibian Peacekeeping Experience." *Terrorism* 16 (January/March 1993): 61–74.

Diehl, Paul F., Daniel Druckman, and James Wall. "International Peacekeeping and Conflict Resolution: A Taxonomic Analysis with Implications." *Journal of Conflict Resolution* 32, no. 1 (February 1998): 33–55.

Dobbie, Charles. "A Concept for Post–Cold War Peacekeeping." *Survival* 36, no. 3 (Autumn, 1996): 121–48.

Dorn, Walter. "Blue Sensors: Technology and Cooperative Monitoring in UN Peacekeeping." SAND 2004–1380. Albuquerque, NM: Sandia National Laboratories, April 2004.

Dorn, Walter L. *Competition for Empire: 1740–1763.* New York: Harper, 1940.

Downs, George. *Collective Security beyond the Cold War.* Ann Arbor, MI: University of Michigan Press, 1994.

Downs, George W., and Keisuke Iida. "The Theoretical Case Against Collective Security," APSA paper (September 1992).

Downs, George W., and David M. Rocke. *Tacit Bargaining, Arms Races, and Arms Control.* Ann Arbor, MI: University of Michigan Press, 1990.

Downs, George W., David M. Rocke, and Randolph M. Siverson, "Arms Races and Cooperation." In *Cooperation under Anarchy,* edited by Kenneth Oye. Princeton, NJ: Princeton University Press, 1986.

Doyle, Michael W. *UN Peacekeeping in Cambodia: UNTAC's Civil Mandate.* International Peace Academy Occasional Paper Series. Boulder, CO: Lynne Rienner, 1995.

———. "Authority and Elections in Cambodia." In *Keeping the Peace: Multidimensional UN Operations in Cambodia and El Salvador,* edited by Michael W. Doyle, Ian Johnstone, and Robert C. Orr. Cambridge, England: Cambridge University Press, 1997.

Duffield, John S. "NATO Force Levels and Regime Analysis." *International Organization* 46, no. 4 (Autumn 1992): 819–55.

———. *Power Rules: The Evolution of NATO's Conventional Force Posture.* Stanford, CA: Stanford University Press, 1995.

Durch, William. "Paying the Tab: Financial Crises." In *The Evolution of UN Peacekeeping: Case Studies and Comparative Analysis,* edited by William J. Durch. New York: St. Martin's Press, 1993.

Durch, William J., ed. *The Evolution of UN Peacekeeping: Case Studies and Comparative Analysis.* New York: St. Martin's Press, 1993.

———. *UN Peacekeeping, American Politics and the Uncivil Wars of the 1990s.* New York: St. Martin's, 1996.

Eckstein, Harry. "Case Study and Theory in Political Science." In *Handbook of Political Science,* vol. 7, edited by F. I. Greenstein and N. W. Polsby. Reading, MA: Addison-Wesley, 1975.

Elrod, Richard B. "The Concert of Europe, A Fresh Look at an International System." *World Politics* 27, no. 2 (January 1976): 159–74.

Evangelista, Matthew. "Cooperation Theory and Disarmament Negotiations in the 1950s." *World Politics* 42, no. 4 (July 1990).

———. "Transnational Relations and Security Policy." *International Organization* 49, no. 1 (Winter 1995): 502–28.

———. *Unarmed Forces: The Transnational Movement to End the Cold War.* Ithaca, NY: Cornell University Press, 1999.

Evans, Peter B., Harold K. Jacobson, and Robert D. Putnam, *Double-Edged Diplomacy: International Bargaining and Domestic Politics.* Berkeley, CA: University of California Press, 1993.

Evron, Yair. *War and Intervention in Lebanon: The Israeli-Syrian Deterrence Dialogue.* London: Croom Helm, 1987.

Falkenrath, Richard A. *Shaping Europe's Military Order: The Origins and Consequences of the CFE Treaty.* CSIA Studies in International Security No. 6. Cambridge, MA: MIT Press 1995.

Fearon, James D. "Signaling versus the Balance of Power and Interests: An Empirical Test of a Crisis Bargaining Model." *Journal of Conflict Resolution* 38, no. 2 (June 1994): 236–69.

———. "Domestic Political Audiences and the Escalation of International Disputes." *American Political Science Review* 88, no. 3 (September 1994): 577–92.

———. "Rationalist Explanations for War." *International Organization* 49, no. 3 (Summer 1995): 379–414.

———."Bargaining, Enforcement and International Cooperation." *International Organization.* 52, no. 2 (Spring 1998): 269–305.

Fearon, James D., and David D. Laitin. "Explaining Interethnic Cooperation." *American Political Science Review* 90, no. 4 (December 1996): 715–35.

Fetherston, A. B. *Towards a Theory of United Nations Peacekeeping.* New York: St. Martin's, 1994.

Filson, Darren, and Suzanne Werner. "A Bargaining Model of War and Peace: Anticipating the Onset, Duration, and Outcome of War." *American Journal of Political Science* 46, no. 4 (October 2002): 819–38.

Findlay, Trevor. *Cambodia: The Legacy and Lessons of UNTAC.* SIPRI Research Report No. 9. Oxford, England: Oxford University Press, 1995.

Finel, Bernard I., and Kristin Lord. "The Surprising Logic of Transparency." In

Power and Conflict in the Age of Transparency, edited by Bernard I. Finel and Kristin Lord, New York: Palgrave, 2000.

———. "Transparency and World Politics." In *Power and Conflict in the Age of Transparency,* edited by Bernard I. Finel and Kristin Lord. New York: Palgrave, 2000.

Finer, Samuel E. "State- and Nation-Building in Europe: The Role of the Military." In *The Formation of National States in Western Europe,* edited by Charles Tilly. Princeton, NJ: Princeton University Press, 1975.

Fisher, Roger, William Ury, and Bruce Patton. *Getting to Yes: Negotiating an Agreement without Giving In.* 2nd ed. New York: Penguin, 1991.

Fishman, J. S. *Diplomacy and Revolution: The London Conference of 1830 and the Belgian Revolt.* Amsterdam, Netherlands: CHEV, 1988.

Florini, Ann. "The Evolution of International Norms." *International Studies Quarterly* 40, no. 3 (September 1996): 363–89.

———. "A New Role for Transparency," *Contemporary Security Policy* 18, no. 2 (August 1997): 51–72.

———. "The End of Secrecy." *Foreign Policy* 111 (Summer 1998): 50–63.

Florini, Ann M. *The Third Force: The Rise of Transnational Civil Society.* Washington, DC: Carnegie Endowment for International Peace, 2000.

Flynn, Gregory, and David J. Scheffer. "Limited Collective Security." *Foreign Policy* 80 (Fall 1990): 77–101.

Fondation Hirondelle. "Blue Sky—Fact Sheet" and "Communiqué de Presse." 3 Août 2000. Available at www.hirondelle.org.

Forsberg, Randall. "The Freeze and Beyond." In *The Future of Arms Control,* edited by Desmond Ball and Andrew Mack. Sydney, Australia: Australian National University Press, 1987.

Fortna, Virginia Page. "The United Nations Angola Verification Mission I." In *The Evolution of UN Peacekeeping: Case Studies and Comparative Analysis,* edited by William Durch. New York: St. Martin's, 1993.

———. "United Nations Transition Assistance Group." In *The Evolution of UN Peacekeeping: Case Studies and Comparative Analysis,* edited by William Durch. New York: St. Martin's, 1993.

Freison, Kate. "The Politics of Getting out the Vote in Cambodia." In *Propaganda, Politics, and Violence in Cambodia: Democratic Transition under United Nations Peace-keeping,* edited by Steve Heder and Judy Underwood. Armonk, NY: M. E. Sharpe, 1996.

Friedman, Thomas L. "African Madness." *New York Times,* January 31, 1996, p. A17.

Gaddis, John Lewis. *The United States and the Origins of the Cold War, 1941–1947.* New York: Columbia University Press, 1972.

———. *The Long Peace: Inquiries into the History of the Cold War.* Oxford, England: Oxford University Press, 1987.

———. "The Long Peace: Elements of Stability in the Postwar International System." In *The Cold War and After: Prospects for Peace,* edited by Sean M. Lynn-Jones. Cambridge, MA: MIT Press, 1991.

———. "International Relations Theory and the End of the Cold War." *International Security* 17, no. 3 (Winter 1992/93): 5–58.

Gagnon, Jr., V. P. "Ethnic Nationalism and International Conflict: The Case of Serbia," *International Security* 19, no. 3 (Winter 1994/95): 130–66.

Garthoff, Raymond L. *Detente and Confrontation: American-Soviet Relations from Nixon to Reagan.* Washington, DC: Brookings Institution Press, 1985.

Geertz, Clifford. *The Interpretation of Cultures.* New York: Basic Books, 1973.

Gensberg, Alexis. "Mediating Inequality: Mediators' Perspectives on Power Imbalances in Public Disputes." Manuscript, Program on Negotiation, Harvard Law School, Cambridge, MA, 2003.

George, Alexander L. "Case Studies and Theory Development." In *Diplomacy: New Approaches in History, Theory, and Policy,* edited by Paul Gordon Lauren. New York: Free Press, 1979.

George, Alexander L., and Andrew Bennett. *Case Studies and Theory Development in the Social Sciences.* Cambridge, MA: MIT Press, 2005.

George, Alexander L., and Timothy McKeown. "Case Studies and Theories of Organizational Decision Making." In *Advances in Information Processing in Organizations.* Vol. 2. Greenwich, CT: JAI Press, 1985.

Gerring, John. *Social Science Methodology: A Critical Framework.* Cambridge, England: Cambridge University Press, 2001.

———. "What Is a Case Study and What Is It Good For?" *American Political Science Review* 98, no. 2 (May 2004): 341–54.

Gershoy, Leo. *From Despotism to Revolution: 1763–1789.* New York: Harper, 1944.

Gertz, Bill. "U.S. Commander in Korea Sees North Near Disintegration." *Washington Times,* March 16, 1996, p. 7.

Geva, Nehemia, and Alex Mintz, ed. *Decisionmaking on War and Peace: The Cognitive-Rational Debate.* Boulder, Co: Lynne Rienner, 1997.

Ghali, Mona. "United Nations Emergency Force II, 1973–1979." In *The Evolution of UN Peacekeeping: Case Studies and Comparative Analysis,* edited by William Durch. New York: St. Martin's, 1993.

Gibler,. Douglas, M. "East or Further East?" *Journal of Peace Research* 36, no. 6 (November 1999): 627–37.

Gildea, Robert. *Barricades and Borders: Europe, 1800–1914.* Oxford, England: Oxford University Press, 1987.

Gilpin, Robert. *War and Change in International Politics.* Cambridge, England: Cambridge University Press, 1981.

Glaser, Charles L. "Political Consequences of Military Strategy: Expanding and Refining the Spiral and Deterrence Models." *World Politics* 44, no. 4 (July 1992): 497–538.

———. "Future Security Arrangements for Europe: Why NATO Is Still Best." In *Collective Security beyond the Cold War,* edited by George Downs. Ann Arbor, MI: University of Michigan Press, 1994.

Glenny, Misha. "Yugoslavia: The Revenger's Tragedy." *New York Review of Books,* August 13, 1992.

Goldstein, Judith and Robert O. Keohane. "Ideas and Foreign Policy: An Analytical Framework." In *Ideas and Foreign Policy: Beliefs, Institutions, and Political Change,* edited by Judith Goldstein and Robert O. Keohane. Ithaca, NY: Cornell University Press, 1993.

Goodby, James E. "A New European Concert: Settling Disputes in CSCE." *Arms*

Control Today 21, no. 1 (January/February 1991): 3–8.

———. "Commonwealth and Concert: Organizing Principles of Post-Containment Order in Europe." *Washington Quarterly* 14, no. 3 (Summer 1991).

Graybeal, Sidney, and Michael Krepon. "Making Better Use of the Standing Consultative Commission." *International Security* 10, no. 2 (Fall 1985): 183–99.

Green, Donald P., and Ian Shapiro. *Pathologies of Rational Choice Theory: A Critique of Applications in Political Science.* New Haven, CT: Yale University Press, 1994.

Grieco, Joseph M. "Anarchy and the Limits of Cooperation: A Realist Critique of the Newest Liberal Institutionalism." *International Organization* 42, no. 3 (Summer 1988): 485–507.

Grieco, Joseph M. *Cooperation among Nations: Europe, America, Non-tariff Barriers to Trade.* Ithaca, NY: Cornell University Press, 1990.

Grimsted, Patricia Kennedy. *The Foreign Ministers of Alexander I: Political Attitudes and the Conduct of Russian Diplomacy, 1801–1825.* Berkeley, CA: University of California Press, 1969.

Gruner, Wolf. "Was There a Reformed Balance of Power System of Cooperative Great Power Hegemony?" *American Historical Review* 97, no. 3 (June 1992): 725–32.

Gulick, Edward Vose. *Europe's Classic Balance of Power.* New York: Norton, 1955.

Gurtof, Mel. "South Korea's Foreign Policy and Future Security: Implications of the Nuclear Standoff." *Pacific Affairs* 69, no. 1 (Spring 1996): 8–31.

Haas, Ernst. "The Reconciliation of Conflicting Colonial Policy Aims: Acceptance of the League of Nations Mandate System." *International Organization* 6, no. 4 (November, 1952): 521–36.

———. "Types of Collective Security: An Examination of Operational Concepts." *American Political Science Review* 49, no. 1 (March 1955): 40–62.

———. "Words Can Hurt You; or, Who Said What to Whom About Regimes." Reprinted in *International Regimes,* edited by Stephen D. Krasner. Ithaca, NY: Cornell University Press, 1983.

———. "Regime Decay: Conflict Management and International Organizations, 1945–1981." *International Organization* 37, no. 2 (Spring 1983): 189–256.

Haggard, Stephan, and Beth A. Simmons. "Theories of International Regimes." *International Organization* 41, no. 3 (Summer 1987): 491–517.

Hamilton, Keith, and Richard Langhorne. *The Practice of Diplomacy: Its Evolution, Theory, and Administration.* New York: Routledge, 1995.

Hampson, Fen Osler. *Nurturing Peace: Why Peace Settlements Succeed or Fail.* Washington, DC: United States Institute of Peace Press, 1996.

Hamza, Khidhir. "Inside Sadaam's Secret Nuclear Program." *Bulletin of the Atomic Scientists* 54, no. 5 (September/October 1998): 26–33.

Harbottle, Michael. *The Impartial Soldier.* London: Oxford University Press, 1970.

———. *The Blue Berets.* London: Leo Cooper, 1975.

Hart, B. H. Liddell. "Aggression and the Problem of Weapons." *English Review* (July 1932): 71–78.

Hart, Parker T. *Two NATO Allies at the Threshold of War; Cyprus: A Firsthand*

Account of Crisis Management, 1965–1968. Durham, NC: Duke University Press, 1990.

Hartmann, Frederick H. *Basic Documents of International Relations*. Westport, CT: Greenwood, 1951.

Hassall, Arthur. *The Balance of Power, 1715–1789. Period VI*. New York: MacMillan, 1898.

Hawes, John. "Open Skies: Beyond 'Vancouver to Vladivostok.'" Stimson Center Occasional Paper, No. 10. December 1992.

———. "Open Skies: From Ideas to Negotiation." *NATO Review: Web Edition*. 38, no. 2 (April 1990): 6–9. Accessed March 5, 2002 at www.nato.int/docu/review/1990/9002–02.htm.

Heder, Steve. "The Resumption of Armed Struggle by the Party of Democratic Kampuchea: Evidence from National Army of Democratic Kampuchea 'Self-Demobilizers.'" In *Propaganda, Politics, and Violence in Cambodia: Democratic Transition under United Nations Peace-Keeping*, edited by Steve Heder and Judy Underwood. Armonk, NY: M. E. Sharpe, 1996.

Heder, Steve, and Judy Legerwood. "Politics of Violence: An Introduction." In *Propaganda, Politics, and Violence in Cambodia: Democratic Transition under United Nations Peace-Keeping*, edited by Steve Heder and Judy Underwood. Armonk, NY: M. E. Sharpe, 1996.

Heininger, Janet E. *Peacekeeping in Transition: The United Nations in Cambodia*. New York: Twentieth Century Fund Press, 1994.

Henze, Paul B. "Ethiopia and Eritrea in Transition: The Impact of Ethnicity on Politics and Development," RAND no. P-7937. Santa Monica, CA: Rand Corporation, 1995.

Herrmann, Richard K. "Image Theory and Strategic Interaction in International Relations." In *Oxford Handbook of Political Psychology*, edited by David O. Sears, Leonie Huddy, and Robert Jervis, chap. 9. Oxford, England: Oxford University Press, 2003.

Heyman, Jeffrey. "The Story of Radio UNTAC: The United Nations First Peace-Keeping Radio Station." *Monitoring Times* 13, no. 10 (1994).

Higgins, Rosalyn. *United Nations Peacekeeping: Documents and Commentary, Europe 1946–1979*. Vol. 4. Oxford, England: Oxford University Press, 1981.

Hinsley, F. H. *Power and the Pursuit of Peace: Theory and Practice in the History of Relations Between States*. Cambridge, England: Cambridge University Press, 1967.

Hoag, Malcolm. "On Stability in Deterrent Races." *World Politics* (July 1961): 505–527.

Hoffman, Stanley. *Organisations Internationales et Pouvoirs Politiques des Etats*. Paris: Armand Colin, 1954.

Holborn, Hajo. *The Political Collapse of Europe*. New York: Knopf, 1961.

———. *A History of Modern Germany: 1648–1840*. Princeton, NJ: Princeton University Press, 1964.

Holbraad, Carsten. *The Concert of Europe: A Study in German and British International Theory, 1815–1914*. London, England: Longman, 1970.

Holsti, Kalevi J. *Peace and War: Armed Conflict and International Order 1648–1989*. Cambridge, England: Cambridge University Press, 1991.

————. "Governance with Government: Polyarchy in Nineteenth-Century European International Politics." In *Governance Without Government: Order and Change in World Politics,* edited by James N. Rosenau and Ernst-Otto Czempiel. Cambridge, England: Cambridge University Press, 1992.

Holsti, Ole R. *Crisis, Escalation, War.* Montreal, Canada: McGill-Queens University Press, 1972.

Holsti, Ole R., P. Terrence Hopmann, and John D. Sullivan. *Unity and Disintegration in International Alliances.* New York: Wiley, 1973.

Hoover, J. Jeffrey. "The Society and its Environment." In *Cyprus: A Country Study,* 3rd ed., edited by Frederica M. Bunge. Washington, DC: American University Press, 1980.

Howard, Roger. *Iran in Crisis? Nuclear Ambitions and the American Response.* London and New York: Zed Books, 2004; distributed in the United States by Palgrave Macmillan.

Hume, Cameron, "Perez de Cuellar and the Iran-Iraq War." *Negotiation Journal* 8, no. 2 (April 1992): 173–84.

Huntington, Samuel P. "Arms Races: Prerequisites and Results." In *The Use of Force,* 3rd ed., edited by Robert J. Art and Kenneth N. Waltz. Lanham, MD: University Press of America, 1988.

Huth, Paul K. "Deterrence and International Conflict: Empirical Findings and Theoretical Debates." *Annual Review of Political Science* 2 (1999): 25–48.

Ikenberry, G. John. *After Victory: Institutions, Strategic Restraint, and the Rebuilding of Order after Major Wars.* Princeton, NJ: Princeton University Press, 2001.

Inbar, Efrain, *Regional Security Regimes: Israel and Its Neighbors.* Albany, NY: State University of New York Press, 1995.

Ingrao, Charles. "Paul W. Schroeder's Balance of Power: Stability or Anarchy?" *The International History Review* 16, no. 4 (November 1994): 661–80.

International Peace Academy and Center on International Cooperation. "Refashioning the Dialogue: Regional Perspectives on the Brahimi Report on UN Peace Operations." International Peace Academy, New York, April 2001.

International Institute for Strategic Studies. *The Military Balance, 1993–1994.* London: Oxford University Press, for the IISS, 1993.

————. *The Military Balance, 1995–96.* London: Oxford University Press, for the IISS, 1995.

Jabri, Vivienne. *Mediating Conflict: Decision-making and Western Intervention in Namibia.* Manchester, England: Manchester University Press, 1990.

James, Alan. *Peacekeeping in International Politics.* New York: St. Martin's, 1990.

————. "Internal Peacekeeping: A Dead End for the UN?" *Security Dialogue* 24, no. 4 (December 1993): 359–68.

Jarque, Xavier, Clara Ponsati, and Jozsef Sakovics. "Mediation: Incomplete Information Bargaining with Filtered Information." *Journal of Mathematical Economics* 39, no. 7 (September 2003): 803–30.

Jelavich, Barbara. *Russia's Balkan Entanglements, 1806–1914.* Cambridge, England: Cambridge University Press, 1991.

Jervis, Robert. "Hypotheses on Misperception." In *American Foreign Policy:*

Theoretical Essays, edited by G. John Ikenberry. Glenview, IL: Scott, Foresman, 1989. Reprint from *World Politics* 20, no. 3 (April 1968).

——. *The Logic of Images in International Relations.* New York: Columbia University Press, 1970.

——. *Perception and Misperception in International Politics.* Princeton, NJ: Princeton University Press, 1976.

——. "Cooperation under the Security Dilemma." *World Politics* 32, no. 2 (January 1978): 167–214.

——. "Security Regimes." *International Organization* 36, no. 2 (Spring 1982). Reprinted in *International Regimes,* edited by Stephen D. Krasner. Ithaca, NY: Cornell University Press, 1983.

——. "From Balance to Concert: A Study of International Security Cooperation." In *Cooperation under Anarchy,* edited by Kenneth Oye. Princeton, NJ: Princeton University Press, 1986.

——. "War and Misperception." *Journal of Interdisciplinary History* 18, no. 4 (Spring 1988): 675–700.

——. "Models and Cases in the Study of International Conflict." *Journal of International Affairs* 44, no. 1 (Spring/Summer 1990): 81–102.

——. "A Political Science Perspective on the Balance of Power and the Concert." *American Historical Review* 97, no. 3 (June 1992): 716–24.

——. "International Primacy: Is the Game Worth the Candle?" *International Security* 17, no. 4 (Spring 1993): 52–67.

——. "Arms Control, Stability, and Causes of War." *Political Science Quarterly* 108, no. 2 (Summer 1993): 239–53.

Jervis, Robert, Richard Ned Lebow, Janice Gross Stein, et al. *Psychology and Deterrence.* Baltimore, MD: Johns Hopkins University Press, 1985.

Jette, Dennis C. *Why Peacekeeping Fails.* New York: Palgrave 2001.

Joffe, Josef. "Collective Security and the Future of Europe: Failed Dreams and Dead Ends." *Survival* 34, no. 1 (Spring 1992): 36–50.

Johnson, Stephen. "Public Diplomacy Needs a Commander, Not a Spokesman." *Heritage Foundation Research.* WebMemo no. 869, September 30, 2005, at www.heritage.org/Research/NationalSecurity/wm869.cfm.

Kagan, Korina. "The Myth of the European Concert: The Realist-Institutionalist Debate and Great Power Behavior in the Eastern Question, 1821–41." *Security Studies* 7, no. 2 (Winter 1997–98): 1–57.

Kam, Ephraim. *Surprise Attack: The Victim's Perspective.* Cambridge, MA: Harvard University Press, 1988.

Kang, David C. "Rethinking North Korea." *Asian Survey* 35, no. 3 (March 1995): 253–67.

Kaufmann, Stuart J. "Spiraling to Ethnic War: Elites, Masses, and Moscow in Moldova's Civil War." *International Security* 21, no. 2 (Autumn 1996): 108–38.

Keck, Margaret E., and Kathryn Sikkink. *Activists Beyond Borders: Advocacy Networks in International Politics.* Ithaca, NY: Cornell University Press, 1998.

Keefe, Eugene K. "Historical Setting." In *Cyprus: A Country Study,* 3rd ed., edited by Frederica M. Bunge. Washington, DC: American University Press, 1980.

Kegley, Charles W., and Gregory A. Raymond. *When Trust Breaks Down: Al-*

liance Norms and World Politics. Columbia, SC: University of South Carolina Press, 1990.

Kende, Istvan. "The History of Peace: Concept and Organizations from the Late Middle Ages to the 1870s." *Journal of Peace Research* 26, no. 3 (1989): 233–47.

Kennedy, Paul. *The Rise and Fall of Great Powers: Economic Change and Military Conflict from 1500 to 2000.* New York: Random House, 1987.

Keohane, Robert O. "The Demand for International Regimes." In *International Regimes,* edited by Stephen D. Krasner. Ithaca, NY: Cornell University Press, 1983.

———. *After Hegemony: Cooperation and Discord in the World Political Economy.* Princeton, NJ: Princeton University Press, 1984.

———. *Neorealism and Its Critics.* New York: Columbia University Press, 1986.

———. *International Institutions and State Power: Essays in International Relations Theory.* Boulder, CO: Westview, 1989.

———. "Institutional Theory and the Realist Challenge after the Cold War." In *Neorealism and Neoliberalism: The Contemporary Debate,* edited by David A. Baldwin. New York: Columbia University Press, 1993.

Keohane, Robert O., and Lisa L. Martin. "The Promise of Institutionalist Theory." *International Security* 20, no. 1 (Summer 1995): 39–51.

Khong, Yuen Foong. *Analogies at War: Korea, Munich, Dien Bien Phu, and the Vietnam Decisions of 1965.* Princeton, NJ: Princeton University Press, 1992.

Khoo, Nicholas, and Michael L. R. Smith. "A 'Concert of Asia?'" *Policy Review* 108 (August/September 2001).

Kim, Samuel S. "North Korea in 1994: Brinkmanship, Breakdown, and Breakthrough." *Asian Survey,* 35, no. 1 (January 1995): 13–27.

Kim, Taewoo. "South Korea's Missile Dilemma." *Asian Survey* 39, no. 3 (May–June 1999): 486–503.

King, Gary, Robert O. Keohane, and Sidney Verba. *Designing Social Inquiry: Scientific Inference in Qualitative Research.* Princeton, NJ: Princeton University Press, 1994.

Kissinger, Henry A. *A World Restored: Metternich, Castlereagh, and the Problems of Peace, 1812–1822.* Boston, MA: Houghton Mifflin, 1973.

———. *Years of Upheaval.* Boston, MA: Little, Brown, 1982.

Kluth, Andreas. "In Praise of Rules: A Survey of Asian Business." *The Economist,* April 7, 2001.

Knorr, Klaus. "Threat Perception." In *Historical Dimensions of National Security Problems,* edited by Klaus Knorr. Lawrence, KS: University Press of Kansas, 1976.

Knorr, Klaus, and Patrick Morgan. *Strategic Military Surprise: Incentives and Opportunities.* New Brunswick, NJ: Transaction, 1983.

Koremenos, Barbara, Charles Lipson, and Duncan Snidal, eds. *The Rational Design of International Institutions,* special issue of *International Organization* 55, no. 4 (Autumn 2001).

Kraehe, Enno E. "A Bipolar Balance of Power." *American Historical Review* 97, no. 3 (June 1992): 707–15.

Krasner, Stephen D. "Regimes and the Limits of Realism: Regimes as Autonomous Variables." In *International Regimes,* edited by Stephen D. Krasner. Ithaca, NY: Cornell University Press, 1983.

———. "Structural Causes and Regime Consequences: Regimes as Intervening Variables." In *International Regimes,* edited by Stephen D. Krasner. Ithaca, NY: Cornell University Press, 1983.

Krasznai, Marton. "Cooperative Bilateral Aerial Inspections: The Hungarian-Romanian Experience." In *Open Skies, Arms Control, and Cooperative Security,* edited by Michael Krepon and Amy E. Smithson. New York: St. Martin's, 1992.

———. "Scenarios for Co-operative Aerial Observations in Support of Crisis Prevention and Post-conflict Settlement: Lessons from the Bosnia Experience." Comments prepared for a seminar titled "Perspectives for Co-operative Aerial Observation and the Treaty on Open Skies," at the Stockholm International Peace Research Institute (SIPRI), Stockholm, Sweden, November 30–December 1, 2004, available at www.sipri.org/contents/director/esdp/KrasznaiOS.html.

Krepon, Michael, and Amy E. Smithson. "Introduction" in Michael Krepon and Amy E. Smithson. *Open Skies, Arms Control, and Cooperative Security.* New York: St. Martin's, 1992.

Kühne, Winrich, with Jochen Prantl. "The Security Council and the G8 in the New Millennium: Who is in Charge of International Peace and Security?" Paper presented to Stiftung Wissenschaft und Politik (SWP), Research Institute for International Affairs, 5th International Workshop, June 30–July 1, 2000, Berlin, Germany.

Kupchan, Charles A., and Clifford A. Kupchan. "Concerts, Collective Security, and the Future of Europe." *International Security* 16, no. 1 (Summer 1991): 114–61.

Kydd, Andrew. "Game Theory and the Spiral Model." *World Politics* 49, no. 3 (April 1977): 371–400.

Kydd, Andrew, and Barbara F. Walter. "Sabotaging the Peace: The Politics of Extremist Violence." *International Organization* 56, no. 2 (Spring 2002): 263–96.

Lachowski, Zdzislaw. "Conventional Arms Control and Security Cooperation in Europe." In *SIPRI Yearbook 1994.* Oxford, England: Oxford University Press, for the Stockholm International Peace Research Institute (SIPRI), 1994.

———. *Confidence and Security-Building Measures in the New Europe.* SIPRI Research Report No. 18. Oxford, England: Oxford University Press, 2004.

Laipson, Ellen. "Government and Politics." In *Cyprus: A Country Study.* 4th ed. Washington, DC: Government Printing Office, 1993.

Lake, David., "Beyond Anarchy: The Importance of Security Institutions." *International Security* 26, no. 1 (Summer 2001): 129–60.

Lake, David A., and Robert Powell. "International Relations: A Strategic-Choice Approach." *Strategic Choice and International Relations.* Princeton, NJ: Princeton University Press, 1999.

Langhorne, Richard. "The Development of International Conferences, 1648–1830." *Studies in History and Politics* 2, no. 2 (1981–1982).

———. "The Regulation of Diplomatic Practice: The Beginnings to the Vienna Convention on Diplomatic Practice, 1961." *Review of International Studies* 18, no. 1 (January 1992).

Lauren, Paul Gordon. *Diplomats and Bureaucrats: The First Institutional Responses to Twentieth-Century Diplomacy in France and Germany.* Stanford, CA: Hoover Institution Press, 1976.

———. "Crisis Prevention in Nineteenth-Century Diplomacy." In *Managing U.S.-Soviet Rivalry: Problems of Crisis Prevention,* edited by Alexander L. George. Boulder, CO: Westview, 1983.

Layne, Christopher. "Lord Palmerston and the Triumph of Realism: Anglo-French Relations, 1830–1848." In *Paths to Peace: Is Democracy the Answer?* edited by Miriam Fendius Elman. Cambridge, MA: MIT Press, 1997.

Legerwood, Judy. "Patterns of CPP Political Repression and Violence during the UNTAC Period. In *Propaganda Politics and Violence in Cambodia: Democratic Transition under United Nations Peace-Keeping,* edited by Steve Heder and Judy Legerwood. Armonk, NY: M. E. Sharpe, 1996.

Lehmann, Ingrid A. *Peacekeeping and Public Information: Caught in the Crossfire.* London: Frank Cass, 1999.

Levi, Michael A., and Michael E. O'Hanlon. *The Future of Arms Control.* Washington, DC: Brookings Institution, 2005.

Levy, Jack S. "Misperception and the Causes of War, Theoretical Linkages and Analytical Problems." *World Politics* 36, no. 1 (October 1983): 76–99.

———. "The Causes of War: A Review of Theories." In *Behavior, Society, and Nuclear War,* edited by Philip E. Tetlock, Jo L. Husbands, Robert Jervis, Paul C. Stern, and Charles Tilly. New York: Oxford University Press, 1989.

———. "The Theoretical Foundations of Paul W. Schroeder's International System." *The International History Review* 16, no. 4 (November 1994): 715–44.

———. Loss Aversion, Framing Effects, and International Theory." In *Handbook of War Studies II,* edited by Manus I. Midlarsky. Ann Arbor, MI: University of Michigan Press, 2000.

———. "Political Psychology and Foreign Policy." In *Oxford Handbook of Political Psychology,* vol. 1, edited by David O. Sears, Leonie Huddy, and Robert Jervis. Oxford, England: Oxford University Press, 2003.

Levy, Tali. "The 1991 Cambodia Settlement Agreements." In *Words over War: Mediation and Arbitration to Prevent Deadly Conflict.* Lanham, MD: Rowman and Littlefield, for the Carnegie Corporation of New York, 2000.

Lewis, William H. *Military Implications of United Nations Peacekeeping Operations.* Washington, DC: National Defense University Press, 1993.

Lichbach, Mark Irving. "Information, Trust, and Power: The Impact of Conflict Histories, Policy Regimes, and Political Institutions on Terrorism." Draft paper, University of Maryland, College Park, MD, October 15, 2004.

Lijphart, Arend. "The Comparable-Cases Strategy in Comparative Research." *Comparative Political Studies* 8, no. 2 (July 1975): 158–77.

Lind, Michael. "Peacefaking: The Case Against U.N. 'Peacemaking'" *The New Republic,* November 8, 1993.

———. "Twilight of the U.N." *The New Republic,* October 30, 1995.

Lindley, Dan. "Collective Security Organizations and Internal Conflicts." In *The International Dimensions of Internal Conflict,* ed. Michael Brown. Pp. 537–68. Cambridge, MA: MIT Press, 1996.

———. "UNFICYP and a Cyprus Solution: A Strategic Assessment." Working Paper, Defense and Arms Control Studies Program, MIT, Cambridge, MA, May 1997.

———. "Transparency and the Effectiveness of Security Regimes: A Study of Concert Europe Crisis Management and United Nations Peace Keeping." Ph.D. diss., MIT, Cambridge, MA, 1998.

———. "Assessing the Rule of U.N. Peacekeeping Force in Cyprus." In *The Work of the U.N. in Cyprus: Promoting Peace and Development,* edited by Oliver P. Richmond and James Ker-Lindsay. New York: Palgrave, St. Martin's, 2001.

———. "Untapped Power? The Status of U.N. Information Operations." *International Peacekeeping* 11, no. 4 (Winter 2004): 608–24.

———. "The Arrogance of the Dogmatic Left and Right." October 26, 2005. Available at www.nd.edu/~dlindley/handouts/arroganceofleftandright.html.

Lindley, Dan, and Ryan Schildkraut. "Is War Rational? The Extent of Miscalculation and Misperception as Causes of War." Draft paper. 2006.

Lipson, Charles. "The Transformation of International Trade: The Sources and Effects of Regime Change." In *International Regimes,* edited by Stephen D. Krasner. Ithaca, NY: Cornell University Press, 1983.

———. "International Cooperation in Economic and Security Affairs." *World Politics* 37, no. 1 (October 1984): 1–23.

———. "Is the Future of Collective Security Like the Past?" In *Collective Security beyond the Cold War,* edited by George Downs. Ann Arbor, MI: University of Michigan Press, 1994.

———. "Are Security Regimes Possible? Historical Cases and Modern Issues." In *Regional Security Regimes: Israel and Its Neighbors,* edited by Efrain Inbar. Albany, NY: State University of New York Press, 1995.

———. *Reliable Partners: How Democracies Have Made a Separate Peace.* Princeton, NJ: Princeton University Press, 2003.

Liska, George. *Nations in Alliance: The Limits of Interdependence.* Baltimore, MD: Johns Hopkins University Press, 1962.

Lowenthal, Mark M., and Joel S. Wit. "The Politics of Verification." In *Verification and Arms Control,* edited by William C. Potter. Lexington, MA: Lexington Books, 1985.

Luard, Evan. *International Society.* New York: New Amsterdam Books, 1990.

Luck, Edward. "Making Peace." *Foreign Policy,* no. 89 (Winter 1992–93): 137–55.

Lyons, Gene M. "A New Collective Security: The United Nations in Theory and Practice." *Washington Quarterly* 17, no. 2 (Spring 1994).

Lyons, Terrence. "Great Powers and Conflict Resolution in the Horn of Africa." In *Cooperative Security: Reducing Third World Wars,* edited by I. William Zartmann and Victor A. Kremenyuk. Syracuse, NY: Syracuse University Press, 1995.

MacDonald, Scott B. "Transparency in Thailand's 1997 Economic Crisis: The Significance of Disclosure." *Asian Survey* 38, no. 7 (July 1998): 688–702.

Mack, Andrew. "Conclusion: The Future of Arms Control." In *The Future of Arms Control,* edited by Desmond Ball and Andrew Mack. Sydney, Australia: Australian National University Press, 1987.

Mackinlay, John. *The Peacekeepers: An Assessment of Peacekeeping Operations at the Arab-Israeli Interface.* London: Unwin Hyman, 1989.

Madden, Jane. "Namibia: A Lesson for Success." In *Building International Com-*

munity: Cooperating for Peace Case Studies, edited by Kevin Clements and Robin Ward. St. Leonards, Australia: Allen Unwin, 1994.

Mahoney, James, and Gary Goertz. "The Possibility Principle: Choosing Negative Cases in Comparative Research." *American Political Science Review* 98, no. 4 (November 2004): 653–69.

Maier, Franz Georg. *Cyprus: From the Earliest Time to the Present Day,* translated by Peter Gorge. London: Elek, 1968.

Mandelbaum, Michael. *The Fate of Nations: The Search for National Security in the Nineteenth and Twentieth Centuries.* Cambridge, England: Cambridge University Press, 1988.

Marquardt, James. "Why Transparency In International Relations Is Not What It Appears to Be." Ph.D. diss., Department of Political Science, University of Chicago, Chicago, IL, 1998.

———. "Open Skies: Not a Moment Too Soon." *Bulletin of the Atomic Scientists* 58, no. 1 (January/February 2002): 18–20.

Marquardt, Jim. "What is Transparency?" International Studies Association-Midwest Meeting, September 1995.

Marston, John. "Cambodian News Media in the UNTAC Period and After." In *Propaganda, Politics, and Violence in Cambodia: Democratic Transition under United Nations Peace-keeping,* edited by Steve Heder and Judy Underwood. Armonk, NY: M.E. Sharpe, 1996.

———. "Neutrality and the Negotiation of an Information Order in Cambodia." In *Forging Peace: Intervention, Human Rights and the Management of Media Space,* edited by Monroe E. Price and Mark Thompson. Bloomington, IN: Indiana University Press, 2002.

Martin, Lisa L. *Coercive Cooperation: Explaining Multilateral Economic Sanctions.* Princeton, NJ: Princeton University Press, 1992: 143–78.

———. "Institutions and Cooperation: Sanctions During the Falklands Islands Conflict." *International Security* 16, no. 4 (Spring 1992).

May, Ernest R. "Conclusions: Capabilities and Proclivities." In *Knowing One's Enemies: Intelligence Assessment Before the Two World Wars,* edited by Ernest R. May. Princeton, NJ: Princeton University Press, 1986.

Mazarr, Michael J. "Going Just a Little Nuclear: Lessons from North Korea." *International Security* 20, no. 2 (Autumn 1995): 92–122.

McCausland, Jeffrey D. "'Squaring the Circle': Cooperative Security and Military Operations." INSS Occasional Paper 45. USAFA, CO: USAF Institute for National Security Studies, July 2002.

McDonald, Robert. "The Cyprus Problem." Adelphi Paper 234. London: International Institute for Strategic Studies, 1989.

Mearsheimer, John J. "Back to the Future: Instability in Europe after the Cold War." *International Security* 15, no. 1 (Summer 1990): 5–56.

———. "The False Promise of International Institutions." *International Security* 19, no. 3 (Winter 1994–95): 5–49.

———. "A Realist Reply." *International Security* 20, no. 1 Summer 1995): 82–93.

Medlicott, W. N. *Bismarck, Gladstone, and the Concert of Europe.* London: University of London/Athlone Press, 1956.

Mei, Zhou. *Radio UNTAC of Cambodia: Winning Ears, Hearts, and Minds.* Bangkok, Thailand: White Lotus Press, 1994.

Meleagrou, Eleni, and Birol Yesilada. "The Society and Its Environment." In *Cyprus: A Country Study,* edited by Eric Solsten, 4th ed. Washington, DC: Government Printing Office, 1993.

Mertus, Julie, and Mark Thompson. "The Learning Curve: Media Development in Kosovo." In *Forging Peace: Intervention, Human Rights and the Management of Media Space,* edited by Monroe E. Price and Mark Thompson. Bloomington, IN: Indiana University Press, 2002.

Mill, John Stuart. *The Logic of the Moral Sciences.* London: Duckworth, 1987.

Miller, Benjamin. "Explaining Great Power Cooperation in Conflict Management." *World Politics* 45, no. 1 (October 1992): 1–46.

———. "Explaining the Emergence of Great Power Concerts." *Review of International Studies* 20, no. 4 (October 1994): 327–48.

Miller, Steven E. "Politics over Promise: Domestic Impediments to Arms Control." *International Security* 8, no. 4 (Spring 1984): 67–90.

Milner, Helen. "International Theories of Cooperation among Nations: Strengths and Weaknesses." *World Politics* 44, no. 3 (April 1992): 466–96. Review article.

———. *Interests, Institutions, and Information: Domestic Politics and International Relations.* Princeton, NJ. Princeton University Press, 1997.

Mitchell, Ronald. "Sources of Transparency: Information Systems in International Regimes." *International Studies Quarterly* 42, no. 1 (March 1998): 109–30.

Moore, Christopher W. *The Mediation Process: Practical Strategies for Resolving Conflict.* 2nd ed. San Francisco, CA: Jossey-Bass, 1996.

Morgan, Patrick. "The Opportunity for Strategic Surprise." In *Strategic Military Surprise: Incentives and Opportunities,* edited by Klaus Knorr and Patrick Morgan. New Brunswick, NJ: Transaction, 1983.

Morgan, Tabitha. "Cyprus Keeps Its Hidden Barrier." *BBC News,* October 5, 2005. Available at news.bbc.co.uk/2/hi/europe/4313016.stm.

Morgenthau, Hans J. *Politics among Nations: The Struggle for Power and Peace.* 5 ed. rev. New York: Knopf, 1973.

Morrow, James D. "Capabilities, Uncertainty, and Resolve: A Limited Information Model of Crisis Bargaining." *American Journal of Political Science* 33, no. 4 (November 1989): 941–72.

———. "The Forms of International Cooperation." *International Organization* 48, no. 3 (Summer 1994): 387–425.

———. "Modeling the Forms of International Cooperation: Distribution vs. Information." *International Organization* 48, no. 3 (Summer 1994): 387–423.

Mowat. R. B. *Europe, 1715–1815.* New York: Longmans, Green, 1929.

Mueller, John. "A New Concert of Europe." *Foreign Policy* 77 (Winter 1989–90): 3–16.

Mueller, Timothy A., Lt. Col, USAF. "Developing National Security Policy in the 'Gorbachev Era.'" Washington, DC: National War College, 31 March 1989, pp. 1–27. Available at www.ndu.edu/library/n3/SSP-89-016.pdf.

Neuffer, Elizabeth. "Greek, Turkish Foes Clash on Cyprus." *Boston Globe,* August 11, 1996, p. A2.

———. "Turkish Troops Kill Protester as Strife Worsens on Cyprus." *Boston Globe,* August 15, 1996, p. A1.

Newhouse, John. *Cold Dawn: The Story of SALT.* Washington, DC: Pergamon-Brassey's, 1989.

Nichols, Irby C., Jr. *The European Pentarchy and the Congress of Verona, 1822.* The Hague, Netherlands: Martinus Nijhoff, 1971.

Nicholson, Harold. *The Congress of Vienna, A Study in Allied Unity: 1812–1822.* New York: Harcourt, Brace, 1946.

Norman, Colin. "Iraq's Bomb Program: A Smoking Gun Emerges." *Science,* November 1, 1991, pp. 644–45.

Oakley, Robert B. "A Diplomatic Perspective on African Conflict Resolution." In *African Conflict Resolution: The U.S. Role in Peacemaking,* edited by David R. Smock and Chester A. Crocker. Washington, DC: United States Institute of Peace Press, 1993.

Odom, William "How to Create a True World Order: Establish a Concert of Great Powers." *Orbis* 39, no. 2 (Spring 1995): 155–72.

Olson, Mancur. *The Logic of Collective Action: Public Goods and the Theory of Groups.* Cambridge, MA: Harvard University Press, 1971.

———. *The Rise and Decline of Nations: Economic Growth, Stagflation, and Social Rigidities.* New Haven, CT: Yale University Press, 1982.

Omond, G.W.T. "Belgium: 1830–1839." In *The Cambridge History of British Foreign Policy: 1783–1919,* vol. 2, edited by Sir A. W. Ward and G. P. Gooch. New York, NY: Macmillan, 1923.

Ostrom, Elinor. *Governing the Commons: The Evolution of Institutions for Collective Action.* Cambridge, Cambridge University Press.

Oye, Kenneth. "Explaining Cooperation under Anarchy: Hypotheses and Strategies." In *Cooperation under Anarchy,* edited by Kenneth Oye. Princeton, NJ: Princeton University Press, 1986.

Papadapoulos, Andrestinos N. "Cyprus: A Case Study, Peace-Making and Peace-Keeping by the United Nations." Working paper, Nicosia, Cyprus, 1969.

Papp, Daniel S. "The Angolan Civil War and Namibia." In *Making War and Waging Peace: Foreign Intervention in Africa,* edited by David R. Smock. Washington, DC: United States Institute of Peace Press, 1993.

Patrick, Richard A. *Political Geography and the Cyprus Conflict: 1963–1971.* Waterloo, Canada: Department of Geography, University of Waterloo, 1976.

Peden, G. C. *British Rearmament and the Treasury: 1932–1939.* Edinburgh, Scotland: Scottish Academic Press, 1979.

Peou, Sorpong. *Conflict Neutralization in the Cambodia War: From Battlefield to Ballot Box.* Oxford, England: Oxford University Press, 1997.

Perlez, Jane. "U.S. Did Little to Deter Buildup as Ethiopia and Eritrea Prepared for War." *New York Times,* May 22, 2000.

Philips, Walter Alison. *The Confederation of Europe: A Study of the European Alliance, 1813–1823, as an Experiment in the International Organization of Peace.* 2nd ed. New York: Longmans, Green, 1920.

Pollack, Kenneth M. *The Threatening Storm: The Case for Invading Iraq.* New York: Random House, 2002.

Posen, Barry R. *The Sources of Military Doctrine*. Ithaca, NY: Cornell University Press, 1984.

———. "Crisis Stability and Conventional Arms Control." *Daedalus* 120, no. 1 (Winter 1991): 217–32.

———. "The Security Dilemma and Ethnic Conflict." In *Ethnic Conflict and International Security*, edited by Michael E. Brown. Princeton, NJ: Princeton University Press, 1993.

Potter, William C., ed. *Verification and SALT: The Challenge of Strategic Deception*. Boulder, CO: Westview, 1980.

Powell, Robert. "Bargaining Theory and International Conflict." *Annual Review of Political Science* 5 (2002): 1–30.

———. "The Inefficient Use of Power: Costly Conflict with Complete Information." *American Political Science Review* 98, no. 2 (May 2004): 231–41.

Prendergast, John, and Mark Duffield, "Liberation Politics in Ethiopia and Eritrea." In *Civil Wars in Africa: Roots and Resolution* edited by Taiser M. Ali and Robert O. Matthews. Montreal, Canada: McGill-Queens University Press, 1999.

Pregenzer, Arian L., Michael Vannoni, and Kent L. Biringer. "Cooperative Monitoring of Regional Security Agreements." SAND96–1121. Albuquerque, NM: Sandia National Laboratories, November 1996.

Purcell, H. D. *Cyprus*. London: Ernest Benn, 1969.

Putnam, Robert D. "Diplomacy and Domestic Politics: The Logic of Two-Level Games." Reprinted in *Double-Edged Diplomacy: International Bargaining and Domestic Politics*, edited by Evans, Peter B., Harold K. Jacobson, and Robert D. Putnam. Berkeley, CA: University of California Press, 1993.

Quandt, William B. *Peace Process: American Diplomacy and the Arab-Israeli Conflict since 1967*. Washington, DC: Brookings Institution, and Berkeley, CA: University of California Press, 1993.

Radio Netherlands Media Network Dossier. "Peace Radio: Outside Africa." Updated September 25, 2002, at www.rnw.nl/realoradio/dossiers/html/peaceradio rest.html.

Rathjens, George. "The Dynamic of the Arms Race." In *Scientific American, Progress in Arms Control?* San Francisco, CA: W. H. Freeman, 1979.

Ratner, Steven R. "The United Nations in Cambodia: A Model for the Resolution of Internal Conflicts?" In *Enforcing Restraint: Collective Intervention in Internal Conflicts,* edited by Lori Fisler Damrosch. New York: Council on Foreign Relations Press, 1993.

Reed, Pamela L., J. Matthew Vaccaro, and William J. Durch. *Handbook on United Nations Peace Operations*. Handbook No. 3. The Henry L. Stimson Center, Washington, DC, April 1995.

Reed, William. "Information, Power, and War." *American Political Science Review* 97, no. 4 (November 2003): 633–41.

Reich, Bernard. *Quest for Peace: United States-Israel Relations and the Arab-Israeli Conflict*. New Brunswick, NJ: Transaction, 1977.

Reinicke, Wolfgang H. *Global Public Policy: Governing without Government?* Washington, DC: Brookings Institution, 1998.

Reiter, Dan. "Exploring the Bargaining Model of War." *Perspectives on Politics* 1, no. 1 (March 2003): 27–43.

Rendall, Matthew. "Russia, the Concert of Europe, and Greece 1821–29: A Test of Hypotheses about the Vienna System." *Security Studies* 9, no. 4 (Summer 2000): 52–90.

Rendall, Matthew Tobias. "Russia, the Concert of Europe, and the Near East, 1821–41: A Status Quo State in the Vienna System." Ph.D. diss., Columbia University, New York, 2000.

Rich, Norman. *Great Power Diplomacy: 1814–1914.* New York: McGraw-Hill, 1992.

Richardson, Louise. "The Concert of Europe and Security Management in the Nineteenth Century." In *Imperfect Unions: Security Institutions over Time and Space,* edited by Helga Haftendorn, Robert O. Keohane, and Celeste A. Wallander. Oxford, England: Oxford University Press, 1999.

Rikhye, Indar Jit. *The Theory and Practice of Peacekeeping.* London: Hurst, for the International Peace Academy, 1984.

Rikhye, Indar Jit, Michael Harbottle, and Bjorn Egge. *The Thin Blue Line: International Peacekeeping and Its Future.* New Haven, CT: Yale University Press, 1974.

Rosecrance, Richard. "A New Concert of Powers." *Foreign Affairs* 71, no. 2 (Spring 1992): 64–82.

Rosecrance, Richard N. *Action and Reaction in World Politics: International Systems in Perspective.* Boston, MA: Little, Brown, 1963.

Rostow, W. W. *Open Skies: Eisenhower's Proposal of July 21, 1955.* Austin, TX: University of Texas Press, 1982.

Rubinstein, Ariel. "Perfect Equilibrium in a Bargaining Model." *Econometrica* 50, no. 1 (January 1982): 97–109.

———. "A Bargaining Model with Incomplete Information about Time Preferences." *Econometrica* 53, no. 5 (September 1985): 1151–72.

Rudolf, James D. "National Security." In *Cyprus: A Country Study,* 3rd ed., edited by Frederica M. Bunge. Washington, DC: American University Press, 1980.

Ruggie, John Gerard. "International Regimes, Transactions, and Change: Embedded Liberalism in the Postwar Economic Order." Reprinted in *International Regimes,* edited by Stephen D. Krasner. Ithaca, NY: Cornell University Press, 1983.

Ruggie, John Gerard. "Multilateralism: The Anatomy of an Institution." *International Organization* 46, no. 3 (Summer 1992): 379–415.

Sagan, Scott D. *The Limits of Safety: Organizations, Accidents, and Nuclear Weapons.* Princeton, NJ: Princeton University Press, 1993.

Salem, Norma. "The Constitution of 1960 and Its Failure." In *Cyprus, A Regional Conflict and Its Resolution,* edited by Norma Salem. New York: St. Martin's, for the Canadian Institute for International Peace and Security, 1992.

Salerno, Reynolds M., et al. "Enhanced Peacekeeping with Monitoring Technologies." SAND2000-1400. Albuquerque, NM: Sandia National Laboratories, June 2000.

Sambanis, Nicholas. "The United Nations Operation in Cyprus: A New Look at the Peacekeeping-Peacemaking Relationship." *International Peacekeeping* 6, no. 1 (Spring 1999): 79–108.

Sartori, Anne E. *Deterrence by Diplomacy*. Princeton, NJ: Princeton University Press, 2005.

Schear, James A. "Riding the Tiger: The United Nations and Cambodia's Struggle for Peace." In *UN Peacekeeping, American Politics and the Uncivil Wars of the 1990s*, edited by William J. Durch. New York: St. Martin's, 1996.

Schelling, Thomas C. *Arms and Influence*. New Haven, CT: Yale University Press, 1966.

Schelling, Thomas C., and Morton H. Halperin. *Strategy and Arms Control*. Washington, DC: Pergammon-Brassey's, 1985; originally published in 1975.

Schenk, H. G. *The Aftermath of the Napoleonic Wars: The Concert of Europe—an Experiment*. New York: Howard Fertig, 1967.

Schiff, Zefev, and Ehud Ya'ari. *Israel's Lebanon War*, edited and translated by Yair Evron. New York: Simon and Schuster, 1984.

Schroeder, Paul W. *Austria, Great Britain, and the Crimean War: The Destruction of the European Concert*. Ithaca, NY: Cornell University Press, 1972.

———. "Alliances, 1815–1945: Weapons of Power and Tools of Management." In *Historical Dimensions of National Security Problems*, edited by Klaus Knorr. Lawrence, KS: University Press of Kansas, 1976.

———. "Quantitative Studies in the Balance of Power: A Historian's Reaction." *Journal of Conflict Resolution* 21, no. 1 (March 1977): 3–22.

———. "The 19th-Century International System: Changes in the Structure." *World Politics* 28, no. 2 (January 1986): 1–26.

———. "Did the Vienna Settlement Rest on a Balance of Power?" *American Historical Review* 97, no. 3 (June 1992): 687–706.

———. *The Transformation of European Politics: 1763–1848*. Oxford, England: Oxford University Press, 1994.

———. "Historical Reality vs. Neo-Realist Theory." *International Security* 19, no. 1 (Summer 1994): 108–46.

———. "Balance of Power and Political Equilibrium: A Response." *The International History Review* 16, no. 4 (November 1994): 745–57.

Schultz, Kenneth A. "Domestic Opposition and Signaling in International Crises." *American Political Science Review* 92, no. 4 (December 1998): 829–44.

———. "Do Democratic Institutions Constrain or Inform? Contrasting Two Institutional Perspectives on Democracy and War." *International Organization* 53, no. 2 (Spring 1999): 233–66.

Scott, H. M. "Paul W. Schroeder's International System: The View from Vienna." *The International History Review* 16, no. 4 (November 1994).

Scoville, Herbert, Jr. "A Leap Forward in Verification." In *SALT: The Moscow Agreements and Beyond*, edited by Mason Willrich and John B. Rhinelander. New York: Free Press, 1974.

Seaman, L.C.B. *From Vienna to Versailles*. London: Routledge, 1988. First published in 1955.

Sharp, Jane M. O. "Restructuring the SALT Dialogue." *International Security* 6, no. 3 (Winter 1981–82): 144–76.

Shay, Robert Paul, Jr. *British Rearmament in the Thirties: Politics and Profits*. Princeton, NJ: Princeton University Press, 1977.

Signorino, Curtis S. "Simulating International Cooperation under Uncertainty:

The Effects of Symmetric and Asymmetric Noise." *Journal of Conflict Resolution* 40, no. 1 (March 1996): 152–205.

Siilasvuo, Ensio. *In the Service of Peace in the Middle East, 1967–1979.* London: Hurst, 1992.

Silber, Laura, and Allan Little. *Yugoslavia: Death of a Nation.* New York: Penguin, 1997.

Simpson, John, and Darryl Howlett. "The NPT Renewal Conference: Stumbling toward 1995." *International Security* 19, no. 1 (Summer 1994): 41–71.

Slantchev, Branislav L. "The Power to Hurt: Costly Conflict with Completely Informed States." *American Political Science Review* 97, no. 1 (February 2003): 123–33.

———. "The Principle of Convergence in Wartime Negotiations." *American Political Science Review* 97, no. 4 (November 2003): 621–32.

Smith, Alastair, and Allan C. Stam. "Bargaining and the Nature of War." *Journal of Conflict Resolution* 48, no. 6 (December 2004): 783–813.

Smith, Hugh. "Intelligence and UN Peacekeeping." *Survival* 36, no. 3 (Autumn 1994): 174–92.

Smith, Roger K. "Explaining the Non-Proliferation Regime: Anomalies for Contemporary International Relations Theory." *International Organization* 41, no. 2 (Spring 1987): 253–81.

Smoke, Richard. *War: Controlling Escalation.* Cambridge, MA: Harvard University Press, 1977.

Smyser, W. R. "Vienna, Versailles and Now Paris: Third Time Lucky?" *Washington Quarterly* 14, no. 3 (Summer 1991).

Snyder, Glenn H., and Paul Diesing. *Conflict among Nations: Bargaining, Decision-Making, and System Structure in International Crises.* Princeton, NJ: Princeton University Press, 1977.

Snyder, Jack. *The Ideology of the Offensive: Military Decision-Making and the Disasters of 1914.* Ithaca, NY: Cornell University Press, 1984.

———. "Science and Sovietology: Bridging the Methods Gap in Soviet Foreign Policy Studies." *World Politics* 40, no. 2 (January 1988): 169–93.

———. *Myths of Empire: Domestic Politics and International Ambition.* Ithaca, NY: Cornell University Press, 1991.

Snyder, Jack, and Karen Ballentine. "Nationalism and the Marketplace of Ideas." *International Security* 21, no. 2 (Fall 1996): 5–40.

Song, Jin. "The Political Dynamics of the Peacemaking Process in Cambodia." In *Keeping the Peace: Multidimensional UN Operations in Cambodia and El Salvador,* edited by Michael W. Doyle, Ian Johnstone, and Robert C. Orr. Cambridge, England: Cambridge University Press, 1997.

Sorel, Albert. *L'Europe et la Révolution Française.* Vol. 8. 7th ed. Paris: Plon, 1908.

———. *The Eastern Question in the Eighteenth Century: The Partition of Poland and the Treaty of Kainardji.* New York: Howard Fertig, 1969.

Spector, Leondard S., and Jacqueline R. Smith. *Nuclear Ambitions: The Spread of Nuclear Weapons 1989–1990.* Boulder, CO: Westview, 1990.

Spitzer, Hartwig. "The Open-Skies Treaty as a Tool for Confidence Building and Arms Control Verification." Expanded version of a paper for the 18th ISODARCO Summer Course, Siena, Italy, July 29–August 8, 1996.

Spitzer, Hartwig and Raael Wiemker. "Perspectives for Open Skies: Technical,

Operational, and Political Aspects." Paper presented at Fourth International Airborne Remote Sensing Conference and Exhibition. 21st Canadian Symposium on Remote Sensing. Ottawa, Ontario, June 21–24, 1999.

Stedman, Stephen John. *Peacemaking in Civil War: International Mediation in Zimbabwe, 1974–1980.* Boulder, CO: Lynne Rienner, 1991.

———. "Spoiler Problems in Peace Processes." *International Security* 22, no. 2 (Fall 1997): 5–53.

Stegenga, James A. *The United Nations Force in Cyprus.* Columbus, OH: Ohio State University Press, 1969.

Stein, Arthur. "Coordination and Collaboration, Regimes in an Anarchic World." In *International Regimes,* edited by Stephen Krasner. Ithaca, NY: Cornell University Press, 1983.

Stein, Janice Gross. "Detection and Defection: Security 'Regimes' and the Management of International Conflict." *International Journal* 40, no. 4 (Autumn 1985): 599–627.

Strayer, Joseph R. *On the Medieval Origins of the Modern State.* Princeton, NJ: Princeton University Press, 1970.

Stromberg, Roland N. *Collective Security and American Foreign Policy: From the League of Nations to NATO.* New York: Frederick A. Praeger, 1963.

Swahn, Johan. "International Surveillance Satellites: Open Skies for All?" *Journal of Peace Research* 25, no. 3 (September 1988): 229–44.

Talbott, Strobe. *Endgame: The Inside Story of SALT II.* New York: Harper and Row, 1979.

———. "Scrambling and Spying in SALT II." *International Security* 4, no. 2 (Autumn 1979): 3–21.

Taylor, A.J.P. *The Struggle for Mastery in Europe: 1848–1918.* Oxford, England: Oxford University Press, 1954.

Temperley, H.W.V. *A History of the Peace Conference of Paris.* Vol. 6. London: Oxford University Press, 1924.

Temperley, Harold. *The Foreign Policy of Canning, 1822–1827: England, The Neo-Holy Alliance, and the New World.* London: G. Bell, 1925.

Temperley, Harold, and Lillian M. Penson, eds. *Foundations of British Foreign Policy from Pitt (1792) to Salisbury (1902).* Cambridge, England: Cambridge University Press, 1938.

Tetlock, Philip E., and Aaron Belkin, eds. *Counterfactual Thought Experiments in World Politics: Logical, Methodological, and Psychological Perspectives.* Princeton, NJ: Princeton University Press, 1996.

Thayer, Carlyle A. "The United Nations Transitional Authority in Cambodia: The Restoration of Sovereignty. In *Peacekeeping and Peacemaking: Towards Effective Intervention in Post–Cold War Conflicts,* edited by Tom Woodhouse, Robert Bruce, and Malcolm Dando. New York: St. Martin's, 1998.

Theodolou, Mike. "Arms Buildup in the Aegean." *Christian Science Monitor,* February 2, 1996.

Thomas, Raju G. C., ed. *The Nuclear Non-Proliferation Regime: Prospects for the 21st Century.* New York: St. Martin's, 1998.

Thompson, Kenneth W. "Collective Security Reexamined." *American Political Science Review* 47, no. 3 (September 1953): 753–72.

Thompson, Mark, and Monroe Price. "Introduction" to *Forging Peace: Inter-*

vention, Human Rights and the Management of Media Space, edited by Monroe E. Price and Mark Thompson. Bloomington, IN: Indiana University Press, 2002.

Tilly, Charles. "Reflections on the History of European State-Making." In *The Formation of National States in Western Europe*, edited by Charles Tilly. Princeton, NJ: Princeton University Press, 1975.

Touval, Saadia. *The Peace Brokers: Mediators in the Arab-Israeli Conflict, 1948– 1979*. Princeton, NJ: Princeton University Press, 1982.

Trevelyan, George Macaulay. *British History in the Nineteenth Century and After (1782–1919)*. 2nd ed. London: Longmans Green, 1937.

Tucker, Jonathan B. "Negotiating Open Skies: A Diplomatic History." In *Open Skies, Arms Control, and Cooperative Security*, edited by Michael Krepon and Amy E. Smithson. New York: St Martin's, 1992.

United Nations. *The Blue Helmets: A Review of United Nations Peace-Keeping*. 2nd ed. New York: United Nations, 1990.

———. Office for Disarmament Affairs, *Report of the Secretary-General: Study on Ways and Means of Promoting Transparency in International Transfers of Conventional Arms*. New York: United Nations, 1992.

———. *The United Nations and Cambodia, 1991–1995*. United Nations Blue Book Series, vol. 2. New York: United Nations, 1995.

———. *The United Nations and the Iraq-Kuwait Conflict, 1990–1996*. United Nations Blue Book Series, vol. 9. New York: United Nations, 1996.

———. *The Blue Helmets: A Review of United Nations Peace-Keeping*. 3rd ed. New York, NY: United Nations, 1997.

———. *Report of the Panel on United Nations Peace Operations*. A/55/305-S/ 2000/809. New York: United Nations, August 2000. Also known as the Brahimi Report.

———. *Implementation of the Report of the Panel on United Nations Peace Operations*. New York: United Nations, October 16, 2001, A/56/478 and December 21, 2001, A/56/732.

———. *Reports of the Secretary-General*. Various operations. Various release dates. Operations include: MONUC, UNDOF, UNFICYP, UNIFIL, UNMEE, UNMIK, UNTAC, and UNTAG. This includes progress reports, special reports, bi-annual reports, and so forth, each focused on the specific operation at hand.

———. UNDOF. Various internal documents. *Golan Journal*. Various issues.

———. UNFICYP. Various internal folders and documents (situation reports, diplomatic memos, standard operating procedures, immediate reports, etc), press releases, and, the *Blue Berets*. Various issues.

———. UNTAG. Radio Programme transcripts, UNTAG Information Service. Various dates.

United Nations Chronicle. Various articles. Various dates.

United States Congress, Office of Technology Assessment (OTA). *Verification Technologies: Cooperative Aerial Surveillance in International Agreements*, OTA-ISC-480. Washington, DC: U.S. Government Printing Office, 1991.

United States Department of the Army. *U.S. Army Handbook for Cyprus*. Washington, DC: Department of the Army, 1964.

United States Department of State. "Background Notes: Cambodia, January 1996." Available at gopher://gopher.state.gov.

―――. "Background Notes: Namibia, April 1995." Available at gopher://gopher .state.gov.

United States Senate, Subcommittee to Investigate Problems Connected with Refugees and Escapees, Committee on the Judiciary. *Crisis on Cyprus*. Washington DC: Government Printing Office, 1974; reprinted in 1975 by the American Hellenic Institute.

Urquhart, Brian. "The United Nations: From Peace-Keeping to a Collective System?" In *Adelphi, Paper 265*. London: International Institute for Strategic Studies, Winter 1991–92.

Van Evera, Stephen. "The Cult of the Offensive and the Origins of the First World War." In *Military Strategy and the Origins of the First World War*, edited by Steven E. Miller. Princeton, NJ: Princeton University Press, 1985.

―――. "Why Cooperation Failed in 1914." In *Cooperation under Anarchy*, edited by Kenneth Oye. Princeton, NJ.: Princeton University Press, 1986.

―――. "Hypotheses on Nationalism and War." *International Security* 18, no. 4 (Spring 1994): 5–39.

―――. *Guide to Methods for Students of Political Science*. Ithaca, NY: Cornell University Press, 1997.

―――. *Causes of War: Power and the Roots of Conflict*. Ithaca, NY: Cornell University Press, 1999.

Vertzberger, Yaacov. "India's Strategic Posture and the Border War Defeat of 1962: A Case Study in Miscalculation." *Journal of Strategic Studies* 5, no. 3 (September 1982): 370–92.

Wagner, R. Harrison. "War and the State: Rethinking the Theory of International Politics." Draft paper, University of Texas, Austin, TX, October 2005.

Wainhouse, David W. *International Peace Observation: A History and Forecast*. Baltimore, MD: Johns Hopkins Press, 1966.

Walt, Stephen M. *The Origins of Alliances*. Ithaca, NY: Cornell University Press, 1987.

―――. "Testing Theories of Alliance Formation: The Case of Southwest Asia." *International Organization* 42, no. 2 (Spring 1988): 275–316.

―――. "Revolution and War." *World Politics* 44, no. 3 (April 1992): 321–68.

Walter, Alison Philips. *The Confederation of Europe: A Study of the European Alliance, 1813–1823, as an Experiment in the International Organization of Peace*, 2nd ed. New York: Longmans, Green, 1920.

Walter, Barbara F. *Committing to Peace: The Successful Settlement of Civil Wars*. Princeton, NJ: Princeton University Press, 2002.

Walter, Barbara F., and Jack Snyder. *Civil Wars, Insecurity, and Intervention*. New York: Columbia University Press, 1999.

Walters, F. P. *A History of the League of Nations*. London: Oxford University Press, 1965. Originally published in 1952.

Waltz, Kenneth N. *Theory of International Politics*. New York: Random House, 1979.

Wang, Jianwei. *Managing Arms in Peace Processes: Cambodia*. UNIDIR/96/17. New York: United Nations, 1996.

Ward, Michael Don. *Research Gaps in Alliance Dynamics*. Monograph Series in World Affairs. 19, Book 1. Denver, CO: University of Denver, 1982.

Warner, Edward L., III, and David A. Ochmanek. *Next Moves: An Arms Control Agenda for the 1990s*. New York: Council on Foreign Relations Press, 1989.

Webster, C. K. *British Diplomacy 1813–1815: Select Documents Dealing with the Reconstruction of Europe*. London: G. Bell, Ltd., 1921.

Webster, C. K., and Sydney Herbert. *The League of Nations in Theory and Practice*. Boston, MA: Houghton Mifflin, 1933.

Webster, Sir Charles. *The Congress of Vienna: 1814–1815*. New York: Barnes and Noble, 1969. Originally published by the British Foreign Office in 1919.

———. *The Foreign Policy of Castlereagh, 1815–1822: Britain and the European Alliance*. London: G. Bell, 1947. First published in 1925.

———. *The Foreign Policy of Palmerston, 1830–1841: Britain, the Liberal Movement, and the Eastern Question*. Vol. 1. London: G. Bell, 1951.

Weiss, Thomas G. *The United Nations and Civil Wars*. Boulder, CO: Lynne Rienner, 1995.

Weiss, Thomas G., David P. Forsythe, and Roger A. Coate. *The United Nations and Changing World Politics*. Boulder, CO: Westview, 1994.

Weiss, Thomas G., and Meryl A. Kessler. "Superpowers and Conflict Management." *Third World Quarterly* 12, nos. 3 and 4 (1990–91): 124–46.

Wendt, Alexander. "Anarchy Is What States Make of It: The Social Construction of Power Politics." *International Organization* 46, no. 2 (Spring 1992): 391–425.

Wentz, Larry, et al., ed. *Lessons for Kosovo: The KFOR Experience*. Washington, DC: Department of Defense Command and Control Research Program, 2002.

Wheeler-Bennett, John W. *The Pipe Dream of Peace: The Story of the Collapse of Disarmament*. New York: Howard Fertig, 1971.

White, George W. "Transylvania: Hungarian, Romanian, or Neither?" In *Nested Identities: Nationalism, Territory, and Scale,* edited by Guntram H. Herb and David H. Kaplan. Lanham, MD: Rowman and Littlefield, 1999.

———. *Nationalism and Territory: Constructing Group Identity in Southeastern Europe*. Lanham, MD: Rowman and Littlefield, 2000.

Wilson, Richard. "Nuclear Proliferation and the Case of Iraq." *Journal of Palestine Studies* 20, no. 3 (Spring 1991): 5–15.

Wimhurst, David. "Preparing a Plebiscite under Fire: The United Nations and Public Information in East Timor." In *Forging Peace: Invention, Human Rights and the Management of Media Space,* edited by Monroe E. Price and Mark Thompson. Bloomington, IN: Indiana University Press, 2002.

Wirth, Timothy E. "Confidence and Security-Building Measures." In *Conventional Arms Control and East-West Security,* edited by Robert D. Blackwill and F. Stephen Larrabee. Durham, NC: Duke University Press, for the Institute for East-West Security Studies, 1989.

Wohlforth, William C. "The Perception of Power: Russia in the Pre-1914 Balance." *World Politics* (April 1987): 353–81.

Wohlforth, William Curti. *The Elusive Balance: Power and Perceptions during the Cold War*. Ithaca, NY: Cornell University Press, 1993.

Wohlstetter, Roberta. *Pearl Harbor: Warning and Decision*. Stanford, CA: Stanford University Press, 1962.

Wolfers, Arnold. *Discord and Collaboration: Essays on International Politics*. Baltimore, MD: Johns Hopkins Press, 1962.

Woodward, Bob. *Plan of Attack*. New York: Simon and Schuster, 2004.

Wright, Quincy. *A Study of War*. Abridged. Chicago, IL: University of Chicago Press, 1964.

Wright, Robert. "Bold Old Vision: The Case for Collective Security." *The New Republic*, January 25, 1993.

Yoroms, Gani Joses, and Emmanuel Kwesi Aning. "West African Regional Security in the Post-Liberian Conflict Area: Issues and Perspectives." CDR Working Paper 97.7, November 1997, Institute for International Studies, Department for Development Research (Former Centre for Development Research), Copenhagen, Denmark.

Young, Oran. "Regime Dynamics: The Rise and Fall of International Regimes." In *International Regimes,* edited by Stephen D. Krasner. Ithaca, NY: Cornell University Press, 1983.

———. "The Effectiveness of International Institutions: Hard Cases and Critical Variables." In *Governance without Government: Order and Change in World Politics,* edited by James N. Rosenau and Ernst-Otto Czempiel. Cambridge, England: Cambridge University Press, 1992.

Zacher, Mark W. "The Conundrums of Power Sharing: The Politics of Security Council Reform." Paper prepared for the conference on the "United Nations and Global Security," January 18–19, 2003, Centre of International Relations, Liu Institute for Global Issues, University of British Columbia, Vancouver, BC, Canada.

Zartman, I. William. *Ripe for Resolution: Conflict and Intervention in Africa*. Updated. New York: Oxford University Press, 1985.

Zartman, I. William, and Jeffrey Z. Rubin. "Symmetry and Asymmetry in Negotiation." In *Power and Negotiation,* edited by I. William Zartman and Jeffrey Z. Rubin. Ann Arbor, MI: University of Michigan Press, 2000.

Zartman, I. William, and Saadia Touval. "International Mediation: Conflict Resolution and Power Politics." *Journal of Social Issues* 41, no. 2 (1985): 27–45.

Zelikow, Philip. "The New Concert of Europe." *Survival* 34, no. 2 (Summer 1992): 12–30.

Interviews

NEW YORK/U.N.

The following interviews took place in New York between April 16 and 26, 1996 at the U.N. headquarters unless otherwise noted.

Lubbers, Ruud, former Prime Minister, Netherlands, at the Rockefeller Foundation; 4/16

Doyle, Dr. Michael, Senior Fellow, International Peace Academy at the Academy; 4/19

Eckhard, Fred, Senior Liaison Officer, Department of Peacekeeping Operations; 4/19

Kimball, Eliza, Senior Political Affairs Officer, Department of Peacekeeping Operations; 4/19

Annabi, Hedi, Director, Africa Division, Department of Peacekeeping Operations; 4/22

Breed, Henry, Political Affairs Officer, Department of Peacekeeping Operations; 4/23

Carlson, Stan, Chief, Situation Center, Department of Peacekeeping Operations; 4/23

Verheul, Adriaan, Political Affairs Officer, Department of Peacekeeping Operations; 4/23

Yacoumopoulou, Lena, Film/Video Archives, Department of Public Information; 4/23–24

de Albuquerque, Joao Lins, Media Division, Department of Public Information; 4/24

Gomez, Joao Carlos, Media Division, Department of Public Information; 4/24

Kennedy, Kevin, Chief, Peace and Security Section, Department of Public Information; 4/24

Whitehouse, Steve, Video Section, Department of Public Information; 4/24

Kawakami, Takahisa, Principal Officer, Asia and Middle East Division, Department of Peacekeeping Operations; 4/25

Schottler, Frederick, Information Officer, Peace and Security Section, Department of Public Information; 4/25

El-Amir, Ayman, Chief, Radio Section, Department of Public Information; 4/26

Titov, Dmitry, Principal Officer, Department of Peacekeeping Operations; 4/26

CYPRUS/UNFICYP

The following interviews took place on Cyprus between May 6 and June 6, 1996. Except for the government, embassy, and other sources clearly indicated, most interviews took place with UNFICYP personnel in UNFICYP headquarters and other UNFICYP facilities. I had numerous casual conversations with many of these sources and other UNFICYP personnel.

Rokoszewski, Waldemar, Spokesman, UNFICYP; 5/6, 6/6

Vartiainen, ATP Ahti, Brigadier General, Force Commander, UNFICYP; 5/7

Talbot, Ian, Colonel, Chief of Staff, UNFICYP; 5/8

Feissel, Gustave, Chief of Mission UNFICYP, Deputy SRSG; 5/8

Parker, Nick, Lt. Colonel, Chief Operations Officer, UNFICYP; 5/9, 5/14

Snowdon, Andrew, Lt. Colonel, Commanding Officer, Sector Two; British Contingent, UNFICYP; 5/10

Barnard, Andrew, Major, Battery Commander, UNFICYP; 5/10

Skinner, Lieutenant, UNFICYP; 5/10

Jones, Elwyn, Bombardier, UNFICYP; 5/10

Tereso, Jorges, Lt. Colonel, Chief Humanitarian Officer, UNFICYP; 5/14

Petrides, Thalia, Director, European Affairs, Cyprus Ministry of Foreign Affairs; 5/15

Theophanous, Andreas, Dr., Director, Center for Research and Development, Intercollege; 5/15

Pantelides, Leonides, Dr., Political Officer, Cyprus Problem Division, Cyprus Ministry of Foreign Affairs; 5/16

Cowie, Raymond, Bombardier, UNFICYP; 5/24

Walsh, Major, Battery Commander, UNFICYP; 5/24–25

Fetter, David, Military Attache, U.S. Embassy, Cyprus; 6/4

Koenig, John, First Secretary, Political Affairs, U.S. Embassy, Cyprus; 6/4

Lister, John, Second Secretary, Political Affairs, U.S. Embassy, Cyprus; 6/4

Plumer, Aytug, Under-Secretary; Ministry of Foreign Affairs and Defense, "TRNC;" 6/5

Altiok, Asim, Director/Representative, Consular and Minority Affairs Dept., "TRNC;" 6/5

Schmitz, Peter, Senior Advisor, UNFICYP; 6/6

SYRIA/UNDOF

The following interviews took place with UNDOF personnel in Syria at UNDOF headquarters and various positions in the Golan Heights from May 20 to May 22, 1996.

Luijten, Sander, Captain; 5/20

Seng, Jeffrey, Major; 5/20

Kawazu, Ken-Ichi, Captain, Deputy Military Public Information Officer; 5/20

Deschambault, Richard, Captain/Major, Military Public Information Officer; 5/20

Kosters, Johannes, Major-General, Force Commander; 5/21

Mixuliszyn, Romuald, Major, Doctor and Chief Medical Officer; 5/21

Holder, Lt. Colonel, Chief Military Personnel Officer; 5/21

Thaller, Stefan, Lt. Colonel, Chief Operations Officer; 5/21

Moidl, Werner, Captain, Operations Duty Officer; 5/21

Torping, Mats, Lt. Colonel, Chief, Observer Group Golan; 5/21

Binas, Lech, Lt. Colonel, Chief Liaison and Protocol Officer; 5/21

Yakcich, Antonio, Lt. Colonel; 5/21

Perez-Berbain, Francisco, Major; 5/21

(non-attribution), Polbatt Commander; 5/22

Gruber, Captain, Commander, 3rd Company, Ausbatt; 5/22

Klinger, Sergeant; 5/22

ISRAEL/UNDOF/UNTSO/UNIFIL

These interviews with U.N. personnel from UNDOF, UNTSO, and UNIFIL took place in Israel at U.N. facilities in the locations indicated from May 27 to May 31, 1996.

Carnapas, Zenon, Senior Advisor, UNTSO, Jerusalem; 5/27

Knight, Bob, Major, Deputy Chief of Operations Officer, UNTSO, Jerusalem; 5/28

Kapetanovic, Lt. Commander, Senior Operations Officer, UNTSO, Jerusalem; 5/28

Oksanen, Jaakko, Colonel, Deputy Chief of Staff, UNTSO, Jerusalem; 5/28

Kupolati, R. M., Major-General, Chief of Staff, UNTSO, Jerusalem; 5/28

Hossinger, Helmut, Lt. Colonel, Chief Military Personnel Officer, UNTSO, Jerusalem; 5/28

French, Anthony, Senior Legal Advisor, UNTSO, Jerusalem; 5/28

Bernard, Manfred, Captain, UNTSO/OGG-T, Tiberias; 5/30

Martin, Ray, Lt. Colonel, UNTSO/OGG-T, Tiberias; 5/30

Kuppens, Tom, Captain, UNTSO/OGG-T, Tiberias; 5/30

Chase, Bob, Major, UNTSO/OGG-T, Tiberias; 5/30

Pack, Major, Duty Officer, UNIFIL, Nahariya; 5/31
Lindvall, Mikael, Press and Information Officer, UNIFIL, Nahariya; 5/31

Other Interviews and Correspondence

In chronological order, telephone interview unless otherwise noted:

Susan Allee, Senior Political Affairs Officer and desk officer for UNDOF, U.N. Department of Peacekeeping Operations, July 16, 2003.

Chris Coleman, Team Leader for UNMEE, U.N. Department of Peacekeeping Operations, January 29, 2003.

Email correspondence with Dr. Hansjoerg Biener, Universität Erlangen-Nürnberg, Nürnberg, Denmark, January 2003.

Dario Baroni, Desk Officer, Fondation Hirondelle, Geneva, Switzerland, January 28, 2003.

David Wimhurst, U.N. DPKO, October 24, 2003.

Susan Manuel, Chief of Section, Peace and Security Programs, U.N. Department of Public Information, November 24, 2003.

Simon Davies, December 19, 2003., Info Officer, UNDPKO.

David Smith, Chief of Information to the UN Mission in the Democratic Republic of the Congo (MONUC), Feb 4, 2003.

Email correspondence Timothy Carney, November 10, 2003 and Stephen Heder November 10, 2003.

Tory Holt, Senior Associate, Henry L. Stimson Center, Washington, DC, January 28, 2003.

Caroline Earle, Research Analyst, Henry L. Stimson Center, Washington, DC, January 28, 2003.

Susan Manuel, January 29, 30, 2003.

Colonel Mike Dooley, Joint Logistics Officer, U.S. Army Peacekeeping Institute, Carlisle Barracks, PA, January 29, 2003.

William Durch, Senior Associate, Henry L. Stimson Center and former Project Director for the Panel on U.N. Peace Operations, May 16, 2003.

Eleanor Beardsley, Press Officer, UNMIK, and Senior Editor, Focus Kosovo, Kosovo; email correspondence January 2003, also, November 3, 2003.

Frederick M. Schottler Information Officer, Peace and Security Section, Department of Public Information; November 10, 2003 and email correspondence February, 2, 2003.

John Darby, Professor of Comparative Ethnic Studies, Joan B. Kroc Institute for International Peace Studies at the University of Notre Dame, conversation November 2, 2005.

Francis X. Stenger, Deputy Division Chief for implementation of the Open Skies Treaty at the DoD Defense Threat Reduction Agency (DTRA); November 3, 2005; series of emails November 2005.

Index

ABMT. *See* Anti-Ballistic Missile Treaty
African Union (AU), 2, 50, 52
Agreed Framework, 234–35
Ahtissari, Martti, 150
Aix-la-Chapelle, Congress of, 66n.26, 69
Aix-la-Chapelle, Treaty of, 65
Alexander I (Tsar of Russia): Greek revolt
    against the Turks, reaction to, 73–75;
    the Poland-Saxony crisis, actions during,
    1–2, 67–69; Spanish rebellion, proposed
    reaction to, 71–72; Troppau Protocol,
    promotion of, 65, 66n.26
ambient transparency, 19, 21, 182–83, 230
America: Seven Years War in, 58–60. *See
    also* United States
Anderson, Matthew, 74
Angola, 142–44, 206
Anti-Ballistic Missile Treaty (ABMT),
    52–53, 224–27
AOS/AOLs. *See* Areas of Separation and
    Limitation
Areas of Separation and Limitation
    (AOS/AOLs), 118–20, 124–30
arms control regimes: beliefs about trans-
    parency held by advocates of, 21; mini-
    case studies of, 52–53, 215–16; nuclear
    weapons in Iran, Iraq, and North Korea,
    228–36; Open Skies (*see* Open Skies
    regimes); Strategic Arms Limitation
    Treaties (SALT I and SALT II), 52–53,
    224–28
Aronson, Shlomo, 121–24
Asad, Hafiz al-, 124–25
ASEAN. *See* Association of Southeast Asia
    Nations
Asia Watch, 167
Association of Southeast Asia Nations
    (ASEAN), 2, 50, 52, 192
AU. *See* African Union
Australia, 158
Austria: Concert of Europe, formation of,
    64–65; Greek revolt against Turkish
    rule, response to, 72–74; liberal rebel-
    lion in Naples, intervention in, 70, 72;
    Poland, first partition of, 60–62; Poland-

Saxony crisis, actions regarding, 2,
    66–68

balance of threat theory, 64
Baradei, Muhammad el-, 231
bargaining/bargaining theory: forums and,
    180–81; hostilities, leading to, 216; in-
    sufficient monitoring/incomplete infor-
    mation, impact of, 26, 28–29; negative
    effects of transparency and, 10; by the
    North Koreans, 235–36; realpolitik as a
    form of hard, 13, 69, 80, 190; themes in
    the literature regarding, 8
Beardsley, Eleanor, 205–6
Belgian independence, crisis of, 48, 75–80
beneficent coercion, 40
Blainey, Geoffrey, 27–29
Blue Sky radio station, 205
bluffing, 26–27
Bonaparte, Napoleon. *See* Napoleon I
    (Emperor of France)
Brahimi report, 198–201, 213–14
Britain: Belgian independence, crisis of, 48,
    75–79; Concert of Europe, formation of,
    64–66; Cyprus, independence of and crisis
    on, 86–87; Department for International
    Development, 210; Greek revolt against
    Turkish rule, reaction to, 72–74; Iranian
    nuclear activities, concern regarding,
    231; Iraq, insufficient transparency and
    the attack on, 233; liberal rebellions in
    Naples and Spain, reactions to, 69–72;
    Namibian independence, member of
    Contact Group regarding, 143; Nuclear
    Non-Proliferation Treaty and, 228;
    Poland-Saxony crisis, reaction to, 2, 66,
    68; Radio Okapi, funding of, 211; Seven
    Years War, lead-up to in America,
    58–60; Troppau Protocol, rejection of,
    66, 71; World War I, willingness to
    enter, 28
Broglie, Victor Duc de, 79
Buddhist party, 168
Bush, George H. W., 218, 223
Bush, George W., 230, 233

Cambodia: de-mining in, 163; the Mixed Military Working Group (MMWG) in, 159–60; the Paris Peace Accords, negotiation of, 156–59; UN peacekeeping forces in (*see* United Nations Advance Mission in Cambodia; United Nations Transitional Authority in Cambodia)

Cambodian People's Party (CPP), 168, 175, 179. *See also* State of Cambodia (SOC) party

Canada, 143

Canning, George, 71

Capo d'Istria (or Capodistrias), Count Ioannis. *See* Kapodístrias, Ioánnis Antónios

Carnapas, Zenon, 137

Carney, Timothy, 157, 174

Carter, Jimmy, 230, 234

case studies, the: comparative method applied to, 44–46; data richness as a selection criterion, 49–50; findings from, 12–14, 180–87; hypotheses applied to (*see* hypotheses); mini-case studies of additional regimes, 52–53, 215–16; policy implications of, 14–15, 190–95; scholarly and policy importance as a selection criterion, 50–52; selection of, 10–12, 46–53; variance as a selection criterion, 46–49

Castlereagh, Viscount Robert Stewart: Metternich's anticipated meeting with, 55; the Poland-Saxony crisis, actions during, 2, 67–68; Russian intervention in Greece, actions to thwart, 73–74; transparency promoted by the Concert, hope for, 64, 66, 80, 185

Ceausescu, Nicolae, 222

Central Intelligence Agency, U.S., 231

Chase, R. H., 131n.37

Chaumont, Treaty of, 64

Chayes, Abram, 18n.4

Chayes, Antonia Handler, 18n.4

Chea Sim, 175

cheating/defection, 38–39, 41, 187. *See also* monitoring/verification

China, People's Republic of: India, attack on, 28; the Iranian nuclear weapons program and, 230; Khmer Rouge in Cambodia, support for, 155–56, 158; North Korean disarmament, diplomatic efforts

regarding, 235; the Nuclear Non-Proliferation Treaty and, 228

Clandestine Radio, 211

Clerides, Glafkos Ioannou, 102

Clinton, Bill, 202

coerced transparency, 19–21, 80, 232–33

coercion, beneficent, 40

Cold War, the: arms control and, 225–27; arms race as a security spiral, 36–37; Cambodia and the end of, 156; transparency during, 225

Coleman, Chris, 203

commitment problems, 25

comparative case study method, 44–46. *See also* methods

compliance. *See* monitoring/verification

Concert of Europe: Belgian independence, crisis of, 48, 75–80; case studies from, 10–11, 46–48, 50–51, 56, 62–63; continuing policy and scholarly importance of, 50–51 (*see also* forum diplomacy); effectiveness of, debates between optimists and pessimists regarding, 12, 74, 81, 84–85; end of, 63n.17; findings regarding transparency in, 12–13, 56–57, 80–85, 185–86; formation of, 63–66; the Greek revolt against Turkish rule, 72–75; liberal rebellions in Naples and Spain, 69–72; multilateral crisis management forum, as model of, 2, 55, 85; the Poland-Saxony crisis, 1–2, 12, 66–69

confrontational transparency, 19, 21

Congo, Democratic Republic of: forum diplomacy in, 192; UN peacekeeping operation in, 52, 202, 206–9, 213

Congress, U.S., Office of Technology Assessment (OTA), 19n.4

Congress of Aix-la-Chapelle, 66n.26, 69

Congress of Verona, 70–71, 73

Congress of Vienna: Concert of Europe, as birthplace of, 64; the Poland-Saxony crisis at, 1–2, 12, 66–69

Contact Group, 143

Conventional Forces in Europe Treaty (CFE), 52

cooperation: anticipated transparency and, hypotheses regarding, 24–27; monitoring/verification and, 38 (*see also* monitoring/verification); theory regarding, 7; trans-

parency and, hypotheses regarding, 27–33
cooperative transparency, 18–21
CPP. *See* Cambodian People's Party
crisis management: the Concert of Europe as a model of, 1–2, 55, 85; crises, definition of, 45; in the eighteenth century, 55–62; spiral model and, 35–36; study of, 3–10; transparency as a tool of (*see* transparency); by the United Nations (*see* United Nations). *See also* security regimes
Crisp, Jeff, 149–50
Crocker, Chester, 144
Cuba, 143
Cyprus: Greek-Turkish conflict on, beginnings of, 86–87; police cooperation with UNFICYP, limited, 107, 109; rogue behavior on, 39; Turkish Republic of Northern Cyprus, declaration of, 97n.24; UN peacekeeping force on (*see* United Nations Peacekeeping Force in Cyprus)

Darby, John, 186n
Dayan, Moshe, 125
defection from regimes and agreements. *See* cheating/defection
defensive optimistic miscalculation, 28, 30
Delimitation Commission, 59–60
Desert Fox, 233
Diesing, Paul, 45
Dinwiddie, Robert, 60
diplomacy: in the eighteenth century, 57–58; public (*see* public diplomacy). *See also* negotiations
disinformation. *See* misinformation
Downs, George, 36
Doyle, Michael, 13, 39, 51n.85, 167
DPI. *See* United Nations, Department of Public Information
DPKO. *See* United Nations, Department of Peacekeeping Operations
Duffield, John, 6
Duquesne, Ange Duquesne de Meneville, Marquis, 60

Eckhard, Fred, 149n.20
Economic Community of West African States (ECOWAS), 50, 52

Economidou, Katie, 111
Economist, 192
ECOWAS. *See* Economic Community of West African States
Egyptian-Israeli disengagement, 120
eighteenth century: crisis management during, 55–62; diplomacy of, 57–58; Poland, the first partition of, 47, 60–62; Seven Years War in America, 58–60
Eisenhower, Dwight, 217
elections: in Cambodia, 1, 14, 168, 171–75; in Namibia, 144, 146–51
England. *See* Britain
Eritrea, UN peacekeeping mission in. *See* United Nations Mission in Eritrea and Ethiopia
Ethiopia, UN peacekeeping mission in. *See* United Nations Mission in Eritrea and Ethiopia
ethnic conflict, 37, 194–95
European Broadcasting Union, 204
European Union (EU), 52
Evangelista, Matthew, 110n.57

Fearon, James D., 8n.16, 27, 39, 51
fears: in Cambodia, 171–74; effect of transparency on, 186–87; hypotheses regarding, 35–38; in Namibia, 148–50; of UN information operations, 213–14. *See also* worst-case assumptions
Federation of American Scientists, 52
Feissel, Gustave, 111
Ferdinand VII (King of Spain), 70–71
Fetherston, A. B., 88
Findlay, Trevor, 158
Finel, Bernard, 10
Florini, Ann, 10, 18n.4
Fondation Hirondelle, 202, 205, 208–9, 211
formal cooperative transparency, 19, 21
Fortna, Virginia Page, 143
Fort Necessity, 59
forum diplomacy: advantages of, 14–15, 55; in Congo, 192; policy implications of findings regarding, 184, 190–92; as a tool for crisis management (*see* Concert of Europe); as a vehicle for power politics, 190–91
France: Belgian independence, reaction to crisis of, 48, 75–79; Cambodia, actions

France *continued*
in, 155–56; foreign ministry during the
eighteenth century, 57; Greek revolt
against Turkish rule, reaction to, 73;
Iranian nuclear activities, concern regarding, 231; liberal rebellions in Naples
and Spain, reactions to, 70–72; Namibian independence, member of Contact
Group regarding, 143; Napoleonic wars,
63–65; Nuclear Non-Proliferation
Treaty and, 228; Poland-Saxony crisis,
reactions to, 2, 66–68; Seven Years War,
lead-up to in America, 58–60
Frederick II "the Great" (King of Prussia),
61
Front Uni National pour un Cambodge
Independent, Neutre, Pacifique, et Cooperatif (FUNCINPEC), 165, 168–69, 173,
175, 179
FUNCINPEC. *See* Front Uni National
pour un Cambodge Independent,
Neutre, Pacifique, et Cooperatif

Gaddis, John Lewis, 9, 37, 189n.6, 225
Germany, 28, 143, 231. *See also* Prussia
Gerring, John, 51
Golan Heights: cease-fire initiated on,
119n.2; UN peacekeeping force on (*see*
United Nations Disengagement Observer
Force)
Goldstein, Judith, 45n.72
Gorbachev, Mikhail, 218, 225
Great Britain. *See* Britain
Greece: crisis on Cyprus, actions regarding,
86–87; the peacekeeping force on Cyprus
and (*see* United Nations Peacekeeping
Force in Cyprus); revolt against Turkish
rulers, 72–75
Grey Wolves, 108
Grimstead, Patricia Kennedy, 73
Group of Seven/Eight, 50
Gulf War of 1991, 228, 230

Haggard, Stephan, 6
Hale, Nathan, 52–53
Hardenburg, Prince Carl Vincent von, 1–2,
67–68
Heder, Stephen, 172n.51, 174
Heng Samrin, 155
Holland. *See* Netherlands, the
Holsti, Kalevi J., 58

Holy Alliance, Treaty of, 65
Hughes, Karen, 193
human rights, 166–67
Hungary, 222
Hun Sen, 155–58, 161, 168, 179
Hutus, 40
hypotheses, 20–22, 42–43; anticipated
transparency hinders cooperation (H2′),
26–27; anticipated transparency promotes cooperation (H2), 24–26; the
Concert of Europe, summary of findings
regarding, 80–85; methodology for testing, 44–46 (*see also* methods); opposing
and conditional effects of transparency,
logic of including in, 33–35, 45; regimes
provide transparency (H1), 22–24;
regimes spread misinformation (H1′),
22–24; summary of findings regarding,
12–14, 180–87; transparency about the
regime increases its effectiveness (H6),
41–42; transparency confirms fears
(H4′), 37–38; transparency hinders cooperation and causes conflict (H3′),
31–33; transparency promotes cooperation and prevents conflict (H3), 27–31;
transparency reduces cheating, rogue,
and spoiler problems (H5), 38–41;
transparency reduces unwarranted fears
and worst-case assumptions (H4),
35–37; UNDOF, summary of findings
regarding, 138–41; UNFICYP, summary
of findings regarding, 111–17; UNTAC,
summary of findings regarding, 176–79;
UNTAG, summary of findings regarding,
151–54

IAEA. *See* International Atomic Energy
Agency
India, 28, 191, 229
Indonesia, 156, 158
INF. *See* Intermediate-Range Nuclear
Forces Treaty
informal cooperative transparency, 19, 21
information: availability of through transparency (*see* transparency); conditions
and the potential effectiveness of transparency, 181–84; counterpropaganda,
use of, 173; filtering in mediation, question of, 186, 189; forum diplomacy as
means to quicken the exchange of, 55;
identification of the exchange of, 23–24;

incomplete as a cause/deterrent of war, 27–35; incomplete as encouraging defection and provocation, 38; intelligence-gathering, 162; intergroup *vs.* intragroup, availability of, 39; mechanisms for the exchange of, 23; in the Paris Peace Accords, special attention paid to, 157; sharing of through surveillance (*see* Open Skies regimes); spreading of incorrect (*see* misinformation); uncertainty regarding (*see* uncertainty)

information operations: bureaucratic problems, 212–13; fears associated with, 213–14; hardware capabilities, 211; impediments to, 209–14; of MONUC, 202, 206–9, 213; objectives potentially achieved by, 197; personnel problems, 209–10; policy recommendations regarding, 193–95; status of at UN headquarters level (the Brahimi report), 198–201, 213–14; status of in the field, 201–9; trends in the U.N.'s use of, 197–98; of UNMEE, 193n.15, 201–3; of UNMIK, 201, 204–6; of UNTAC, 51n.85, 168–75, 195, 205; of UNTAG, 146–51, 154, 195

Institute for Science and International Security (ISIS), 230

institutionalism/institutionalists: in the Concert of Europe, scholarly claims regarding, 81, 84; security studies and, 5–9

intelligence transparency, 19, 21

Intermediate-Range Nuclear Forces (INF) Treaty, 225, 227

International Atomic Energy Agency (IAEA): background on, 229–30; Iran and, 230–31; Iraq and, 231–33; North Korea and, 234–36; nuclear weapons activities, role of transparency in constraining, 52–53, 228

international political economy (IPE), 5–6

international relations/international relations theory: balance of threat theory, 64; diplomacy in the eighteenth century, 57–58; future research on transparency, need for, 187–90; institutionalism/institutionalists, 5–9, 81, 84; realism/realists/rationalist theory, 28–29, 31–33, 84; realpolitik, 13, 69, 80, 190; regime theory, 5–9 (*see also* security regimes)

IPE. *See* international political economy

Iran, 228, 230–33

Iraq, 228–29, 232–34

Iraq War, 233–34

Isaac, Tasos, 108

Israel: Golan Heights, UN peacekeeping force on (*see* United Nations Disengagement Observer Force); Iraq, insufficient transparency and the attack on, 228, 232; nuclear capability of, 32; the Nuclear Non-Proliferation Treaty and, 229; Syria, negotiation of disengagement agreements with, 119–26, 186, 189

Israeli Defense Forces (IDF), 135–36

James, Alan, 140

Japan, 158, 170–71, 235

Jervis, Robert, 6, 9, 38–39, 51, 84

Joseph, Robert, 231

Kabila, Laurent, 206

Kagan, Korina, 84

Kapodístrias, Ioánnis Antónios, 73–74

Kennedy, Kevin, 179

Keohane, Robert O., 6, 45n.72

Khmer People's National Liberation Front (KPNLF), 169

Khmer Rouge, 1, 155–56, 158–65, 167–69, 172–74, 178

Khmer Rouge radio, 174

Kissinger, Henry, 31; Alexander's response to the Greek revolt against the Turks, interpretation of, 74; Poland-Saxony crisis at the Congress of Vienna, interpretation of, 69; realist interpretation of the Concert by, 84; the Syria-Israel disengagement agreement, negotiation of, 31, 119–21, 123–26, 140, 186, 189

Kleovoulou, Athanasios, 104

Koenig, John, 99

Korea, Democratic People's Republic of, 191, 228–29, 233–36

Korea, Republic of, 235

Kosovo, UN peacekeeping operation in, 52, 201, 204–6

Kosovo Liberation Army (KLA), 205

Kosters, Johannes C., 131–32, 137

Krasznai, Marton, 223

Kupchan, Charles, 6, 9, 84

Kupchan, Clifford, 6, 9, 84

Kydd, Andrew, 189

Laitin, David D., 39
Lake, David, 6
League of Nations, 52–53, 142
Ledgerwood, Judy, 172n.51
Lehmann, Ingrid, 51n.85, 173n.53, 179
Leveson-Gower, Granville (1st Earl Granville), 76
Levy, Jack, 35
liberal institutionalists. *See* institutionalism/ institutionalists
Lipson, Charles, 6, 9, 84
Lodding, Jan, 229
Lon Nol, 155
Lord, Kirsten, 10
Louis-Philippe (King of France), 76
Louis XV (King of France), 59
Luanda Agreement, 192
Luck, Gary, 191
Luxemburg, 75–77

Mackinlay, John, 121, 127nn.29–30, 129n.30, 131–32, 136–37, 140
Makarios III, 86–87
Marquardt, James, 10
Martin, Ray, 134
methods: comparative case study, 44–46; crises, function of focus on, 45; hypotheses (*see* hypotheses); process-tracing, 44–45; purposes of, 17. *See also* case studies, the
Metternich, Count Wenzel Lothar, 55, 68, 70–71, 73–74
Mill, John Stuart, 47
Milles Collines, 40
Milosevic, Slobodan, 40, 154, 204
misinformation: Alexander I, use of to manipulate, 72–75; Cambodia, used in, 172–74; as "negative noise," 40n.60; purposes of a peacekeeping operation, about the, 41–42; by security regimes, findings regarding, 184; spread through transparency mechanisms, 24
Missile Technology Control Regime (MCTR), 52
Mitchell, Ronald, 10
MMWG. *See* United Nations Mixed Military Working Group
monitoring/verification: in arms control regimes, 215–16, 226–27; cooperation promoted and cheating deterred through, 38; hypotheses regarding transparency

and, 25–26; of nuclear weapons activities, 228–35; skeptical countries, impossibility of satisfying, 228, 231; by UNDOF on the Golan Heights, 118, 129–34; by the UN in Cambodia, 157–58
MONUC. *See* United Nations Organization Mission in the Democratic Republic of Congo
Moore, Christopher W., 186n
Morrow, James D., 31
Mount Ejo Declaration, 145

Namibia: Congo rebellion, involvement in, 206; elections held in, 144, 146–51; independence for, beginnings of, 142–44; as South West Africa, 142; UN peacekeeping force in (*see* United Nations Transition Assistance Group)
Naples, 69–72
Napoleon I (Emperor of France), 63–65
National Union for the Total Independence of Angola (UNITA), 148–49
NATO. *See* North Atlantic Treaty Organization
negotiations: arms control agreements, 224–27; the bilateral Open Skies Treaty between Hungary and Romania, 223; diplomacy in the eighteenth century, 57–58; filtering information in mediation, question of, 186, 189; the Open Skies Treaty, 217–19; the Paris Peace Accords, 156–59, 178; phases of, 31; the Syria-Israel disengagement agreements, 119–26, 186, 189; third-party mediators, 125n.23
Netherlands, the, 75–79
NGOs. *See* nongovernmental organizations
Nixon, Richard, 123
nongovernmental organizations (NGOs): combating hate radio, efforts regarding, 211; Fondation Hirondelle, 202, 205, 208–9, 211; UNMIK and, 205
North Atlantic Treaty Organization (NATO): Cyprus, proposed action in response to crisis on, 86–87; Open Skies proposal by, 218–19; replacement of, 3–4
North Korea. *See* Korea, Democratic People's Republic of
NPT. *See* Nuclear Non-Proliferation Treaty

Nuclear Non-Proliferation Treaty (NPT), 52–53, 228–30, 232, 234–36

October War, 119
offensive optimistic miscalculation, 28, 30
Office of Technology Assessment (OTA), 19n.4
Oksanen, Jaako, 137n.51
Omond, G. W. T., 77
opacity: dangers of highlighted by the Seven Years War in America, 58–60; effects on miscalculation, deterrence, and war, 33–35; secrecy as a reason to value, 216
Open Skies regimes: anticipated transparency, as example of, 215, 223; the bilateral treaty between Hungary and Romania, 222–23; idea of and negotiations regarding, 216–19; the multilateral treaty, 52–53, 219–20, 223; overflights, effects of, 220–23
Open Society Institute, 211
optimistic miscalculation, 27–28, 30
Organization for Security and Cooperation in Europe (OSCE), 52, 204–5
Organization of African Unity (OAU), 50, 52, 202
Organization of American States (OAS), 52
OSCE. See Organization for Security and Cooperation in Europe
Ottoman Empire, 72–75. See also Turkey
Oye, Kenneth, 29

Pakistan, 191, 229, 230
Palmerston, Viscount Henry Temple, 76
Panayi, Stelios, 101–4
Pantelides, Leonides, 99, 106
Paris, Second Treaty of, 65
Paris Peace Accords, 156–59, 178
Parker, Nick, 106
peacekeeping operations: policy recommendations for, 192–95; self-transparency of, 41–42; of the United Nations (see United Nations)
People's Liberation Army of Namibia (PLAN), 144
Petrides, Thalia, 106
Phnom Penh Post, 169
Plumer, Aytug, 99, 107
Poland: crisis during the Congress of

Vienna regarding, 1–2, 12, 66–69; first partition of, 47, 60–62
policy/policymakers' concerns: implications of the case studies for, 14–15; recommendations regarding forum diplomacy, 190–92; recommendations regarding peacekeeping operations, 192–95; security regimes, interest in, 3–5; UNFICYP, applicable to, 116–17
Pol Pot, 155, 167
Portugal, 71
Posen, Barry, 32–33
Powell, Robert, 27
Price, Monroe, 51n.85
prisoner's dilemma, 32
process-tracing, 44–45, 47
proffered transparency, 19, 21
Prussia: Belgian independence, reactions to crisis of, 75–77, 79; Concert of Europe, formation of, 64–66; Poland, first partition of, 60–62; Poland-Saxony crisis, reactions to, 1–2, 66–69; Troppau Protocol signed by, 66, 70. See also Germany
public diplomacy, 3, 9, 14, 182, 188, 193
Public Information Strategic Deployment Stocks (SDS), 211
Putin, Vladimir, 219

Quadruple Alliance, 65

Radford, Arthur, 217
radio: Blue Sky station, 205; Khmer Rouge, 174; Milles Collines, 40; in Namibia by UNTAG, 145–50; non-governmental organizations and, 211 (see also Fondation Hirondelle); policy recommendations regarding, 194–95; UNMEE broadcasts, 203. See also information operations
Radio Okapi, 202, 208, 211, 213
Radio Television Kosovo (RTK), 204–5
Radio UNTAC, 169–72, 174–75, 177–79, 205
Rathjens, George, 36
realism/realists/rationalist theory, 28–29, 31–33, 84
realpolitik, 13, 69, 80, 190
"Refashioning the Dialogue," 200–201
regime theory, 5–9. See also security regimes

Reich, Bernard, 122, 127n.29
Rendall, Matthew, 84
Report of the Panel on United Nations Peace Operations (Brahimi report), 198–201, 213–14
Revolution in Military Affairs (RMA), 33n.42
Ritter, Scott, 232–33
Rocke, David, 36
rogues, 39–41, 59–60, 187
Rokoszewski, Waldemar, 103
Romania, 222
RTK. *See* Radio Television Kosovo
Rubin, Jeffrey Z., 126
Russia: Belgian independence, reactions to crisis of, 75–77; Concert of Europe, formation of, 64–65; diplomatic representatives during the eighteenth century, 57; Greek revolt against Turkish rule, reactions to, 72–75; Iranian nuclear weapons program and, 230–31; liberal rebellions in Naples and Spain, reactions to, 69–72; North Korean disarmament, diplomatic efforts regarding, 235; Nuclear Non-Proliferation Treaty, 228; Open Skies proposals, 219–21; Poland, first partition of, 60–62; Poland-Saxony crisis, reactions to, 1–2, 66–69. *See also* Union of Soviet Socialist Republics
Russo-Turkish War, 60–61
Rwanda, 206–7

SALT I & II. *See* Strategic Arms Limitation Treaties
Sambanis, Nicholas, 94n.22, 193n.14
Sanderson, John, 173
Sartori, Anne E., 27n.20, 229n.33
Saxony, 1–2, 12, 66–69
Schear, James A., 161–62
Schroeder, Paul W., 69, 74, 77–78, 81
Schwartzkopf, Norman, 230
Search for Common Ground, 211
Second Treaty of Paris, 65
secrecy, 216, 224
security regimes: arms control regimes (*see* arms control regimes); case studies of (*see* case studies, the; Concert of Europe; United Nations Disengagement Observer Force; United Nations Peacekeeping Force in Cyprus; United Nations Transitional Authority in Cambodia; United

Nations Transition Assistance Group); cooperative transparency and, 18–21; defined, 2; formality of, variation in, 46–48; hypotheses regarding (*see* hypotheses); as independent variable, 20; Open Skies (*see* Open Skies regimes); secrecy vs. transparency in, 216, 224. *See also* crisis management
self-transparency, 41
Seven Years War, 58–60
Shirley, William, 59
Signorino, Curtis S., 40n.60
Sihanouk, Norodom, 155, 157–58, 160, 168
Siilasvuo, Ensio, 122–23, 127
Simmons, Beth A., 6
Siverson, Randolph, 36
Smith, David, 208
SNC. *See* Supreme National Council
Snyder, Glenn H., 45
SOC. *See* State of Cambodia party
societal transparency, 110–11
Solomos, Solomos, 108
SORT. *See* Strategic Offensive Reduction Treaty
South Africa, 142–44, 150, 229
South Korea. *See* Korea, Republic of
South West Africa, 142. *See also* Namibia
South West African Police (SWAPOL), 144
South West Africa People's Organization (SWAPO), 142–45, 150–51
South West Africa Territorial Force, 145
Soviet Union. *See* Union of Soviet Socialist Republics
Spain, 69–72
spiral model, 35–36
spoilers, 40–41, 187, 201
Standing Consultative Commission (SCC), 226
State of Cambodia (SOC) party, 157–59, 161–69, 172–73, 175, 185. *See also* Cambodian People's Party
Stenger, Francis, 221, 223
Stewart, Lord Charles, 70
Strategic Arms Limitation Treaties (SALT I & II), 52–53, 224–28
Strategic Arms Reduction Treaties (START I & II), 227
Strategic Offensive Reduction Treaty (SORT), 224, 227
Strayer, Joseph R., 57n.4
Studio B92, 154

Supreme National Council (SNC), 156–57
SWAPO. *See* South West Africa People's Organization
Switzerland, 211
Syria: Golan Heights, state of forces on, 133–34n.45; Golan Heights, UN peacekeeping force on (*see* United Nations Disengagement Observer Force); Israel, negotiation of disengagement agreements with, 119–26, 186, 189; "peacekeeping," objection to the term, 118n

Talbot, Ian, 107
Talleyrand-Perigord, Prince Charles-Maurice de, 67–68, 79
Temperley, Harold, 71
Thailand, 164, 169
third-party mediators, 125n.23
Thompson, Mark, 51n.85
Thornberry, Cedric, 146–48
threat assessments, impact of transparency on, 37
Tito, Josip, 222
Torping, Mats, 137
transparency: arms control regimes and (*see* arms control regimes); background information conditions and the potential effectiveness of, 181–84; case studies of (*see* case studies, the; Concert of Europe; United Nations Disengagement Observer Force; United Nations Peacekeeping Force in Cyprus; United Nations Transitional Authority in Cambodia; United Nations Transition Assistance Group); categorizing, alternative approaches to, 18–19n.4; cognitive misperceptions and, 36 (*see also* worst-case assumptions); in the Concert of Europe, summary of findings regarding, 80–85; crisis management in security regimes, role in, 2–3; definition of, 17–20; as dependent and independent variable, 20; diplomacy as a means of increasing, 57; distributional effects of, 26, 189, 215–18; effects on miscalculation, deterrence, and war, 33–35; examples of promoting peace through, 1–2; findings regarding, 12–14, 180–87; future research on, 187–90; hypotheses regarding (*see* hypotheses); information and, 22–23, 179 (*see also* information); negative effects of, potential for, 10, 22, 31–33; nuclear weapons and, 228–36; opacity as the inverse of (*see* opacity; uncertainty); optimists *versus* pessimists regarding the effects of, 21–22, 33–35, 188–89; policy implications of findings regarding, 14–15, 190–95; societal, 110–11; as a tool of security regimes, reasons to study, 5, 8–10; types of, 18–21; in the UNDOF, scholar and practitioner assessments of, 136–37, 140; UNDOF and, summary of findings regarding, 138–41; UNFICYP and, summary of findings regarding, 111–17; UNTAC and, summary of findings regarding, 176–79; UNTAG and, summary of findings regarding, 151–54
Transylvania, 222
Treaty, Second of Paris, 65
Treaty of Aix-la-Chapelle, 65
Treaty of Chaumont, 64
Treaty of the Holy Alliance, 65
"TRNC." *see* Turkish Republic of Northern Cyprus
Troppau Protocol, 65–66, 70–72
Tucker, Jonathan B., 217n.1
Turkey: Cyprus, beginnings of conflict with Greece on, 86–87; Cyprus, peacekeeping force on (*see* United Nations Peacekeeping Force in Cyprus); the Grey Wolves, 108; Poland, first partition of, 60–62. *See also* Ottoman Empire
Turkish Republic of Northern Cyprus ("TRNC"), 97–99, 103, 107

Uganda, 206
UN. *See* United Nations
UNAMIC. *See* United Nations Advance Mission in Cambodia
uncertainty: about a peacekeeping operation's purposes, 41–42; arms control as reducing, 215, 224; as a cause of war, 27, 31–33; exploitation of by hate-mongers, 40; security spirals worsened by, 35–36; worst-casing as a result of, 42
UNDOF. *See* United Nations Disengagement Observer Force
UNFICYP. *See* United Nations Peacekeeping Force in Cyprus
UNHCR. *See* United Nations High Commissioner for Refugees
unilateral transparency, 19, 21, 182–83

Union of Soviet Socialist Republics: arms control agreements and, 224–27; Cambodia, actions in, 155–56; defection from the ABM Treaty by, fears of, 39; Namibia, cooperation with the U.S. in bringing peace and independence to, 143–44; NATO or UN intervention in Cyprus conflict, concerns regarding, 86–87; Open Skies proposals and, 217–19. *See also* Russia

United Arab Emirates, 203

United Kingdom. *See* Britain

United Nations (UN): Congo, facilitation of forum diplomacy in, 192; Department of Peacekeeping Operations (DPKO), 200, 209–10, 212; Department of Public Information (DPI), 200, 209–12; information operations in peacekeeping missions (*see* information operations); intelligence-gathering operations by, wariness of, 162, 201, 213; Namibian independence, pre-UNTAG efforts to promote, 142–43; North Korean cooperation with the IAEA, resolution urging, 234; peacekeeping case studies, 11–15, 46, 48–52 (*see also* United Nations Disengagement Observer Force; United Nations Peacekeeping Force in Cyprus; United Nations Transitional Authority in Cambodia; United Nations Transition Assistance Group); peacekeeping in the 1990s, varying interest levels in, 3–5; personnel and costs of peacekeeping operations, 5; policy recommendations for peacekeeping operations, 192–95; Security Council passage of Resolution 687, 232; as a security regime, prominence of, 51–52; Sinai front of the October War, helping to bring peace to, 119; transparency in peacekeeping operations, lessons regarding, 15; types of peacekeeping operations, 11

United Nations Advance Mission in Cambodia (UNAMIC), 159–60

United Nations Civilian Police (UN-CIVPOL), 144, 147

United Nations Disengagement Observer Force (UNDOF): Areas of Separation and Limitation, 118–20, 124–30; boundary lines, finalizing of and measuring/marking, 127n.30, 129n.30; as case study, 11, 118–19; complaints at lower levels investigated by, 132–33n.41; disengagement negotiations, factors contributing to the success of, 123–26; findings from the case study, 13, 138–41, 181, 186; formation of, negotiation of the disengagement agreement and, 119–26; information exchange limited through mediation by, 31; mandate and initial operations of, 126–29; monitoring/verification by, 129–34 (*see also* United Nations Truce Supervision Organization); size and nationality composition of the current, 129n.32; transparency provided by, scholar and practitioner assessments of, 136–37, 140; violations confronted by, 134–36

United Nations Emergency Force I (UNEF I), 140

United Nations High Commissioner for Refugees (UNHCR), 164

United Nations Interim Administration Mission in Kosovo (UNMIK), 52, 201, 204–6

United Nations Interim Force in Lebanon (UNIFIL), 131

United Nations Logistics Base (UNLB), 208, 211

United Nations Military Working Group, 126, 127n.30, 129n.30

United Nations Mission in Eritrea and Ethiopia (UNMEE): data and scholarship on, 50; failure of, 181; information, failure to exploit opportunities regarding, 193n.15, 201–3; as a mini-case study, 52; policy implications of this study applicable to, 15

United Nations Mixed Military Working Group (MMWG), 159–60

United Nations Monitoring, Verification, and Inspection Commission (UN-MOVIC), 234

United Nations Organization Mission in the Democratic Republic of Congo (MONUC), 52, 202, 206–9, 213

United Nations Peacekeeping Force in Cyprus (UNFICYP): as case study, 11, 86; demonstrations and crowd control, 107–9; the early years of, 87–89; find-

ings from the case study, 13, 111–17, 181–84, 186; formation of, 86–87; humanitarian activities and societal transparency, 109–11; the liaison system, 91; overview of, 90–93; Roccas Bastion, conflict over construction at, 97–100; the status quo as base truth, maintenance of, 91–93;
> violations: antagonisms, 93–95; violations: construction, 95–100; violations: moves forward and local agreements, 105–7; violations: shooting and weapons, 100–104

United Nations Special Commission on Iraq (UNSCOM), 19–20, 232–33

United Nations Transitional Authority in Cambodia (UNTAC): the Advance Mission in Cambodia, 159–60; as case study, 11, 155; civil control, supervision of, 165–66; civilian mandate of, 163–75; elections, organization and conduct of, 168; elections promoted through transparency by, 1, 14; findings from the case study, 13–14, 176–79, 181, 185–87; human rights, promotion and protection of, 166–67; information operations of, 51n.85, 168–75, 195, 205; military mandate of, 161–63; origins of, 155–60; Paris Peace Accords, negotiation of, 156–59; personnel and cost of, 160; refugee repatriation by, 164; rehabilitation and reconstruction by, 164–65

United Nations Transition Assistance Group (UNTAG): as case study, 11, 142; civilian component of, 146–51; findings from the case study, 13–14, 151–54, 181, 186–87; the information campaign, 146–51, 154, 195; mandate and operations of, 144–51; military component of, 145; as a model for many subsequent multifunctional peacekeeping missions, 51n.85; origins of, 142–44; personnel involved and cost of, 145; unwarranted fears, using information to overcome, 148–50

United Nations Truce Supervision Organization (UNTSO): boundary lines, assisting with measuring and marking, 127n.30; inspections and monitoring/

verification by, 130–32, 135, 137; monitoring/verification of buffer zone since the 1967 war, 119; size and nationality composition of the Golan Heights observer force, 129n.32; supplementation of UNDOF by, 126n.27

United States: arms control agreements and, 224–27; Cambodia, actions regarding, 155–56; Cold War arms race spiral, action based on misinformation in, 36–37; Cyprus, reaction to conflict on, 86–87; Iran, relations with, 230–31; Iraq, insufficient transparency and attacks on, 228, 233–34; Namibian independence, support for peaceful transition to, 143–44; North Korea, relations with, 191, 234–36; the Nuclear Non-Proliferation Treaty and, 228; Open Skies proposals and, 217–21; public diplomacy, lack of respect for, 193; Radio Okapi, funding of, 211; Syria-Israel disengagement negotiations, leverage brought to bear on, 123–26. See also America

UNLB. See United Nations Logistics Base

UNMEE. See United Nations Mission in Eritrea and Ethiopia

UNMIK. See United Nations Interim Administration Mission in Kosovo

UNSCOM. See United Nations Special Commission on Iraq

UNTAC. See United Nations Transitional Authority in Cambodia

UNTAG. See United Nations Transition Assistance Group

UNTSO. See United Nations Truce Supervision Organization

Van Evera, Stephen, 18, 27
Vartiainen, ATP Ahti, 101, 111
Verheul, Adrian, 122
verification. See monitoring/verification
Verona, Congress of, 70–71, 73
Vienna, Congress of 1814-1815 at. See Congress of Vienna
Vietnam, 155–56, 158
Voice of Democratic Kampuchea, 174

Walt, Stephen M., 64
Walter, Barbara, 189–90

war, causes of, 27–35
West Germany, 143. *See also* Germany
Wimhurst, David, 200, 208
worst-case assumptions: effect of transparency on, 186–87; in SALT II, 226; security spirals and, 35–37; uncertainty as source of, 42. *See also* fears

Yacoumopoulou, Lena, 149, 154

Zaire, 206. *See also* Congo, Democratic Republic of
Zambia, 142
Zartman, I. William, 126
Zimbabwe, 206